HUNGARY

GYULA NÉMETH

HUNGARY

A COMPLETE GUIDE

HIPPOCRENE
BOOKS, INC.
NEW YORK

171 Madison Ave
New York, N.Y. 10016

Edited by Gyula Németh
Written by
Péter Gál
Zoltán Halász
István Koroknay
Vera Kovács
Gyula Németh
Tibor Sebestyén
András Székely
Ferenc Zákonyi

Translated from the Hungarian by Charles Carlson
Translation revised by George Maddocks
Map and illustrations by Tamás Biczó
Design by László Tasnádi

Fourth, revised edition

© Gyula Németh
Reprinted 1990
ISBN 0-87052-592-1

Published in co-production with Corvina Books, Budapest
This edition for distribution in the USA and Canada

CONTENTS

HUNGARY: A LITTLE BACKGROUND

HUNGARY: THE LAND AND ITS PEOPLE 11
A BRIEF HISTORY 12
A CHRONOLOGICAL TABLE 18
A SHORT HISTORY OF HUNGARIAN CIVILIZATION 19
SOME PROMINENT FIGURES OF CULTURE AND HISTORY . 26

A DETAILED GUIDE

Budapest 31

THE HISTORY OF THE CITY 31
BUDA 36
The Castle District and the Royal Palace 36
Víziváros, Óbuda, Margaret Island, Aquincum and the
Római-part 47
Gellért Hill and surroundings. The southern section of
Buda 57
The Buda Hills 59
PEST 60
The Inner City 60
The Kiskörút 69
The Nagykörút 73
Andrássy út and the City Park 75
Rákóczi út 80
From Újpest to Csepel 82

The Danube Bend 83

THE RIGHT BANK OF THE DANUBE 84
Szentendre 84
Visegrád 88
Esztergom 92

THE LEFT BANK OF THE DANUBE 98
Vác 100

Transdanubia 105

NORTHERN TRANSDANUBIA 108
Tatabánya 109
Tata 109
Győr 112
Mosonmagyaróvár 117
WESTERN TRANSDANUBIA 118
Sopron 118
Kőszeg 124
Szombathely 126

Zalaegerszeg 131
Nagykanizsa 132
CENTRAL TRANSDANUBIA 133
Székesfehérvár 134
Veszprém 138
Pápa 142
EASTERN AND SOUTHERN TRANSDANUBIA 143
Dunaújváros 144
Szekszárd 145
Pécs 147
Mohács 153
Kaposvár 154

Lake Balaton 155

THE NORTHERN SHORE 158
Balatonakarattya 158
Balatonkenese 159
Balatonfűzfő 159
Balatonalmádi 160
Balatonfüred 162
Nagyvázsony 166
Tihany 167
Balatonszepezd 172
Révfülöp 173
Balatonrendes 173
Badacsony 173
Tapolca 176
Sümeg 177
Keszthely 178
Hévíz 182
THE SOUTHERN SHORE 183
Siófok 183
Zamárdi—Szántód 186
Balatonföldvár 187
Balatonszárszó 187
Balatonszemes 187
Boglárlelle—Balatonlelle 188
Boglárlelle—Balatonboglár 189
Fonyód 190
Balatonfenyves 191
Balatonmáriafürdő 191
Balatonberény 192
THE LITTLE BALATON 192

The Great Plain 193

THE REGION BETWEEN THE DANUBE AND THE TISZA . . . 193
Kalocsa 194
Baja 197
Kiskunhalas 198
Kecskemét 199
Nagykőrös 202
Kiskunfélegyháza 202
Szentes 203

Szeged 204
Cegléd 209
Jászberény 209
Szolnok 210
THE REGION BEYOND THE TISZA 211
Makó 212
Hódmezővásárhely 213
Orosháza 214
Békéscsaba 214
Gyula 215
Szarvas 216
Karcag 218
The Hajdúság 218
Hajdúszoboszló 219
Debrecen 220
The Hortobágy 223
The Nyírség 226
Nyíregyháza 226

Northern Hungary 229

THE CSERHÁT MOUNTAIN RANGE 229
Balassagyarmat 229
Salgótarján 234
THE MÁTRA MOUNTAIN RANGE 234
Gyöngyös 235
Eger 237
THE BÜKK MOUNTAIN RANGE 242
Miskolc 244
Kazincbarcika 249
Ózd 250
THE AGGTELEK MOUNTAIN RANGE 250
Aggtelek—Jósvafő 250
THE ZEMPLÉN MOUNTAIN RANGE 252
Szerencs 253
TOKAJ-HEGYALJA 254
Tokaj 256
Sárospatak 257
Sátoraljaújhely 260

PRACTICAL INFORMATION

TRAVEL INFORMATION 262
FORMALITIES 263
Visas 263
Customs concessions and currency regulations 263
Car papers 263
Health regulations 264
TRAVEL TO HUNGARY 264
TRANSPORT 265
Motoring 265
Railways 266
Long-distance buses 266
Air travel 266
Boats 266
Public transport 267

ACCOMMODATION 267
EATING OUT 267
   Hungarian cuisine 267
   What to drink 268
   Csárda-inns and taverns 269
   Confectioner's 269
   Mealtimes and eating habits 269
SIGHTSEEING 269
NATIONAL HOLIDAYS 270
REGULAR EVENTS 270
HUNTING, ANGLING, RIDING 271
SHOPPING 271
POSTAL SERVICES 273
NEWSPAPERS 273
MEDICAL TREATMENT 273
INSURANCE 273

Appendix 274

TOURIST DIRECTORY 274
DIRECTORY OF PLACE NAMES 292

HUNGARY:
A LITTLE BACKGROUND

HUNGARY:
THE LAND AND ITS PEOPLE

Hungary is situated in Central Europe at approximately an equal distance from the Equator and the North Pole and lies between 16° and 23° longitude East and 45° 48' and 48° 40' latitude North. Occupying an area of 93,032 sq.km, Hungary makes up less than 1% of all Europe and ranks sixteenth in size among the European countries.

It extends 528 km from east to west and 268 km from north to south.

SURFACE OF THE LAND

Almost two-thirds of the territory of Hungary consists of fertile plains no more than 200 m above sea level, and barely 2% of the land lies 400 m above sea level. The country's highest peak, Kékestető (1,015 m), is in the Mátra Mountains, the lowest point (78 m) is near Szeged.

Hungary is divided into three large regions: Transdanubia (Dunántúl), the Great Plain (Alföld) and Northern Hungary.

The Danube Bend (Duna-kanyar) is situated at the point where the three large regions of Hungary meet, forming a harmonious unity.

HYDROGRAPHY

Hungary belongs to the drainage basin of Europe's second longest river, the Danube. The 417 km long Hungarian section of the river is completely navigable (140 kilometres of this section form part of the Hungarian–Czechoslovak border). The 579 km Hungarian section of the Tisza is likewise mostly navigable. Spreading over an area of 596 sq. km, Lake Balaton is the largest lake of Central and Western Europe. Its length is 77 km, its average width is 5 km, and its maximum width is 14 km, the narrowest section, between Tihany and Szántód, is only 1.5 km. Its average depth is between 2 and 3 m, and its deepest point is 12.4 m. Lake Velence, the country's second largest lake (27 sq. km), lies between Budapest and the Balaton.

Hungary is rich in mineral and medicinal waters. Today there are about 500 natural springs and newer ones are continually being discovered and put into use.

CLIMATE

Hungary is situated in the temperate zone, with both moderate maritime and mild Mediterranean air currents influencing its climate. Temperatures above 30°C may occur in July and August but generally do not last very long. The average temperature during these months is between 20° and 21°C. January is the coldest month, but even then the average temperature does not fall below—1°C. Hungary has a rather low rainfall, which exceeds an annual average of 600 mm only in Transdanubia. Nevertheless, sudden downpours and storms are frequent during the summer. The number of sunny hours is high, exceeding 2,000 hours per annum in some regions of the country. July and August are the two sunniest months, with almost 300 hours of sunshine.

PLANT AND ANIMAL LIFE

There are 2,165 flowering-plant species in Hungary. Field crops cover much of the land, 13.6% of which is forests, mostly oak and beech (only 6% are coniferous). There are 32,000 animal species in Hungary, including 450 vertebrates.

POPULATION

The population of Hungary is 10,590,000. Hungary is one of the more densely populated countries of the Continent with 114 people per sq.km. The population of the capital is 2,115,000. There are eight cities besides Budapest with a population of over 100,000 (Miskolc, Debrecen, Szeged, Pécs, Győr, Nyíregyháza, Kecskemét and Székesfehérvár).

In addition to the Hungarian population, German, Slovak, South Slav and

Rumanian national minorities also live in Hungary. Some five million Hungarians live outside Hungary: approx. 3.5 million in the neighbouring countries,
the rest scattered all over the world, the largest number residing in the USA.

A BRIEF HISTORY

At the end of the ninth century, around A.D. 895, mounted nomadic people comprising an alliance of seven tribes occupied the Carpathian Basin, an area that
had been inhabited since prehistoric times. The half-million-year-old skull frag-
ment found at Vértesszőlős (western Hungary) is one of the oldest finds connected with prehistoric man. But a large number of objects dating from Late
Stone Age and Copper Age cultures, such as clay statues, pottery, weapons, etc.,
have also survived. Around the fifth century B.C. Scythians drove their horses
over the fields of the Carpathian Basin. Later on Celts settled in the area. Like the
inhabitants of ancient Britain, the Celts were brought under Roman supremacy
when the Romans in A.D. 10 turned what is now western Hungary into a Roman
province bearing the name Pannonia.

Beginning in the third century, waves of migrations advancing towards the
west followed in rapid succession: Germanic tribes, Lombards, Gepids, as well
as Goths lived here. It is also possible that the area served as the seat of King
Attila, the founder of the Hunnish Empire, in the middle of the fifth century. In the
seventh century the Carpathian Basin again fell to a nomadic people, but this
time it was the Avars, whose rule was broken by Charlemagne around 800.
Except for two small Slavic principalities, no state of any importance was
founded on this territory after the downfall of the Avar Empire.

The conquering Magyars arrived with one of the last waves of the great migrations. Leaving their proto-Finno-Ugric homeland situated somewhere between
the Volga Bend and the Ural Mountains, and travelling through the Caucasus
and along the Black Sea, the Hungarian tribes finally arrived at the Carpathian
Mountains where they gradually, and relatively peacefully, occupied the Basin
from a north-easterly and south-easterly direction. The conquerors elected
Árpád as head of the Magyar tribe. The name of this tribe was later to pass on to
the whole nation as well as to the country itself. Árpád and his followers brought
the inhabitants of the Carpathian Basin under their control, and it was these people who, together with the lower ranks of the Hungarians, afterwards cultivated
the land, herded the cattle, and fished and hunted in a country covered at that
time by forests and rich in fish and aquatic birds. Some of their ranks, however,
were more intent on fighting and consequently conducted a number of plundering military campaigns. Fighting with bows and arrows, these swift Magyar
riders—partly acting as allies of the princes of Western Europe and partly for the
sake of plundering—turned up everywhere in Europe from the Pyrenees to the
Byzantine Empire. They finally suffered decisive losses at the hands of German
mounted troops at Merseburg in 933 and at Augsburg in 955. Prince Géza
(972–997) finally had to decide whether Hungary was to remain pagan or identify
itself with feudal Europe, that is, accept Christianity or succumb to decadence.

THE AGE OF KING STEPHEN I
AND THE KINGS OF THE HOUSE OF ÁRPÁD (1001–1301)

King Stephen I (St. Stephen, c. 997–1038), the son of Géza, swore obedience to
the Pope like his father before him, and was crowned on Christmas Day in the
year 1000. During the four decades of his rule, Stephen I effected the organization of the Hungarian state, partly by using Slavic and Western European states
as examples.

After Stephen's death, monarchs from the House of Árpád were to rule Hungary for the next three centuries (until 1301). During this period Hungary was
able to emerge as an important state, managing successfully to defend its borders against the emperors of the Holy Roman and Byzantine Empires. By the
twelfth century the area of Hungary was around 3–400,000 sq. km, and its population included, besides Hungarians, Slovaks, Croatians, Germans, Rumanians
and Turkish-speaking Cumans. Hungary was thus a conglomerate of many
nationalities speaking different languages.

The first years of the Hungarian state were spent in one continuous war fought
for the purpose of strengthening the royal power and Christianity. In 1222 the so-
called Golden Bull, a Hungarian document comparable to the Magna Carta,
listed the rights of the nobility. This bull also strengthened the citizenry, the
medieval intellectuals, and the clergy. In 1241 the Mongol invasion brought

a halt to the country's development. With the exception of a few fortified cities, all of Hungary was virtually destroyed, and it was left to King Béla IV (1235–1270) to rebuild the country. Hungary started to regain its strength in the second half of the century, and royal decrees and orders for the building of cities contributed to the cultural development as well.

THE PERIOD BETWEEN 1301 AND 1526 AND THE BATTLE OF MOHÁCS

The House of Árpád died out in 1301 and kings from other related families came to the throne of Hungary: the Italian–French Anjou kings, Charles Robert and Louis I (the Great) in the fourteenth century, followed by Sigismund of Luxembourg, Matthias Corvinus (Hunyadi), and later the members of the Polish––Lithuanian House of Jagiello; and finally monarchs from the House of Habsburg, beginning in the sixteenth century. Besides agriculture, which took an upswing in the fourteenth century, the country's economy developed around its foreign trade and goldmining. The Hungarian king, ruling with a strong hand, formed an alliance with the Czech and Polish rulers against the competition offered by the merchants from Vienna. During the reign of Louis the Great (1342–1382) as well as on several following occasions, Poland and Hungary had common kings. Hussite doctrines became widespread in Hungary during the rule of Sigismund of Luxembourg (1387–1437), and in 1437 the first large-scale peasant uprising broke out in Transylvania. Above all, there was the growing danger from the Ottoman Turks. In 1444 Ulászló, who also ruled Poland as Wladyslaw III Jagiello, fell in the Battle of Várna. János Hunyadi, the elected viceroy of Hungary, managed in 1456 at Nándorfehérvár (the present-day Belgrade) to stop the Turkish advance for the next seventy years. (In this way the Hungarians as well as the Balkan nations struggling against the Turks gained a common hero, the leading figure of many folk ballads.) In 1458 Matthias Corvinus, the son of János Hunyadi, was chosen king, and it was during his reign (1458–1490) that Hungarian history reached one of its golden periods. There were four million inhabitants living in Hungary during this period, as many as in England, a much larger country. Matthias centralized his power by curbing the authority previously exercised by rival lords, and introduced uniform taxes with which he could pay his mercenaries, largely composed of the defeated Hussites and known after its commander, "Black John" Haugwitz as the "Black Army", which afterwards occupied Vienna in 1485. It was Matthias who made the splendour of the courts of Buda and Visegrád famous in far-away countries and who also became a liberal patron of scholarship and the arts. Renaissance art and culture flourished in the country during his reign, partly because of the influence of his second wife, Beatrice of Aragon, and the Italian artists and scholars she invited to Hungary. There was not one successor to Matthias who would have been able to continue the work of this great king in counterbalancing the relative backwardness of the Hungarian cities and the lack of a strong middle class. In their striving for power, the noblemen kindled discord and placed all burdens on the serfs. Turkish expansion, in the meanwhile, was becoming more and more of a threat, so much so that in 1514 a crusade was preached against them. The landowners, however, hindered the military drives aimed at defending the country until finally the peasant army that had collected became infuriated at waiting idly around. Finally, with György Dózsa, a man who had been elevated to the rank of a nobleman for his bravery, at their head, the peasants turned against the landowners. After a few initial successes, the uprising (1514) was cruelly crushed, and the nobility turned its revenge on the captured leaders. A law was passed depriving the serfs of all liberty of movement, an act which forced most of the peasantry back to conditions they had lived under several centuries earlier.

The decisive battle against the Turks took place in 1526 near Mohács, in southern Hungary. In this battle King Louis II fell and a large part of the Hungarian army likewise perished. The Turks did not make full use of their victory, and it was not until one and a half decades later that they occupied Buda, the capital of the country, and went on to subject an appreciable part of the country to their control. The final victory enjoyed by the Turks was hastened by the fact that the Hungarian nobility was not united. Some of the nobles wanted Ferdinand of Habsburg on the throne, while others would have preferred János Zápolya, who put down the Dózsa peasant rebellion, or his son.

THE TURKISH OCCUPATION AND ANTI-HABSBURG SENTIMENTS

With the Turkish capture of Buda in 1541, the country was torn into three parts and a long period of partition began. The part lying west and north of the Danube, a section called "Royal Hungary", fell into Habsburg hands and took its orders from Vienna. The Habsburgs and the Turks took turns at making their influence felt in Transylvania, and it was only in the first third of the seventeenth century, when there existed the principalities of István Bocskai and Gábor Bethlen—leaders who in 1625 were allies with the Danes, Dutch and British—that a touch of relative independence came to this section of the country. The central part of the country fell completely under Turkish rule. The origins of some of the territorial differences seen in present-day Hungary go back to this period, when the economic life of the western section was much more stable than that of the Great Plain, an area that was ruthlessly exploited by the Turks to the very last.

Hungarian, Croatian and Slovak mercenary troops from the border castles on the periphery of the occupied territory as well as troops partly recruited from the western states belonging to the Habsburg Empire more than once succeeded in standing up to the advancing Turks. In 1523 Captain Miklós Jurisich forced the Turks to retreat at the Castle of Kőszeg. The Castle of Eger in 1552 managed under the command of Captain István Dobó to hold up under odds many times greater, and in 1566 Miklós Zrínyi defended Szigetvár until his heroic death. Other great lords, however, managed to prosper, partly because of the looting they were able to carry out while the war was going on, and partly because of the continual upheavals caused by the long struggle between the Reformation and the Counter-Reformation. As a result of these struggles, many aristocrats acquired even larger holdings for favours done for the emperor and the Prince of Transylvania at the expense of the other magnates and especially at the expense of the country they had plundered.

It became increasingly clear by the 1650s that the Habsburgs regarded the kingdom of Hungary as nothing more than one of their provinces, a kind of "buffer state". This was recognized by the military commander and writer Miklós Zrínyi, the 17th-century descendant of the hero of Szigetvár, and later by the lower-gentry peasant class which considered Hungary to be "bleeding between two heathens". This realization served as the basis of political movements such as the uprising led by Imre Thököly (1657–1705). In 1686 Buda was liberated by the united forces of the Christian world, and within a few years the Turks were expelled from the rest of the country. This act, however, did not bring about the freedom the country had so earnestly longed for. The oppressive Counter-Reformation policies of the imperial court, which were also directed towards Germanization, turned the various classes living in the country, serfs and nobles alike, more and more against Vienna. Ferenc Rákóczi II came to the forefront of the movement in 1703. Coming from a Transylvanian family of nobles, Rákóczi, a man who was later chosen Prince of Transylvania, enjoyed the status of being one of the country's most powerful landowners. For eight years he fought his War of Independence. It was, however, due to the numerical superiority of the opposing forces, the irreconcilable conflicts between the serfs and nobles and treason within the ranks that his struggle met with defeat in 1711. Rákóczi died in exile in Turkey.

Following the failure of the Rákóczi War of Independence, Hungary became a province of the Habsburg Empire. Part of the nobility pledged their "lives and blood" to the emperor, and this pledge he made use of to the full. For example, Hungarian Hussars occupied Berlin under the leadership of Field Marshal András Hadik during the Seven Years' War (1756–1763). The reward for this service, however, did not result in any decrease of political dependence, only in a certain degree of economic development. Since Maria Theresa and her son Joseph II were the representatives of enlightened absolutism, under their rule Hungary took great steps forward both economically and culturally. The country's first factories were built, the rights of the peasantry were defined and public education was introduced. However, the necessity of bourgeois development and the national consciousness, which had been suppressed, put more of a strain on the existing framework. In 1795, the Hungarian Jacobins proclaimed the ideals of equality and fraternity, for which seven of them paid with their lives.

The movement for making Hungarian the official language of the state started at the beginning of the nineteenth century, and with it came a new chapter in the struggle for an independent Hungary. This era represented an awakening of a national culture and politics, for, beginning in 1825, it was mostly the county delegates of the lesser nobility who, in their fight for progress, urged the enactment of reforms at every session of parliament and also advocated improvements for the serfs. The greatest politicians of the time such as Count István Széchenyi and the outstanding orator and publicist Lajos Kossuth, leaders pos-

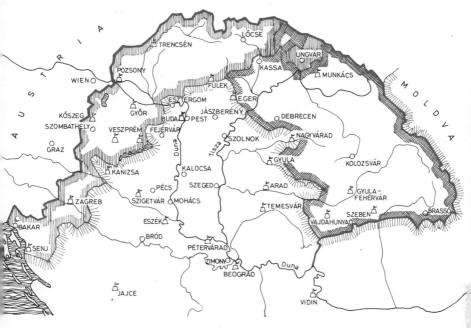

Tripartite Hungary under Turkish domination

sessing versatile organizational capabilities, strove for industrial development and the modernization of agriculture. These two men, although they differed in their political views, shared an interest in English culture. Széchenyi's reform programme called for bridge construction, horse breeding, etc., interests which he acquired during a trip to England. Széchenyi also invited experts from England to help carry out his reforms. Kossuth studied English while he was held a political prisoner by the Habsburgs. He was mainly interested in the traditions of parliamentary democracy. Since the bourgeoisie continued to represent only a narrow class with limited power, it was the more enlightened members of the nobility who understood the historical development of the times and who led the struggle for an anti-feudal, capitalist transformation. It was during this period that the first railway and steamship were put into operation, the first permanent bridge was built between Buda and Pest, the power of the press was increased, and books announcing the reforms were published and smuggled into the country from Germany to avoid Austrian censorship.

THE PERIOD FROM THE 1848–1849 WAR OF INDEPENDENCE TO THE FIRST WORLD WAR

The spring of the reform movement also brought with it a revolution in 1848. On March 15, a group of radical intellectuals, led by the "March Youths" under the leadership of the poet Sándor Petőfi and his companions, along with other citizens of Pest, took to the streets. In Pozsony (Bratislava), the seat of parliament at that time, deputies passed a law liberating the serfs. The first responsible Hungarian government was instituted. The Viennese court, although reluctant, accepted Hungarian demands, but on its encouragement, Jellačić, the governor of Croatia, attacked the young state. In the victorious battle fought against Jellačić (September 29, 1848), the revolution turned into a war of independence. Adverse relations between the Hungarian government and the Imperial family surfaced when the Hungarian army, upon hearing of the revolution in Vienna, began to march towards Austria for the purpose of helping the inhabitants of the Austrian capital. The Viennese revolution was put down, and the Hungarian troops were stopped at Schwechat. But during the War of Independence, the Imperial forces were unable to gain a decisive victory over the Hungarian army. When parliament declared the deposition of the House of Habsburg in April 1849 in Debrecen, Francis Joseph I appealed for help to the Russian tsar, who sent an army across the Carpathians. Finally, in August 1849, the combined Austrian and Russian forces forced the Hungarians to lay down their arms. Kossuth, the leader of the revolutionary government, emigrated together with many of his companions.

Savage reprisals followed, and the country was dismembered once more. However, after Austria's defeat in Italy in 1859, the Austrian government wished to bring about a compromise, an effort that was also necessitated by the "passive resistance" shown by the people of Hungary. Finally, in 1867 the Viennese government came to terms with the representatives of the Hungarian parliament. This "Compromise", or *Ausgleich,* as it is often called, which could be described as a series of mutual concessions between the Austrian capitalists and the large Hungarian landowners, was drawn up by the well-known jurist, Ferenc Deák. After his public relations trips to England and North America, Lajos Kossuth, while living as an émigré in Italy, vehemently opposed the Compromise, and in his so-called "Cassandra letter" pointed out that should it go through, the people of the Habsburg Empire desiring independence would regard the Hungarians as the greatest oppressors after the Austrians and that they would take revenge when the time came for the inevitable collapse of the Empire. Those in power, however, would not listen to Kossuth, and in 1867 the Austro–Hungarian Monarchy was formed with the Austrian emperor Francis Joseph I as the lawful king of Hungary. Hungary maintained a separate government and ministries, though the key ministries of defence, foreign affairs, and finance remained common to the two sides. This half century, which lasted from 1867 to 1918, known as the "Age of Dualism", was marked by the rapid development of capitalism.

The pace of development was characterized by the fact that the population of Budapest, after Óbuda, Buda and Pest were united in 1872–1873, grew, during the last decades of the nineteenth century, to four times its previous size. It was during this period that the buildings characterizing the city's present-day skyline were built: the Baroque-style Royal Palace, the Matthias Church, the Fishermen's Bastion, the Basilica, the Opera House, and the Parliament building. The first underground railway on the Continent was also constructed during this period, based on the model provided by the London Underground, and the system of boulevards presently seen in Pest was constructed. The larger cities outside Budapest, such as Szeged, Debrecen and Pécs, owe their present-day appearances largely to construction work done during this period. Industry made great strides forward; this was particularly true of industrial fields connected with agriculture as well as machine production and light industry.

In 1896, the Dual Monarchy celebrated the Millennium of the Conquest or settlement of Hungary, and proclaimed that the country was progressing on the right road within the framework of the monarchy. However, the people under the Habsburg Empire—Czechs, Slovaks, Rumanians, Croatians—were struggling more and more for independence, and considered both the Austrians and Hungarians as their oppressors.

The first decade of the twentieth century was characterized by the movements of the workers and peasants and the non-Hungarian minorities. Then, as a part of the Austro–Hungarian Empire, Hungary entered the war as an ally of the German Empire in June, 1914.

THE HUNGARIAN REPUBLIC OF COUNCILS AND THE HORTHY REGIME

World War I brought heavy destruction on Hungary; hundreds of thousands fell on the Italian and Russian fronts. More and more people joined parties and organizations professing left-wing principles. In Budapest on October 31, 1918 the workers and soldiers won a bourgeois democratic revolution, and with this act, the monarchy was overthrown. Two weeks later Hungary, like Austria, became a republic. Mihály Károlyi (1875–1955), who was a pacifist, pro-Allied politician during the war, became the leader of the Hungarian government and later of the republic. Károlyi was an aristocratic landowner, but when he became Prime Minister of the Republic, he personally divided his large holdings among the peasants.

Many of the Hungarian prisoners of war captured in Russia became members of the Communist Party, and upon their return to Hungary, they organized the Communist Party of Hungary, choosing Béla Kun as their leader. The bourgeois government found itself experiencing more and more economic and political problems following the lost war, and on March 21, 1919, it handed over its power to the united Communist and Social Democratic Party which soon proclaimed the Hungarian Republic of Councils.

The new republic introduced various economic and social welfare measures and in doing so endeavoured at an extremely rapid pace to do away with many flagrant social injustices. Industrial plants were nationalized and cooperatives were organized on the land owned by the large landowners. Cultural values were also popularized; publishing houses printed inexpensive series of works, and private collections were opened to the populace. Well-known Hungarian writers, thinkers and artists also gave their support to the Hungarian Republic of Councils; one such example was György Lukács, the world-famous philosopher.

Economic difficulties, the counter-revolution within and intervention by the Allies all led to the downfall of the Hungarian Republic of Councils in August, 1919, after only 133 days of existence. In March, 1920, Admiral Miklós Horthy was elected regent. In theory he restored the monarchy, but he would not allow the last Habsburg ruler, Charles IV, to return to Hungary.

The 1920 Treaty of Trianon resulted in two-thirds of the territory belonging to historical Hungary being annexed to Austria, Czechoslovakia, Rumania and Yugoslavia. As a result, the country, which had already been ravaged by war, lost territories with important industrial and mining resources.

Although the inflation ravaging the country after the war was overcome with the help of foreign loans, the world economic crisis reduced the country's achievements to nothing. The successive reactionary governments, who were still hoping for a recovery of the territories that had been lost as a result of the Treaty of Trianon, became more and more oriented in their foreign policy towards Italian and German fascism. As a result of the so-called Vienna Awards agreed upon in 1938 and 1940, Hungary did recover certain territories that had been annexed to Rumania and Slovakia, but, as a result, the country was drawn into the Second World War.

THE SECOND WORLD WAR

The German High Command made use of its Hungarian ally when it attacked Yugoslavia and then the Soviet Union. During the war, the Germans increasingly recruited Hungarian military forces and made use of whatever was produced on Hungarian soil. Hundreds of thousands of Hungarian soldiers fell, and almost half a million Hungarians of Jewish origin lost their lives in concentration camps or in forced labour. The extreme right-wing parties, eager to serve Hitler, became strong especially after March 19, 1944, when the Germans occupied Hungary, thus preventing a possible separate peace for Hungary. The Germans clearly knew that there were English-oriented politicians in the Hungarian government, politicians who were co-operating with the British secret service and who would have liked to have seen Hungary give herself up to the Allies. In October, 1944, Horthy actually tried to pull out of the war, but his attempt met with failure. The fascist Arrow Cross Party took over power with German help. While the first provisional national assembly and government of a new liberated Hungary had already been at work in Debrecen since December 1944, units consisting of Hungarian fascists as well as the German army were continuing the meaningless war, causing immeasurable suffering to the people and leaving appalling devastation in their wake. By April 4, 1945, however, the Soviet Red Army had driven out the Germans from the whole country. This marked the beginning of a new era in the life of the country.

A CHRONOLOGICAL TABLE

895–896	Hungarian tribes under the leadership of Árpád conquer the territory of present-day Hungary
997–1038	Stephen I organizes the State and strengthens the power of the Church
1241–1242	The Mongol invasion
1308–1382	Anjou kings on the throne of Hungary
1387–1437	The reign of Sigismund of Luxembourg
1437	Peasant revolt led by Antal Budai Nagy
1456	János Hunyadi defeats the Turks at Nándorfehérvár (the present-day Belgrade)
1458–1490	The reign of King Matthias Corvinus
1514	Peasant revolt led by György Dózsa
1526	Decisive Turkish victory at Mohács
from 1526	The Habsburgs on the throne of Hungary
1541	The Turks occupy Buda
16th to 17th centuries	Battles fought against the Turks
17th century	Wars of independence fought against the Habsburgs
1683–1699	Expulsion of the Turks from Hungary
1703–1711	The Rákóczi War of Independence
1795	Execution of the leaders of the Hungarian Jacobin Movement
March 15, 1848–August 13, 1849	The Bourgeois Revolution, followed by the War of Independence against the Habsburgs
1867	"Compromise" with the House of Habsburg
1914–1918	Hungary participates in the First World War
October 30–31, 1918	Bourgeois Democratic Revolution
November 24, 1918	The Communist Party of Hungary is formed

March 21–Aug. 1, 1919	The Hungarian Republic of Councils.
1919–1944	Regime of Miklós Horthy
1920	The Treaty of Trianon: Hungary loses two-thirds of its former territory
April 11, 1941	Attack on Yugoslavia
June 27, 1941	Declaration of war against the Soviet Union
March 19, 1944	German occupation of Hungary
October 11, 1944	Horthy tries to conclude an armistice and to withdraw from the war
October 16, 1944	The fascist Arrow Cross Party seizes power
December 22, 1944	Provisional National Assembly and Government are formed in Debrecen
March 17, 1945	Enactment of the Land Reform
April 4, 1945	The Germans are driven out of the entire country
February 1, 1946	Hungary is declared a republic
February 10, 1947	Signing of the Peace Treaty
August 1, 1947–	The beginnings of planned economy
August 20, 1949	New Constitution; People's Republic of Hungary
December 14, 1955	Hungary is accepted into the United Nations
October 23, 1956–	Uprising against Hungarian stalinism
November 4, 1956	
March 17, 1969	The "Budapest Summons", prelude to the European Security Conference which convened in Helsinki in 1975
1985	European cultural forum in Budapest
October 23, 1989	Republic of Hungary proclaimed

A SHORT HISTORY
OF HUNGARIAN CIVILIZATION

For a long time archeologists engaged in research on the life and beliefs of the Magyars who settled in the Carpathian Basin at the end of the 9th century thought that the evidence lay only in the graves of horsemen dressed in silver-mounted clothing and carrying ornamental weapons. More recent views, however, support the claim that the Hungarians as early as the period of the Conquest were in command of an important agricultural civilization, one which went on to develop even further as they made contact with the Slavic population. The Hungarians also made their livelihood through fishing. Linguistic evidence indicates that the Hungarians developed their fishing techniques while they were living in the area of the Urals, where they also practised hunting; Herodotus mentions in his account that the Finno-Ugric peoples living in the forests of Russia hunted with horses and dogs. It is also possible that they were acquainted with vine-growing. According to evidence provided by loanwords in Hungarian, agriculture as practised by the Hungarians developed before the Conquest, while the Magyars were in contact with Turkic peoples. Other loanwords denoting agricultural and everyday activities are of Slavic origin and thus provide evidence for believing that at one time the Hungarians assimilated to the Slavic population.

King Stephen I put a stop to the marauding expeditions of the early Hungarians, and his priests wiped out paganism with fire and sword. Strict laws forced the people to settle down. The king deliberately invited foreigners to the country: German priests as well as Italian wine workers, whose name has been preserved by several settlements in the Tokaj wine region, Muslim and Jewish merchants, French architects, Walloon citizens and semi-nomadic Cumans. From the fourteenth and fifteenth centuries onwards, the population increase that took place among the citizens of German extraction represented the most significant foreign influence, especially in Buda. These "newcomers" sooner or later adapted to their new Hungarian surroundings.

SCIENCE

The many-sided foreign influence exerted on Hungary did not seem to impede the emergence of a characteristically Hungarian culture. One of Europe's first universities was founded at Pécs in 1367, and the Buda printing-press set up by **András Hess** in 1472 is one of the earliest such workshops. Before the university of Pécs came into existence, there were Hungarian students attending colleges in Paris, Bologna and Padua and later, from the fifteenth and sixteenth centuries onwards, colleges in Vienna, Cracow, Göttingen, and other cities outside Hungary had Hungarian students as well.

The language of science in the Middle Ages was Latin; nevertheless, a scientific work written in Hungarian appeared in the middle of the seventeenth century: the Magyar Encyclopedia of **János Apáczai Csere** (1653). The writing of this work presupposed an educated, literary language, and as early as the fifteenth century, we have the beginnings of a writing on grammar and style. The complete Protestant and Catholic translations of the Bible that appeared at the turn of the seventeenth century created a generally-accepted, rich vernacular. Later, many people occupied themselves with polishing and refining the language, the printer and typographer **Miklós Tótfalusi Kis,** for example, who made his home in Transylvania after working in Holland.

The works written by **János Sajnovics** (1770) and **Sámuel Gyarmathi** (1791) on the Finno-Ugric linguistic relationship were the first attestations of scientifically-grounded comparative linguistics, written even before the works of Sir William Jones and Franz Bopp appeared. The activities of **Alexander Kőrösi de Csoma,** who sought after traces left by the early Hungarians, were especially significant in the field of investigating Buddhism and the languages of Asia. His "Tibetan Dictionary" (1834) is still considered a basic handbook. During the mid-19th century **Antal Reguly** worked among the small Finno-Ugrian peoples living in the region of the Urals and returned from his trip with a rich linguistic and ethnographic collection.

Hungarian science began to develop seriously at the end of the eighteenth century and the beginning of the nineteenth, even though circumstances often made it impossible for significant inventions and discoveries to find the necessary financial support to make their practical application possible. For example, it happened that simultaneously with, but independently of, Gauss and Lobachevski, **János Bolyai** worked out the principles of non-Euclidean geometry

in a remote Transylvanian village around 1830, while the physicist and teacher, **Ányos Jedlik,** formulated the principle of the dynamo in 1856, ten years before Siemens and Wheatstone. Only a few were fortunate enough, particularly at the turn of the nineteenth century and the beginning of the twentieth, to succeed in finding their place in their native homeland. Included among them were Edison's associate, **Tivadar Puskás,** who established the first telephone exchange (1881), **Donát Bánki,** the technician who invented the pulverizer (1892), **Kálmán Kandó,** the designer of the electric locomotive, **Loránd Eötvös,** the geologist who invented the torsion pendulum used in prospecting for oil and the mathematicians **Lipót Fejér** and **Frigyes Riesz.** The best-known representative of medical science was **Ignác Semmelweis,** the "saviour of mothers", who discovered a protective measure against puerperal (child-bed) fever. Many other Hungarian physicians are held in high esteem by medical science, from **Frigyes Korányi,** one of the pioneers of physiotherapy, to the pair of authors who wrote a modern anatomical atlas used throughout the world, **Ferenc Kiss** and **János Szentágothai.**
    Possibilities were even greater for inventors living at the beginning of the twentieth century: **Oszkár Asbóth**'s helicopter first took off in 1927 outside Budapest and **Albert Szent-Györgyi,** later to become a Nobel Prize winner, who, at present engaged in cancer research in the United States, extracted industrially manufacturable Vitamin C from paprika grown near Szeged (1932). However, the field was still not wide enough to allow for much of the potential talent available to reveal itself, and this was especially true under the unfavourable atmosphere of the Horthy regime. Among those who emigrated in 1919 as a result of the White Terror were the Nobel Prize winner physicist **George Hevesy,** who discovered the element known as hafnium, **Dénes Gábor,** who discovered what is called holography, the perfect three-dimensional picture, the aeroplane designer and one of the pioneers of aviation, **Tódor Kármán,** and **Péter Goldmark,** the inventor of colour television and the long-playing record. A number of Hungarian natural scientists managed to succeed only in America—for example, the physicist **Leo Szilárd,** the mathematician who worked on cybernetics, **John von Neumann,** and the Nobel Prize winner **Eugene Wigner,** as well as the "father of the hydrogen bomb", **Edward Teller.**

LITERATURE

The first literary remains after the old poetry preserved by oral tradition go back to the Middle Ages. These include the Latin chronicles and a sermon written in Hungarian around 1200. The first piece of Hungarian poetry is the "Ó-magyar Mária-siralom" (The Old Hungarian Lament of Mary) that was composed around 1300. **Janus Pannonius,** the humanist poet who lived in the second half of the fifteenth century, wrote his poetry in Latin, but from the sixteenth century onwards, the language of poetry became Hungarian. The first poet to write in the Hungarian vernacular was **Bálint Balassi** (1554–1594), the minstrel of love and the soldier's life, who died a hero's death struggling against the Turks. Travelling minstrels sang their songs about the battles of the sixteenth century. Songs composed by the most famous minstrel, **Sebestyén Tinódi Lantos,** were even published (1554). The battle fought against the Turks inspired **Miklós Zrínyi** in the seventeenth century to write an epic poem called "Szigeti veszedelem" (The Siege of Sziget). **Gáspár Károli**'s Protestant version of the Bible appeared during the Reformation and Counter-Reformation (1590), and in 1626 the Catholic translation emerged from the pen of **György Káldi** as did a countless number of polemic sermons, pamphlets, verses, and dramas.
    The literature of the end of the seventeenth century and the beginning of the eighteenth was again connected with political events. Sentiments felt by the "kuruc" soldiers who fought in the War of Independence (1703–1711) first led by Imre Thököly and then by Ferenc Rákóczi II were expressed in spirited and bitter songs, and books written in Latin and French by the exiled prince after the failure of the War of Independence as well as the epistolary chronicle of **Kelemen Mikes,** who was in exile together with the prince, are also worthy of mention here. One of the most interesting prose forms to develop during the period was the memoir, which flourished in Transylvania.
    The influence of French Enlightenment reached Hungary in the second half of the eighteenth century during the reign of Maria Theresa. Its influence was manifested especially in the Voltairian works of young squires performing bodyguard service in Vienna and in the poems of **Mihály Csokonai Vitéz** (1773–1805).
    At the turn of the nineteenth century the movement, initiated by the classicist poet and translator **Ferenc Kazinczy** (1759–1831), for developing the Hungarian national language, opened up new perspectives for literary development. A whole series of translations were prepared, and the first Hungarian novels,

literary almanacs and journals appeared. An important movement was started among the intellectuals against the efforts of the Viennese Court to make German the official language. The goal of the movement all above was to develop the Hungarian literary language, and within a short time, this effort produced Hungarian literary translations as well. In this way the Hungarian public was introduced to numerous German, English and French poets and writers. On many occasions translations were made of the English and French by using German translations. The text of "Hamlet", for example, was turned into Hungarian at that time on the basis of the German translation.

The "heroic period" of the Hungarian theatre had its beginnings around 1790—at first in Transylvania, then in the other parts of the country—although a small number of Hungarian and Latin plays had in fact existed earlier. The best writers of the age considered the development of a national drama to be of the utmost importance. The first permanent theatre to produce its plays in Hungarian opened in Kolozsvár (Cluj–Napoca, Rumania), and this was soon followed by similar theatres in Miskolc (1823) and Balatonfüred (1831). The Hungarian Theatre of Pest, which was built through public contributions, opened in 1837. This theatre later became the National Theatre.

The first classical works of Hungarian literature were written around 1820: the odes of **Dániel Berzsenyi** (1776–1836), the poems and noble-spirited discourses of **Ferenc Kölcsey** (1790–1838), the poet who wrote the words of the Hungarian National Anthem, the nationally-spirited romantic epic poems and dramas of **Mihály Vörösmarty** (1800–1855), the plays of **Károly Kisfaludy** (1788–1830), which are still performed today, and the immortal drama of national literature, "Bánk bán" by **József Katona** (1797–1830). During the period preceding 1848, a movement resembling the Young Italy movement emerged in Hungary among the circle of young intellectuals.

A poet of world-wide literary importance, **Sándor Petőfi** (1823–1849), was the representative of spirited revolutionary lyricism. Petőfi was one of the men who prepared and furthered the cause of the 1848 revolution. He was a major in the War of Independence and the adjutant of the famous Polish revolutionary and Hungarian general, József Bem. He met his death on the battlefield. It was in the lyric and epic poetry of his older friend and comrade during the revolution, **János Arany** (1817–1882) that Petőfi's dream was fulfilled: in literature, the people emerged victorious. **Imre Madách,** the author of the epic drama "The Tragedy of Man", was also one of the supporters of the 1848 revolution.

The romantic novelist **Mór Jókai** (1825–1904), also a friend of Petőfi, whose lifework includes more than one hundred volumes, glorified the society of his age, a society that emerged from the dualism following the Compromise of 1867. The greatest writers and poets of the age, such as **László Arany** (1844–1898) and **János Vajda** (1827–1897), however, viewed the Hungarian world with pessimism. In his poetry, Vajda expressed his conviction that the nobility who clung to the traditions of feudalism must not be in positions of leadership in a modern state. **Kálmán Mikszáth** (1849–1910) expressed the same thought even more strongly through the medium of his humorous, ironic prose, which later, however, became more and more gloomy. **Endre Ady** (1877–1919), who brought revolutionary change to Hungarian lyric poetry through his poems and militant newspaper articles, pursued the traditions established by Petőfi by raising the theory and practice of struggle for social progress into the realm of poetry. Both his stay in Paris and his acquaintance with modern French poetry (Verlaine, Baudelaire) had great influence on his creative genius.

The life of the peasantry was depicted by **Zsigmond Móricz** (1879–1942), whose art, following his experiments with lyric novels and Expressionism, was at its best in his realistic novels portraying the life of the people. Other great Hungarian literary figures of the period also turned their interests towards social problems. The pain that was felt because of the state of the country penetrated the grievances even of poets committed to solitude. For example, **Dezső Kosztolányi** (1885–1936), who began his career as a Parnassian master of language, wrote one of his most beautiful novels "Édes Anna" (Anna Édes) about the hopeless future of servant girls. The last monumental poem "Jónás könyve" (The Book of Jonah) written by **Mihály Babits** (1883–1941) before his death called attention to the approaching surge of fascism. Mihály Babits was the editor-in-chief of "Nyugat", a journal of middle-class humanism; his translations into Hungarian include that of the "Divine Comedy". **Attila József** (1905–1937), an outstanding figure of twentieth-century Hungarian lyricism, was led into the ranks of the workers' movement and the illegally-functioning Communist Party by the anxiety he felt for the future of the people. Destitution and discord finally led him to suicide. The description of the worker's life is made universal in the poetry and prose of **Lajos Kassák** (1887–1967), a representative of the Hungarian avant-garde. He founded the progressive though short-lived journals "Tett" and "MA". **Miklós Radnóti's** (1909–1944) last profoundly humanistic poems were composed in fascist war camps; it was a fascist bullet which put an end to his life. Many, such as **József Lengyel, Béla Balázs** and **Béla Illés,** were forced to emigrate. Almost every outstanding representative of twentieth-century Hungarian literature was heavily influenced by French culture, which in itself was a kind of protest against German and Italian (fascist) orientation. The poets of the periodical "Nyugat" consciously adapted the verses written by the French symbolists. Attila József, who was a student at the Sorbonne during the twenties, was influenced by the Surrealists; Radnóti was affected in his artistic development by a trip to Paris, governed at that time by the Popular Front, his experience with the solidarity of the Spanish left-wing, and African culture with which he became acquainted in Paris.

The literature of the country emerged on new foundations after the end of the Second World War. A verse written at that time refers to the end of the forties as the age of the "radiant breezes". Although the period between 1950 and 1955 fractured the development of literature, the traditional interest in society continued to thrive, and after 1957, modern Hungarian literature received new impetus through poets such as **Gyula Illyés, Sándor Weöres, Ferenc Juhász,** poets who wrote in a variety of voices and whose merits are recognized abroad. Also adding their weight to this impetus were philosophically profound novelists such as **Tibor Déry, László Németh, József Lengyel,** successful dramatists such as **István Örkény, Ferenc Karinthy,** and essayists like **Miklós Szabolcsi, István Sőtér** and **Endre Illés.**

VISUAL ARTS

Mosaic floors from villas once standing in the Roman province of Pannonia, ornamental statues from the same era, and numerous masterpieces of Roman handicraft are unearthed almost daily by Hungarian archeologists. Every people who lived here during the period of migrations, from the Scythians to the Avars, left behind objects of exquisite craftsmanship made of gold and precious stones.

The **ornamental art** produced by the conquering Magyars shows traces of Iranian metalwork and textile craftsmanship, but this art shortly yielded to Romanesque-style architecture and handicrafts. The most beautiful monuments from the later period include a royal city that has been preserved only in fragments **(Esztergom),** well-reconstructed cathedrals **(Pécs, Veszprém),** and village churches from the twelfth and thirteenth centuries **(Lébénymiklós, Karcsa).** Decorative statues have been preserved on the outer walls of some of these churches **(Ják),** while the original frescoes appear in the interior of others **(Feldebrő).** Gothic art reached Hungary in the middle of the thirteenth century, and the mature forms of Gothic art flourished in the courts of the Anjou kings (14th century) and later during the age of Sigismund (first half of the 15th century). How these various architectural styles were built over one another is well demonstrated by the exhibition appearing in the Buda Castle Museum. Although the most beautiful medieval monuments are found outside the borders of present-day Hungary, there are a number of beautiful Gothic churches and chapels preserved inside the country **(Nyírbátor, Sopron, Siklós).** Included among the monuments preserved from the royal court as well as those exemplifying urban Gothic architecture are the Anjou well at Visegrád, the synagogue at Sopron, and a group of houses near the Castle of Buda belonging at one time to the citizenry. Frescoes have been preserved at Esztergom and Velemér, and quite recently extremely valuable fragments of Gothic statues once standing in Buda have been found, fragments reminiscent of Burgundian sculpture. Priceless objects of metalwork, including chalices, crucifixes and crowns, as well as illuminated codices, are preserved in museums such as the National Museum of Budapest or the Treasury in the Cathedral of Esztergom.

Monuments from the Renaissance have been preserved in Buda Castle and among the ruins of the Palace of Visegrád. Renaissance creations bearing Italian features include the **Bakócz Chapel** added by the papal candidate Archbishop Tamás Bakócz to the Cathedral of Esztergom at the beginning of the sixteenth century, the carved pews belonging to the Gothic church of Nyírbátor, and the stall preserved in the National Museum. During the period of Turkish occupation a simpler Renaissance form superseded the marble buildings. (The village churches, for example, were covered with panels painted in flower designs, and flower ornamentation appeared on the walls of mansions and palaces, reflecting both late Renaissance and Baroque influence, such as the "Sub rosa" room of the Castle of Sátorpatak.) The greatest master of this sixteenth-century style in painting was the **Master M. S.,** whose works are exhibited in the Hungarian National Gallery in Budapest and the Christian Museum in Esztergom.

Castles and manor houses were destroyed during the stormy years between the sixteenth and eighteenth centuries. Such talented artists as **Jakab Bogdány,** the painter of the English royal court, sought their fortunes abroad. Only the art of **Ádám Mányoki,** the portraitist from the court of Ferenc Rákóczi II, excels during this period (*c.* 1700). The stately Baroque churches built in the seventeenth and eighteenth centuries were expressions of the power of Catholicism, and the Baroque manor-houses from this same period give evidence of the power and wealth of the new aristocracy, such as the Esterházys. Among the best architects of the period were **András Mayerhoffer** (1690–1771), who designed and planned the manor-house at Gödöllő, **Jakab Fellner** (1722–1780), who constructed the secondary school at Eger, and their pupils. The interior ornamentation of these buildings was done by well-known German and Italian sculptors and painters, such as **Franz Anton Maulbertsch,** the famous Austrian painter, whose most beautiful works can be seen in Hungary in the Church of Sümeg, for example, or the outstanding sculptor **Georg Raphael Donner.**

National art, however, began a course of development only in the nineteenth century. The first works of national art were characterized by the neo-Classical style; these included the National Museum built by **Mihály Pollack** (1773–1855), the mansions in Pest built by **József Hild** (1789–1867), and the cathedrals of Esztergom and Eger; and lastly, the Chain Bridge (Lánchíd) in Budapest, designed by the Scotsman **Adam Clark** and finished by his namesake **William Tierney Clark.** A taste imitating the Romantic and historical styles was later to dominate in architecture. This style is represented, for example, by the Vigadó (Municipal Concert Hall) of **Frigyes Feszl** (1821–1884), the neo-Renaissance Opera House of **Miklós Ybl** (1814–1891), and the neo-Romanesque Fishermen's Bastion (Halászbástya) of **Frigyes Schulek** (1841–1919). Particularly interesting is the work of **Ödön Lechner** (1845–1919), an architect who strove after the creation of a unique Hungarian architectural style (the Budapest Museum of Applied Arts). Sculpture started to develop as a result of the work of **István Ferenczy** (1792–1856), a pupil of Thorvaldsen, only later to reach perfection in the Romantic art of **Miklós Izsó.** The large commissions of the end of the century, however, went to the representatives of academic sculpture (**György Zala,** the Millennium Monument in Budapest). The romantic "historic" painting of the years around 1860, which served to keep national consciousness alive, became the style of the establishment, and was represented in the works of **Viktor Madarász** (1830–1917), **Bertalan Székely** (1835–1910) and others. Opposing the neo-Baroque artists who were brought up in the Munich School—as for example **Gyula Benczúr** (1844–1920)—were artists like **Mihály Munkácsy** (1844–1900), who became world-famous during his lifetime, producing his best paintings around 1875, especially works depicting village life which, though painted in Paris, bear evidence of a particular kind of Eastern European realism. There was also the landscape painter **László Paál** (1846–1879), as well as **Pál Szinyei Merse** (1845–1920), who was urged into retirement by the baffling reception he experienced after reaching the limits of the Impressionistic outlook. László Paál was one of the outstanding representatives of the Barbizon School of painting.

A large number of Hungarian painters from Munich left the Bavarian capital after 1896 and founded an artists' colony in Nagybánya (now in Rumania), a colony which followed the examples set forth by the "purely naturalistic" and realistic school of French painting, and which influenced most of the Hungarian artists for decades to come. Uniquely individual groups of painters also emerged on the Great Plain, groups which derived their inspiration mostly from the region itself, and the life of the people living there. In Budapest Expressionism and Cubism gained adherents among the members of the group of painters known as the "Nyolcak" (the Group of Eight), and a workshop that kept pace with the most recent international trends of that time was organized by the poet **Lajos Kassák** (1887–1967). The impact of this workshop also left its mark—by means of the journal "MA"—on the works produced by artists such as the architect **Marcell Breuer, László Moholy-Nagy,** who taught in the Bauhaus, and **Victor Vasarely,** the founder of op art, artists who left the country after 1919 because of the stifling atmosphere generated by the Horthy regime.

Between the two world wars architects had only limited opportunities to apply new techniques, but the very best of them, including **Béla Lajta** (1873–1920), **Aladár Árkay** (1868–1932), **Farkas Molnár** (1897–1945) or **Lajos Kozma** (1884–1948), who was an outstanding interior architect, nevertheless managed to design some remarkable buildings. **Gyula Derkovits** (1894–1934), the greatest painter of his age, developed his art from Expressionism to a universal realism. A worker who became an artist, Derkovits lived in appalling poverty and virtually starved to death. The other great painter from that period was **Tivadar Csontváry Kosztka** (1853–1919), the lonely genius, who created his huge painted visions at the beginning of the century, but it was only from the middle of the twenties that his art was able to affect his contemporaries, and the world recognized the genius of this "Rousseau of the Danube" only at the end of the fifties. In addition to Derkovits and Csontváry, mention should also be made of the pictures and prints of the socialist **István Dési Huber** (1895–1944) and **Sándor Ék** (1902–1975), as well as the statues of **Ferenc Medgyessy** (1881–1958), who was so fond of the massive Maillol forms. Among the great artists of the period following the thirties were **Pál Pátzay** and **Zsigmond Kisfaludi Strobl** (1884–1975), who made well-known portraits of members of the royal family of England and of Bernard Shaw. Not so well known were the groups that were formed in Szentendre (on the Danube Bend), one of the most popular of whom was **Lajos Vajda** (1908–1941).

The importance of art works connected with architectural complexes built for the public grew in art after 1945. Examples are the frescoes of **Endre Domanovszky** (1907–1974) in Dunaújváros, the mosaics of **Jenő Barcsay** in Szentendre, the statues of **Jenő Kerényi** (1908–1975) and **József Somogyi**, and the figurines and statues of **Imre Varga** and **Miklós Borsos**. Béla Czóbel, József Egry (1883–1951), **István Szőnyi** (1894–1960) and **Aurél Bernáth**, leading figures in the legacy left by post-Impressionism, worked with renewed vigour for a considerable period of time after 1945.

Two internationally recognized names need to be mentioned in connection with modern applied arts: **Géza Gorka** (1894–1971), who united folk art and modern forms in the works he created with a virtuoso glaze technique, and **Margit Kovács** (1902–1977), who excelled with her charming figures and building ceramics that emphasize in their form the technique of the potter's wheel.

MUSIC

The performances of musicians and minstrels were much enjoyed in the courts of the kings of the House of Árpád, and later, court music was as much a part of the Gothic way of life in Hungary as it was anywhere else in Europe. We have knowledge of songs written down in the sixteenth century, including the songs of **Sebestyén Tinódi Lantos,** which live on in today's folk music. Collections of secular and ecclesiastical music and collegiate songs have been preserved from the seventeenth and the eighteenth centuries. In the eighteenth century, we can already speak of a serious musical life. **Joseph Haydn** lived and composed from 1761 to 1790 in the Baroque Esterházy Palace at Fertőd. Around 1780 a unique Hungarian musical style was created from the music played while soldiers were being recruited. What emerged from this was the romantically flavoured Hungarian music that can be heard in the compositions of **János Bihari** (1764–1827), **János Lavotta** (1764–1820), and **Antal Csermák** (1779–1822). Later, dances originated from the recruiting music, as for example, the fast and slow *csárdás* and the dignified and ceremonial *palotás*.

National music was created in the nineteenth century by **Ferenc Erkel** (1810–1893), the composer of the operas "Bánk bán" and "László Hunyadi", and it was he who set the National Anthem to music. The celebrated composer and pianist **Ferenc (Franz) Liszt** (1811–1886), who for a long time lived abroad, contributed significantly to the development of Hungarian musical life, and established a musical academy.

At the turn of the century, folk music came close to being forgotten through the popularity gained by the pseudo-folk song compositions known as the Hungarian popular song. It was at this time that **Béla Bartók** (1881–1945), together with his colleague **Zoltán Kodály** (1882–1967), investigated and collected pieces of musical folklore, subjecting them to serious scientific study, and elevated these to the highest artistic level by introducing them into modern music. Bartók's orchestral works and concertos, his chamber music, stage productions ("Bluebeard's Castle", "The Wooden Prince", "The Miraculous Mandarin") and folk song improvizations raised Hungarian music to new heights and saved folk music from oblivion. The activities carried out by Zoltán Kodály in composition and ethno-musicology were combined with his organizational efforts involving music education. The high level reached today by modern Hungarian music, musical education among young people, and new generations of artists and composers, all owe something to Kodály's efforts.

Hungarian music today is, on the one hand, continuing on the foundations laid by Bartók, combined with national traditions and universal trends, and on the other, seeking new directions. This is particularly true of the modern Hungarian operas, "Blood Wedding", "Hamlet" and "Samson" by **Sándor Szokolay,** and the works of **Emil Petrovics** ("C'est la guerre", "Lysistrate", "Crime and Punishment"). Both young and older composers of instrumental music have likewise made an international name for themselves. These include the following: **Pál Kadosa, Endre Szervánszky, András Mihály, György Kurtág, Endre Székely, András Szőllősy, Rudolf Maros, Zsolt Durkó, Attila Bozay,** and **István Láng.** But we meet numerous Hungarian names among the ranks of conductors, instrumental artists, singers, ballet dancers, and choreographers living in all parts of the world. Likewise, conductors, orchestras and artists from all over the world come to Hungary to give guest performances in Budapest's two opera houses and concert halls.

Musical life outside Budapest is also lively. There are opera companies and symphony orchestras in Pécs, Szeged, and Debrecen; and the modern Ballets of Pécs and Győr have gained an international reputation. Each year in August the Summer Festival in Szeged attracts huge audiences.

FOLK CUSTOMS AND FOLK ART

With the spread of the modern life-style, old **folk customs** are gradually sinking into oblivion in Hungary. Games and ceremonies connected with significant events of the year or a person's life are, however, still very much alive in the more isolated villages. The children's Bethlehem procession, itself a remnant of the medieval nativity plays, is popular around Christmas time; the magic of *regölés* (an ancient Hungarian folk custom at Christmas and New Year), which brings two people together for the purpose of marrying them, can be traced directly to shaman texts of the pagan period. (By casting various magic spells, it can be foretold in each home on New Year's Eve who will be the fiancé of each marriageable daughter.) Winter carnivals are also celebrated, just like Easter, when young men sprinkle the girls with water, while the girls present the young men with painted Easter eggs, braided sweet bread *(kalács)* and brandy *(pálinka)*. A long time ago, fires were lit on June 24 (St. John's Eve), and the people had to jump across them. There were also other holidays and festivals celebrated by the villagers in connection with the harvest, the vintage and other types of work. Some of these are still preserved today, such as the killing of a pig early in December, a time for entertaining guests.

Births, christenings, proposals, marriages, funerals and periods of mourning were all accompanied by their own special kind of ritual. Children, for example, were not very long ago given a "protective name" or nickname before christening to ward off evil spirits, and in certain places, masked guests appeared at weddings. In Southern Hungary there are places where the colour of the clothing worn during mourning is white. Many other examples could also be cited here. The Carnival Sunday procession *(busójárás)* is a particularly colourful folk custom that is preserved even today. The original purpose of this procession was both to celebrate the expulsion of the Turks and the beginning of spring.

In the villages, a gypsy orchestra usually plays at dances and weddings, but the peasant tradition of using the zither orchestra is still alive. (Gypsy music is synonymous neither with the rhythmical music of the gypsies, which does not use instruments, nor with Hungarian folk music, but is, rather, connected with a pseudo-folk musical form evolved for entertainment.)

The melodies of Hungarian **folk songs,** which employ a musical scale consisting of five tones (pentatonic), show the influence of Slovak, Southern Slavic and Rumanian folk songs. The basic structure and melody line of the Hungarian folk song is, however, related to Turkish and even Mongolian music. From the end of the last century onwards, a considerable amount of material has been collected and made public from this vast storehouse of melodies. Efforts to record the words of songs and folk ballads, however, started much earlier. Particularly inspiring were the Székely ballads which were recorded in the mountains of Transylvania and preserved medieval traditions. The power and refinement of these ballads can be compared to the folk poetry of the Scots and the Bretons. Research into ethno-musicology has also revealed ballads of this kind on the Great Plain and elsewhere. There is also a vast storehouse of Hungarian folk tales, an enumeration of which could fill two thick volumes.

DECORATIVE ARTS

The **decorative folk arts** are very popular in Hungary. Pieces of peasant furniture are usually decorated with engravings and carvings, leaving the wood in its original colour (chairs, benches, clothes-hangers put together with laths). Trousseau chests are painted with flower designs on a blue background, and are called "tulip chests". The carvings done by shepherds living on the Great Plain and in Transdanubia are especially beautiful. Salt-cellars and other useful articles are made out of wood and horn, and are frequently adorned with figural ornamentation, for example, of *betyár*s (outlaws). Spinning and weaving are done by the girls, and the blouses they make are decorated with many different kinds of embroidery work, simple black and white designs (South-eastern Hungary and Transdanubia) or colourful flower decorations (the neighbourhood of Kalocsa and the area around Mezőkövesd). The flower design they employ can adorn outer garments as well and is used, for example, on the _szűr,_ a long felt coat made by Hungarian shepherds, overcoats made out of animal hide, and vests. The so-called "clean rooms" of peasant houses are decorated with embroidered and hand-woven tablecloths, pillows, and curtains. Then there is modern folk pottery, preserving medieval traditions, such as terracotta, or black vases from Nádudvar, colourfully-painted plates, dishes, jugs, coloured or green wine mugs shaped like men, or jug-like vessels _(bokály)_ without a pouring lip.

The state is trying to preserve the legacy left by folk art. Through state support, many folk artists are engaged either independently or in cooperatives in making different kinds of articles for both use and decoration. Their products are sold by special chain stores, and outstanding folk artists are presented with high honours, just like any other distinguished artist.

SOME PROMINENT FIGURES OF CULTURE AND HISTORY

ADY, ENDRE (1877–1919): lyrical poet and journalist, who revived Hungarian poetry at the beginning of the 20th century.

APÁCZAI CSERE, JÁNOS (1625–1659): philosophical and pedagogical writer, editor of the first Hungarian encyclopedia.

ARANY, JÁNOS (1817–1882): greatest Hungarian epic poet and composer of ballads, outstanding translator of literary works.

ASBÓTH, OSZKÁR (1891–1960): engineer, one of the inventors of the helicopter (1928).

BABITS, MIHÁLY (1883–1941): poet, short-story writer, translator of literary works, and essayist.

BAJCSY-ZSILINSZKY, ENDRE (1888–1944): one of the leaders of the national antifascist movement during the Second World War. He was executed by the Hungarian Arrow Cross.

BALASSI, BÁLINT (1554–1594): poet, first outstanding representative of lyric poetry written in Hungarian.

BARTÓK, BÉLA (1881–1945): one of the great figures of modern music.

BOLYAI, JÁNOS (1802–1860): mathematician, who revolutionized geometry.

CSOKONAI VITÉZ, MIHÁLY (1773–1805): poet of the Age of Enlightenment.

CSONTVÁRY KOSZTKA, TIVADAR (1853–1919): self-taught painter, who ingeniously expressed his intuitive imagination in his paintings.

DERKOVITS, GYULA (1894–1934): painter and graphic artist, who immortalized the life and struggles of the proletariat.

DÉRY, TIBOR (1894–1977): one of the outstanding prose writers of Hungarian literature.

DOBÓ, ISTVÁN (d. 1572): Captain of Eger Castle, who in 1552 defended the Castle against the Turks in a heroic struggle.

DÓZSA, GYÖRGY (?1474–1514): leader of the Peasant revolt of 1514.

EÖTVÖS, LORÁND (1848–1919): physicist, the inventor of the torsion pendulum named after him.

ERKEL, FERENC (1810–1893): composer, pianist, founder of the Hungarian National Opera, and first director of the State Opera House.

FEJÉR, LIPÓT (1880–1954): one of the greatest mathematicians of the present century, who achieved results of fundamental importance mainly through his research into the theory of function.

FELLNER, JAKAB (1722–1780): architect, master of neo-Classical and late Baroque architecture.

FERENCZY, ISTVÁN (1792–1856): sculptor, representative of neo-Classicist sculpture.

FRANKEL, LEÓ (1844–1896): one of the founders of the First International, minister of the Paris Commune, chief organizer of the General Workers' Party of Hungary.

HESS, ANDRÁS: printer, founder of the first printing-press in Hungary (Buda, 1473).

HILD, JÓZSEF (1789–1867): architect, one of Hungary's outstanding neo-Classicist architects.

HUNYADI, JÁNOS (?1407–1456): heroic commander of the battles fought against the Turks.

ILLYÉS, GYULA (1902–1983): poet, short-story writer, dramatist, a representative of the populist writers' movement.

JANUS PANNONIUS (1434–1472): poet, bishop, first Hungarian representative of secular Latin lyrical poetry in Hungary.

JEDLIK, ÁNYOS (1802–1895): designer of the first electro-magnetic motor.

JÓKAI, MÓR (1825–1904): romantic novelist, whose works have run into hundreds of Hungarian and foreign editions.

JÓZSEF, ATTILA (1905–1937): most outstanding representative of modern revolutionary lyrical poetry.

KANDÓ, KÁLMÁN (1869–1931):

mechanical engineer, one of the pioneers of the electric railway, designer of the electric locomotive named after him.

KARINTHY, FRIGYES (1887–1938): writer, poet, critic and translator, creator of philosophical-satirical Hungarian prose.

KASSÁK, LAJOS (1887–1967): poet, artist, editor of the activist journal entitled "MA".

KATONA, JÓZSEF (1791–1830): dramatist, author of "Bánk bán".

KODÁLY, ZOLTÁN (1882–1967): composer, musicologist, one of the great pioneers of music education.

KORÁNYI, FRIGYES (1827–1913): doctor and medical researcher, who made an international name for himself through the results he achieved in the field of physiotherapy.

KOSSUTH, LAJOS (1802–1894): governor of Hungary during the 1848–1849 Hungarian War of Independence, outstanding orator and statesman.

KOSZTOLÁNYI, DEZSŐ (1885–1936): poet, translator of literary works, prose writer, a significant artist of form and language.

KŐRÖSI CSOMA, SÁNDOR (1784–1842): orientalist, the first European researcher to do work on Tibet, he compiled the first English--Tibetan dictionary.

KUN, BÉLA (1886–1939): one of the leading political figures of the Hungarian Republic of Councils.

LISZT, FERENC (FRANZ) (1811–1886): one of the forerunners of modern music, founder of the Budapest Academy of Music.

LUKÁCS, GYÖRGY (1885–1971): philosopher, literary historian, aesthetician.

MADÁCH, IMRE (1823–1864): dramatist, his major work is "The Tragedy of Man", which has been translated into English and other major languages.

MARTINOVICS, IGNÁC (1755–1795): leader of the Hungarian Jacobin Movement; he was put to death, together with the other leaders of the organization.

MATTHIAS CORVINUS (1440–1490): son of János Hunyadi, king of Hungary from 1458.

MEDGYESSY, FERENC (1881–1958): sculptor, master of Hungarian realistic folk sculpture.

MIKSZÁTH, KÁLMÁN (1847–1910): ironic novelist and writer of short stories.

MÓRICZ, ZSIGMOND (1879–1942): journalist and realistic novelist, outstanding representative of 20th-century Hungarian prose.

MUNKÁCSY, MIHÁLY (1844–1900): painter, outstanding master of 19th-century realism.

NÉMETH, LÁSZLÓ (1901–1975): novelist and playwright, master of psychological and realistic works on social conditions.

ÖRKÉNY, ISTVÁN (1912–1979): outstanding figure of modern Hungarian prose, especially drama. His two most famous plays, "The Family Tóth" and "Catsplay", have been successfully staged in many parts of the world.

PETŐFI, SÁNDOR (1823–1849): lyrical poet; his revolutionary poetry made him one of the leading figures of the 1848–49 Revolution and War of Independence; he died on the battlefield.

POLLACK, MIHÁLY (1773–1855): architect, a significant figure of Hungarian neo-Classical architecture.

PUSKÁS, TIVADAR (1845–1893): electrical technician, inventor, associate of Edison; he set up the first Hungarian telephone exchange and invented the telephonograph.

RADNÓTI, MIKLÓS (1909–1944): poet who died a martyr, translator of literary works, outstanding representative of Hungarian anti-fascist lyricism.

RÁKÓCZI II, FERENC (1676–1735): Prince of Hungary and Transylvania, leader of the national War of Independence that took place between 1703 and 1711.

RIESZ, FRIGYES (1882–1958): world-famous mathematician, one of the pioneers of functional analysis.

RIPPL-RÓNAI, JÓZSEF (1861–1927): painter, Hungarian representative of attempts at post-Impressionism and *art nouveau*.

SEMMELWEIS, IGNÁC (1818–1865): physician, university professor, investigated and found the cause of puerperal fever, he worked out a preventive measure to treat the disease.

STEPHEN I (975–1038): first king of Hungary, crowned in the year 1000.

SZÉCHENYI, ISTVÁN (1791–1860): one of the leaders of the Reform Movement that evolved during the 1820s; one of the initiators of Hungary's cultural and economic development.

SZINYEI MERSE, PÁL (1845–1920): artist, pioneer of the *plein-air* style of painting.

TÁNCSICS, MIHÁLY (1799–1884): writer and politician of revolutionary democracy, one of the pioneers of socialist thought.

TELEKI, SÁMUEL (1845–1915): researcher on Africa, discoverer of Lakes Rudolf and Stefania as well as a volcano named after him; he was among the first to climb Mt. Kilimanjaro.

THÖKÖLY, IMRE (1657–1705): prince of Northern Hungary, leader of the anti-Habsburg movement at the end of the 17th century.

TÓTH, ÁRPÁD (1886–1928): poet, translator of literary works, short-story writer.

TÜRR, ISTVÁN (1825–1908): the Hungarian-born chief-of-staff of Garibaldi. He took part in working out the plans for the building of the Panama Canal.

VÖRÖSMARTY, MIHÁLY (1800–1855): lyric, epic and dramatic poet who wrote in the romantic style.

YBL, MIKLÓS (1814–1891): architect, prolific representative of Hungarian eclecticism.

ZRÍNYI, MIKLÓS (1620–1664): politician, military commander, poet and political writer, author of the first great Hungarian national epic "Szigeti veszedelem" (The Siege of Sziget).

KEY TO THE MAPS

- ▦ Railway station
- ▣ Long-distance coach terminal
- ⬆ Landing-stage, pier
- Ⓜ Metro station
- Ⓗ Hotel
- Ⓜ Motel
- ⌂ Tourist hostel
- ⒤ Tourist bureau, travel office
- ⊚ Post office
- �m Museum, gallery
- Ⓑ Library
- ⒩ College, academy
- ♥ Theatre
- 🎭 Open-air theatre
- ✕ Restaurant
- Inn *(csárda)*
- Ethnographical Museum

- Café-bar, bar
- ▦ Department store
- Market
- Ⓟ Parking
- Petrol station
- Ⓣ Service station
- Baths, thermal baths
- Beach, open-air pool
- ▲ Campsite
- Nature conservation area
- Fishing
- Look-out tower
- Ⓞ Cave
- Ruins
- Ⓡ Roman ruins
- Castle
- † ✱ ⛪ ⛪ Church, chapel
- ⊖ No entry

A DETAILED GUIDE

Budapest

Budapest, the capital of Hungary (population: 2,115,000), is situated on the two banks of the Danube and covers an area of 525.6 sq.km. **Buda,** lying on the west (or right) bank of the river, comprises almost one-third (173.2 sq.km) of the area; while **Pest,** which is situated on the east (or left) bank, occupies two-thirds (352.4 sq.km). Administratively, Budapest is divided into 22 districts, city management being responsible for the capital's City Council and 22 district municipal councils. Districts I–III, XI, XII and XXII are situated on the Buda side of the Danube, Districts IV–X and XIII–XX on the Pest side, and District XXI on the northern tip of Csepel Island.

The length of the Danube passing through the capital is 28 km, the width of the river is between 300–400 m. Its average depth is between 3 and 4 m, only at one place does it reach 10 m. The two banks are connected by six road and two railway bridges.

Budapest is situated at the point where mountainous Transdanubia (Dunántúl) and the Great Plain (Alföld) meet. Much of Buda is built on hills and is surrounded on the north, west, and south by the forest-covered Buda Mountain Range. Pest lies on a gently sloping plain. The city's fortunate geographical situation enables the visitor to Budapest to enjoy a beautiful panorama from the more distant heights of the rocky **Gellért Hill** (235 m), which extends to the shores of the Danube, **Castle Hill** (Várhegy; 167 m), the **Rózsadomb** (195 m), and the Buda Mountain Range. The highest peak, **János Hill**, rises 529 m above sea level. The Danube is 96, the Inner City 100 m above sea level.

The Hungarian capital is one of the most important traffic centres of Eastern Europe.

THE HISTORY OF THE CITY

Archeological evidence indicates that a settlement existed in the area of present-day Budapest as far back as the 4th century B.C. The area between the Danube and the Buda Mountain Range was also inhabited during both the Bronze Age and the Iron Age. Communities of various sizes were established by the Illyrians and Celts between the 10th and 5th centuries B.C. During the Ist century A.D., Roman legions, in extending the boundaries of their empire as far as the Danube, occupied the Celtic settlement Ak-Ink ("abundant waters") in northern Buda, which had a fully-developed handicrafts industry and an urban-type civilization. The Roman city of Aquincum, the capital of the province of Lower Pannonia, grew up on the site of the Celtic settlement. A smaller fortified settlement that functioned as an advanced Roman bridgehead, Contra-Aquincum, was established on the east bank of the Danube at a place known as Barbaricum, near what is now the Pest end of Elizabeth Bridge.

Aquincum attained the height of its glory during the 2nd and 3rd centuries. The Emperor Hadrian later had a magnificent marble palace built in Aquincum while he was still governor of Pannonia. Two amphitheatres have remained since Roman times, and excavations have revealed a drainage system, baths, a hypocaust and villas. Owing to the weakening of the Roman Empire as well as to increasing attacks from outside, Aquincum started to decline during the 4th century, and its population sharply decreased. By the time the Roman legions had left at the beginning of the 5th century and had handed Pannonia over to the Huns, only a portion of the former 25,000–30,000 inhabitants of Aquincum remained.

At the time of the migrations the sovereign tribe of Avars lived for two centuries in the area of present-day Pest. Following Charlemagne's victory over the Avar Empire, a Bulgarian-Slav population settled in the area of the Danube crossing.

After the Magyar Conquest, which took place in the Carpathian Basin at

the end of the 9th century, significant centres of trade developed on both banks of the Danube, and with the establishment of the monarchy, Buda (not present-day Buda, but what is known today as Óbuda) became a royal city. After the 13th-century Mongol invasion (1241–1242), King Béla IV (1235–1270) constructed a city surrounded by a wall on the Castle Hill in Buda and moved there what had remained of the population, as well as the new settlers. A royal palace was also built on Castle Hill, and in 1255 the monarch raised Castle Hill to the rank of a city known as Buda. (From that time on the former Buda was known as Óbuda—Old Buda.) Pest continued to develop as an independent city on the east bank of the river, and it became a centre for crafts and commerce.

Beginning in 1286 feudal Diets were held on Rákos-mező in Pest. King Louis the Great of the House of Anjou bestowed staple rights on Buda, and at the turn of the 15th century Sigismund of Luxembourg built on Castle Hill what was called Friss Castle, one of the most beautiful architectural complexes of the age. The golden age of the medieval city culminated under the rule of King Matthias Corvinus. The king completed the Royal Palace with a sidewing in Renaissance style and had it decorated with statues and paintings by Hungarian and Italian artists. Codices were prepared for the library in the miniature workshops of Buda and Florence, and less than two decades after Gutenberg, in 1473, the András Hess Press was working in Buda, by that time one of the cultural, commercial, and political centres of Europe. A workshop manufacturing Italian style faience also operated in the city.

Buda's development was interrupted in the 16th century by a tragic turn of events in Hungarian history. After the Hungarian defeat at Mohács, the city finally fell in 1541 into the hands of the Turks and the three communities on the banks of the Danube (Pest, Buda, Óbuda) lived under Turkish domination until 1686, when the forces of the Christian league under the leadership of Charles of Lorraine drove the Turks out. Ottoman domination had marked an age of decline and destruction. Palaces and churches were destroyed, no new buildings, with the exception of baths, were erected, and only the castle walls were reinforced. The fire that broke out in the wake of the siege of 1686 completed the destruction.

Following the expulsion of the Turks, the population of Buda, Pest and Óbuda consisted of scarcely one thousand persons. The three towns were, however, re-populated with Hungarian, German, Serbian and Slovak settlers in the following decades. In the 18th century when industrialization got under way, trade was already flourishing. In place of the Royal Palace that had been destroyed, a new palace was erected. Many churches and palaces were built, first in a Baroque and later in a neo-Classical style. Buda became the military and administrative centre, and in 1777 the University was moved from Nagyszombat (now Trnava, Czechoslovakia) to Buda, and in 1784 to Pest.

In the first decades of the 19th century the city's rate of development accelerated. It was during this so-called Age of Reform (1825–1848) that institutes and public buildings were established. Much of this was due to the initiative of Count István Széchenyi, who was engaged in the civil transformation of the country. Under his direction the first permanent bridge, the Chain Bridge (Lánchíd), was built linking Buda with Pest, the first railway line was opened, the Hungarian Academy of Sciences was founded, and a steamship began operating on the Danube. Széchenyi was also the first man to raise the idea of uniting the three cities. After the Revolution of March 15, 1848 broke out, Parliament convened in Pest (until then it had met in Pozsony [now Bratislava, Czechoslovakia]), and the first Hungarian ministry responsible to Parliament also functioned there. On the proposal of Lajos Kossuth, the government of the 1848–49 War of Independence agreed on, and provided for, the unification of the three cities.

The revolution was followed by the anti-Habsburg War of Independence. At the beginning of 1849 the Austrians entered the city, but in May the Hungarian troops recaptured Buda Castle. The autocracy that followed the defeat of the War of Independence upset the realization of many plans, including the unification of the three cities. Nevertheless, a few fundamental achievements of the struggle for freedom survived, and as a result of these bourgeois reforms, development had already accelerated during the years of oppression. The population of Buda, Pest, and Óbuda was 54,000 in 1799, 100,000 in 1848, 270,000 in 1869, and in 1890 it already exceeded half a million.

The process of industrialization speeded up, especially after the 1867 Compromise with the Habsburgs. The law of 1872 proclaiming the unification of Buda, Pest, and Óbuda, on the basis of which Budapest was born in 1873, further increased the significance of the city.

The Habsburg Monarchy collapsed

at the end of World War I. On March 21, 1919, the Hungarian Republic of Councils was proclaimed. After the defeat of the Republic of Councils, and under the twenty-five years of Miklós Horthy's regime, steadily increasing social conflicts left their mark on the life of the capital.

In 1930 the population of the capital already exceeded one million. The inner part of present-day District XIII (Újlipótváros), the outskirts of District XIV, as well as the elegant residential parts of Districts XI, XII, and II were all developed during that period. But meanwhile, an increasingly large part of the population found itself in serious financial difficulties as a result of the economic crises of the thirties and the many constricting measures of the war. The city suffered serious damage as a consequence of the aerial bombardments of the Second World War and of the almost two-month-long siege during the winter of 1944–45. The Nazis blew up all the city's bridges and removed equipment and raw materials from the factories. In the course of the siege, 74% of buildings in the city were damaged and more than one-third were destroyed. The Soviet Red Army liberated all Budapest by February 13, 1945.

In the years following the liberation, the capital rose rapidly from its ruins. The outer districts were joined to it in 1950. During the next years, modern residential estates were built. An east-west Metro (Underground) line has been completed, and now that a north-south line is largely completed, the development of mass transportation is rapidly progressing. The main roads leading to the capital have been rebuilt and the road system has been modernized.

While a large modern city was being created, care was also taken to preserve historic monuments from the past. For example, numerous remains of Aquincum dating back to Roman times were brought to light during excavations carried out in conjunction with the rebuilding of the northeast section of Óbuda. The remains were placed in exhibition rooms set up in the basements or ground floors of new buildings. The largest historic building complex, Buda Castle, which was destroyed by fire during the battles fought in the winter of 1944–45, has been restored on the basis of thorough archeological research, and it can be attributed to just this type of research that many valuable areas dating back to the Middle Ages have come to light underneath later superstructures.

Finding one's way about the capital is facilitated by the easily recognizable configuration of the city. One glance at the map will show that the boulevards situated on both sides of the Danube curve from one Danube bridge to the other. In Buda the thoroughfare going round Castle Hill stretches from Margit-híd (Margaret Bridge) to Erzsébet-híd (Elizabeth Bridge) and is lengthened by a branch that goes towards the south to Petőfi-híd (Petőfi Bridge). Another thoroughfare surrounds Gellért Hill, and the two are joined in the south by a main road leading to the Balaton and Vienna, and in the north by a main road running towards the Buda Mountains and in the direction of Aquincum and Szentendre.

On the Pest side, the Kiskörút (Little Boulevard), as it is called, runs roughly from Marx tér to the Szabadság-híd (Liberty Bridge), the Nagykörút (Great Boulevard) from the Margit-híd (Margaret Bridge) to the Petőfi-híd (Petőfi Bridge), and the outer boulevard roughly from the Árpád-híd (Árpád Bridge) to the southern railway bridge. A still wider curved outer belt is now under construction. Broad thoroughfares lead radially from the bridges of the Danube to the different parts of the city, and other roads that lead out of the city.

BUDA

The Castle District and the Royal Palace

The Castle District (Várnegyed), surrounded by protective walls and ramparts, is situated on the plateau of **Castle Hill,** which is 167 m high. In the Middle Ages the northern two-thirds of the plateau were occupied by the so-called **Citizens' Town;** the southern third was occupied by the former royal residence. Although the historic city area has been destroyed many times over the centuries, the street arrangement of the Castle District as well as its basic housing scheme still follow the medieval city plan. After the Turkish occupation, the city was rebuilt using the walls of old houses, and it was only during the recent reconstructions that many medieval buildings, buried beneath later constructions, came to light.

The chief streets lying in the Castle District are: Úri utca, Országház utca, Táncsics Mihály utca, Fortuna utca all running in a north-south direction from the Bécsi kapu (Vienna Gate) and Kapisztrán tér towards the centre of the Castle District, and Szentháromság (Trinity) tér.

The **Bécsi kapu** (Vienna Gate) was built in place of a demolished 18th-century gate. The **National Archives** (Országos Levéltár, built between 1915 and 1918) rise beside the Vienna Gate. Opposite the Archives are some 18th-century houses and in front of them an ornamental fountain preserves the memory of Ferenc Kazinczy, the leader of the Language Reform that took place at the turn of the 19th century. The **Lutheran church** in Bécsi kapu tér was built in 1896.

The two-storied neo-Classicist palace housing the present-day **Museum of Military History** stands in the vicinity of Bécsi kapu tér in Kapisztrán tér (the entrance to the museum is at **Tóth Árpád sétány 40**). The oldest historic monument in **Úri utca (No. 55)** is the solitary tower of the **Church of St. Mary Magdalene,** built in the 13th century. This was the only Christian church in Buda during the first period of the Turkish occupation. The Catholics and Protestants took turns using it, and later the Turks turned it into a mosque. All that remained after the devastations of World War II was the four-storied Gothic tower. The simple Baroque building standing at **Úri utca 53** was a Franciscan monastery, well known because the leaders of the Hungarian Jacobin movement were imprisoned here in 1795. Ignác Martinovics and his companions were led from here to the Vérmező (Field of Blood) beneath Castle Hill and there were put to death. (The spot was named after this event, and a stone plaque marks the place of execution.)

Gothic *sedilia,* the characteristic features of medieval lay architecture, can be found in the gateways of many buildings in **Úri utca.** The house at **No. 19** was the residence of Pipo of Ozora (known originally as Filippo Scolari), one of the wealthy patrons of the Renaissance. The entrance to a **cave system** reaching deep into Castle Hill can be found at **No. 9.**

Országház utca received its name from the fact that building **No. 28** was the old Parliament building, where feudal Diets were held. The premises are now used by certain institutes of the Hungarian Academy of Sciences, and scientific conferences and international congresses are held in the former national assembly Empire hall. **Országház utca 20** was built in the Gothic style at the end of the 14th century and was rebuilt in the Baroque style in 1771. A relief on the façade of **Fortuna utca 6** portrays Cupid. The street was named after the 18th-century Fortuna Restaurant, the building of which today houses the **Museum of Hungarian Commerce and Catering**. The materials on exhibit display the

The Castle District and Watertown

Buda Castle seen from the east (woodcut by Michael Wolgemuth, late 15th c.)

development of catering in Hungary from the Roman age to the middle of the 20th century. Among the items of interest are the original furnishings of a Hungarian csárda (inn) and a 19th-century confectioner's shop. The beautiful relief on the façade of house **No. 9** is the work of Ferenc Medgyessy (1881–1958).

In the Middle Ages the Jewish quarter was situated in the neighbourhood of the present-day **Táncsics Mihály utca**. Remains of a medieval synagogue and cemetery were found and uncovered under **No. 26;** they can be seen in the **Museum** established *in situ*. **No. 9** was originally an ammunitions dump and then a prison. It was here that Lajos Kossuth was imprisoned between 1837 and 1840, and Mihály Táncsics in 1847–48, the latter being freed from his captivity as a result of the revolution of March 15, 1848. Beethoven stayed at **No. 7** while he was giving concerts in Buda. The **Institute of Musicology** of the Hungarian Academy of Science and the **Bartók Archives** are housed here.

A statue of Pope Innocent XI stands in the middle of **Hess András tér**. It was erected in memory of the assistance the Pope offered in organizing an international military force which helped expel the Turks in the 1680s. The square itself bears the name of the first printer in Buda whose printing shop operated here in the 1470s. The wrought-iron red hedgehog over the gate of **No. 3** indicates that in the house known as the **Red Hedgehog Inn** there used to be a tavern, once the only public lodging house in Buda. Also in Hess András tér stands the **Budapest-Hilton**. The remaining walls and sanctuary of a medieval Dominican monastery and the Gothic tower of the 13th-century Church of St. Nicholas have been incorporated into its walls. The replica of King Matthias' monument at Bautzen in the German Democratic Republic on the wall of the tower is a reminder of the fact that the Buda Academy founded in 1477 by King Matthias operated here. There was probably a miniature workshop in the vicinity where the miniatures of the Corvina codices were prepared. The houses opposite the tower also preserve historic monuments from the Middle Ages.

A panorama of the residential areas of Buda and of the Buda Hills unfolds to strollers on the western edge of Castle Hill from the **Tóth Árpád sétány,** which runs parallel to the protective wall. There are some old cannons on the northern part of the promenade **(No. 40)** in front of the

Museum of Military History. The rooms of the museum exhibit a collection of flags, weapons, and uniforms, as well as woodcuts, paintings, and statues connected with military history.

Glancing down into the valley from the rampart promenade, which is adorned with circular bastions, it is possible to follow closely the section of the system of roads called **Mártírok útja,** that begins at the Buda end of the Margaret Bridge and runs as the continuation of the Nagykörút (Great Boulevard) of Pest, towards the south. Mártírok útja leads into **Moszkva tér,** one of the main traffic centres of Buda. Directly below Castle Hill runs **Attila út,** which, together with **Krisztina körút** running almost parallel to it, surrounds the extensive **Vérmező Park.** On the western edge of the park is situated the **Southern Railway Station** (Déli pályaudvar), the terminal for trains going to Lake Balaton and other destinations in Western Hungary. The western terminal of the east–west line of the Metro is also located here. **Alkotás utca** begins at the railway station and leads to where the Balaton motorway M7 begins, and Krisztina körút leads towards the south to Elizabeth Bridge.

From Tóth Árpád sétány through Szentháromság utca we reach **Szentháromság tér,** at one time the centre of Buda's city life.

The **former City Hall (No. 2)** with its corner balcony and clock tower was built on medieval foundations in the Baroque style according to the plans of Venerio Ceresola, Matthias Kayr, and Máté Nepauer. The statue of Pallas Athene standing on the corner of the building was originally part of a fountain belonging to one of the public wells in the Castle District (the work of Carlo Adami, 18th century). The **equestrian statue** in front of the building portrays András Hadik, Maria Theresa's Hungarian general, who with his hussars held Berlin to ransom during the Austrian War of Succession in 1757.

Once again we can see characteristic Gothic sedilia in the gateways of houses **No. 5 and 7,** Szentháromság utca. The **Ruszwurm Confectioner's** has operated at **No. 7** since 1827.

The Baroque **Trinity Column** (by Fülöp Ungleich) in Szentháromság tér was erected out of gratitude by the survivors of a plague epidemic in 1712–13 and since then has more than once been enlarged and recon-

Bécsi kapu tér

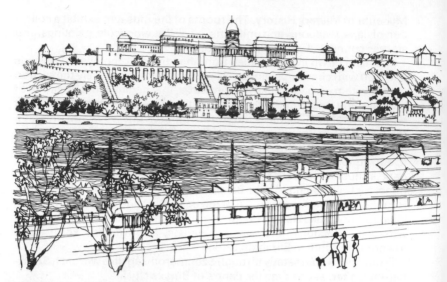

structed. The **relief of St. Rosalia** seen on the column is the work of Antal Hörger, from 1738.

The building on the north side of the square designed in a neo-Gothic eclectic style was built between 1901 and 1905 according to the plans of Sándor Fellner. Earlier it housed the Ministry of Finance, now it serves various cultural institutions.

One of the most outstanding monuments of the Castle District—and indeed of the whole city—is the **Church of Our Lady,** popularly known as the **Matthias Church.** The church was built in the 13th century by Béla IV and reconstructed as a hall church in the 14th century, when the southern "Mary Door" was also added. King Matthias Corvinus had the church rebuilt in 1470, and his coat of arms can be seen today on the façade of the tower, hence the church's other, more popular, name. The Matthias Church was used by the Turks as their main mosque. It was later seriously damaged, and its roof collapsed during the liberation siege of 1686. In the 18th century the church was rebuilt in the Baroque style. Its present appearance was achieved in the 19th century when Frigyes Schulek completely reconstructed the church. Schulek had the 18th-century Baroque sections of the building removed, and remodelled the exterior, largely by reproducing the original Gothic sections unearthed during demolitions. The damage the church suffered during the Second World War was repaired between 1954 and 1968.

Charles Robert of the House of Anjou was crowned king in the Matthias Church in 1308, King Matthias Corvinus married Catherine Podebrad here in 1463, and Beatrice of Aragon in 1470, after the death of his first wife. Francis Joseph I and Charles IV of the House of Habsburg were crowned in the Matthias Church in 1867 and 1916 respectively. Ferenc Liszt's monumental work, the "Coronation Mass", was composed in 1867 for the coronation.

From outside the most beautiful part of the church is the 80 m high, stone-laced Gothic south tower. The main door ending in a slightly pointed arch is situated between this tower and a stocky two-storied tower with four turrets, called the Béla Tower. The Mary Door on the south façade is decorated with a 14th-century relief depicting the death of the Virgin Mary.

Inside, a marble statue portraying the Virgin and the infant Jesus stands in the south window of the Loreto Chapel (17th century). The sarcophagi of Béla III and his wife, Anne de Châtillon, rest in the Trinity

View of Buda with Castle Hill

Chapel, opening from the north aisle. Frigyes Schulek designed their tombs in 1898, when the remains were moved from Székesfehérvár to Buda. The neo-Gothic high altar of the church is also the work of Schulek.

Near the chancel, in the former crypt, we find a museum of stonework remains, including medieval carvings. The crypt, together with the gallery and St. Stephen's chapel, houses a collection of ecclesiastical art, including old goblets, pyxes, various works of the goldsmith's art, chasubles, and replicas of the Hungarian royal crown and orb.

Doorway with sedilia in the Castle District (Úri utca 40)

Szentháromság tér with the Matthias Church and the (Budapest) Hilton in the background

An **equestrian statue of** the founder of the state, **(St.) Stephen I,** stands in front of the south façade of the Matthias Church (Alajos Stróbl, 1906).

The plateau of Castle Hill is bordered on the east by the **Fishermen's Bastion** (Halászbástya) with its towers and stairways. Its name is derived from the fact that it was built between 1901 and 1903 over a former fish market and fishermen's village. Frigyes Schulek, in planning it, created an unusual mixture of neo-Romanesque and neo-Gothic styles. A beautiful panorama of the capital unfolds from the pleasant terraces and balconies of the Bastion, a panorama which offers fine subjects for the photographer's lens. Below the Fishermen's Bastion, in a bend of the road, stands the bronze statue of János Hunyadi (the work of István Tóth), the military commander who in 1456 repulsed the Turkish attack at Nándorfehérvár (today's Belgrade), and who was the future King Matthias's father. Still further down, the streets of Watertown (Víziváros) wind in and out. The Danube below, Margaret Island to the north, Gellért Hill to the south, on the opposite bank the Parliament building with its dome and towers, and behind it the vast numbers of houses situated in Pest complete the view.

There are also a few interesting medieval architectural monuments in **Tárnok utca,** a street leading from Szentháromság tér. The Gothic merchant houses **Nos. 14 and 16** were restored by removing the Baroque superstructures that had been added later. It was even possible to reconstruct the old graffiti.

The oldest coffee-house in Buda, the "Korona" (Crown), is situated on the south side of **Dísz tér,** the building of the **Castle Theatre** (Várszínház) stands in **Színház utca (No. 1–3).** The original theatre building, which was in turn a monastery, a mosque, and then a Baroque church, was rebuilt in Louis XVI style by Farkas Kempelen in 1787. The theatre was opened the same year, and in 1790 the first performance in Hungarian was given here by the company of László Kelemen, a pioneer of the Hungarian theatre. On May 7, 1800 Beethoven gave a concert here. The theatre building was burned down during the fighting of 1944–45, and was opened again in 1978 after reconstruction. The statue of a national guardsman standing in Dísz tér recalls the soldiers who fought in the 1848–49 War of Independence (the work of György Zala); the "Hussar looking at his sword" nearby is the work of Zsigmond Kisfaludi Strobl.

THE ROYAL PALACE

Following the devastations of the Second World War the former Royal Palace was reconstructed so that many medieval parts, damaged during earlier remodelling, were again made visible. The southern fortification system and others rose again as a result of these reconstructions. It consists of the Mace Tower, the round bastion on the south, and the Gothic gate tower which greets those arriving at the southern entrance of the Royal Palace from the direction of Szarvas tér. The "turbaned" Turkish tombstones lying below the walls are a reminder of the time when Buda was the seat of the Turkish Pasha of Buda.

The earliest precursor of the Royal Palace was a royal residence of only moderate size built in the second half of the 13th century by Béla IV. The Anjou kings later enlarged the palace; the foundations of the István Tower that have been uncovered and the successfully reconstructed crypt of the Royal Chapel are monuments from that age. Many sections from the time of Sigismund of Luxembourg, such as the huge Knights' Hall, have been recreated. The interior of the palace was rebuilt by Matthias Corvinus originally in a Gothic and later in a Renaissance style, after which he began construction of the huge Renaissance wing added to the northeast section. The palace fell into ruins during the Turkish occupation and was finally destroyed in the great siege of 1686. Between 1715 and 1723 a smaller palace was built on the ruins, and by 1770, under the reign of Maria Theresa, part of the palace had been completed, to the plans of Jean-Nicolas Jadot, Franz Anton Hillebrandt and Ignác Oracsek. On March 3, 1800, Joseph Haydn conducted his oratorio "The Creation" in the ceremonial hall of the palace. One of the wings as well as the middle part were destroyed by fire in 1849 when the palace was occupied by Hungarian troops participating in the War of Independence. The whole building was renovated and enlarged during the 1850s. The neo-Baroque form of the building complex is the result of wide-scale construction work directed by Miklós Ybl and later by Alajos Hauszmann between

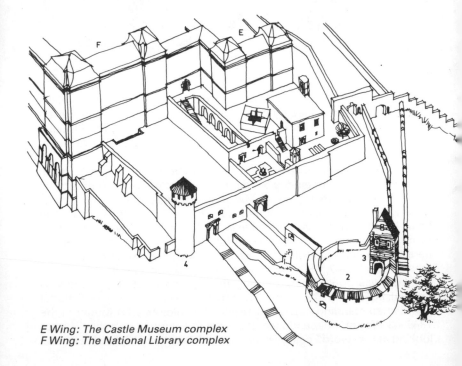

E Wing: The Castle Museum complex
F Wing: The National Library complex

1869 and 1903. The palace was burned down and its roof collapsed during the Second World War. It was rebuilt with a modern interior by incorporating walls that had not been destroyed. The uncovered medieval sections were renovated (one section can be seen in the Castle Museum), and further excavations are constantly being carried out. Newer layers, statues presumed to be of the Anjou age, and building remains are being unearthed in the course of these excavations. Among the sections reconstructed it is advisable first to examine the fortifications on the outside—the round bastion, the Mace Tower, the ramparts, and the castle garden. Inside the Castle Museum, the Knights' Hall dating back to the age of Sigismund, the Royal Chapel, and the Museum of Stonework Finds are well worth a visit.

Cultural institutions have been given a home in the newly constructed buildings of the Royal Palace. The **Castle Museum** (Wing E) has an exhibition on its main floor entitled "Two Thousand Years of Budapest" with

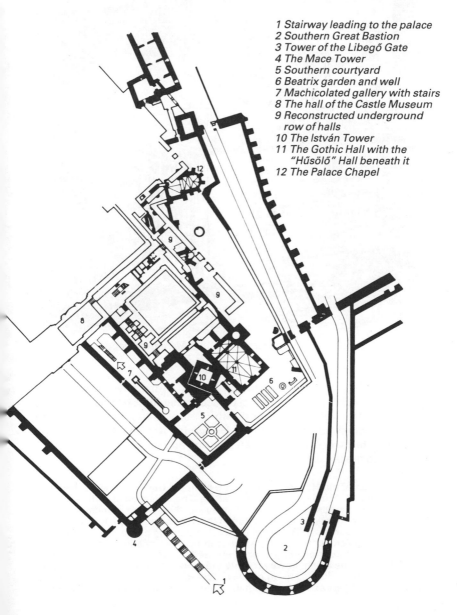

1 Stairway leading to the palace
2 Southern Great Bastion
3 Tower of the Libegő Gate
4 The Mace Tower
5 Southern courtyard
6 Beatrix garden and well
7 Machicolated gallery with stairs
8 The hall of the Castle Museum
9 Reconstructed underground
  row of halls
10 The István Tower
11 The Gothic Hall with the
   "Hűsölő" Hall beneath it
12 The Palace Chapel

View towards the north with the Parliament and Margaret Bridge

historical documents relating to the history of the city; in the reconstructed halls of the medieval royal palace archeological finds, paintings,
articles used in every-day life, and 14th-century statue fragments can be
seen. The collections housed in the **Hungarian National Gallery** (Wings
B, C, D) contain works of Hungarian painting and sculpture from the Middle Ages to the present.

The exhibition of old Hungarian art in the National Gallery presents medieval
stone sculptures, paintings and painted altars. The collection of 19th- and 20th-
century sculpture has been put on display on the stairway landings. These
include the neo-Classical statues made in the 19th century by **István Ferenczy,**
the terracotta figures of **Miklós Izsó** portraying dancing peasants, and the 20th-
century master **Ferenc Medgyessy**'s Etruscan-inspired creations, among others.
    Nineteenth-century painting makes up the bulk of the material on the first
floor. (For the time being, however, only the works of a few of the most important masters and schools are on display.) The Romantic works of **Mihály Munkácsy** (to the left) are examples of outstanding 19th-century painting. Masters of

14th-century busts from the
Castle Museum

plein-air painting are **Pál Szinyei Merse, László Mednyánszky** and **Károly Ferenczy.** Trends in painting that made their appearance at the turn of the century influenced the art of **Károly Kernstok** and **József Rippl-Rónai.**

There is a fine selection of early 19th-century paintings on the first floor: portraits, landscapes, genre pictures and excellent *Biedermeier* works, including **Károly Markó's** canvases.

Hungarian Baroque painting (which may be seen as a continuation of this exhibition) is represented primarily by pictures made for the former palaces of the aristocracy. Exhibits include Ádám Mányoki's famous portrait of the Transylvanian Prince Ferenc Rákóczi II. Paintings by the masters of other 19th-century schools may be seen in the row of courtyard rooms encircling the staircase.

An exhibition on the second floor presents the works of the **Nagybánya school** including Simon Hollósy, Károly Ferenczy, Béla Iványi Grünwald, János Thorma and others, who, unlike the representatives of the so-called academic trend, worked under the influence of direct experience.

Works of 19th- and 20th-century masters are also on view in the **medallion exhibition.**

The **graphic art collection** preserves more than 30,000 plates. Of these, the most beautiful ones from 1800 down to the present are on display.

Contemporary art is presented by temporary exhibitions. The Baroque hall and the domed hall are often the scene of concerts of chamber music.

The Castle has been given accommodation in Wing A. The **National Széchényi Library** has its new home in the palace's East Wing (Wing F).

Víziváros, Óbuda, Margaret Island, Aquincum and the Római-part

VÍZIVÁROS (WATERTOWN)

The centre of Budapest's—as well as of Hungary's—road system is **Clark Ádám tér,** situated at the Buda bridgehead of the Chain Bridge. The exact centre is marked by a statue, the "0-kilometre stone" (by Miklós Borsos, 1971) in front of the tunnel which goes under Castle Hill. All kilometre signs lining the country's main roads indicate the distance from this point. (Adam Clark was a Scottish engineer, who directed the construction of the Chain Bridge in the middle of the 19th century and then built the tunnel connecting the western parts of Buda with the city [See p. 60].) The square itself may have been an important place as early as two thousand years ago, for at that time the route leading along the Roman *limes* to Aquincum ran here. It is probable that Fő utca, the main street connecting Óbuda with Víziváros, the part of the city situated beneath Castle Hill, was constructed later on the traces of the Roman road.

The vicinity of **Fő utca** has preserved some of the former atmosphere of Víziváros to this day. The **Capuchin church** located in the area was built at the turn of the 18th century on the spot where a Turkish mosque once stood. The church gained its present-day appearance in 1856 when it was remodelled in the Romantic style (Frigyes Feszl, Károly Gerster, and Ferenc Reitter). The picturesque house at **No. 20** with its corner balcony is built in the *zopfstil* or Louis XVI style, as is the Hikisch House on **Batthy-**

Batthyány tér—detail

ány tér (No. 3). The two-storied palace built in the Rococo style standing
on the same place **(No. 4)** housed the "White Cross Inn" in the 18th century; here the inhabitants of Buda held joyful carnival festivities. The
stage-coach to Vienna left from nearby Gyorskocsi (Express coach) utca.

The two-steepled **St. Anne's Church** standing on the south side of
Batthyány tér was built between 1740 and 1762 in the Baroque style (by
Cristoph Hamon, Máté Nepauer and Michael Hamon). The ornate high
altar is the work of Karl Bebo; above the entrance are statues of the Virgin
and St. Anne. (There is a delightful café on the Danube side of the church,
and a Metro station is situated underneath the square, from where a suburban railway, the HÉV, runs to the north towards Aquincum and Szentendre.)

Continuing further along Fő utca is the Baroque-style church at No.
41–43, formerly **a church for the nuns of the order of St. Elizabeth,** and
there is a former convent and hospital building beside it. Today these
function as a social welfare home for the aged. The **Király Baths,** situated
a few minutes' walk north in Fő utca, were built by the Pashas Arslan and
Sokolli Mustapha between 1566 and 1570. After the Turkish withdrawal
the baths were rebuilt in the Baroque style. In the 19th century the König
family (König meaning "king", or *király* in Hungarian) became the owners of the baths and enlarged them with the addition of neo-Classical
wings. The domed building was rebuilt between 1955–1957, freeing the
Turkish building complex from the later secondary structures and
renovating the remaining Baroque and neo-Classical sections. Near the
baths **(No. 90)** stands the **Flórián Chapel,** which was built in 1759–1760 to
the plans of Máté Nepauer and which has been a Greek Catholic church
since 1920. Inside there are Baroque altars and Rococo pulpits. The
Ministry of Foreign Affairs is situated on the corner of Fő utca and Bem
tér, and the **Foundry Museum (No. 20)** provides a point of interest in Bem
József utca, a street leading off Fő utca. Abraham Ganz, an industrialist of
Swiss origin, established his first foundry here in the 19th century, and
the museum of the Hungarian smelting industry was given a home in the
former building of the Ganz factory.

Bem József tér carries the name of the heroic Polish general who
fought in the 1848–49 War of Independence and whose statue stands in
the square (János Istók, 1936). Fő utca, just like Bem rakpart (quay) run-

Óbuda and Margaret Island

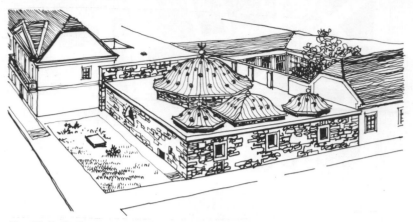

The Király Baths

ning parallel to it, runs into Mártírok útja, which continues on to Margaret Bridge. To the left, several streets lead up to **Rózsadomb** (Hill of Roses). **Mecset utca** opens to the right from the first steep street (Rómer Flóris utca). The tomb at **Mecset utca 14** is the **tomb of Gül Baba,** reverently cared for by the capital and frequently visited, not only by Muslims, but by Hungarians and foreigners alike. **Mártírok útja** then bends to the south. Along the way it is worth while stopping to look at **No. 23,** a former Franciscan church and monastery, at **No. 66,** the commemorative plaque which draws one's attention to the remaining section of the former city-wall; and **No. 85,** which was a military prison during the Horthy regime, where many anti-fascist resistors were tortured and put to death. In memory of these patriots the name of the former Margit körút was changed to Mártírok útja (Street of Martyrs). The boulevard runs to Moszkva tér, a traffic centre for trams and buses taking passengers into the Buda Mountain Range and arriving from various sections of Pest and Buda. The square also has a major Metro station.

From Margaret Bridge, **Frankel Leó út** is the continuation of Fő utca. Frankel Leó út received its name from the 19th-century figure of the Hungarian labour movement, once minister of the Paris commune. Some well-known thermal baths and public swimming pools are located in this area: the **Lukács Pool and Thermal Baths (No. 25–29),** the **Császár Baths (No. 31–33),** and the modern **Komjádi Béla Sports Pool** next to it (entrance from the Danube side). Natural thermal springs gushing out along a geological fault-line where the Buda hill country and the plains meet have for a long time attracted those seeking convalescence and recreation. At the time of the Turkish occupation a bathing-establishment known as Barát (Friar) Dergemine's Baths was built where the Lukács Baths now stand, and one known as Veli Bey's baths was situated in the area of the Császár Baths. In 1699 a fire gutted a large section of the old Turkish bath buildings. However, the middle section of the Császár Baths, the swimming-pool dating back to Turkish times, survived. Among the present-day bath buildings, the one housing the Lukács Baths was built in 1924 by using parts of the building dating back to the 19th century. The neo-Classical building of the Császár Baths was built in 1806 and 1841–1848 according to the plans of József Hild. The Komjádi Sports Pool was opened in 1976. It has a 50×21 m pool (27 °C) and a grandstand seating 2,000 people. Its locker rooms can accommodate 600 men and 400 women.

The **National Institute of Rheumatology and Physiotherapy** (Országos Reuma-Fizioterápiás Intézet) was established in the vicinity of the thermal baths **(Frankel Leó út 17–19.)** The neo-Classical houses at **No. 36–46** and **50** on the other side of Frankel Leó út were spa-hotels in the middle of the last century. Today a modern health and convalescent home of the trade unions stands above them on the side of the Rózsadomb. The "Malomtó" Espresso opposite the baths received its name from the fact that a small mill-pond (malomtó) covered with water lilies and nurtured by the water of the thermal springs, is situated beside it.

ÓBUDA

Frankel Leó út continues towards Óbuda, District III of the capital, which has literally become "two-faced" during the past few years. Here, in a milieu recalling the city's most distant past with Roman ruins and small-town streets, it has taken only ten years for one of Budapest's newest and most up-to-date housing developments to spring up.

In the Middle Ages, while the town was still being formed, the predecessor of present-day Óbuda was its first significant settlement. It was still called Buda then, and it was the city of royalty. Stones of the former Roman city were used in its construction. Palaces were built in this city on the bank of the Danube as well as a royal residence, but only a few remains of walls have been found by archeologists. Since the time following the Mongol Invasion, when Béla IV had the royal residence moved to Castle Hill, Óbuda's importance gradually declined (although it still remained for some time the residence of the royal ladies). After the Turkish occupation, it was reborn only as a characteristic market-town settlement, although a few important industrial plants—notably a ship factory—were later established in the area. Óbuda was a famous wine-producing area up to the end of the 19th century.

An atmosphere nostalgically reminiscent of the past still hovered at the beginning of the century over the small houses and cosy restaurants of Óbuda constructed both in the Baroque and the *zopfstil* (Louis XVI style).

The present-day new building development began near the Árpád Bridge and now stretches to the foot of the Buda Hills. A large portion of old Óbuda was demolished to make way for the construction of the new residential area, but a few characteristic islands of historic monuments have been preserved. Today these monuments radiate some of the atmosphere once pervading this part of the city. At the same time that excavations were being carried out for further constructions, more valuable finds dating back to the Roman Age were uncovered. Today these finds enrich the collection of the Aquincum Museum.

The **Roman Catholic Parish Church (Óbudai u. 2),** built by the Zichy family between 1744 and 1749, recalls the mood of Baroque Óbuda. The statues of the church are the work of Karl Bebo. The neo-Classical building of the **Óbuda Synagogue (Lajos u. 163)** was planned in the last century by András Landherr.

Fő tér, the east side of which **(No. 1)** is occupied by the multistoried farm building of the former **Zichy mansion,** has remained an enclosed "historic monument island", as the Hungarians call it. The Baroque mansion itself stands in the courtyard. Today it is the cultural centre of the district (exhibitions, garden concerts in summer, etc.).

The house called the **Kerek Ház (Harrer Pál u. 44–46)** is a characteristic landmark built at the end of the 18th century. At one time the two-storied house was a silk mill. The partially ruined building has been rebuilt and will serve cultural purposes.

Óbuda's Baroque historic monument which preserves modern collections belonging to the Budapest History Museum was formerly a Trinitarian monastery; today it is the **Kiscelli Museum (Kiscelli u. 108)**. After the dissolution of the order in the 18th century, the buildings became the property of the Treasury and then passed into the ownership of the capital.

Connected to the city by the Árpád Bridge on the north and by Margaret Bridge on the south, lying between two branches of the Danube, is **Margaret Island** (Margitsziget).

MARGARET ISLAND

is 2.5 km long and at its broadest part there is a huge park 500 m wide. The island is one of Budapest's most popular places for walking, bathing, amusement, and sports.

It is likely that once the Romans occupied the island, for remains of villas and watchtowers dating back to Roman times have been found here. During the Middle Ages the Templars of St. John built a castle-monastery in the southern part of the island. A convent of the Dominican order was also established here, in which King Béla IV's daughter, (St.) Margaret, lived and died. It was from her that the island, at one time called Rabbit Island, received its present name. The medieval buildings were destroyed during the Turkish occupation, and only since the end of the 18th century has the island become a well-cared-for park. The owner of the island at that time, Palatine Joseph, planted rare flowers, trees and plants, and had summer homes built here. At the end of the 19th century, deep-drilling operations brought medicinal thermal water to the surface, and Margaret Island subsequently developed into an internationally-known bathing and recreation area.

Árpád Bridge spans the Danube at the northern tip of Margaret Island, and there is a road leading from it to the island. The length of the bridge is almost 2 km, and its length over the water is 928 m. It was completed in 1950, but has since been enlarged.

Private cars can be driven onto the island only across the Árpád Bridge and only as far as the car park next to the Grand Hotel. However, any part of the island can be reached by means of bus, taxi, or micro-bus service.

The **Hotel Thermal** was built on the northern part of the island near the road leading to the Árpád Bridge, next to the charming **Japanese Garden**. The **Grand Hotel Ramada** is situated nearby. The **Open-air Theatre of the State Opera House,** where opera and ballet performances and concerts are held every summer, is situated in the centre of the island. The stage, which is surrounded by ancient trees, has an area of 1,400 sq.m. The **Water Tower** overlooking the outdoor theatre was built in 1911.

The former **Premonstratensian chapel** near the Grand Hotel is a reconstructed historic monument of medieval origin. The 12th-century Romanesque church was destroyed during the Turkish occupation and was reconstructed in 1930–31 by making use of the remaining walls. (The south wall of the nave with the two windows ending in a semicircle is from the original building.) Busts of prominent Hungarian authors and artists line the

Detail of Margaret Island

neighbouring promenades. In the middle of the island, ruins of a 13th-century **Franciscan church** have survived. Recent excavations have uncovered additional sections of the sanctuary, the sacristy, and the former monastery. Next to it stand walls of Palatine Joseph's former palace. The **church of the Dominican nuns** (east of the Water Tower) is another monument worthy of interest. The evidence of the unearthed remains suggests that is was originally one-aisled with an octagonal tower on its western side. Beside it there stand the remains of the convent yard, the cloisters and convent halls.

The island can be approached from the south across the 638 m long **Margaret Bridge,** built in 1872–76 according to the plans of E. Gouin. The underground passageway leading from the bridge to Margaret Island was added in 1901. The bridge was blown up by the fascists at the end of 1944, during rush-hour. It was rebuilt in 1946–48. (The No. 6 and 4 tram stops are situated at the entrance to the island. Bus No. 26 carries passengers to the island from Marx tér.)

A **bronze monument** (by István Kiss) erected in 1972 in commemoration of the hundredth anniversary of the unification of Pest, Buda, and Óbuda greets visitors arriving at the south entrance of the island. Behind it there is a **fountain** illuminated every night in colour.

On the left-hand side of the island (on the bank towards Buda) is situated the **Pioneer's Stadium,** a sport stadium for children of the capital which can seat up to 3,000 spectators.

The next sports establishment is the **National Sports Swimming-Pool,** the scene of international swimming competitions and water polo matches. The builder, Alfréd Hajós, was a swimming champion at the first modern Olympic Games held in 1896. The establishment has one indoor and two outdoor pools with a high diving board and seats 6,000 spectators. Except during times of training and competitions, the swimming-pool is open to the general public.

The ship-harbour (Casino Restaurant and café) situated on the bank of the island facing Pest is about level with the Sports Swimming-Pool. Boathouses line the shady, grassy holiday park intersected by paths, and a small zoo soon follows. Across the island, on the bank facing Buda, is situated the **Palatinus Outdoor Public Swimming-Pool** with cold and warm water pools, and a swimming-pool with artificial waves. The bathing facilities cover an area of 70,000 sq.m and can accommodate up to 20,000 persons.

Across Margaret Island, in Óbuda, we find the remains of Aquincum, which dates back to Roman times.

AQUINCUM

Aquincum's ruins and monuments are dispersed over a large area, for once there was both a larger and a smaller Roman settlement here. The larger one was designated as the garrison town, upon which present-day Óbuda (District III) was built. Its ruins were discovered by chance during demolition work and building excavations, one of the most important being the **amphitheatre** situated in the area bordered by Nagyszombat utca, Korvin Ottó utca, Szőlő utca and Viador utca. The amphitheatre was unearthed between 1937 and 1940, when the houses built there in the 17th to 18th centuries were being demolished. It dates from around A.D. 160 and was able to hold up to 16,000 spectators. The 131 m×110 m structure was one of the largest amphitheatres ever built in the Roman provinces. During the Age of Migrations in the 4th century, the amphitheatre was converted into a fortress, and according to archeological evidence,

Ground-plan of Aquincum

1 Entrance
2 Museum building
3 The covered lapidary
4 Basilica
5 Large public baths
6 Market-place (macellum)
7 Double baths
8 Mithras altar
A–F: Stone-paved streets of the city

bloody battles repeatedly arose over its ownership. (There are sugges-
tions that the amphitheatre at Aquincum could have been the Etzelburg
that figures in the "Nibelung's Ring".)

The remains of a larger Roman building have been discovered, together with valuable mosaics, in the so-called **Hercules Villa (Meggyfa u.
21).** In the gardens of a new school, mosaic floors depicting scenes from
the story of Hercules can be seen in their original place, under protective
covers. From the point of view of museology, this is certainly an interesting solution for preserving remains such as the Roman baths discovered

in the basement of the modern apartment building at **Korvin Ottó utca 63.** The premises of the baths were converted into a museum called the **Táborvárosi Museum,** and Roman agricultural implements, tools, and other useful items have been placed there on exhibition. Remains of the public baths of the legionary camp were unearthed at **Flórián tér 3–7.** Relics of Roman medicine have been placed here on exhibition. Remains of a **sepulchral chapel,** a *cella trichora* from a 4th-century cemetery, can be seen at the intersection of Raktár utca and Hunor utca. Early Christian inhabitants of the area were buried around the chapel.

In contrast to the few remains of the garrison town, archeologists were able to uncover much of the Roman civilian settlement for, when excavations were begun, this area was still a vacant field. Sporadic excavations have been carried on ever since and are still proceeding. For instance, a section of the Roman aqueduct has been uncovered along Szentendrei út. Historic objects found during excavations have been collected and placed on exhibition in the **Aquincum Museum (Szentendrei út 139),** the building standing in the middle of the field containing the ruins of the civilian town. Excavations carried out in this area have uncovered the middle section of the Roman city. The public baths are in front of the museum building, and the walls of a meat market and other shops are spread out next to it. To the left of the museum are the remains of private homes, ornamental courtyards and private baths, as well as the remains of smaller public baths and the Shrine of Mithras. There are also remains of private homes behind the museum, and to the right are the remains of workshops, more private homes, baths and a shrine. It is possible to see Roman mosaics, reconstructed wall-paintings and furniture on the exhibition premises situated in the south section of the ruins.

The Aquincum Museum

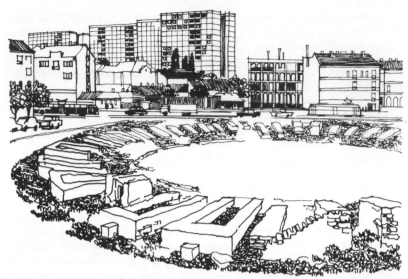

The amphitheatre in Óbuda's garrison town

The **exhibitions in the museum** are as follows: in the central hall there are documents connected with the history of the civilian city of Aquincum, as well as documents concerned with the organization of the settlement; Hall 2 (to the right) contains historic objects connected with industrial and agricultural occupations, financial management, and commerce; Hall 3 displays objects connected with urbanization—historic relics of the water system, the drainage system, and road building, and documents relating to building technology and home furnishings; Hall 4 (to the left) contains objects connected with culture and art such as the only Roman organ that can still be played (one showcase contains the original bronze parts, and another the reconstructed organ); while in Hall 5 there are documents of religious life and burial customs. Headstones and stone monuments lie under the colonnades surrounding the museum building.

The **amphitheatre of the civilian city** lies outside the excavation site belonging to the museum, on the other side of the railway embankment. This one is much smaller than the amphitheatre of the garrison town (length: 55 m; original capacity: 6,000 spectators). The amphitheatre was built in the 2nd century.
North of Aquincum: about 1 km from the excavation site and the museum—a large recreation area called

RÓMAI-PART (ROMAN SHORE)

stretches between the bank of the Danube and the hillside. The **Római Outdoor Swimming-Pool and Camping-Site,** as well as the Motel Venus, are situated near the HÉV suburban railway station. The soft, lukewarm spring water that feeds the swimming-pools was used for bathing by the Romans. The large, grassy open fields and old trees make the Roman Shore one of the most enjoyable outdoor bathing areas of the city.

On the hillside, one stop after the Roman Swimming-Pool, are the **Csillaghegy Outdoor Pool,** and on the shore of the Danube, the **Pünkösdfürdő Outdoor Pool.**

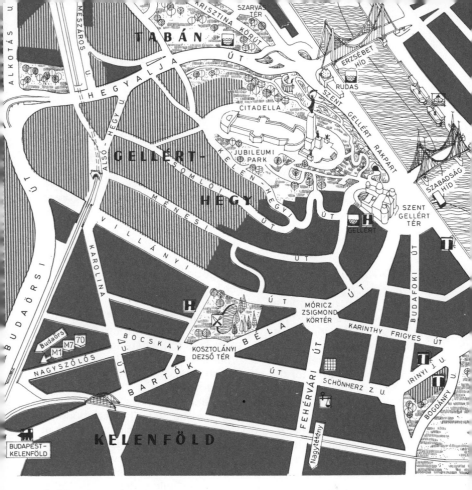

Gellért Hill and South Buda

Gellért Hill and surroundings
The southern section of Buda

Running from Clark Ádám tér towards the south, **Lánchíd** (Chain Bridge) **utca** passes alongside a row of arcades in the middle of which there is a ceremonial ascent beginning with a flight of stairs and then winding upwards. This is the so-called **Várkert-bazár** (the Castle Garden Bazaar, the work of Miklós Ybl). The historic building in the style of Louis XVI located at **Apród utca 1–3** is the birthplace of Ignác Semmelweis (1818–1865), the physician who discovered the cause of puerperal fever. Today the building houses the **Semmelweis Museum of Medical History** (Semmelweis Orvostörténeti Múzeum), which exhibits documents connected with the history of Hungarian medicine from the 16th century to the present, a memorial room dedicated to Semmelweis, and a reconstructed pharmacy from the past called the Gömöri Pharmacy. Semmelweis's grave and monument are situated in the courtyard.

Apród utca ends at **Szarvas tér,** where there is a relief depicting a deer over the entrance to the neo-Classical house at **No. 1,** which contains the "Aranyszarvas" (Golden Stag) Restaurant. The Baroque **Church of St. Catherine** (1728–36) stands nearby where a Turkish mosque once stood. The group of statues (István Kiss, 1961) in **Dózsa György tér,** at the beginning of Attila út just below Castle Hill, preserves the memory of the leader and members of the Peasant Uprising of 1514. Opposite, below the **Nap-**

The Castle Museum, Nagytétény

hegy (Sun Hill) runs **Krisztina körút,** a large boulevard stretching as far as the **Krisztina City Parish Church,** which was originally built in the style of Louis XVI and then remodelled eclectically.

There was once a ferry crossing the Danube at the foot of Gellért Hill, and it was here that the precursor of medieval Buda came into existence.

On the northern slope of Gellért Hill (235 m), where today there is a well-cared-for recreation park, a romantic city district called the Tabán was once located, this for the most part consisted of little old broken-down houses, cobblestone streets and small inns. The Tabán was demolished between the two world wars and now only a few old houses survive. Still standing, for example, are the neo-Classical building located at **Döbrentei utca 9,** the Louis XVI-style building standing at **No. 15,** and the building housing the **Rác Baths,** at the edge of the park.

From Gellért Hill a beautiful panorama unfolds to the visitor out for a leisurely stroll on its paths and terraces. The **Citadella** situated on the summit is not a medieval structure, for it was built in 1850 by the Habs-burgs, following the suppression of the Hungarian War of Independence, to keep the Hungarian capital under surveillance. The walls of this struc-ture are 4 to 6 m high, up to 3 m thick, and stretch 200 m from east to west. The Citadella was the home of a garrison for half a century, then in 1899 it became the property of the capital and consequently lost its fortress-like character. At the end of World War II, during the 1944–45 battles fought for the liberation of Budapest, the German fascist occupants fired upon the city from here, as well as from Castle Hill.

The **Liberation Monument** was erected in 1947 (the work of Zsigmond Kisfaludi Strobl).

The **statue of Bishop Gellért** (Gerard) facing the Danube (by Gyula Jan-kovits, 1901) rises above the eastern foot of the hillside facing the Danube. It was here that this missionary from Italy, who was asked to come to Hungary by King Stephen, suffered a martyr's death in a pagan uprising at the beginning of the 11th century.

A geological fault-line stretches below Gellért Hill, from which medici-nal springs gush forth. To the south of Elizabeth Bridge lie the **Rudas Baths** with a cupola dating back to Turkish times. The well-houses situ-ated in the park around it call attention to the medicinal springs. Situated below the south slope of Gellért Hill, at the Buda bridgehead of Liberty Bridge, is an internationally known spa-hotel, the **Hotel Gellért.** The medicinal baths of the hotel, as well as the outdoor pool with artificial waves and the indoor effervescent baths are all fed by natural thermal spring water.

The **Technical University** campus is situated to the south of Gellért Hill, along the Danube. It is one of Europe's oldest institutions for higher tech-nical education.

Beginning at Gellért tér, **Bartók Béla út** passes through the main traffic centre of south Buda, the **Móricz Zsigmond körtér,** and runs towards the south-western outskirts of the city. Among the modern residential areas beginning at Móricz Zsigmond körtér, Fehérvári út running towards the south leads among the hills of **Budafok,** well-known in the past for its wine. Budafok, with its kilometres-long wine cellars and wine-drinking establishments, was a separate community until it was joined to the capital in 1950, when it became District XXII. The main attraction of **Nagytétény,** which is the southernmost part of Buda, is the Baroque **Castle Museum (XXII, Csókási Pál u. 9),** the premises of which contain exhibitions of Hungarian and European furniture of various periods. The furniture is shown just as it would appear in a private house, supplemented by carpets, stoves, and other contemporary furnishings. There is a glazed tile collection in the Gothic basement.

The Buda Hills

The hill country upon which a large part of Buda was built belongs to the Buda range surrounding the city. Proceeding towards the southern and particularly the western and northern parts of Buda, one passes almost

Buda Hills

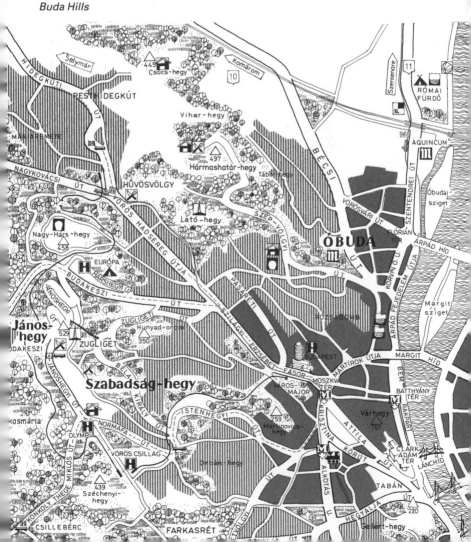

unnoticeably from densely-built areas to districts of villas and gardens and beyond them to thickly-wooded country, a paradise for excursions. It is possible to reach the woods of the Buda Hills by car, bus, tram, the Cogwheel Railway, a chair-lift, as well as by the Pioneer Railway in barely half an hour.

The northernmost peak of the chain of hills is the **Hármashatár-hegy** (497 m), the upper slopes of which offer a beautiful panorama of the city. Under favourable weather conditions, there is lively glider activity here. The **stalactite cave of Pálvölgy** (Pálvölgyi cseppkőbarlang, II., Szépvölgyi út 162) is situated on the southern part of the dolomite mountain chain. Some electrically-lighted sections of the cave are open to the general public.

The chain of hills comprising **Szabadság-hegy** (Liberty Hill), **Széchenyi-hegy** and **János-hegy** is connected on the west to the residential parts of Buda. The wooded plateau of Szabadság-hegy is a popular recreation park extending over 10 sq.km with trade union and company-owned rest homes. The **Hotel Panorama** is situated on the summit of Széchenyi-hegy, and not far away, in the immediate vicinity of the ski grounds is the **Hotel Olympia**. In the winter the best ski grounds, including a ski-lift, in the vicinity of Budapest can be found here. The narrow-gauge **Pioneer Railway** (Úttörővasút) begins at Széchenyi-hegy, and its 12 km-long track winds among the most beautiful sections of the Buda Hills to its terminus at Hűvösvölgy. (The conductors of the little train are schoolboys and girls—"pioneers"—who are being trained for railway service by means of special courses.) The **cable line of the Libegő** chair-lift connects the highest peak of the range, János-hegy (529 m) with Zugliget **(Zugligeti út 93)**. The **Cogwheel Railway** (Fogaskerekű) carries passengers from **Szilágy Erzsébet fasor** (opposite the Hotel Budapest) up to Szabadság-hegy, while bus services connect the recreation areas among the Buda Hills with the city. **Zugliget** and **Hűvösvölgy** can be approached from Moszkva tér by tram. Two main roads, **Budakeszi út** and **Hárshegyi út** running parallelly (Hotel Európa, Hotel Rege, campsite), lead towards many popular strolling and excursion destinations.

PEST

The Inner City

On the left bank of the Danube, where Pest now stands, there once stood the Roman fortress of Contra-Aquincum, which was situated near the present-day Elizabeth Bridge. The fortress was established in A. D. 294 by the Romans to protect the Danube-crossing leading to Aquincum against the Barbarians. The settlement around the Roman fortress which came into existence in the centuries following the Magyar Conquest was annihilated during the 13th-century Mongol invasion. Situated opposite the new royal seat of Buda on Castle Hill, Pest afterwards developed into a thriving city of commerce and handicrafts. The medieval city extended as far as the present-day Kiskörút (Little Boulevard), and walls were built round it. However, the walls were demolished during the widespread development programme that began at the end of the 18th century. Remains of the walls can still be seen embedded in the partitions of houses built later along Múzeum körút. The area of the Inner City of Pest, situated between the Liberty Bridge and Chain Bridge and surrounded by the Kiskörút, is roughly the same as the area of the medieval city. Known today as District V, the Inner City has, however, expanded beyond the medieval city limits and now reaches as far as Margaret Bridge.

The Inner City Parish Church with Elizabeth Bridge

The centre of the Inner City is **Elizabeth Bridge** (Erzsébet-híd), whose predecessor was built between 1897–1903. It was blown up, along with the other bridges on the Danube, by the Germans at the end of World War II. The bridge was rebuilt in its present form as a cable bridge. Its length is 380 m. The **Inner City Parish Church** is situated at the Pest end of the Elizabeth Bridge. Built in a Romanesque style during the 12th century from stones of former Roman walls, this church is the oldest building in Pest. Its south wall was built on top of the southern boundary wall of the Roman *castrum*. Remains of the 12th-century building can still be discovered on the wall of the south tower. At the end of the 14th century the church was converted into a Gothic hall church, and in the second half of the 15th century chapels were added on the north and south. The church was used as a mosque during the Turkish occupation, a relic of this being the **Turkish prayer-niche** (mihrab) at the end of the row of niches running on the right. The church was first rebuilt between 1725–1739 in the Baroque style, then it was restored at the end of the 19th century under the direction of Imre Steindl, the architect who designed the Parliament building. Between 1932–1944 a number of walled-in historic remnants were unearthed. The present appearance of the church is the result of restoration work since 1948. The most beautiful part is the Gothic sanctuary with an inlaid door on the south side and the 19 sedilia under the sanctuary windows. Among the chapels opening out of the nave, the fourth chapel on the left side contains a Renaissance monstrance cubicle from around 1500, which belonged to András Nagyrévi, the parish priest. The Renaissance monstrance cubicle of the city of Pest with the city's coat of arms and figures of the mayor and his wife, is in the fourth chapel on the right side of the nave.

Uncovered remains of Contra-Aquincum can be examined in a small park in nearby **Március 15. tér**. In **Petőfi tér** there stands a bronze statue of the poet Sándor Petőfi (1882, by Adolf Huszár after sketches by Miklós Izsó). The late Baroque building of the **Hungarian Orthodox Church** was rebuilt by Miklós Ybl towards the end of the last century. The **Hotel Duna Inter-Continental** stands at the north end of the square.

Forming a continuation of the Elizabeth Bridge axis, **Szabadsajtó útja** runs into busy **Felszabadulás tér**. Until the turn of the century only narrow streets and old alleys existed here, but with the construction of the bridge, city planning opened the east-west thoroughfare. This section of the Inner City was developed at that time, but its present appearance has been determined by the underground road system built between 1974–1976 and the Metro station at Felszabadulás tér.

Apartment houses built in the *art nouveau* style at the turn of the century line Felszabadulás tér on the north and south. On the north side where it runs into Váci utca, is **Kígyó utca,** one of the most popular shopping streets of the Inner City. A **Franciscan church** stands on the eastern side of the square, on the corner of Károlyi Mihály utca, with the "Fountain of the Naiads" (Ferenc Uhrl, 1899) in front of it. The medieval church was converted into a Turkish mosque and was later rebuilt in the Baroque style. It was consecrated in its present form in 1743. Its eclectic tower was completed only in 1861–1863. The *al secco* murals in the church are for the most part the work of Károly Lotz (from 1894–1895). The embossed memorial plaque (Barnabás Holló, 1905) on the side wall facing Kossuth Lajos utca commemorates the memory of Baron Miklós Wesselényi, the "flood mariner", whose rescue work saved large numbers of people imperilled during a flood that inundated Pest and a large part of Buda and Óbuda in 1838.

The neo-Renaissance building at **Károlyi Mihály utca 10** is the **Library of the Eötvös Loránd University of Arts and Sciences** (Egyetemi Könyvtár), which preserves Corvina codices and valuable first editions in its collection. House **No. 16** was **the palace of the Count Károlyi family.** Following the defeat of the 1848–49 War of Independence Count Haynau, who had been appointed Commander by the Habsburgs, directed bloody reprisals against the city from here, and Lajos Batthyány, the president of the first ministry responsible to Parliament in 1848 and who was executed on October 6, 1849, was taken prisoner here. The palace was presented to the nation by the widow of Count Mihály Károlyi, the leader of the 1918 Bourgeois Revolution, and at present it is the home of the **Petőfi Literary Museum.**

The buildings housing the **political science and law faculty of the Eötvös Loránd University** stand in **Egyetem tér.** The university was established in 1635 by Péter Pázmány, the archbishop of Esztergom, and functioned in Nagyszombat (now Trnava, Czechoslovakia) for almost 150 years before it was transferred to Buda in 1770, and then to Pest in 1785. The most beautiful Baroque historic building in Pest, the **University Church,** stands on the corner of Eötvös Loránd utca next to the university building. The church was built by András Mayerhoffer between 1725 and 1742, and its beautifully-contoured towers were completed in 1768 and 1781 respectively. The sculptured gate is the work of unknown monks of the Order of St. Paul; the wood carvings on the ornate Baroque stalls and the statues adorning the high altar were carried out by József Habenstreit; the opulent wood carvings on the pews and choir doors are the work of Brother Félix Tatirek. The pulpit is an outstanding example of Hungarian Baroque.

Kossuth Lajos utca is the busiest street of the Inner City. The houses lining it were for the most part built at the turn of the century. Kossuth Lajos utca was originally called Hatvani utca, because it continued beyond the walls of the city on the highway leading towards the towns of Hatvan and Miskolc. It was given its present name at the end of the last century. The historical interest of the building at **No. 3** lies in the fact that the Landerer and Heckenast Printing Press, which printed the first publications of the free press on March 15, 1848, Sándor Petőfi's famous "National Song" and the "Twelve Points" containing the demands of the Hungarians for bourgeois reform, once operated here.

In the middle of **Vörösmarty tér,** which can be reached via Váci utca, stands a statue of the poet Mihály Vörösmarty (1800–1855), between spreading trees and flower beds. Eclectic buildings erected at the turn of the century and the beginning of the present century line the square on three sides. On the fourth side is the modern office building completed at the beginning of the 1970s which houses the headquarters of the Hunga-

rian Federation of Musicians, the Hungarian P.E.N. Club, book publishers, and institutes of music, art, and other cultural fields. The concert
booking office, a gallery of painting, sculpture, and industrial arts and
a record store are situated on the ground floor of the building. The other
side of the complex, with its façade facing the Danube, is the **Vigadó**
(Municipal Concert Hall) built in the Romantic style between 1859–1864
on the basis of plans by Frigyes Feszl. The statues adorning the façade
are the work of Károly Alexy, while the frescoes on the main stairway
were painted by Károly Lotz and Mór Than. For three quarters of a century concerts, ballets, and celebrations were held in the Vigadó. Ferenc
Liszt, Brahms, Béla Bartók and many other notable artists have given
concerts within its walls. The building was burned down during the Second World War. Its reconstruction was completed at the beginning of
1980 and it serves again as the scene of many concerts. Its gallery is used
for staging temporary exhibitions.

The terminal point of the so-called **"little underground"** is also situated
in Vörösmarty tér. This was the very first underground railway to be built
on the Continent. It was opened in 1896, during the festivities celebrating
the millennium of the Magyar Conquest of Hungary. The adjective "little" was attached to the name during the last few years, after the fist full-
size Metro line was opened. The 4.5 km-long subway line, line No. 1, connects with the Metro at Deák tér. It has since been extended to one of the
city's outer suburbs and since 1974 it has been running on new rails with
new coaches. One of the original eighty-year-old coaches has been
placed in a museum that can be reached from an underground passage
beside the Metro station at Deák tér.

Next to the underground railway station **(Vörösmarty tér 7)** we find the
Gerbeaud Confectioner's, named after its former owner, who was of
Swiss origin. The pastry-shop was originally founded in the 19th century
by Henrik Kugler. Today it is furnished in period style and is a favourite
spot with residents of Budapest. The old utensils, kettles, and moulds
exhibited in one of the rooms bring back recollections of the confectioner's trade of the past century.

Running parallel to the Danube from Vörösmarty tér to Dimitrov tér,
Váci utca is cut into two by the Elizabeth Bridge–Kossuth Lajos utca axis,
but the two halves of the street are also very different in appearance and
character. In the 18th century Váci utca was the main thoroughfare of
Pest; today, much of it is a pedestrian precinct and a popular rendezvous
for strolling and shopping. (The section of Váci utca situated to the south
of the Elizabeth Bridge, however, is no more than a busy, rather narrow
residential street.) The "Inn of the Seven Electors" was formerly situated
at **No. 9.** Magnificent balls were held here, and Ferenc Liszt, then an eleven-year-old child prodigy, gave a concert in the ceremonial hall in 1823.
The building was rebuilt several times, and at present it is the home of the
Pesti Theatre. No. 11, the façade of which is covered with coloured Zsolnay ceramics, was built at the turn of the century by Ödön Lechner in collaboration with Gyula Pártos. **No. 20.** is the new **Hotel Taverna.** The large
building complex located at the place where Váci utca and Pesti Barnabás utca meet houses the **Faculty of Arts of the Eötvös Loránd University.** The **University Theatre** is also located in this building complex. The
two-storied Baroque mansion opposite the university at **Pesti Barnabás
utca 2** was built in 1775. Since 1831 it has been a restaurant, and today it
is called the **Százéves** ("One Hundred Year Old") **Restaurant.**

Petőfi Sándor utca, which runs parallel to Váci utca, leads from Felszabadulás tér to Martinelli tér. The Baroque church leaning with its
single tower against the modern **main post office building** on the south
side of **Martinelli tér** is the former **Servite Church.** The church was built

between 1725–1732 but has been renovated many times since. The present façade and tower date back to 1871. The house at **Martinelli tér 5** with its ceramic decorations represents a striking example of Hungarian architecture at the beginning of the century. It was designed by Béla Lajta between 1910 and 1912. The **City Hall** stands at **Városház utca 9–11;** this street opens from the south-east side of the square. Built between 1727 and 1735 according to the plans of Anton Erhardt Martinelli, the City Hall is the largest Baroque building in Budapest. Originally it served as a home for disabled soldiers, then was converted into a barracks for grenadiers at the end of the 18th century. It has been the City Hall since 1894. In the same street **(No. 7)** we find the headquarters of the Pest County Council. The two-storied neo-Classical palace was built between 1838 and 1841 to the plans of Mátyás Zitterbarth, Jr.

The **Katona József Theatre** is located at **Petőfi Sándor utca 6.** The passage through **Nos. 2–4** next door is called the **Paris Arcade** (Párizsi udvar) and it leads to the row of stores in **Kígyó utca,** and **Haris köz.** (One of the underpasses leading to the south section of the Inner City begins at the Paris Arcade and another is located at the entrance to the Elizabeth Bridge.)

Business street (Kígyó utca) in the Inner City

That part of the Danube embankment which stretches in a southerly direction from the Elizabeth Bridge to Liberty Bridge is called **Belgrád rakpart**. An **international ship landing-stage** is situated here. The memorial plaque on the wall of **Váci utca 43** commemorates that in November, 1714 Charles XII of Sweden spent the night here while he was travelling on horseback from Constantinople to Stralsund. At **Váci utca 47** is the Baroque **Church of St. Michael.** Continuing towards Dimitrov tér, the Serbian Orthodox church opening from **No. 66** (whose actual address is Szerb u. 6) deserves attention. In 1690 a group of Serbs fleeing from the Turks settled in Pest and soon established themselves in this area. The Baroque church, which they built between 1730 and 1755, together with its beautiful garden, is a characteristic historic monument of old Pest.

District V includes an area to the north much younger than the ancient town core, which upon the construction of the Chain Bridge (1842–1849) became the centre of traffic between those parts of the city lying on the two banks of the Danube. This section was surrounded by neo-Classical buildings in the first half of the last century, but they have for the most part disappeared since then. Only a few buildings have remained in two streets that run parallel to the Danube, **Apáczai Csere János utca 3, 7,** and **15** and **Dorottya utca 11.** Both these streets lead to the **Chain Bridge,** the oldest bridge over the Danube. Construction of the bridge was planned for the first decades of the 19th century, when it became a vital necessity to connect (as well as to unite) Buda and Pest. It was István Széchenyi who undertook the task of building the bridge. In England, he became personally acquainted with the advantages and disadvantages of different kinds of technical procedures, and it was on his proposal that William Tierney Clark, an English engineer, was commissioned to draft the plans. Actual construction began in 1842 under the direction of Adam Clark, the designer's Scottish namesake, and in 1849 the bridge was opened. Adam Clark afterwards settled down in Hungary, and his descendants, who intermarried with Hungarians, played an important role in Budapest's economic and social life. The square at the Buda bridgehead of the Chain Bridge bears his name. The plans and construction work of the **Tunnel,** which is situated on the road leading from the bridge, are also connected with the name of Adam Clark.

The large square situated at the Pest bridgehead of the Chain Bridge is **Roosevelt tér;** at its south end there is a smaller square called **Eötvös tér;** here stand two hotels built in 1981, the Hotel Forum and the Atrium-Hyatt. One of the most striking buildings contained in the row of houses forming the eastern border of Roosevelt tér was built in the *art nouveau* style and is called the **Gresham Palace** (Zsigmond Quittner, 1906). The ground floor of the building is occupied by the offices of the Budapest Tourist Agency and a Chinese restaurant.

The neo-Renaissance palace housing the **Hungarian Academy of Sciences** (Magyar Tudományos Akadémia, Ágost Stüler, 1862–1864) stands on the north side of the square. In front of the building is a statue of **István Széchenyi** (1791–1860), the founder of the Academy. In 1825 Széchenyi pledged a year's income from his property to found the Academy, and in 1830 the "Hungarian Learned Society" came into existence. This event is immortalized by a marble plaque on the wall of the Academy building. (There had been several similar initiatives during the 18th century but, because of the lack of financial means, none of them proved viable under the conditions of political oppression.) Opposite the statue of Széchenyi stands the statue of **Ferenc Deák** (1803–1876), the statesman who brought about the Compromise of 1867 (see p. 16).

The quay on the Danube bank that begins at the Chain Bridge is called **Széchenyi rakpart,** and it leads, as does **Akadémia utca** running parallel

The Hungarian Academy of Sciences

to it, in which the neo-Classical buildings **Nos. 1** and **3** are historic monuments, to **Kossuth Lajos tér.**

This is the northernmost part of the Inner City, a section where state institutions, banks, headquarters of large companies and elegant apartment houses were built at the turn of the century. Earlier, this area was called Lipótváros, after the Habsburg Archduke Leopold. (Several other sections of the city were also named after archdukes of the House of Habsburg. At that time the designation denoted not only a geographical concept, but also a way of life.)

The domed neo-Gothic **Parliament** rising on the banks of the Danube in Kossuth Lajos tér (Imre Steindl, 1880–1902) is 268 m long. Its greatest width is 123 m and the dome is 96 m high. There are 10 courtyards, 27 gates, and 29 stairways. The outer walls are adorned with 88 statues depicting Hungarian monarchs, commanders, and famous warriors. A ceremonial stairway with stone lions on either side leads up to the main entrance.

The rotunda located in the middle section of the Parliament building is used for receptions. South of it is the Parliament chamber. The chamber of the former Upper House to the north is the scene of congresses and conferences. The official premises of the Council of Ministers and other leading government bodies are also located in the Parliament building. The ground floor facing the Danube is occupied by the Parliament halls adorned with frescoes, paintings, and tapestries by Mihály Munkácsy, Károly Lotz, Gyula Rudnay and other artists. (Group visits are organized by travel agencies.) The building also houses the Parliamentary Library.

In a small square in front of the north façade of the Parliament stands **the statue of Mihály Károlyi** (Imre Varga, 1975), the former president of the 1918–1919 Hungarian Republic and a radical politician (1875–1955), who was forced into exile after 1919.

Kossuth Lajos tér, which has an area of 65,000 sq.m, is the site of three more statues. In the northern part of the square stands the **monument of Lajos Kossuth** (1802–1894), the leader of the 1848–1849 War of Inde-

Parliament with the statue of Kossuth

pendence, and the governor of the country. The principal figure is the work of Zsigmond Kisfaludi Strobl, the subordinate figures are the work of András Kocsis and Lajos Ungvári (1952). In the southern part of the square stands the **equestrian statue of Ferenc Rákóczi II** (1676–1735) (János Pásztor, 1937), the leader of the anti-Habsburg War of Independence at the beginning of the 18th century. Standing in the small park south of the building of Parliament is the statue of **Attila József,** the great 20th-century Hungarian poet (László Marton, 1980).

The eclectic building opposite the Parliament, on the east side of the square **(No. 12),** is the **Ethnographical Museum** built between 1895 and 1896 according to the plans of Alajos Hauszmann. The statues on the façade are the work of Károly Senyei, János Fadrusz, and György Zala. The painting on the ceiling of the marble stairway is by Károly Lotz.

The permanent exhibitions of the Ethnographical Museum are as follows: a presentation of the way of life, culture and art of the Hungarian peasantry; relics of peasant work and occupations as well as the historical relics of festivities and Hungarian folk art. Another exhibition presents the principal stages and more significant forms in the development of human society, with selected examples from Asia, Africa, the South Sea Islands, Indonesia, Australia, and America. Collections originating from the Siberian Finno-Ugrian peoples, who are linguistically related to the Hungarians, include those of Antal Reguly and others. The early New Guinea collections of Lajos Bíró and Sámuel Fenichel, and the old East African and Central African collections of Sámuel Teleki and Emil Torday respectively, are also situated here.

Szabadság tér is only a few steps from Kossuth Lajos tér. This square was established at the place where a barracks called the Újépület (New Building) once stood, and where many who took part in the unsuccessful 1848–1849 War of Independence were imprisoned and executed, including Count Lajos Batthyány, who for a time had been Prime Minister. (There is an **eternal light** burning in his memory at the end of **Aulich utca.**) Following the demolition of the barracks at the turn of the century, a spacious square provided with a park was constructed here. In the northern section of the square stands a **memorial obelisk** dedicated to the Soviet soldiers who fell in the battles for the liberation of the capital. In the southern section of the park stands a well ornamented with reliefs

(Ede Telcs, 1930). A bronze memorial (Farkas Dózsa, 1934) dedicated to the patriots who were executed in the Újépület was erected on a stone pedestal in the park.

The headquarters of the **Hungarian Television** on the west side of Szabadság tér are housed in the eclectic building which was once the Stock Exchange. Opposite, on the east side of the square, stands the building of the **Hungarian National Bank,** which is also eclectic in style. Both buildings are the work of Ignác Alpár (1905). Another building of the Hungarian National Bank situated behind the first—in Rosenberg házaspár utca—was designed in a beautiful and characteristically Hungarian *art nouveau* style (Ödön Lechner, 1900).

The Kiskörút

begins at the Pest bridgehead of Liberty Bridge and describes a gentle semicircle. This "Little Boulevard", which marks the boundary of the Inner City, follows the outline of the former city wall and runs into the avenue-like Bajcsy-Zsilinszky út at Deák Ferenc tér. Today, Deák Ferenc utca closes off the old heart of the city towards the Danube at this point.

The 331 m long **Liberty** (Szabadság) **Bridge** was built in 1894–1896 to the plans of János Feketeházy. The **Budapest University of Economics** at the Pest bridgehead was built between 1870 and 1874 to the plans of Miklós Ybl, the building—which was originally a customshouse—has been a university only since 1951. Supported by ten pillars, the middle balcony of the building extends along the second floor. The ten allegorical statues standing there are the work of Ágoston Sommer.

The Kiskörút from Dimitrov tér to Kálvin tér bears the name of Marshal Tolbuhin. An interesting patch of colour at **Tolbuhin körút 1–3** is the **Large Market Hall,** which was originally the central food market hall of the capital. However, since a much larger market was established on the island of Csepel, the Large Market Hall has been serving only retail provisions to the consumers.

There are a few old houses on the even-numbered side of Tolbuhin körút worth mentioning: the **Gabler House (No. 2),** for example, where the Nádor Hotel operated at the beginning of the 19th century, and a section of the old city wall that has remained intact and has been incorporated into the back partition of the house **(No. 16).**

On **Kálvin tér,** near one of the stations on the north–south Metro line, stands a **Calvinist church** (József Hofrichter and József Hild, 1818–1830) built in the neo-Classical style. The stone lion on the historic building situated in the neighbourhood at **No. 9** recalls the fact that the "Inn of the Two Lions" once stood here. It was also here that Hector Berlioz, during his stay in Pest, is alleged to have heard the "Rákóczi Song" from which he composed his famous "Rákóczi March". The beautiful neo-Baroque palace located near Kálvin tér where Baross utca begins houses the **Municipal Szabó Ervin Library.** The library, which boasts a collection of 1.5 million volumes, has over 40,000 books about the capital.

In **Múzeum körút 14–16,** the section of the Kiskörút stretching from Kálvin tér to Kossuth Lajos utca, is the neo-Classical palace of the **Hungarian National Museum** (Mihály Pollack, 1837–47). The museum, which recalls so many historic memories, houses the country's very first public collection, which dates back to 1802 when Count Ferenc Széchényi presented his library and collection of medals to the nation. On March 15, 1848 a mass meeting took place in the open area in front of the museum, which proclaimed the demands of the nation for bourgeois reform. The

The Hungarian National Museum

memorial plaque on one of the retaining walls of the grand stairway states that Sándor Petőfi recited his "National Song" from here, and the "Twelve Points" of the radical young intellectuals, stipulating the freedom of the press, independent government, and so on are said to have been read here to the crowd. In 1848–1849 the Upper House of Parliament met in the ceremonial hall of the museum and sessions were again held there after the Compromise of 1867 until the Parliament building was finished.

A mezzanine, supported by eight Corinthian columns, is situated above the grand staircase; above the mezzanine is a tympanum. The frescoes adorning the walls and ceilings of the staircase with its pair of railings behind the spacious vestibule are the work of Mór Than and Károly Lotz.

The permanent exhibitions of the Hungarian National Museum are as follows:
In the vestibule on the main floor are stone monuments from the Roman and Middle Ages.
On the first floor is **the history of the Hungarian nation down to the age of the Magyar Conquest.** Hall 1: Prehistory; Hall 2: New Stone Age; Hall 3: Bronze Age; Hall 4: Late Bronze Age; Hall 5: Iron Age; Halls 6–8: Roman Age; and in the corridor are monuments from the Age of Migrations.
The history of Hungary from the Conquest of the country to 1849 is represented on the second floor. In the corridor: the age of the Conquest; Hall 1: age of Sigismund and Matthias; Hall 2: age following the reign of Matthias, to 1526; Hall 3: the country during its division into three parts under Turkish occupation; Hall 4: Ferenc Rákóczi II and his age; Hall 5: the breakdown of feudalism; Hall 6: the Reform Age; Hall 7: the 1848–1849 War of Independence.
The Hungarian crown and the coronation regalia are on display in the large hall.

Mineralogical and zoological materials from the **Museum of Natural Sciences** (Természettudományi Múzeum) are also on exhibition in the museum building.
At the main entrance to the **Museum Gardens** stands the **statue of János Arany,** the outstanding epic poet and translator of the 19th century (Alajos Stróbl, 1893). The supporting figures are heroes from Arany's masterpiece, the "Toldi Trilogy". Busts of several great figures of Hungarian history, science and literature, as well as a bust of Garibaldi and sev-

eral Roman stone monuments (a column from the Roman forum is included among them) are on exhibit in the park.

The **Hungarian Radio** building lies behind the National Museum. The area also includes various cultural institutions situated in former town houses of the aristocracy.

The **Faculty of Natural Sciences of the Eötvös Loránd University (Múzeum körút 4–8)** was built between 1880 and 1883 to the plans of Imre Steindl.

The intersection of Múzeum körút and the Kossuth Lajos utca–Rákóczi út axis is one of the busiest spots in Budapest, not only above, but also below ground, since there is an important Metro station here.

The next section of the Kiskörút is called **Tanács körút**. A **synagogue** with two onion-shaped towers is situated at the corner of the first side street, **Dohány utca**. The synagogue was built between 1854 and 1869 to the plans of Lajos Förster. A cemetery surrounded by a row of arcades adjoins the Byzantine–Moorish style chapel, where the victims of fascism, the dead of the 1944–1945 ghetto, rest in mass graves. Adjoining the chapel there is also a **Heroes' Chapel** which preserves the memory of the Jewish heroes of World War I (Deli and Faragó, 1929–1932), and the **National Museum of Jewish Religion and History.**

The section of the Kiskörút that follows the former city wall runs to **Deák Ferenc tér**. The neo-Classical building of the **Lutheran Church** standing in Deák tér was built between 1799 and 1809 to plans by Mihály Pollack and János Kraus. The main façade was later rebuilt by József Hild. The adjoining building (No. 4–5) houses the **National Lutheran Museum,** where, in addition to valuable works of the goldsmith's craft, a facsimile of Martin Luther's will may also be seen. (The original is preserved in the archives of the Lutheran Church.)

Some of the long-distance coaches depart from the big bus terminal on the eastern end of **Engels tér,** which adjoins Deák tér. The inner city terminal of the airport bus service is also located here, behind the terminal building. The **Danubius Fountain** (Miklós Ybl and Leó Feszler, 1880–1883) in the middle of the square symbolizes the Danube and its tributaries. **József Attila utca,** which leads to the Chain Bridge, closes off Engels tér from the north.

Bajcsy-Zsilinszky út extends from Deák tér to Marx tér and bears the name of one of the leading figures of the bourgeois resistance movement of World War II. Lined with eclectic and *art nouveau* apartment houses built at the turn of the century, this street leads to the **Western Railway Station** (Nyugati pályaudvar).

At the opening of Népköztársaság útja, its façade facing towards the Danube, stands **St. Stephen's Parish Church,** popularly known as the Basilica. Construction was begun in 1851 according to plans by József Hild. After Hild's death Miklós Ybl continued with the construction in 1868 on the basis of modified plans, and following Ybl's death, József Kauser took over. The Basilica was finally dedicated in 1905.

This neo-Renaissance church has two frontal towers. The dome is 96 m high; the area on which the church was built covers altogether 4,147 sq.m; and it can hold 8,500 persons. Above the main gate is a bust of St. Stephen made of Carrara marble; above the bust is a mosaic picture designed by Bertalan Székely and Mór Than. The statues inside, in front of the four pillars supporting the dome, are the work of Alajos Stróbl, János Fadrusz, and Károly Senyei. The mosaics on the dome were designed by Károly Lotz, while the statue of St. Stephen on the high altar is the work of Alajos Stróbl. The five bronze reliefs around the high altar depicting scenes from the life of St. Stephen are by Ede Mayer.

Bajcsy-Zsilinszky út leads into the Nagykörút at Marx tér.

The Nagykörút

The 4 km long **Nagykörút** (Great Boulevard) extends in a semicircle through the most densely-populated sections of Pest, from the Margaret Bridge to the Petőfi Bridge. A real "folklore" has grown up around the Nagykörút during its barely hundred-year-old history, from poems to prose, chansons and dance songs. Not because there are historic monuments or other items of interest to be seen, but rather because the Nagykörút has been a pulsating artery in the life of the city ever since it came into existence in the second half of the 19th century, built, for the most part, where a muddy branch of the Danube once ran. The rapid development of the city demanded room, and for this reason this branch of the river was filled in and apartment houses were built on both sides as part of a plan for uniform city development. The boulevard was finished by 1896 for the thousandth anniversary of the Magyar Conquest, which was celebrated with great pomp and ceremony. Today it embraces the densely populated districts V—IX.

The ratio between the height of the eclectic buildings lining the Nagykörút and the width of the thoroughfare is somehow "of human proportion", and it is for that reason, perhaps, that the Nagykörút is so alluring. The boulevard consists of four sections: Szent István körút, Lenin körút, József körút, and Ferenc körút.

Szent István körút begins at the Pest bridgehead of Margaret Bridge and runs to Marx tér.

At **Szent István körút 14** stands one of the most important homes of Hungarian prose theatre, the **Vígszínház.** Busts of Miklós Zrínyi, a 17th-century poet and general, and of Sándor Petőfi, stand in front of the main entrance.

The first point of interest on **Lenin körút,** which extends from Marx tér to Rákóczi út, is the steel-framed **Western Railway Station,** built between 1874–1877 by the atelier of Gustave Eiffel, the builder of the Paris Eiffel Tower. The Western Railway Station was erected on the spot in Marx tér where once stood the original station building, from which the first Hungarian train ran—from Pest to Vác—on July 15, 1846. The iron structure, a valuable historical monument, was reconstructed in 1979. This was followed by the full reconstruction of the station and its vicinity (Metro station, underpasses, department store).

The **Madách Theatre** is located in the section of Lenin körút **(No. 29–33)** that follows **November 7. tér.** Several hundred metres north of the boulevard, on **Hevesi Sándor tér,** is situated the country's leading prose theatre, the **National Theatre.**

Proceeding further along the Nagykörút towards Rákóczi út, we see the eclectic New York (today Hungária) palace, which was designed by Alajos Hauszmann and built between 1891 and 1895. Rebuilt in the original style on the ground floor of the building in premises once occupied by the New York Coffee-house is the **Hungária Café and Restaurant.** On the other floors are editorial offices of newspapers and book-publishing houses. The coffee-house was the meeting-place for writers, journalists and actors for three quarters of a century. Poems, short stories and plays were born beside its marble tables, and discussions and debates continued far into the night. The many caricatures on the walls and the notes made in the visitors' book by world-famous writers and artists, from Chaliapin to Klemperer and from Thomas Mann to Asturias, still preserve these memories.

József körút is the section of the Nagykörút stretching from Rákóczi út to Üllői út.

Ferenc körút extends from Üllői út to the Petőfi Bridge.

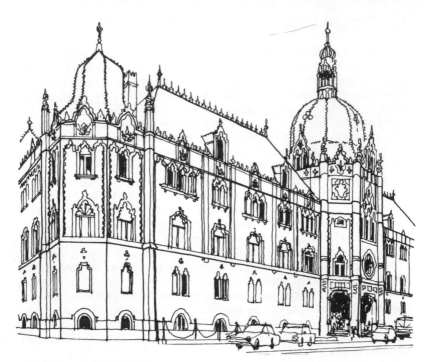

The Museum of Applied Arts

The characteristic, domed building of the **Museum of Applied Arts** with its coloured ceramic decorations rises near the intersection of Ferenc körút and Üllői út **(Üllői út 33–37)**. In building the museum, the designers Ödön Lechner and Gyula Pártos established a new Hungarian architectural style. A blend of Hungarian folk motifs, coloured ceramic decorations and oriental architectural elements, it represents an interesting individual experiment. Under the gigantic dome of the three-storied museum is a large glass-covered exhibition hall. The building is covered with coloured pyrogranite bricks from the Zsolnay factory at Pécs and is decorated with ceramics in Hindu, Islamic and Hungarian folk styles. The Hungarian and foreign applied industrial arts collections of the museum are also rich, the most important of them including furniture, wall-hangings, oriental rugs, goldsmiths' works and clocks; tin, bronze and iron objects; oven, wall and floor tiles; glazed earthenware dishes, works of glass art, porcelain, book bindings, ivory carvings and fans and creations of modern industrial art. The furniture collection includes valuable pieces of 18th-century English furniture.

Petőfi Bridge links the south end of the Nagykörút with the southernmost business parts of Buda (its length is 514 m; it was built in 1933–1937, and rebuilt in 1950–1952). In the course of the 1979 reconstruction work, an underpass system was built at both ends of the bridge.

The Andrássy út and Városliget (City Park)

Andrássy út and the City Park

The 2.5 km long **Andrássy út** (Népköztársaság útja) came into existence
under the name Sugárút (Radial Avenue) as part of a carefully integrated
plan between 1872 and 1876. A competition was opened for construction
of the avenue and a special statute set aside the necessary funds for
appropriations and building operations. The small, winding streets that
existed where this major thoroughfare now runs were pulled down, the
old houses were demolished, and construction was completed at a rapid
pace. From the point of view of city architecture, a carefully planned and
harmonious ensemble came into existence. Lined with gardens, the last
section of the large avenue, which begins at Bajcsy-Zsilinszky út, gradually widens as it proceeds towards the City Park (Városliget) with its
groves and parks.

Worth seeing in the row of eclectic living quarters, which mainly display elements of Renaissance style and which are characteristic of the
section leading from Bajcsy-Zsilinszky út to November 7. tér, are **No. 3,**
where the gateway is adorned with frescoes by Károly Lotz; **No. 5,** where
the gate is adorned with statues and marble columns and where an ornamental fountain stands in the courtyard; **No. 7,** which is adorned with
a relief-frieze and medallions; and **Nos. 8** and **9,** which are also richly
adorned. At No. 22 is the **State Opera House,** built in an Italian neo-
Renaissance style between 1875 and 1884 by Miklós Ybl. The façade is

adorned with statues of Ferenc Liszt and Ferenc Erkel (Alajos Stróbl), among others, and the ceiling frescoes of the main stairway are the creations of Mór Than. The foyer entrance with its arcades is adorned with paintings by Károly Lotz and the upper wall with paintings by Árpád Feszty and Róbert Scholtz. The ceiling pictures in the auditorium were painted by Károly Lotz. The stage is 43 m deep. The Opera House was opened on September 24, 1884; during its nine decades of continuous existence, many of the world's leading conductors have conducted here. The first director was Ferenc Erkel, and Gustav Mahler managed it for some time. Before World War II Sergio Failoni and after him Otto Klemperer were permanent conductors for several years. (There is another opera house in Budapest, the Erkel Theatre [see p. 81] and in the summer opera productions are held in the outdoor theatre on Margaret Island.) For its one-hundredth anniversary, the Opera has been extensively modernized and its art work and auditorium restored.

Ödön Lechner and Gyula Pártos built the palace opposite the Opera House (**No. 25**) in 1883 in which the **State Ballet Institute** (Állami Balettintézet) is located.

Nagymező utca, a street that crosses Népköztársaság útja, and its surrounding neighbourhood, are well known for theatres and places of entertainment. Here are located the **Moulin Rouge** Variety Theatre, the **Operetta Theatre,** the **Radnóti Literary Theatre,** the **Mikroszkóp Theatre** and the **Thália Theatre.** The **Children's Theatre** is in the neighbouring Paulay Ede utca, the **Vidám Színpad** is in Révay utca and the **State Puppet Theatre** is on nearby Jókai tér.

On **Jókai tér** stands a statue (Alajos Stróbl) of the great writer after whom the square is named. There is a statue of the poet Endre Ady (Géza Csorba) in **Liszt Ferenc tér** that begins on the other side of Népköztársaság útja. The building housing the **Academy of Music** on the corner of Liszt Ferenc tér and Majakovszkij utca (**Liszt Ferenc tér 8**) was built between 1904–1907 to the plans of Kálmán Giergl. Situated above the main entrance of the college is a statue of its first president, Ferenc Liszt, a work by Alajos Stróbl.

At the time it was being established, from 1881 to 1886, the Music Academy functioned in a few rooms of Ferenc Liszt's home on Hal tér (today's Irányi utca) on the bank of the Danube. It was later moved to **No. 67** (built between 1877 and 1879) in what is now **Andrássy út.** The Academy of Music has been functioning in its present home since 1907 and serves as the centre for higher musical education—training teachers, artists and composers. The majority of concerts given in the capital are held in the Large Hall of the Academy of Music, which can accommodate up to 1,200 persons, or in the Small Concert Hall. In the foyer of the Large Hall stands a bronze bust (the work of András Beck) of Béla Bartók, who was a teacher in the Music Academy until his emigration.

Andrássy út widens beyond November 7. tér as it continues towards Hősök tere. Here can be found the **former academy of music (No. 67)** where memorial plaques of Ferenc Liszt and Ferenc Erkel hang on the wall. At **No. 69** stands the reconstructed main building of the **State Puppet Theatre** and adjoining it, the neo-Renaissance palace of the **Academy of Fine Arts (No. 71),** the façade of which is embellished with graffiti. In the park of what is known as the **Strawberry Gardens** (Epreskert) (**Bajza u. 41**) are situated studios belonging to the Academy of Fine Arts. There are several monuments to be seen in the area of Strawberry Gardens: from the Matthias Church in Buda before its reconstruction, a Gothic gate, a few stone monuments, and the Baroque Calvary of András Mayerhoffer (built between 1744 and 1749), which was trans-

The Opera

ported from its original place to Strawberry Gardens during the replanning of the city in 1893.

The **Kodály körönd** (earlier it was called just the Körönd—the Circle) received its name from the fact that the great music teacher and composer lived here. The statues standing under the old trees of the square depict four great figures of Hungarian history: Vak Bottyán, one of the leaders of the Rákóczi War of Independence that took place in the 18th century, Miklós Zrínyi and György Szondi, heroes of the 16th-century battles against the Turks, and Bálint Balassi, the first great Hungarian lyric poet, who fell in a battle against the Turks.

The foundations were laid for the collection housed in the **Hopp Ferenc Museum of Eastern Asiatic Art (Andrássy út 103),** by Ferenc Hopp, a Budapest art collector (1883–1919) who brought back with him from his trips to the Far East valuable works of art and who bequeathed his collection of 4,100 items, together with his villa, to the Hungarian state. Since then, material from other Budapest museums (as well as collections, purchases and presentations) have increased the collection to many times its original size. The **Museum of Chinese Art** (Kína Múzeum) **(Gorkij fasor 12)** also forms part of the Hopp Ferenc Museum of Eastern Asiatic Art.

Népköztársaság útja runs into Hősök tere at Dózsa György út.

The **Millennial Monument** situated on **Hősök tere** (Heroes' Square) was erected to commemorate the thousandth anniversary of the Conquest of Hungary. Construction of the monument began in 1897, but it was finished only in 1929. The statues are the work of György Zala, and the architectural details are by Albert Schickedanz. The central point of the monument is a 36 m high column which is crowned by a winged figure. On the pedestal are statues depicting the leader of the conquering tribes, Prince Árpád, as well as the leaders of the seven Magyar tribes. Behind the column is a row of ceremonial columns shaped in a semicircle with statues of outstanding figures of Hungarian history. The order of the statues (from left to right) is as follows: King (St.) Stephen I, Ladislas I, Coloman Beauclerc, Andrew II, Béla IV, Charles Robert, and Louis the Great; General János Hunyadi, King Matthias Corvinus, Princes of Transylvania Gábor Bethlen, István Bocskai and Imre Thököly and Prince Ferenc Rákóczi II, the leader of the 1703–1711 War of Independence, and

Lajos Kossuth. Below each bronze statue is a relief depicting a historical scene taken from the life of each great figure. On top of the colonnade rise the allegorical statues of Labour and Welfare, War and Peace, Science and Art.

On a gigantic stone tablet in front of the Millennial Monument is the **Hungarian War Memorial,** on which stands the following inscription: "In memory of the heroes who sacrificed their lives for our nation's freedom and for national independence".

There are museum buildings standing on both sides of the square. A Corinthian colonnade adorns the façade of the neo-Classical building housing the **Museum of Fine Arts** (Szépművészeti Múzeum). On the tympanum of this building is a reproduction of the "Battle of the Centaurs", one of the reliefs from the Olympian temple of Zeus. The museum building was completed between 1900 and 1916 by Albert Schickedanz and Fülöp Herzog. The collections housed here are as follows:

Egyptian Exhibition: Painted wooden mummy-cases, masterpieces of plastic art of different sizes, for example, a man's portrait made from limestone, reliefs from the wall of a temple built during the 4th century B. C. and a seated bronze statue of the god Imhotep. The small collection provides a good survey of Egyptian art from the Prehistoric Age down to the Roman and Coptic Ages.

Graeco-Roman Collection: The international importance of this collection is due to the abundance of original Greek statues. Works by the finest masters can be found in the Greek vase collection; the terracottas as well as the early Cyprian and the Etruscan and Roman material are also of great value.

Gallery of Old Masters: The Spanish material found in this gallery is some of the most important in all Europe. The Trecento and Quattrocento works in the Italian collection, as well as the Renaissance and Venetian Settecento works are outstanding. The Dutch collection is also rich. Other important works demonstrate French, German and English painting of the 17th and 18th centuries. Outstanding 18th- and 19th-century English landscapes are included in the English collection.

Sculpture Gallery: This section contains a collection of works representing European sculpture from the 4th to the 18th centuries. Pisano, Verrocchio and Leonardo da Vinci are among the great Italian masters represented.

Modern Foreign Picture Gallery: Among the most significant works in this gallery are those of Delacroix, Daubigny, Troyon, Corot, Courbet, Pissarro, Manet, Monet, Gauguin, Renoir, Cézanne, Toulouse-Lautrec and Kokoschka.

Modern Sculpture Collection: Exhibits works of 19th- and 20th-century European sculptors, such as Rodin, Meunier, Maillol and Meštrović.

20th-century Art: The recently opened exhibition shows the work of artists of Hungarian origin living abroad (e.g. Sigismund Kolos-Vary, Nicolas Schöffer, Amerigo Tot, Victor Vasarely and others), and a few works of great contemporary foreign artists (e.g. Hans Arp, Marc Chagall, Oskar Kokoschka, Pablo Picasso, Fritz Wotruba and others).

Department of Prints and Drawings: The collection consists of almost 100,000 items. Periodic exhibitions show the most valuable ones arranged in different groupings.

Reminiscent of a Hellenistic temple, the **Art Gallery** on the opposite side of Hősök tere **(Dózsa György út 37)** was also built by Albert Schickedanz and Fülöp Herzog, in 1895. The halls of the museum house temporary exhibitions.

The **City Park** (Városliget) is a favourite place of resort for the residents of the capital. Until the beginning of the 19th century, this 1 sq. km area was nothing but a sandy, bare, open space; earlier, in the Middle Ages, Diets were held here. Then work was begun in 1817 to convert the area into a park, and since then it has gradually become both open woodland and a popular place of entertainment. The workers of Budapest used to hold processions here, such as May lst celebrations. In 1896, a great millennial exhibition commemorating the thousandth anniversary of the Conquest was held on the grounds of the City Park.

The street beyond Hősök tere which forms a continuation of And-

City Park with the Castle of Vajdahunyad

rássy út and which intersects the Városliget in a straight line, crosses the small bridge over Városliget Lake into the interior of the park. In the summer, one can row on the waters of this artificial lake; in the winter, an ice skating-rink is open in one part of the area. The building complex which consists of 21 different parts and is situated on an island in the middle of the lake, exemplifies historical styles of Hungarian architecture from the Roman age down to the Baroque period. The building was named the **Castle of Vajdahunyad** since its most characteristic sections are reproductions of the Transylvanian Castle of Vajdahunyad (today Hunedoara, Rumania), the former castle of the Hunyadi family. The replica of the main entrance to the Church of Ják, in western Hungary, is a particularly beautiful part of the complex. The building was built on a temporary basis for the Millennial Exhibition of 1896, but it achieved such popularity that it was later rebuilt permanently. A statue of Ignác Alpár (by Ede Telcs), who planned the building, stands in front of the bridge leading to the castle. One of the statues in the courtyard is of Anonymus, King Béla III's scribe, the first Hungarian chronicler (the work of Miklós Ligeti), whose identity has never been successfully established. The entrance to the **Museum of Agriculture** (Mezőgazdasági Múzeum) is located in the Baroque wing of the castle. In the halls of the museum the visitor can become acquainted with Hungarian animal husbandry, silviculture, hunting, fishing and viticulture. The botanical collection of the **Museum of Natural Sciences** (Természettudományi Múzeum) is also located here. A bronze statue of George Washington stands near the lake and the Castle of Vajdahunyad.

The **Széchenyi Medicinal and Open-air Baths** are also situated in the City Park (**Állatkerti körút 11**). The baths were built between 1909 and 1913 by Győző Cziegler and Ede Dvorzsák and were enlarged in 1926. Opposite the main entrance is a statue of the engineer and geologist Vilmos Zsigmondy, who discovered the first medicinal springs of the park in 1877. In 1936 thermal water was again discovered, and it gushes forth today from a depth of 1,256 m and feeds the pools of the Széchenyi Baths with medicinal water of a temperature of 76 °C.

The visitor can enter the 13.7 hectare area of the **Municipal Zoological and Botanical Gardens (Állatkerti körút 8–10)**, through a gate supported by four stone elephants. The zoo is one of Central Europe's oldest. It was opened in 1866 with animals placed in 11 buildings and a number of cages, and was rebuilt and enlarged between 1907 and 1912. The buildings of the Zoological Gardens were damaged during World War II, and most of the animals perished; but after many years of work, it was rebuilt and its livestock replaced. Now it shelters more than 4,000 animals, and 10,000 plants belonging to 1,500 species. European, polar and tropical animals, living creatures found in fresh waters and oceans and flocks of birds all live in an environment as similar as possible to their home surroundings: the brown bear on the side of the "mountain" into which a cave leads; aquatic birds on the shores of a lake; and the hippopotamus in a pond fed by natural thermal spring water. To these favourable conditions can be attributed the fact that the hippopotamus, which does not normally breed in captivity, regularly contributes offspring to the animal inventory of the Budapest Zoo. A favourite sight in the Zoological Gardens is the animal nursery, where lion- and bear-cubs frolic with antelope kids and puppies.

The **Amusement Park** (Vidám Park, **Állatkerti körút 14–16**) was established with a roller-coaster, and many other attractions at the beginning of the century, on the model of the Tivoli in Copenhagen and the Luna Park in Berlin.

Monuments and documents from the history of transportation are on exhibit in the **Transport Museum** located in **Május 1. út 26,** which borders the Városliget on the north-east. Old carriages, locomotives, automobiles, aeroplanes, as well as working models of miscellaneous means of transport can all be seen in the museum. The Adam Clark memorial, including his plans for the Chain Bridge, bridge components he assembled in England and a portrait of the Clark family, a portrait of Adam Clark by Miklós Barabás and an engraving, are also on exhibition in the Transport Museum.

Rákóczi út

Kossuth Lajos utca (see p. 63) is continued beyond the Kiskörút by **Rákóczi út.** At the beginning of the 19th century, when the city boundary was at the present-day Kiskörút, this was the main road to Kerepes and Hatvan, and it was lined with merchants' booths and stalls. Other than these, only the St. Roch Chapel and a city hospital were then standing along this road. The first important public building to be completed in present-day Rákóczi út was the National Theatre. Its opening in 1837 was a great event for Hungarian culture. The theatre has since been

People's Stadium

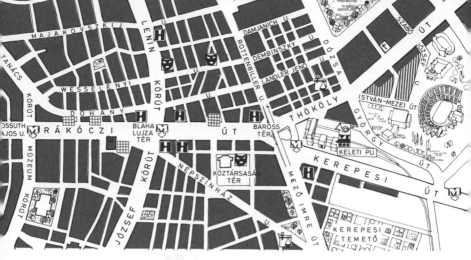

Rákóczi út and the Népstadion (People's Stadium)

demolished, and only one remaining capital and a memorial tablet mark the spot where it formerly stood. The fact that Rákóczi út has become so important a shopping street is due to the fact that in the second half of the 19th century, while the thoroughfare was being developed, it became the natural link with the busy Eastern Railway Station. From the point of view of transport, too, the street is important, for underneath it runs the east-west Metro line; Rákóczi út is in fact the capital's chief eastwest thoroughfare.

The history of the building housing the **Semmelweis Hospital** (earlier the St. Roch Hospital) goes back to the beginning of the 18th century, when it was also a hospital for infectious diseases, well outside the city. The Rókus Hospital was built here in 1796 and was rebuilt and enlarged between 1837 and 1841 by Mihály Pollack. In front of the main entrance to the hospital stands a statue of Ignác Semmelweis, who was the hospital's head doctor. The St. Roch and St. Rosalia chapels beside the hospital were built in 1711.

The intersection of Rákóczi út and the Nagykörút is one of the busiest spots in the capital. The **Erkel Theatre,** Budapest's second opera house, stands on **Köztársaság tér** near the part of Rákóczi út between the intersection and Baross tér. On the eastern side of Baross tér rises the eclectic iron-and-glass-framed structure of the **Eastern Railway Station** (Keleti pályaudvar), built in 1882 from plans by Gyula Rochlitz. Statues of Stephenson and Watt can be seen on the main façade of the station.

Thököly út and Kerepesi út lead eastwards from Baross tér towards the outer suburbs of the city, Rottenbiller utca to the north, and Mező Imre út to the south.

The area behind the Eastern Railway Station is occupied by sports establishments. Between 1949 and 1953 the **People's Stadium** (Népstadion) **(Istvánmezei út 3–5)** was built on the basis of plans by Károly Dávid. It covers 22 hectares, held by 18 steel and concrete pylons, and its grandstand is 30 m high, 50 m wide, and 328 m long. The public can enter the 73,200-seat arena through 50 gateways. Near the People's Stadium is situated the **National Sports Hall** (Nemzeti Sportcsarnok), which can accommodate up to 2,000 spectators (built in 1940 from plans by Gyula Rimanóczy). Located on the Hungária körút side of the People's Stadium, the **Budapest Sports Hall** (Budapest Sportcsarnok) was opened in 1982. The largest covered sports complex of Budapest, it is suited to the staging of every type of indoor sport and also has an artificial ice rink. It can seat 12,500 and is therefore ideal not only for sporting events, but also for concerts and other cultural events designed for large audiences. The

Indoor Hall for Competitions (Fedett Játékcsarnok, 1966) is the scene of handball, basketball and volleyball matches. The **Small Stadium** (Kisstadion) can seat up to 15,000 persons. In addition to sporting matches, concerts are also held here, and in the winter, figure-skating contests and ice-hockey matches. The **Millennial Sports Ground** (Millenáris Sportpálya), which can accommodate up to 20,000 spectators, is situated at the intersection of Thököly út and Szabó József utca.This is where bicycle and motorcycle races are held.

The **Trotting Racetrack and the Galloping Racetrack** are located close by. The **Budapest International Fair** takes place not far from here in **Dobi István út**. Industrial fairs are held here in May and September of every year, and once every five years, there is an **Agricultural Exhibition and Fair**. It was here that the Hotel Expo was built in 1982.

From Újpest to Csepel

Roads lead from the centre of Pest north, east and south to industrial districts and new residential estates. Some of these industrial districts were formerly considered as suburbs; only during the 1950 reorganization did they become part of the capital itself.

Starting from Marx tér, **Váci út** leads through the northern factory district of **Angyalföld**, it leads to **Újpest** (New Pest, District IV), which developed in the 19th century into an important industrial area embracing leather and shoe manufacture, lumber and furniture works, to which was later added the making of electronic and precision instruments and incandescent lamps and machinery. One of the largest new residential parts of the capital has been developed in District XV, **Újpalota**, next to Újpest.

With the demolition of 3,500 obsolete living quarters and the construction of 12,000 new apartments, **Zugló** (District XIV) has been almost completely remodelled. An extension of Rákóczi út, Kerepesi út leads past new residential areas to Rákosszentmihály, Sashalom, and Mátyásföld, which are all situated in District XVI, part of the capital's green belt. **Kőbánya** (where the Budapest International Fair is held), **Kispest** and **Pestlőrinc** are the southeastern industrial districts of the capital (Districts X, XIX and XVIII); these, alongside a thriving development, have still preserved their industrial character. The urban layouts of these areas have, however, undergone certain fundamental changes. Modern residential estates are being built in areas closer to the centre of the city; while the more distantly-situated private family houses, with their gardens, give the appearance of a garden city. The continuation of Üllői út leads out in the direction of Pestlőrinc to **Ferihegy Airport** (Ferihegyi repülőtér).

On the northern tip (26.1 sq.km) of the 47 km long **Csepel Island** is located **Csepel** (District XXI), one of the focal points of Hungarian heavy industry.

Earlier, Csepel was a separate settlement with all the characteristics of a self-contained community. However, after being annexed in 1950 to Budapest.

In addition to the numerous industrial establishments, the **Budapest National Free Harbour** is situated in Csepel.

Besides Csepel and Margaret Island, the capital has three other islands which lie to the north of the city: **Palotai-sziget** and **Népsziget** near the Pest bank of the Danube, and **Óbuda Island** near Óbuda. The later is worthy of mention, since remains of the Emperor Hadrian's palace have been uncovered there. There is also a park towards the north of the island, which can be approached over a small bridge.

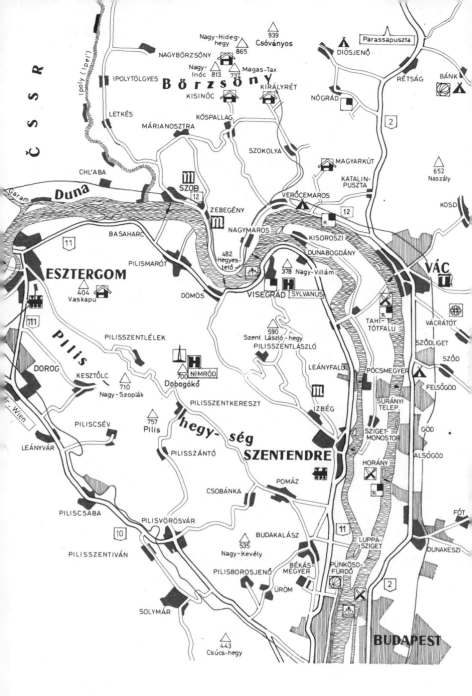

The Danube Bend

The Danube Bend

Rds. 2 and 11 lead from Budapest along the right and left banks of the Danube respectively.

Between the two banks are ferries which transport cars between Viseg-rád and Nagymaros, Basaharc and Szob, and between Vác and Szent-endre Island (Tótfalu), on which the Pokol csárda can be found. A bridge connects Tótfalu with Tahi, on the right bank of the Danube.

The Danube Bend (Duna-kanyar) is an almost 20 km long and particularly wind-ing part of the 417 km Hungarian section of the Danube; but if one includes the many resorts on either side of the Bend itself, one means by the term "Danube Bend" an area which stretches for some 50 or 60 km. The river, whose general direction has been from west to east, changes to a northsouth direction below Esztergom and turns north with a hairpin bend, then, suddenly forming a right angle after Visegrád, continues its course towards the south. Before reaching Budapest the river divides into two branches on either side of Szentendre Island.

On the right bank the Visegrád range follows the river from Esztergom to Szentendre, the Pilis Mountains follow it from the west of Pomáz, and the Buda Hills follow the river as it approaches the capital. On the left bank the slopes of the Börzsöny Mountains run down to the Danube between Szob and Verőce-maros. Willows and forests reaching to the water line the banks of the 31 km long Szentendre Island, creating a romantic scene on both branches of the Danube.

The holiday areas include not only the shores of the river but the neighbouring hilly region as well. Besides the natural beauties of the Danube Bend as well as the possibilities for bathing and walking, the historic monuments of the area are also of interest.

This part of the Danube constituted the *limes*, the boundary of the Roman Empire from the beginning of the 1st century until the first half of the 5th century. A virtual chain of fortifications protected the Danube elbow. But monuments originating from Hungary's Middle Ages are much more significant than those from the Roman age, for several Hungarian monarchs lived on the Danube Bend between the 11th and 15th centuries.

THE RIGHT BANK OF THE DANUBE

The name of **BUDAKALÁSZ** (15 km from Budapest turn left on the road to Szent-endre) is well known because of an archeological discovery made there—a small four-wheeled clay cart (an old drinking vessel) exhibited in the National Museum of Budapest, a discovery which proves that the four-wheeled wagon was made and used in the Danube Valley as early as four thousand years ago. Ruins of a medieval hunting-lodge belonging to the queens of Hungary have been unco-vered at **POMÁZ** (17 km from Budapest) on the road branching off at Budakalász and leading through the villages of the Pilis Mountains. Stone relics from this lodge are at the National Museum of Budapest.

Szentendre

Reached by taking Rd. 11 north of Budapest, or by the suburban express train (HÉV). Lies 19 km from Budapest.

The historic buildings of this picturesque little town were erected by Ser-bian, Dalmatian and Greek families, who found refuge here from the Turks in the 14th and later in the 17th centuries. In predominantly Catholic and partly Protestant Hungary the people fleeing from the Bal-kans were able, under special royal privileges, to form their own Pravos-lav (Orthodox) communities in Hungary.

The old main square of the inner town, the present-day **Fő tér,** is sur-rounded by an ensemble of protected historic buildings and 18th-century Serbian commercial houses.

The group of houses held together by a gabled roof at **Nos. 2–5** (1720 and 1730) consists of five separate houses in Vastagh György utca and houses the **Szentendre Picture Gallery.** The temporary exhibits include 50 years of art by artists who worked or are still working in Szentendre.

The painted iron Rococo **memorial cross** in the middle of the square was erected in 1763 by Serbian merchants out of gratitude for having the town spared from the plague.

An interesting feature of the **Béke Restaurant** building is that it shares a common roof with the neo-Classical house at **No. 18,** the Baroque house at **No. 19/a,** and the Rococo house at **No. 19,** and also that an inn was situated there as early as 1770. **No. 11** is characteristic of town

Szentendre

houses built in the style of Louis XVI. One should also note the Baroque house at **No. 17** and its wrought-iron gate.

It thus happens that some of the finest treasures of Orthodox Church art, which originally came from workshops far beyond the frontiers of Hungary, may be admired less than an hour's drive from Budapest. Two of the town's seven old, protected churches are Catholic, four are Orthodox and one is Calvinist.

The central zone of Szentendre, once a busy merchant town, has fully preserved its 18th-century character: individual buildings, whole street sections and squares exude the atmosphere of the typical 18th-century Dalmatian-Baroque small town.

One of the most important historic buildings of the square and of the whole town is the Orthodox **Blagovestenska Church,** built in the Baroque style in 1752 (probably the work of András Mayerhoffer). Because of the Greek inscription on a grave stone (dated 1759) beside the gate, the church is popularly called the Greek Church. Certain sections of the portal and bell tower are Rococo in style.

The house in the style of Louis XVI beside the church **(No. 6)** was built in 1793 as a Serbian school; today it is the **Ferenczy Museum. Károly Ferenczy** (1862–1927), a Hungarian pioneer of Impressionism in painting, spent his youth in Szentendre. The works of the artist's two well-known children are also on exhibit in the museum: **Noémi Ferenczy**'s (1890–1957) tapestries, the themes of which are for the most part taken from the lives of Hungarian peasants, and **Béni Ferenczy's** (1890–1967) sculptures, medallions, and plaquettes. A few small works of their mother, **Olga Fialka Ferenczy,** have also been placed on exhibit here.

A permanent exhibition containing the life work of the **ceramic artist Margit Kovács** (1902–1977) has been established at the corner of the narrow **Görög utca** and **Vastagh György utca** in a former 18th-century commercial house. By combining modern art forms with the traditions of Hungarian folk art, Margit Kovács created a unique and very popular style of her own. The house itself with its decorative stone-framed gate, Rococo window, and beautiful small courtyard is worthy of attention.

What has remained of a former hoist used by the 18th-century merchants in transporting bales of leather through an opening in the gable into an attic storeroom can still be seen on the gable of **Görög utca 6–8,** a house in the Baroque style. The **memorial cross of the tobacconists** (tanners) on **Szamár Mountain (Bartók Béla u. 10)** preserves the memory of the many tanners who once lived in this house.

The **Catholic Parish Church** is of medieval origin but was reconstructed during the 18th century in the Baroque style. It rises on a small hill near Marx tér. The shape of the windows suggests a late Romanesque style, but Gothic features resulting from a 15th-century reconstruction are also evident in the building. An interesting ornamentation on the outer wall is a more than 700-year-old medieval sundial. In the 18th century the church was owned by Catholic Dalmatians and was called Klisa. The frescoes of the Gothic sanctuary are the collective works of the painters belonging to the local colony of artists. A picturesque view is offered of the walled-in gardens encircling the church: a multitude of tiny houses, their small courtyards full of flowers, the colourful view of small winding streets, alleys, and stairways. The Dalmatians who migrated here from the shores of the Adriatic transplanted a little of their own Mediterranean world to Szentendre. In the vicinity of the church (Templom tér 1), the **Czóbel Béla Collection** exhibits the works presented by the painter to the town.

On the way down the hill it is worthwhile casting a glance at the Baroque **City Hall** with its side wing facing Rákóczi Ferenc utca; the central part of the building was built at the beginning of the 18th century.

The **Belgrade (or Saborna) Church,** the Serbian Orthodox episcopal cathedral built between 1756 and 1764, stands in Alkotmány utca, opening from Fő tér, in a garden surrounded by a wall. The pictures on the magnificent carved Baroque-inspired iconostasis were painted by Vasilije Ostoić of Novi Sad. The red marble altar, the Rococo pulpit and bishop's throne, the two side entrances and the wrought-iron gate (made by Mátyás Ginesser) are all worthy of special attention.

The **Serbian Collection of Ecclesiastical Art** (Szerb Egyháztörténeti gyűjtemény, **Engels u. 5**) can be found next to the rear courtyard of the Belgrade Church in one of the side buildings of the former Serbian Episcopal See. The most beautiful icons belonging to the Hungarian Eastern Slavic churches have been assembled here because many of the churches have not been used since the Serbs returned home. Icons dating back to the 16th to 19th centuries give a picture of Eastern Slav art steeped in Byzantine tradition and attest the influence which the playfulness of Hungarian Rococo exercised on the conservative Byzantine heritage. A synthesis of the two styles is the special feature and most genuine value of Hungarian Eastern Slav ecclesiastical art. Among the icons in the museum, the panel painting of the **Nativity** by the Greek Mitrofan is one of the most outstanding. The **Vladim Virgin** and the **Kazan Virgin** are icons originating from Russia. Codices, ecclesiastical vestments, objects of the goldsmith's art and wood carvings from Mount Athos in Greece

View of Szentendre

complete the exhibition. In its vicinity we find the **Pest County Cultural Centre,** the hall of which is decorated by Jenő Barcsay's large **mosaic.**

Returning from Engels utca to Rákóczi utca, the present **Calvinist Church,** formerly the Opovačka Church, another Eastern Slav building built in the 18th century, meets the eye. (All these churches received their names according to the region from which the congregation of refugees that built them came. The churches were first built of wood and later of stone, and interior ornamentation also depended on whether the congregation was of the Eastern or the Catholic Church.) It is worth-while turning off here up **Sallai Imre út,** then after about 3 km up the gently rising Szabadság forrás út to the **Outdoor Folk Museum** (Szabadtéri Néprajzi Múzeum). (A local bus runs from Szentendre suburban railway station to the Outdoor Folk Museum, and to the Szabadság Springs.)

The exhibition at the outdoor museum is not yet complete, since of all the house types represented in the ethnographic regions of Hungary only those from the Upper Tisza region (northeastern Hungary) and the Kisalföld (northwestern Hungary) have so far been assembled. But even so, the Museum is well worth a visit as it gives a picture of 19th-century Hungarian peasant life.

A visit to **Rab Ráby tér,** situated in the northern section of the town, should not be missed. The Baroque **house at No. 1** was where the civil servant Mátyás Ráby lived in the 18th century during the reign of Emperor Joseph II (1780–1790). His life and tragedy were made legendary by Mór Jókai's romantic novel after which the square was named. On the wall of **No. 3** hangs the emblem of the **locksmiths'guild.** In the 18th century eleven guilds were in operation in the small town where, besides the activity of the merchants, the work of craftsmen was a long-established source of wealth for Szentendre.

Malom utca leads from Rab Ráby tér towards the bank of the Danube. The memorial cross in **Bogdányi út** is a reminder that a wooden church once stood here; the coffin of the Serbian Tsar Lazar, who fell in the Battle of Kosovo in 1389, was placed in the church by refugees who came here in 1690. (The coffin was returned in 1699, after the Treaty of Karlowitz.)

The tanners' church, the **Preobraženska,** which was built between 1741 and 1746, stands in Bogdányi út **No. 40.** The wrought-iron, ornamental garden gate of the church is the work of a local locksmith. Pictures placed in five rows and separated from one another by Corinthian columns adorn the iconostasis. The background work of the pictures is gilded, the carving on the iconostasis is dark green. On August 19 of every year

a traditional Serbian festival is held in the gardens of the church, at which time a tamboura orchestra plays music to a "kolo" dance.

The **Szentendre artists' colony** is situated at the junction of Bogdányi út and Ady Endre út. It was founded in 1928. Béla Czóbel (1883–1976), who divided his time for almost forty years between Paris and Szentendre and who, at the end of his life, donated his works to the city, was one of the prestigious members of the artists' colony, which has opened a gallery for his works (Templom tér). Periodic art exhibitions are held in the town in the **Small Gallery** (Kis Galéria), Bogdányi út 51.

At **Ady Endre utca 5** stands a small museum which exhibits the works (statues, graphic drawings) of the sculptor Jenő Kerényi (1908–1975). Continuing up Ady Endre út towards the north and on over the embankment (you can do it by car) you will reach Pap-sziget, an island covered with shady trees (camp site, small motel, bungalow site, outdoor swimming-pool).

In the district situated south of Fő tér, at **Dumtsa Jenő utca 7** stands the birthplace of the Serbian novelist, Jakov Ignatovič, who supported Hungarian–Serbian friendship in 1848–1849. At **No. 7,** the graphics and paintings of Jenő Barcsay are on exhibit. The **Požarevačka Church** (Hajós utca), surrounded by a stone wall, is noteworthy because of its Byzantine iconostasis and the tombstones in the courtyard. The **Church of Sts. Peter and Paul (Május 1. út),** the town's other Catholic church, was formerly owned by the Dalmatians who called it Ciprovačka.

The **Museum of Roman Stonework Finds** open to the public at **Római sánc utca 7** was established in the area of the former military camp of Ulcisia Castra, the 2nd-century Roman predecessor of Szentendre. One of the museum's main points of interest is stone slab No. 25, which preserves the memory of Septimius Severus Caesar's visit.

A bus line runs from Szentendre to **Lajos-forrás,** the spring 5 km outside the town.

LEÁNYFALU. 7 km along Rd. 11 towards the north is resort area with a warm water outdoor pool, first class camping site, luxury rest-houses, bungalows, villas.

The house of **Zsigmond Móricz** (1879–1942), a 20th-century Hungarian novelist, is situated here. Leányfalu is also a favourite summer retreat for writers and artists living in the capital.

Visegrád

42 km from Budapest on Rd. 11

In the 4th century the Romans built a castrum on the present-day Sibrik Hill, a fortress that was still used in the 9th and 10th centuries by the Slovaks who had settled here. The name Visegrád is Slavonic for high castle. A monastery was built in Visegrád in the 11th century following the Magyar Conquest; the settlement itself became a county capital. After the Mongol Invasion had subsided, construction was begun in 1250 on the lower castle situated near the river bank for the royal family, and later work was begun on the Citadel situated on the mountain. In 1326 Charles Robert, the Anjou king, had the royal seat transferred to Visegrád and had the lower castle converted into a royal palace in the late Gothic style of the Trecento. In 1335 Charles Robert here received the Polish king Casimir and the Czech king John, Rudolf, the Saxon, and Heinrich Wittelsbach, the Lower Bavarian elector, and the representatives of the Teutonic Order, and entered into an international agreement with them by which territorial disputes were resolved between Poland and the Teutonic Order, and international trade routes were delimited. The monarchs Louis the Great (of the House of Anjou) and Sigismund of Luxembourg resided in Buda but the work of construction was continued. In 1438, during the reign of Matthias Corvinus, an envoy of the

Pope wrote a letter from the Palace of Visegrád, which had already been enlarged and ornamented in the Renaissance style by Italian architects, sculptors, and stone masons. The letter was headed: *"Ex Visegrado paradiso terrestri"* ("from Visegrád, a paradise on earth"). Among the humanist writers of the age, the Hungarian Miklós Oláh and the Italian Bonfini also praised the magnificence of the palace.

Under Turkish rule (1543–1686) the palace fell into ruin. After the expulsion of the Turks the people settling in

the area built their homes of stones lying among the ruins. The destruction was completed by nature: over the centuries, landslides on the mountain buried the palace to such an extent that up to 1934, when the ruins were excavated, certain historians, despite the evidence provided by contemporary writers, refused to believe that a famous European palace had once stood here. The 600 m long by 300 m wide palace has still not been completely unearthed, for there are residential houses situated over much of the site.

Remains of the **water bastion** belonging to the lower castle lie next to the pier on the bank of the Danube. The Danube was watched from this 13th-century rondella. The bastion on the bank was connected to the lower castle by a wall which led from here to the citadel on the top of the mountain, and in this way the various fortresses as well as the palace consti-

GROUND-PLAN OF THE ROYAL PALACE OF VISEGRÁD

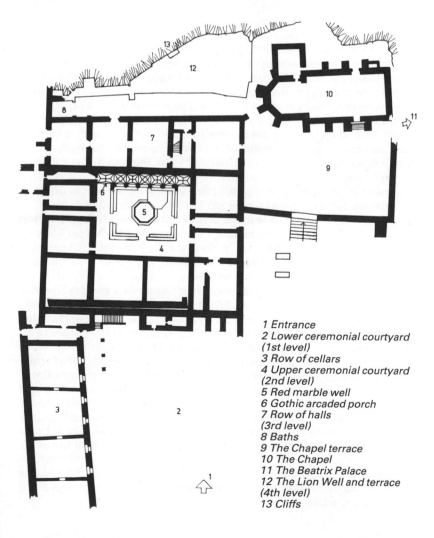

1 Entrance
2 Lower ceremonial courtyard
(1st level)
3 Row of cellars
4 Upper ceremonial courtyard
(2nd level)
5 Red marble well
6 Gothic arcaded porch
7 Row of halls
(3rd level)
8 Baths
9 The Chapel terrace
10 The Chapel
11 The Beatrix Palace
12 The Lion Well and terrace
(4th level)
13 Cliffs

tuted a connected system of fortifications. The stone wall of the battlement can still be seen today on the side of the mountain above the water bastion.

From the 13th-century keep of the **lower castle** the traffic of the road along the Danube bank could be surveyed, and merchants travelling this way were made to pay duty here. The hexagonal-shaped Romanesque tower is one of the most massive old buildings in Hungary. The thickness of the walls varies from 3.5 m to 8 m. (Popular tradition has named the stocky building **Solomon's Tower,** for in the 11th century King Ladislas, in the course of internal struggles over the throne, held the former King Solomon prisoner in Visegrád for a short time, presumably in the castle on Sibrik Hill, since the keep was built only 200 years later.) The 14th-century Gothic, ornamental **Anjou well-head** from the palace courtyard has been erected on the ground floor of the museum established in the tower. A relief known as the **Visegrád Madonna** has been transferred here from the palace chapel.

The area of the **former royal palace** can be approached from **Fő utca 27.** Walking from here through an indoor hallway provided with sedilia, one reaches the **ornamental courtyard,** in the middle of which the Renaissance **Hercules Fountain** stood on an octagonal well-pedestal. The coat of arms of King Matthias adorns the three marble lateral facings that have remained undamaged. The Renaissance **balustrade** above the Gothic hallway of the courtyard convincingly proves how harmoniously the Renaissance reconstruction work completed under the reign of Matthias fitted in with the Gothic parts. One of the points of interest in the rocky courtyard are the remains of a large **sewer.** A stairway and hall lead down to the **lower ceremonial courtyard.** A hallway provided with sedilia leads back to the starting point. From here another narrow stairway leads up to the foundation walls of the chapel, and to a terrace. Walking through a corridor, we reach the so-called **Courtyard of the Lion Fountain.** King Matthias had an ornamental marble fountain provided with a canopy erected here. From the mouths of the two lions on the rear wall, spring water flowed at one time into the marble basins, the supporting columns of which rest on five reclining lions. The remains of the original fountain can be seen in the keep. A reproduction stands in place of the original. The palace baths can also be reached from this courtyard.

The 18th-century Baroque mansion at **Fő utca 41** was a **royal hunting lodge** at the end of the 19th century. The **Chapel of the Virgin Mary** as well as the **Catholic church** on Fő tér are both from the 18th century. Remains of a 4th-century **Roman watchtower** have been discovered at the end of Fő utca next to the stone quarry.

The **Citadel** (as well as the Nagy-Villám lookout tower and the Silvanus Hotel) can be approached from Fő tér along Nagy Lajos utca, Mátyás király út, the Panoráma Highway, or by a local bus line that begins at the Mátyás Statue situated on the bank of the Danube, at the corner of Fő utca and Salamon-torony utca. The ruins of the Citadel and the high walls and towers that have remained give some idea, even now, of the former strength of the fortress, where the royal crown was kept for some time.

The **area around the Citadel,** together with the **Silvanus Hotel and Restaurant,** which offer a magnificent view of the Danube Bend, is today a popular resort area. The Börzsöny and Cserhát mountains on the other side of the Danube are revealed to the visitor from the 278 m high **Lookout tower on Nagy-Villám Hill** not far away. From the lookout tower the road continues towards a motel and a group of summer villas (restaurant, stores) built in the pleasantly-wooded surroundings. Finally, the road returns by the keep of the lower castle to Road 11, which runs along the bank of the Danube.

The Hercules Fountain
in the cour d'honneur

The Lion Well in the Matthias
Corvinus Palace of Visegrád

EXCURSIONS

Visegrád is the centre of the 35,000 hectare **Pilis Park Forest**. Footpaths have been laid through the forest belt and shelters, parking places, and sports grounds have been built. There is a riding-school at **Gizella-major** (pleasure rides in the forest).

Note: Swimming is not permitted in the Visegrád reach of the Danube, but there are excellent pools at the outdoor swimming baths complex located in magnificent woodland area near the **Lepence spring,** about 1.5 km from the ferry-boat crossing. From here through the Pilis Park Forest winds a panoramic road which links up with Rd. 11 at Szentendre.

DÖMÖS: Ruins of an 11th-century monastery; lies 7 km from Visegrád. South of Dömös on the bank of the **Malom Stream** there is a 2–3 km long path leading to a romantic world of rocks (to the left are the **Vadálló Rocks,** and to the right the **Rám Precipice**). **Prédikálószék** (Pulpit Seat) (641 m) towers over the Vadálló Rocks. Climbing it, however, is a difficult task for any tourist.

Esztergom

66 km from Budapest on Rd. 11, 46 km on Rds. 10 and 111 (through Dorog), and 72 km by boat.

The first permanent inhabitants of the area of present-day Esztergom were the Celts in the 4th century B.C. In the 1st century the Romans took possession of the area, calling it Solva Mansio. It was here that the Roman emperor Marcus Aurelius wrote a part of his most famous philosophical treatise, "The Meditations", while he was waging a war against the Germanic Quadi. Around A.D. 970–971, the Hungarian Prince Géza chose the area for his residence, and it was here that the first king of Hungary, Stephen I, was crowned. It was he who completed the conversion of pagan Hungary to Christianity and organized the Hungarian state. The first palace belonging to the kings of Hungary as well as the first basilica were constructed in Esztergom (once known by the medieval Latin name of Strigonium). It was here that in the 12th century the king of Hungary received western European knights on their way to the Holy Land. Among them were Godefroi de Bouillon, the French King Louis VII, and the German-Roman Emperor Friedrich Barbarossa. The 12th century—the time of King Béla III—was Esztergom's golden age. In the midle of the 13th century, following the Mongol Invasion, the monarch of the time (Béla IV) had his residence transferred to Buda. The head of the Catholic Church in Hungary, the Archbishop of Esztergom, remained, however, in the town and moved into the royal palace. During the time of the archbishops János Vitéz and Tamás Bakócz—at the beginning of the 16th century—the city still continued to flourish; scholars and artists of European fame lived in the archbishops' households. Almost the whole city was destroyed, however, during the Turkish occupation (1543–1683). The first "modern" Hungarian lyrical poet, Bálint Balassi, died a hero's death beneath the walls of the castle of Esztergom. Monteverdi, the court musician of the Prince of Mantua, was also in Esztergom at about this time.

At Esztergom the Danube splits into two branches, forming a pleasant island. The **Small Danube branch** is an ideal place for water skiing. There are two hills in the heart of the city: **Castle Hill** and **Szent Tamás** (St. Thomas) **Hill.**

The entrance to the unearthed and reconstructed section of **the medieval royal palace** is on Szent István tér, next to the Basilica. The most beautiful pieces in the stonework museum are a 12th-century ornamental gate, the marble fragments of the **Porta Speciosa,** which adorned the western façade of the **St. Adalbert Cathedral** built in the 12th century. (The cathedral meanwhile fell victim to the ravages of time.) Walking through a passage leading from the stonework museum into a 12th-century vaulted hall, the visitor reaches the oldest living-room in Hungary. The Romanesque portal in the next hall is worthy of special attention. Royal receptions were held in the so-called double hall on the first floor, which later became the study of the archbishop and scholar János Vitéz. The **Hall of Virtues** obtained its name from the themes depicted on its frescoes (by Alberti of Florence) symbolizing Prudence, Temperance, Fortitude, and Justice. The arch is adorned with the signs of the zodiac. (The passageway leading down from the hall belongs to the oldest—10th and 11 th c.—section of the palace. Excavations are still being carried out here.) The 12th-century single aisled, semicircular-arched **royal sanctuary chapel** can likewise be found on the first floor. The rich Gothic vaulting suggests that the chapel may have been built by the French masters who moved here from Burgundy in the 1180s, after Béla III had married Marguerite Capet. The Gothic arch over the sanctuary is one of the earliest historic examples of that style outside France. The most interesting pieces from among the works of stone masonry are the capitals depicting human figures and symbolizing the struggle between Good and Evil. The frescoes of the chapel are of several layers. The earliest layer—on the left

Esztergom

wall of the sanctuary—which depicts a strolling lion, was placed in
a Byzantine palmetto frame; the tree of life grows from under the feet of
the lion. (The use of the Byzantine style can be explained by the Byzantine
upbringing of Béla III.) The frescoes of the nave are of a later period. The
figures of the Apostles in the sedilia date from the mid-14th century.

From the palace the road leads to the **remains of the castle walls**
encircling Castle Hill; on the southeastern section of Castle Hill there is
a drawbridge gate with bastions, which is surrounded from the direction
of the Basilica by the 12th-century **Buda Tower from the direction of the
town and by the 16th-century Suleyman bastion**. The central of the
palace is the so-called **White Tower** built by Béla III. It was originally built

as a keep at the end of the 12th century. The **Danube Rondella** protected the castle from the north. The Danube bank was protected by the bastion network leading up from the **Mattyasovszky Bastion** in József Attila tér.

The dominant feature of Esztergom's city landscape is the **Cathedral** rising on Castle Hill. The porch is formed of Corinthian columns and overlooks Szent István tér. The 118 m long, 40 m wide building is cruciform in shape, and is crowned by a 71.5 m high dome. Work was started on the building in 1822 to the plans of Pál Kühneland and János Packh in the neo-Classical style. József Hild directed the later stage of construction that was finally completed in 1869. The large picture on the main altar was painted by the Italian master Grigoletti after Tizian's "Assumption of the Virgin". The frescoes on the vault of the sanctuary were painted by L. Moralt of Munich. The picture on the secondary altar on the south is the work of Grigoletti, the work on the north altar was begun by Grigoletti and finished by the Viennese Mayer.

The red-marble panelled **Bakócz Chapel** dating from 1507 is joined to the church on the south. The chapel was disassembled in the 19th century into 1,600 numbered pieces and rebuilt into the new cathedral as a side chapel to the plans of Packh. The white marble altar, an outstanding example of Renaissance architecture in Hungary, was carved by the

GROUND-PLAN OF THE ROYAL CASTLE OF ESZTERGOM

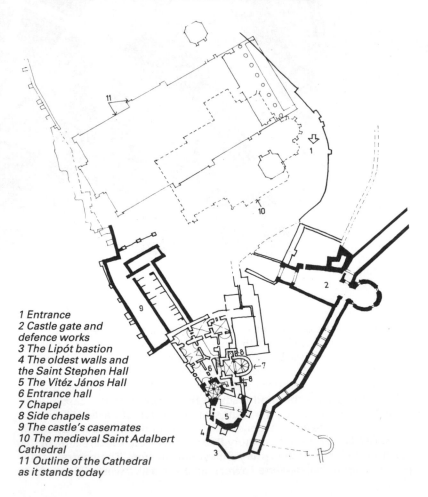

1 Entrance
2 Castle gate and
defence works
3 The Lipót bastion
4 The oldest walls and
the Saint Stephen Hall
5 The Vitéz János Hall
6 Entrance hall
7 Chapel
8 Side chapels
9 The castle's casemates
10 The medieval Saint Adalbert
Cathedral
11 Outline of the Cathedral
as it stands today

The medieval castle and chapel gate, Esztergom

Florentine Andrea Ferrucci in 1519. The chapel is one of the most beautiful examples of Tuscan Renaissance architecture.

The side chapel on the north was erected in honour of the martyr St. Stephen. In the Middle Ages a church named after this martyr stood on the north of the castle at this very same place. The statue of St. Stephen is the work of István Ferenczy, while the statue of Archbishop Ambrus Károly is by Giuseppe Pisani of Mantua.

The **Cathedral Treasury** (Kincstár) established in the 11th century, is in the northwest part of the Basilica; the entrance is inside the church. The treasury was robbed a number of times during the frequent wars, but it is nevertheless still the richest collection of ecclesiastical goldsmith's art and textiles in Hungary. It consists largely of works made in Hungary from the 11th century to the present.

The earliest piece in the collection is a crystal cross of the Carolingian age, but there are also several valuable objects of goldsmith's art from the 18th and 19th centuries. Outstanding pieces in the collection are as follows: a 12th-century **cross container** adorned with Byzantine *cloisonné* enamel pictures; a 13th-cen-

Bakócz Chapel, Esztergom

tury **golden cross** on which the Hungarian kings took the oath; a 16th-century relief work called the **Suki Chalice**; the 15th-century **Széchy Chalice** (both are the work of Hungarian goldsmiths); **horn goblets** from the 15th century; and the 15th-century so-called **Matthias Calvary**. The Gothic upper section of the Calvary was made by a Parisian craftsman, and in 1424 it was presented as a gift by the French Queen Isabelle to the Hungarian royal court. The lower part was commissioned by King Matthias from a Lombard goldsmith. It is adorned with three sphinxes holding Matthias's coat of arms in their claws. Three enamel paintings also adorn the 72 cm high golden calvary, which is set with pearls and precious stones.

A stairway at the entrance to the church leads down to the **crypt**. Stone remains have been placed here of the former St. Adalbert Church, which once stood where the present-day Cathedral is situated.

On either side of **Szent István tér** are the neo-Classical **Archiepiscopal Seminary (No. 21)** and the romantic prebendal houses **(Nos. 4–12)**.

The formerly Franciscan **Watertown** (Víziváros) **Parish Church (Hősök tere)** was built at the beginning of the 18th century, its tower was built in the 1780s. The church is one of the Baroque churches in Hungary which show a marked Italian influence.

The **Christian Museum** (Keresztény Múzeum) is housed in the new Primatial Palace **(Berényi Zsigmond u. 2)**. The collection was established by the two 19th-century prelates, Archbishop János Simor and Bishop Arnold Ipolyi. The main attraction of the museum is the large number of early plaques and the number, unusually large for any museum outside Italy, of Trecento and early Quattrocento paintings.

The works on exhibit in the picture gallery are as follows:

Hungarian panel paintings from the Middle Ages: The Bát altarpiece from 1420 (the legend concerning the conversion of the Alexandrian princess St. Catherine); the valuable winged altar of Tamás of Kolozsvár from 1427.

Late Gothic Hungarian painting: works of the Master of Aranyosmarót I (*c.* 1450), the Master of Aranyosmarót II (*c.* 1460), the Master of Jánosrét (*c.* 1465), the Master of Jakabfalu (*c.* 1480), the Master of Csegöld (1494), and others. The Calvary series from 1506 by Master M.S. of Selmecbánya, are among the outstanding works of Hungarian panel painting. His art represents the peak of the late Gothic period, but the expression of feeling in his representations of nature and man already shows the influence of the early Renaissance.

15th and 16th-century Austrian and German painting is also represented.

The earliest piece in the **Italian Collection,** the Florentine Calvary, was painted in 1270 by an unknown artist. The walls are lined with paintings done by the famous Italian masters of the Trecento and Quattrocento: Giovanni di Bartolommeo Cristiani (*c.* 1370); Vecchietta of Siena (also known as Lorenzo di Pietro, *c.* 1340); Mariotto di Nardo of Florence (*c.* 1390); Taddeo Gaddi (*c.* 1300–1366?); one of Duccio's (*c.* 1255–1319) workshop companions, Giovanni di Paolo of Siena (*c.* 1450); Neroccio di Bartolommeo Landi (1435–1495); Andrea di Bartolo of Siena (*c.* 1410); Pietro Giovanni d'Ambrogio (*c. 1409–1449);* Giovanni Boccati of Umbria (*c.* 1420–1480); Niccolo da Foligno of Umbria (*c.* 1430–1502); Stefano di Verona (*c.* 1374–1451); Marco Palmezzano of Romagna (*c.* 1459–1539); Francesco Pesellino of Florence (*c.* 1422–1457); the Florentine master Marradi (*c.* 1490); Giampietrino of Milan (*c.* 1530); Francesco da Santacroce (*c.* 1550).

The Flemish Collection includes works by Hans Memling (*c.* 1433–1499); a Bruges painter (*c.* 1510), Jan Wellens de Cock (1480–1527), a Brussels painter (from the 1520s), a painter from the Lower Rhine considered to be a pupil of Derick Baegert (*c.* 1500), and Jan van Hemessen (1500–1575).

The finest representatives of German Baroque painting are two masterpieces by J. I. Cymbal and F. A. Maulbertsch.

Among the **Hungarian paintings of the 17th and 18th centuries,** the 17th-century portrait of the poet Bálint Balassi and three paintings depicting scenes from *Kuruc* life (*c.* 1710–1720) are especially worthy of attention. (The *Kuruc* were the soldiers in the insurrectionist armies of Thököly and Rákóczi fighting against Habsburg oppression.)

The most beautiful late Gothic work represented in the **Medieval Hungarian Wood Sculpture Collection** is the **Coffin of Our Lord** which served as the symbolic coffin of Christ in the liturgies of Holy Week. An unknown artist modelled the realistic human figures which emotionally express the drama of Holy Week from actors who took part in contemporary passion plays.

French and Flemish tapestries, handwoven folk-pieces, porcelain and medieval and Baroque wood sculptures complete the fine arts exhibit.

The following can also be seen in Esztergom: the neo-Classical old **Primatial Palace, Berényi Zsigmond utca 1.**; a former Franciscan monastery built in the middle of the 18th century, the present-day **Theological College, Bajcsy-Zsilinszky út 44,** the **Balassi Bálint Museum, Bajcsy-Zsilinszky út 63,** exhibiting monuments connected with the history of the town; the **Cathedral Library, Bajcsy-Zsilinszky út 28,** the historic building of the **Fürdő Hotel, Bajcsy-Zsilinszky út 14.** There is an outdoor thermal bath, between the Fürdő Hotel and the Small Danube. Its water was used by the Romans, and in the 12th century the first public baths in the country were opened here under the management of the Johannite Knights. Located on nearby József Attila tér is the **Volán Szálló,** the town's only other hotel.

The **monument of the Polish King Jan Sobieski** in the middle of the park situated on the bank of the Danube honours the memory of the heroes who fought in the 1683 battle which liberated Esztergom from Turkish rule. (Two thousand Polish soldiers gave their lives for the city.)

The **historic houses in Széchenyi tér** are as follows: **No. 3** built in the Romantic style (1862), **No. 7** in the Baroque style (1768), **No. 15** in the Baroque style (18th century), **No. 19** in the neo-Classical style (1802), **No. 21** in the Romantic style (1860), **No. 24** in the style of Louis XVI (1780), **No. 25** in the style of Louis XVI (1780).

The largest building in the square is that of the **City Hall,** built in the 17th and reconstructed in the 18th century. Rococo elements adorn the windows on the various floors of the Baroque palace. At one time the sword of the city hung on a hook protruding from the balcony of the City Hall, reminding by its symbolism those passing by of the city council's power over life and death. (The leaders of the city had the power of sentencing criminals who had committed a capital offence to death by beheading.) At the end of the 17th century the palace was occupied by Ferenc Rákóczi II's famous general Vak Bottyán ("Bottyán the Blind").

The **old houses in Bottyán János utca** are as follows: the Baroque palace **No. 3,** the former Benedictine monastery **No. 8,** and the Baroque Church of St. Anne **No. 10** adjoined by a former Franciscan monastery, now a secondary school.

Another name for the **Church of St. Anne** on Hősök tere is the "Round" Church. This small masterpiece of neo-Classical architecture (1828–1835, János Packh), originally built as the model of Esztergom's large Basilica, was conceived along the lines of the Roman Pantheon.

On the eastern side of the town on the hill called **Elő-hegy,** stands the **home of Mihály Babits** (1883–1941), one of the most important Hungarian poets, critics and essayists of the 20th century. The house has been converted into a museum.

EXCURSIONS

At **Vaskapu-hegy** adjoining the city, there is a tourist hostel.
DOBOGÓKŐ (38 km on Rd. 11) is a 700 m high resort area with a tourist hostel and the Nimród Hotel, which offers every comfort (with a restaurant and a bar). Light and pleasant walks can be taken on well cared-for forest paths. (In the winter the terrain is suitable for skiing.) The entire Danube Bend can be viewed from the **lookout tower**: the Börzsöny Mountains to the north, in clear weather the Slovak mountains, and under favourable conditions, the High Tátra situated 180 km away. The bronze relief on the natural stone pyramid (on top of Dobogókő) commemorates a 19th-century pioneer of Hungarian mountain tourism, Ödön Téry.
PILISSZENTKERESZT is situated beneath the 757 m high **Pilis-tető**. It is noted for the Kovács Stream Canyon, a narrow, steep village valley at the beginning of which there is a **lime-kiln** operating with ancient techniques. In the Middle Ages a monastery and church of French origin belonging first to the Cistercian order and later to the Paulite order were located near by. A small part of the stone remains unearthed here have been placed beside the **Baroque church** of Pilisszentkereszt. The Pilis forests were the favourite hunting grounds of the medieval kings, who had hunting lodges built there in the Romanesque style. These centres of jollification, however, later became places for asceticism, for the kings gradually handed them over to the monks. (The only monastic order founded in Hungary, the Paulites, had several monasteries in the Pilis Hills.)

THE LEFT BANK OF THE DANUBE

Leaving Budapest by Váci út, the main road leads for about 20 km through an almost continuously built-up area to Vác on Rd. 2, and then on to Szob on Rd. 12.

DUNAKESZI (20 km from Budapest): Its main tourist attraction is the **Alag Riding School**. (One of the most popular rides in Hungary is frequently arranged between Tata in Transdanubia and Alag, across the Gerecse and Visegrád mountains.) **Ruins of a round church** in the Romanesque style (13th century), and then rebuilt in the 15th century in the Gothic style, can be seen at the Alag Mansion.
FÓT (turn-off from Rd. 2 about 5.6 km before Dunakeszi): In the centre is situated the former mansion of Count Károlyi. The boarding-schools and other schools

The church at Fót

built in its park as well as the apprentice workshops today constitute the **Children's Town,** a home for children who are in the care of the state. The neo-Classical mansion was rebuilt by Miklós Ybl in 1847. The **Catholic Parish Church** (Miklós Ybl, 1845–1855) is noted for its style made up of eastern, Arabic, and Moorish ornamental elements. It has four towers and three naves and was completed in 1855. The glass frescoes of the main nave, the pictures in the sanctuary and on the altar, were painted by the Austrian Karl Blaes. The statue of Christ in the crypt was carved from white Carrara marble by the Italian Pietro Tenarari. Organ concerts are occasionally given in the church.

Water-mill in the Botanical Gardens, Vácrátót

GÖD (25 km from Budapest): The Labour Movement Memorial on the outskirts commemorates the fact that the Communists and leftists held underground meetings here during the Horthy regime.

SZŐDLIGET (29 km): a pleasant Danube bathing resort.

SZENTENDRE ISLAND stretches from the northern outskirts of Budapest as far as Visegrád. The island is 31 km long, and has an area of 56 sq.km. It is linked to both banks by ferry-boats, and between Tahi and Tótfalu it is connected to the right bank by a bridge. There are four settlements on the island: the **Horány resort area** belongs to **SZIGETMONOSTOR,** and the resort of **Surány** belongs to the settlement **PÓCSMEGYER.** Remains of a Roman watchtower are situated in Horány on the Vác branch of the Danube. The Szentendre branch of the Danube at **KISOROSZI,** which lies at the northern end of the island, is a pleasant bathing area. There are ruins of a Roman watchtower here on the Vác bank of the Danube. The fourth settlement is **TAHITÓTFALU.** There are many willows along the river bank and the island is well wooded.

VÁCRÁTÓT (turn off on Rd. 203 about 10 km before Vác) is worth visiting because of its **Botanical Gardens.** The 28.5 hectare gardens contain the largest herbarium in Hungary, with 23,000 different kinds of flowers, trees, shrubs, and plants. From the second half of the 19th century onwards, the gardens gradually developed into today's richly-vegetated botanical park. The collection was founded by the landowner Count Sándor Vigyázó, who at the end of his life bequeathed the collection to the Hungarian Academy of Sciences. The capriciously-formed lake, the streams, the artificial ruins, the small waterfalls and the shady forest paths have made the botanical gardens a popular place for visitors in search of rest and recreation. The collection has moreover been further developed by the Academy of Sciences. Vácrátót today maintains relations with 500 botanical gardens abroad.

Some exotic specimens of the gardens well worth seeing are "Cleopatra's needle" from the deserts of Turkestan, a type of pigweed that grows as tall as a man, elephant grass from the Sudan, and a series of tropical palms in the glasshouse. The small mansion standing in the gardens is today a research laboratory. Visitors to the park will find their way about by referring to the map at the entrance.

Vác

34 km from Budapest by bus on Rd. 2, by rail, or 32 km by boat.

Vác's predecessor is mentioned by Ptolemy when he refers to the Jazygian town known as Uvcenum. The town is believed to have developed from a crossing place established on an important route leading across Szentendre Island.

King Stephen I established an episcopal see here, and the Cathedral of Vác, built in the Romanesque style and surrounded by a castle-like fortification, was already standing by the first half of the 11th century. Following the Mongol invasion of 1241, King Béla IV had the castle rebuilt, the town strengthened, and in the 14th century the coin known as the "silver mark of Vác" was already serving as the national currency. The Cathedral of the Inner Castle was rebuilt at this time in the Gothic style.

At the end of the 15th century the humanist Bishop Miklós Báthori enriched the town with Renaissance buildings. Vác fell into Ottoman hands in 1544 and was liberated only in 1686. The medieval town was completely destroyed under Turkish rule. After the Turks had been driven back, the building activities of the 18th-century bishops, the Althan brothers, Károly Esterházy, and Kristóf Migazzi, developed Vác into a small but pleasant Baroque town and it has remained so, even though Vác was the first town linked by railway with the capital.

Konstantin tér was at one time the ecclesiastical centre of the city. In the middle of the quadrangular square rises the **Cathedral** built between 1763 and 1777. Work was started on the Cathedral by the architects Franz Anton Pilgram and Johann Housmann and later Bishop Migazzi and Isidore Canevale from France were commissioned to finish the construction. Considered a model of Hungarian neo-Classicism, the façade of the church is adorned with gigantic Corinthian columns. The six statues standing on the parapet are the work of Josef Bechert, and the frescoes on the dome, which rises where the nave and transepts meet, and those on the main altar were painted by Franz Anton Maulbertsch. Bishop Migazzi, who had in general shown good taste in his plans for the Cathedral, had the fresco on the main altar walled up because it was not to his liking. This fresco, entitled "The Meeting of Mary and Elizabeth", was revealed only later in the course of restoration work. The sanctuary rail is from the former Renaissance cathedral of Bishop Miklós Báthori—since destroyed. The cross of Bishop Migazzi as well as a chasuble from the Maria Theresa period are on display in the treasury of the church. Stone fragments from the cathedral that had previously stood here have been placed in the crypts.

Construction on the corner building of the square **(No. 4)** was started in 1725 with the purpose of creating a **Piarist Monastery** (together with the previously mentioned Piarist Church adjoining it on Szentháromság tér). The wing facing Konstantin tér was only completed in 1781. In the course of the lengthy construction work, the former monastery and grammar school became a mixture of the Baroque and the style of Louis XVI. The Baroque corner building **No. 1** is a secondary school. The houses at **Nos. 10, 11, 13,** and **15** in the square were built in the 1780s.

The entrance to the palace opposite the façade of the Cathedral, which is surrounded by a park, opens from the small **Vak Bottyán tér**. This late Baroque building was completed in 1775 and is considered to be the work of Joseph Meissl (also known by the name Majzel) of Vienna. (Part of it is today a home for the aged.)

The local historical collection, the **Vak Bottyán Museum,** is located in **Múzeum utca,** which opens from Konstantin tér. The few modest stone fragments housed in the museum preserve the memory of magnificent 12th-century Romanesque and 15th-century Renaissance works of

Vác

masonry found in Vác. The main collections comprise 17th- and 18th-century weapons, historical monuments of the Vác guilds, and documents relating to the 1848–1849 Hungarian War of Independence. An 18th-century Baroque **Franciscan Church** is situated at the end of the street in **Géza király tér (No. 18)**. The wood carving on the pulpit of the church is worthy of attention: it is an allegorical portrayal of the Virtues. A modern school stands in the square, where stone remains of the medieval castle can be seen on the grounds.

The small **Szentháromság** (Trinity) **tér** is only a few minutes' walk from Konstantin tér along **Köztársaság út**. A Baroque **statue of the Trinity** (18th century) as well as a former **Piarist church** (first half of the 18th century) are situated here. The ornamentation of the inside of the church includes a Venetian monstrance provided with a mirror.

The most beautiful building in **Március 15. tér** (further ahead on Köztársaság út; those arriving by train can begin their sightseeing tour of the town here) is the **Baroque City Hall,** completed in 1764. A graceful, wrought-iron balcony extends over the gate. The statue of Justice stands on the gable of the roof, the female figures hold the Hungarian and

Bridge over the Gombás Stream, Vác

Migazzi coats of arms. The old coat of arms of the town can be seen on the semicircular arch of the gable. But one is struck primarily not by the ornaments, but rather by the Baroque symmetry of the two-storied palace. The windows of the neighbouring Baroque building **(No. 7–9),** a former monastery belonging to the Order of Mercy, are lattices made in the style of Louis XVI. On the other side of the square **(No. 6)** stands the oldest building in the town, an originally Gothic building which, however, lost its medieval character during 18th-century reconstruction. The Church relinquished the building for the purpose of establishing an **Institute for the Deaf and Dumb,** and this it has remained. Next door there stands the former palace of the grand provost **(No. 4)** built in the style of Louis XVI.

The 18th-century **Rococo Church of the Upper City,** formerly a Dominican church, stands on the north side of the square. The house, reconstructed in the neo-Classical style, at **No. 23** and the Baroque house at **No. 27** opposite the side of the church are both worthy of attention.

A somewhat hidden passage going downhill from the small park in the middle of the square leads to a medieval barrel-vaulted cellar, where wine tasting takes place to the accompaniment of gypsy music.

The **Triumphal Arch** standing in **Köztársaság út** and designed by Canevale was erected by Bishop Migazzi in honour of a reception given in 1764 in Vác for the empress-queen Maria Theresa. (Migazzi was also the Archbishop of Vienna, and as such wanted to please the Queen with a reception excelling the dimensions of the small town in every respect. The prelate even thought of setting up theatrical scenery in front of the dismal houses to dazzle the Queen.)

The **statues on the stone bridge over Gombás Stream** which flows into the Danube, and is situated on the road leading to the town from the south are all historic monuments (1753–1757). South of the bridge stands the **Monument of the Unknown Hungarian Soldier** in memory of the Hungarian heroes of the battle fought at Vác during the 1848–1849 War of Independence. The chapel called the **Chapel of the Seven** built at the beginning of the 18th century closes off the Seven Stations of the Calvary parallel to the main road (before Gombás Stream). The hall of the Cultural Centre located nearby on Lenin út is decorated by a relief by Margit Kovács.

To the right of the memorial there is a grove and a lake for fishing, and a path has been made on the bank of the Danube. The first section of the path is called **József Attila sétány,** at the end of which is a bandstand; then comes **Ady Endre sétány,** which is ornamented by a statue called the "Girl with a Jug" by Sándor Mikus, and finally we reach **Liszt Ferenc sétány,** at the beginning of which there is a ferry crossing to the Pokol csárda on Szentendre Island. The so-called **Pointed Tower,** with windows in the Romanesque style, and remains of medieval town walls are situated at **Liszt Ferenc sétány 12.** The building of the State Penitentiary situated on the river bank was originally intended to serve as an academy for educating young nobles. The Theresianum, however, soon became a barracks and then, at the middle of the 19th century, a penitentiary.

To the north of Vác, Road 12 takes us further along the eastern, outer edge of the Danube Bend.

VERŐCEMAROS (10.5 km from Vác) unites the settlements of Verőce and Kismaros, and its history is interwoven with that of Vác. The Baroque **church** of the settlement of **VERŐCE** as well as the neo-Classical **summer mansion** standing near the Kismaros highway, which serves as a home for old people, were both built by the Bishop of Vác, Kristóf Migazzi, in the 18th century. Today the resort is well known for the **young people's camping site** established at the confluence of the **Morgó** and **Nagyvölgyi streams,** a favourite meeting-place in the summer for the youth of neighbouring countries. Young people setting out from Verőce can easily explore the whole of the Danube Bend. The memorial museum of **Géza Gorka,** an important 20th-century Hungarian ceramist, is located in the settlement of Verőce **(Szamos u. 22). KISMAROS** is one of the most popular starting points for tourists travelling into the Börzsöny mountains. From here a narrow-gauge forest railway leads through the **Valley of the Morgó** to **Királyrét** (Royal Meadows, 10 km from Kismaros), a 350 to 550 m high basin surrounded by mountains. Its name preserves the memories of the medieval centuries when kings came here to hunt and when the beautiful wife of King Matthias, Beatrice of Aragon, bathed in the lake situated near the castle hill.

NAGYMAROS (18 km from Vác): If it were not for documents testifying to the contrary, one could hardly believe that aristocratic palaces once lined its streets. At the time when Visegrád on the opposite bank was the royal seat, Nagymaros developed into a town. It was later destroyed during the Turkish occupation. Today the area is famous for its raspberry crops. Nagymaros is one of the stops of the yearly **International Danube Expedition.** The Gothic **Catholic Church** of Nagymaros was built in the 14th century, the late Gothic framework in the gate is from 1504. The church was rebuilt in the 18th century. The furnishings in the interior are also from this period.

At **ZEBEGÉNY** (8 km from Nagymaros) the Danube turns for the first time towards the south, and the mighty river begins forcing its way through the Visegrád and Börzsöny Mountains. Constrained by the mountains, however, it soon turns to the northeast again. Further on, the Danube river bed virtually disappears when viewed from Zebegény.

The picturesque landscape attracted the great Hungarian painter, **István Szőnyi** (1894–1960), who spent his entire life here. His home is now a **memorial museum,** while the gardens are the scene every summer of a **free school for the fine arts,** attended by foreign artists and art pupils. (A youth camp is situated in the gardens.) The **Catholic Parish Church** was built at the beginning of the 20th century and is a masterpiece of Hungarian *art nouveau.* (It was designed by Károly Kós.)

At **SZOB** (64 km from Budapest) is the railway frontier-post with Czechoslovakia (there is no crossing here for motorists). The late Baroque **Catholic Parish Church** dates from the 18th century, and the building of the **Határ Restaurant** dates from the same period. The **Börzsöny Museum (Hámán Kató u. 14)** exhibits the archeological findings, plant and animal life, the national costumes and folk art of the area, as well as furniture of a room from an old peasant dwelling.

The Miners' Church, Nagybörzsöny
The Danube Bend at Zebegény

Girls from Nógrád

The westernmost mountains belonging to the north-central mountain range consist of the volcanically formed **Börzsöny Mountains.**
NAGYBÖRZSÖNY (20 km north of Szob), where two important church monuments are open to the public, lies on the western edge of the mountain range. Iron, copper and gold were mined in these parts during the Middle Ages, and in the middle of the 14th century mining developed to such an extent here that the king had Nagybörzsöny raised to the rank of a town. The mines, however, were exhausted in a few centuries, part of the population left the area, and the mining town degenerated into a mere village. The **Church of St. Stephen** was built in the first half of the 13th century of trachyte. It is one of the few Romanesque Hungarian village churches that have remained intact. It is solid and almost like a fortress. It has one tower, and the nave has a wooden ceiling. The semicircular sanctuary is adorned on the outside with bearded human heads and is encircled by an arcaded stone parapet. The stone fence surrounding the church dates from the 17th century. The **Miners' Church** (Bányásztemplom) is a Gothic building (15th century) with a gabled façade and buttresses, but no tower. The statue of a lion on the southeast buttress of the vaulted nave is of the same period; the pictures of miners are from the 18th century.
NÓGRÁD (north of Vác on Rd. 2 which then branches off to the west, 20 km): A castle already stood at the eastern edge of the Börzsöny Mountains before the Conquest of Hungary. In the 11th century this fortress became the county capital and as the centuries went by, it was modernized many times. The last occupants of the fortress were the Turks in 1685, at which time a thunderbolt struck the tower, and exploded the gunpowder stored there. The Turks, having no more ammunition, had to surrender the fortress. Today a road leads from the village to the fortress ruins.
DIÓSJENŐ (4 km from Nógrád): Pleasant excursion area with outdoor swimming-pool facilities, fish pond and camp site.
BÁNK (on Rd. 2 from Vác, branching off to the east, 30 km) is famous for the national costumes still worn on holidays by the Slovak population. The house at **Petőfi utca 94** has been converted into a Slovak folk museum. There is a pleasant beach for swimming as well as camping facilities on Bánk Lake.
The interior regions of the **Börzsöny Mountains** can be reached from many directions. The last station on the already-mentioned Kismaros–Királyrét narrow-gauge railway is situated at the foot of **Nagy-Hideg Mountain** (5 km from Királyrét). There is a tourist hostel on the edge of the 865 m high mountain, near the peak. Skiing is a popular sport here in the winter. Apart from the Mátra, snow remains here longer than anywhere else in the country. Another tourist hostel can be found south of Nagy-Hideg Mountain on the 737 m high **Magas-Tax.** The highest mountain of the Börzsöny Mountains is the 939 m high **Mount Csóványos** (on the peak is a shelter). Climbing the peak is, however, recommended only to experienced climbers.

Transdanubia

Connected to Budapest by highways M1—(E75, E60), M7—7(E71), Rd. 6, as well as by Rds. 10 and 70, and Rd. 8 which runs from Székesfehérvár to the western border.

This part of Hungary, which stretches to the west of Budapest, is flanked on the north by the Danube and the Czechoslovak border (along the left bank of the river), on the south by the Dráva and the Yugoslav border, and on the west by the foothills of the Alps and the Austrian border. Mountain ranges, hilly regions, plains, rivers, streams, lakes, ancient and modern settlements alternate throughout Transdanubia. There are historic monuments dating from the Roman age and later periods as well as monuments of Hungarian folk architecture.

The Transdanubian Mountain Range comprises the region's main mountainous area. It is made up of mountains Bakony, Vértes, and Gerecse, as well as the Buda, Pilis, and Visegrád mountains lying on the west bank of the Danube. Mountains of interesting shape, of volcanic origin and covered by a layer of basalt rise on the western boundaries of the central range: the Badacsony, Szent György-hegy and Somló mountains situated on the shores of the Balaton. The foothills of the Alps, the Sopron and Kőszeg mountains, lie on the edge of the western border, while the Mecsek and Villány mountain ranges, rising in isolation from the hilly and plain country in the southeast, provide the area with variety. Throughout the various historical periods, the elevations and hills provided a natural means for building castles and villages. Later on the mineral wealth hidden deep in the mountains as well as in the surrounding areas stimulated the development of industry.

The southern part of Transdanubia is flatter than the northern part. Here the fertile low hill regions of Zala, Somogy, Tolna and Baranya are situated. The more extensive plains are as follows: **Kisalföld** (the "Little Plain") in the northwest, the **Mezőföld, Sárköz,** and **Drávamente** in the east and south.

The Balaton (see p. 155) as well as two other larger lakes, Lake Velence and the Hungarian section of Lake Fertő, also lie in Transdanubia. Its rivers and streams besides the Danube and the Dráva are: the Rába, Rábca, Sió, Kapos, Zala, and other small rivers and brooks.

Many of the towns developed in areas once occupied by the military and civil centres of the Roman province of Pannonia: Sopianae–Pécs, Savaria–Szombathely, Scarbantia–Sopron, Arrabona–Győr, Ad-flexum–Mosonmagyaróvár, Intercisa–Dunaújváros and Alisca–Szekszárd. A number of towns developed as early as the Middle Ages into centres of royal land, because they were strategically and commercially important.

Since Transdanubia is relatively rich in sources of energy (coal, oil, natural gas) and mineral wealth (bauxite, manganese, basalt and uranium), it is economically the most developed and most industrialized area of Hungary (apart from Budapest). The industry of the area is predominantly concentrated on aluminium production and aluminium metallurgy, and contains about half the oil-refining capacity of the country. The chemical industry, as well as the food and other light industries, are also important. Industrialization has speeded up the development of several older towns such as Győr, Szombathely, Veszprém, Kaposvár, Zalaegerszeg, Nagykanizsa and Pécs, and has given life to newer towns (Tatabánya, Oroszlány, Várpalota, Ajka, Dunaújváros and Komló).

The characteristic, traditional branches of agriculture in the area are viticulture and viniculture (the Balaton region, Somló, Sopron, Mór, Szekszárd, and Villány). Horse-breeding (Kisbér, Bábolna, Porva, Kerteskő, Rádiháza) and wine-production also have a wide tourist appeal, just like the game preserves of the hunting forests.

The climate of the region is fairly stable with the average temperature in July ranging from 20°–22° C, and in January, —1° C. (The Balaton has a special microclimate, see p. 155) Motorists should be aware that the prevailing wind direction is north-westerly and that there are frequent snowstorms and blizzards in the winter.

The regions of Transdanubia have no sharply defined boundaries and all divisions are therefore arbitrary, but touristic, geographical and administrative factors have been taken into consideration.

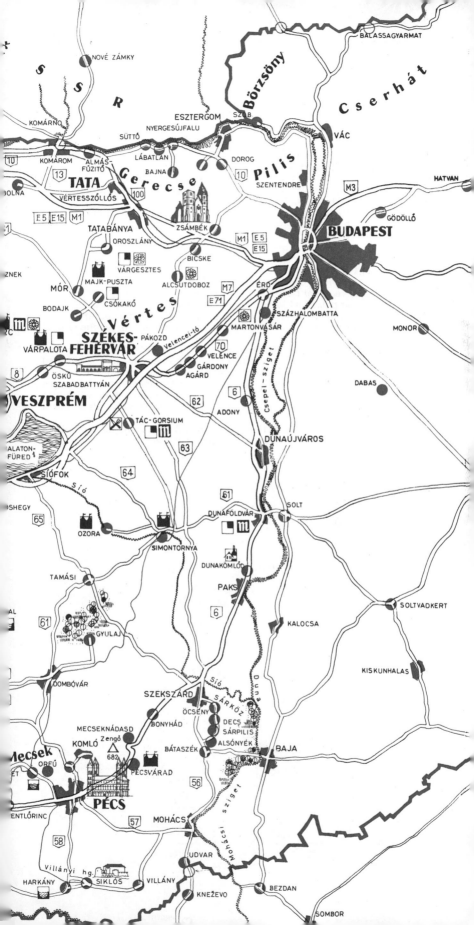

NORTHERN TRANSDANUBIA

Rd. M1—1 (E75, E60) from Budapest, or Rd. 10. By rail: the Budapest
—Hegyeshalom—Vienna main line

The tracts of land lying on both sides of the route mentioned above classified Transdanubia as follows: the Gerecse mountains, a part of the Vértes mountains, and the larger half of the Little Plain (Kisalföld); from an administrative point of view, Komárom County (capital Tatabánya) and Győr-Sopron County (capital Győr), with the exception of Sopron and vicinity.

Komárom county is small but economically important. Its coal-mining provides about one-third of the country's brown coal production. Numerous powerplants as well as a multitude of industrial plants also operate here. The Vértes and Gerecse mountains offer good opportunities for motoring and other excursions. Tata is its tourist centre, though several other settlements also offer cultural institutions of interest for tourists.

In the district around Győr, the abundance of river waters create a particularly alluring scene of regional beauty. This area is rich in historical monuments, almost whole complexes of which greet the visitor, for example, in Győr, Pannonhalma, and Mosonmagyaróvár. In addition, Győr is the country's third largest industrial city after Budapest and Miskolc, as well as the second largest centre of the textile industry.

ZSÁMBÉK (33 km from Budapest on the M1, then north): One of the most important architectural monuments of medieval Hungarian architecture is situated here, the remains of a Romanesque, 13th-century **church** provided with three naves and towers. In 1763 the church was seriously damaged by an earthquake and has not been rebuilt. Adjoining the church there is a **monastery** which was enlarged in the 15th century and houses a museum of stonework finds in one of its halls.

BICSKE (10 km southwest, near M1) A 15th-century **Calvinist church** later rebuilt in the Baroque style, and a 19th-century **observatory tower**.

Ruins of a late Romanesque church,
Zsámbék

Tatabánya

On M1, 56 km from Budapest; 67 km by rail.

The coal fields surrounding it have made Tatabánya an important settlement. At the beginning of the century, the small mining settlement, uniting with three neighbouring communities–Alsógalla, Felsőgalla and Bánhida–developed into a considerable town and has served as the capital of Komárom county since 1950. (Brown coal mining; cement, lime, and aluminium industries.) The new sections of the town, Újváros and Kertváros, have been built since 1945 and have now become the centre of the town.

The Baroque **Catholic church of Alsógalla** was built in the second half of the 18th century. The local **historical museum** is noted for its outstanding collection dealing with the history of industry.

A panoramic road leads from the M1 motorway to the hill where the **Turul statue** stands. (The *turul* is a mythical, eagle-like bird presumably of Asian origin, and the totemic animal of the ancient Magyars.) The huge bronze monument (the full length of the wingspread of the *turul* bird standing on gray natural blocks is 14 m, and the length of the sword of Prince Árpád held in its claws is 12.5 m) was erected in 1896 on the thousandth anniversary of the Magyar Conquest. A beautiful view of Tatabánya can be seen from the monument, as well as of Tata in the distance and the hills of the Vértes mountains situated even further away. It is only a five-minute walk from the historical monument to the **Selim Caves,** where the Turks, according to tradition, massacred hundreds of men from the neighbourhood. The human remains found are actually significant prehistoric archeological finds.

EXCURSIONS

OROSZLÁNY (18 km southwest of Tatabánya) has developed into an industrial town and coal-mining centre since 1945. A steam plant built with a high output capacity operates on the coal produced from the mines.

MAJK-PUSZTA, located a few kilometres from Oroszlány in the heart of the forest, has a unique group of historic buildings. In the 18th century monks from Kamaldul established a settlement here for hermits by making partial use of the remains of a Premonstratensian abbey. The group of buildings consists of a Baroque **mansion** and a **hermitage** (or rather a section of a hermitage) built in the same style, as well as the surviving **tower of a church** demolished at the end of the 18th century.

VÁRGESZTES (16 km from Oroszlány) boasts the ruins of a 14th-century castle. There is also a **tourist hostel** situated on the castle hill.

VÉRTESSZŐLŐS (between Tatabánya and Tata): Finds that caused an international sensation were made in the 1960s, when the **remains of a prehistoric human settlement** thought to be almost half a million years old were discovered In a travertine cave. Apart from that at Heidelberg, this is the oldest such find in Europe. (Footprints made by Early Stone Age man as well as by prehistoric animals can be seen under a protective roof during the summer months. More finds of importance are on exhibit in the National Museum in Budapest.)

Tata

70 km from Budapest on Rds. M1 and 100; 84 km by rail.

Tata and its surroundings, situated between the Vértes and Gerecse mountains, are full of springs, streams, lakes, and canals. As early as the 14th century the area was the scene of knightly tournaments and royal hunting parties. The town reached its golden age in the 15th cen-

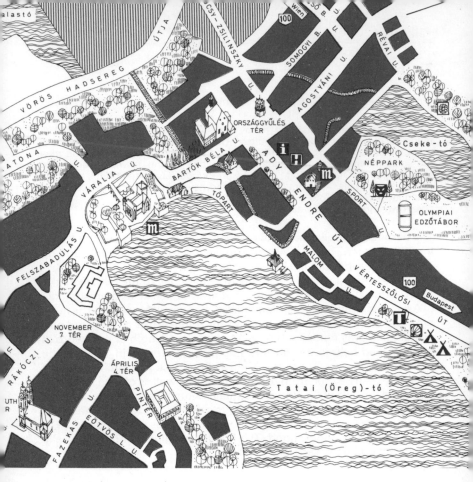

Tata

tury, at which time the castle, one wing of which is still in good condition today, was rebuilt by King Sigismund (later Holy Roman Emperor), and then, in the second half of the 15th century, by King Matthias. In 1510 the Diet convened here. The town played an important role in the Rákóczi War of Independence, and the office of the Chief of Staff of the Hungarian National Army was situated here for some time in 1848—49. The destruction suffered by the town throughout the centuries was replaced by the large-scale construction that took place in the 18th century and which is associated mainly with the name of Jakab Fellner.

A famous faience plant began operating in the town in 1758. Today there are also carpet, shoe and brick factories.

The **Catholic Parish Church,** built by Jakab Fellner and József Grossman between 1751 and 1785, stands in **Kossuth tér.** The former building complex of the Louis XVI style **Esterházy Palace** standing nearby on **November 7. tér** was also built by Fellner. The two-storied main building with its two solid corner towers today houses the town's hospital. Not far from here **(Felszabadulás utca)** the **Museum of Classical Greco-Roman Replicas** has been set up in the former synagogue.

The most important historic building in Tata is the so-called **Old Castle,** standing on the shore of the **Old (Öreg) Lake.** This Gothic fortress with its square ground-plan and four corner towers was seriously damaged during the Turkish wars, and in 1707 the Habsburgs had it burned down because it was used by the *Kuruc* forces in the Rákóczi War of Independence. At the end of the last century its remaining sections were rebuilt in the Romantic style. A **museum** named after **Domonkos Kuny,** a master of faience, has been established in its halls. Besides the archeological and local historical collection, the exhibition of old Tata pottery and ceramic art is also worthy of attention.

A small wooden bridge leads from the Old Castle to the shore of the 230-hectare **Old Lake** rich in fish and fed by warm-water springs. First we reach the **Ornate** (Cifra) **Mill** (Bajcsy-Zsilinszky u. 30), which was built in the 16th century and rebuilt in the Baroque style in 1753. There were many such water-mills in Tata, a large number of which can still be seen today. A good example is Jakab Fellner's **Miklós Mill** (Ady Endre u. 26). Today its completely intact wooden interior houses the **German Minority** (Nemzetiségi) **Museum**. Another fine mill is the **Nepomucenus Mill** (Alkotmány u. 1) which today houses the country's **Modern Gallery**. Among the monuments connected with industry, the thatch-roofed **slaughterhouse** (this, just like the mills, is near the castle) from the Baroque period is worth seeing. A road lined by a row of poplars leads from the lake to **Országgyűlés tér,** in which there stands an octagonal wooden clock tower (1763) with four clock faces.

The city's other lake is **Lake Cseke,** one side of which is occupied by the Amusement Park established in the 18th century and known today as the **People's Park** (Néppark). In 1801 romantic artificial ruins were built on the lake shore. Thirteenth-century capitals from the Benedictine abbey at Vértesszentkereszt as well as some gravestones from the Roman age are built into a structure that imitates the ruins of a three-naved church. **A training camp** for the Hungarian Olympic team has also been established at Lake Cseke. Lake Cseke itself is an angling area. In the vicinity of People's Park the **Kristály Swimming-pool** is open to the general public. It is also worth visiting the former **Capuchin church** built in the Baroque style in 1743–1746 and situated in Bartók Béla út, as well as the former monastery next door. Visit can be made, too, to the former **Piarist monastery** on the shore of the Old Lake, the **Chapel of the Calvary** on Calvary Hill and the 45 m high lookout tower named after Fellner, also situated on Calvary Hill. From these vantage points there is a wide view. The **Fényes Baths** provided with swimming-pools and a sauna is situated north of the town at the Fényes Springs. There is also a first class auto camping-site by the Old Lake.

Rd. 10 leading from Budapest towards Győr stretches over the mountainous terrain between the Buda and Pilis mountains, then over the flat area

Fortified castle, Tata

as far as Dorog, after which it continues along the bank of the Danube. Rd. 100, which runs into the M1 at Tatabánya, branches off at Almás-füzitő.

DOROG (38 km from Budapest) is the third coal-mining centre of the area.
TOKOD (6 km west of Dorog) is known for its **glass factory** and **remains of a Roman castrum**. A small **Roman city** called Crumerum once stood where **Nyergesújfalu** (14 km west of Dorog on Rd. 10) is situated today. Remains of the castrum can still be seen today on Sánc mountain.
LÁBATLAN (5.5 km from Nyergesújfalu on Rd. 10): Cement production here goes back for several centuries. The factory's old furnace is preserved as a historical relic. Today there is a factory for making building units and a modern thin-paper producing factory. The **Calvinist church,** built in the 15th century in the Gothic style but rebuilt as a Baroque church (18th c.) is of interest. Another interesting sight to visit is the 244 m long cave in the **Nagy-Pisznica,** 544 m.
SÜTTŐ (3.5 km from Lábatlan on Rd. 10) is known for its red limestone mining industry.
NESZMÉLY (8 km from Süttő on Rd. 10) is known for its wine production and as a starting point for mountain tours. There are also three interesting caves situated on the side of **Nagy-Somló mountain.** Points of interest are the **Calvinist church** (15th c.), surrounded by a medieval wall, and the **ruins of a castle.** Rd. 100 runs into Rd. 10 at **ALMÁSFÜZITŐ** (aluminium factory and oil refinery).
SZŐNY (6 km from Almásfüzitő): During the old Roman age, Brigetio, one of the most important Pannonian communities, stood where the present-day village now stands. Rich Roman finds were unearthed in Szőny and its vicinity, fragments of frescoes made in the style of Pompeii, a collection of 118 gold medals, stone carvings, and an early Christian cemetery from the 4th century which contains the grave of a bishop. (Kuny Domonkos Museum, Tata, and the National Museum, Budapest.)
KOMÁROM (90 km from Budapest on Rd. 10, 104 km by rail): Until the end of the First World War Komárom and Komárno, a town on the northern bank of the Danube and now belonging to Czechoslovakia, constituted one town. Its strong castle was surrounded by branches of the river and could not be taken either by the Mongols in the 13th century or by the Austrian troops during 1848–1849. In 1920, when the northern part of the town was annexed by Czechoslovakia, the smaller southern part began to develop into an independent town, which has today become important both as a Danube port and as a frontier crossing. (Warm water outdoor pools; thermal hotel and camp site.) The **stonework museum** in the so-called **Igmándi Fortress,** with carvings dating back to the Roman age are worthy of attention.
BÁBOLNA (21 km south of Komárom) is one of the chief centres for horse breeding. The horse ranch founded here in 1779, which is famous throughout Europe, has Arab thoroughbreds, halfbreds, and Lippizaner horses, but considerable racehorse breeding also takes place here. Other branches of production at the Bábolna State Farm are also significant; it was here that the American system of maize production was first introduced in Hungary, and new methods of large-scale poultry breeding are experimented with.

Győr

123 km from Budapest on M1, 142 km by rail.

Győr is situated in the centre of the **Kisalföld** (Little Plain) at the confluence of the Mosoni branch of the Danube (the so-called "Little Danube") and the Rába and Rábca rivers.

According to archeological evidence, the area occupied by the present city of Győr has been inhabited for thousands of years. During the Roman period the city was called Arrabona. In the 11th century it was made an episcopal see and in 1271 the city was given the right to tax goods being passed through its territory. Its medieval castle was not occupied by the Turks until the 1590s, and even then only as a result of treachery. From the 18th century onwards the trading significance of Győr, partly because of its harbour on the Danube, gradually increased, and it soon became the second largest centre of the grain trade in the country after Budapest. Even though later large-scale road and railway constructions lessened the importance of the waterway, in the wake of the industrial development that began in the second half of the 19th century and which reached its height after 1945, Győr became one of the largest industrial centres in the country.

Győr

Szabadság tér can be reached from Road 1 by taking Tanácsköztársaság útja, and Köztársaság tér by taking Lenin út and Kazinczy utca, streets both lined by shops and other commercial premises. At Kazinczy utca 21, the two-storied Baroque Rozália House, built in 1703, was the home of the linguist János Sajnovics, who discovered the Finno-Ugrian origin of the Hungarian language and who was also one of the pioneers of comparative linguistics. The group of buildings in Köztársaság tér came into being in the 17th and 18th centuries, the most important building (No. 15) being the Church of the Carmelites (1721–1725, Martin Witwer). The Baroque façade of this church, with its three statue niches, faces the square; the arms of the order as well as a window are situated above the iron-covered gates. Witwer also planned the interior furnishings of the church. The carved Baroque benches are contemporary, so are the pictures on the altar. Only the ceiling paintings are new. The Baroque Altabak House (No. 12) was commissioned by János Altabak in 1620. The wide arched gate of the house dates from the 17th century; its present form originates from the 18th century. Today, the house at No. 5 is the department of stonework finds of the Xantus János Museum. Monuments from the history of the castle can be seen in the so-called Sforza

Köztársaság tér, Győr

Courtyard, where old casemates of the castle as well as historical monuments from the Roman age are exhibited. The two-storied house at **No. 13** was built between 1778 and 1782 where two medieval houses once stood. The first café in Győr was opened in the second half of the 18th century in the house at **No. 14.**

Káptalan utca leads from Köztársaság tér up to Káptalan-domb. The ancient **Cathedral,** the architecture of which bears the stamp of the styles of many different centuries, was built in the centre of the hill, in **Martinovics tér.** The foundations date from the 11th century, while the building itself was probably completed at the turn of the 13th century. But signs of 13th- and 14th-century construction can be seen on it as well. Around 1404, the Gothic **Héderváry Chapel** was added to it, and between 1635 and 1650, after the damage and fires suffered during the Turkish period, the Cathedral was rebuilt in the Baroque style. In 1823 the main façade was reconstructed in the neo-Classical style. Included among the decoration in the interior are frescoes and altar paintings by F. A. Maulbertsch. The furnishings are mainly Baroque. A silver-gilt reliquary containing a relic from the head of King (St.) Ladislas (1040–1095), an outstanding work of the goldsmith's art from the beginning of the 15th century, is preserved in the Héderváry Chapel. Ecclesiastical objects of great value can be seen in the treasury of the Cathedral, which includes examples of the goldsmith's art, embroidered church vestments, and much else.

The **old keep** on the west side of Chapter Hill was built and reconstructed in the 12th and 14th centuries respectively. The **Bishop's Castle** (Püspökvár) situated around the watchtower is the palace of the Bishop of Győr. There are beautiful Gothic sedilia situated in the corridor under the sturdy tower, and other parts of the palace, later rebuilt in the Baroque style, bear Gothic traces as well. This is true, for example, of the so-called **Dóczy Chapel** (1841) built by Bishop Orbán Dóczy. Several walls and bastions remaining of the **old Castle of Győr** have survived, such as the underground remains of a 13th-century keep. The rest was demolished in the 19th century. A splendid view opens up from the bastions and from the uppermost, 18th-century section of the 14th-century tower.

The house at **Martinovics tér 1–2**, once the mansion of the bishop's steward, now houses a permanent exhibition of the works of Miklós Borsos, one of Hungary's prominent sculptors.

For many centuries **Széchenyi tér** has been the city's main square. The statue of the Virgin Mary standing in the middle of the square was erected in memory of the liberation of Buda (1686). Facing the square is the one-time Jesuit and later **Benedictine church** that was built between 1634 and 1641 on the model of the Il Gesù in Rome, according to the plans of Baccio del Bianco. The present façade of the church dates from 1727. The furnishings, statues, and ceiling frescoes (the latter by Paul Troger) are likewise 18th century, but the secondary altars and the chapel decorations and frescoes date from 1662. The Baroque stucco decorations in the former **Benedictine monastery** next to the church are from 1654. The former Jesuit chemist's shop on the corner of Czuczor Gergely utca is today a **pharmacy museum** and has beautiful interior furnishings.

The three-storied, early Baroque house (1697) standing at **Széchenyi tér 4**, on the corner of Stelczer utca is one of the city's most interesting historical buildings. It is called the **Iron Stump House** because a tree trunk covered with iron plates was placed on the corner of the house and journeying apprentices covered it with nails as a memorial of their stay; for this reason the grocery store opened in the house at the beginning of the 19th century was called "Stock im Eisen".

The Baroque **Abbey House** dating from 1741–1743 and situated at **Széchenyi tér 5,** owes its name to the fact that it served at one time as the city guest-house of the Abbey of Pannonhalma. Today it houses the **museum** named after **János Xantus,** (1825–1894) a scholar who did much research on America and Asia. The collections housed in the museum present the history of Győr and its surroundings as well as archeological and ethnographical relics from the Kisalföld.

In almost every street of the Inner City there are monuments that catch the eye. For example, almost all the houses in **Liszt Ferenc utca** are historic monuments. The building at **No. 1,** built in the style of Louis XVI, is originally from the 16th century. (The inscription above the gateway reads as follows: CURIA NOBILITARIS, i. e., the house at one time belonged to nobility.) The building at **Rákóczi Ferenc utca 1** was once the **Town Hall;** the ground floor section was built in 1562, while the present Baroque appearance of the building dates from a later period. At **Alkotmány utca 4** there is a three-storied Baroque **palace,** formerly the Esterházy and later Bezerédj palace, where Napoleon spent a night in 1809 while outside Győr his troops were defeating the last uprising of the Hungarian nobility. The **picture gallery of the Xantus János Museum** is housed on the first floor of the palace.

Late Baroque and neo-Classical houses can be seen in **Kossuth Lajos utca** which runs through Újváros. (On the island at the confluence of the Rába and the Danube is an outdoor swimming-pool, a beach and a thermal bath.)

Rds. 81, 82, 83, 85 and 14 branch out from Rd. 1 at Győr.

EXCURSIONS

PANNONHALMA (21 km southeast of Győr on Rd. 82) is the seat of the chief abbey of the Benedictine Order in Hungary. The monastery, which stands on a 280 m high hill, was founded by Prince Géza in A.D. 996; its construction was finished by his son King Stephen I. The Chapel of St. Martin was built in its initial form in the 11th century; the second church was finished in 1137. The late Romanesque building, which constitutes the foundation of the present church (reconstructed and enlarged several times throughout the centuries) was conse-

Monastery yard, Pannonhalma

crated in 1224. The oldest section of the church is the crypt consisting of three naves, which shows a transition from the Romanesque to the Gothic style. The building complex was restored at the end of the 19th century by Ferenc Storno in Sopron. The 55 m high neo-Classical tower was built by János Packh in the first half of the 19th century. An appreciable section of the monastery adjoining the church is medieval (13th c.), its final form evolved during the Baroque period. A secondary school and dormitory finished in the early 1940s are also parts of the impressive group of buildings, which are divided by a number of courtyards.

The various **collections** at Pannonhalma are of great value. Rare documents and records from the earliest centuries of the Hungarian state are preserved in the **archives of the main abbey**. Among them is the earliest written record of the Hungarian language, the Latin deed of foundation of the Benedictine Abbey at Tihany dating from 1055, in which a considerable number of Hungarian words (about 100 words consisting of place-names and proper names) occur for the first time. The **library** founded by King (St.) Ladislas possessed more than 70 codices from the 11th century. A number of valuable codices and incunabula as well as rich materials from more recent periods are preserved in ornamented cherry-wood book-cases. Consisting of over 300,000 volumes, the library now houses the fifth largest collection of books in the country. The **art gallery** contains valuable, mostly 16th to 18th-century works, among them a few genuine masterpieces (mainly Italian, German, and Dutch paintings). There are also archeological and stone collections, collections of medal signets and woodcuts, as well as a natural science exhibition.

A vast panorama of the hill country can be seen from the top of the 280 m high hill. (A tourist office is situated near the wrought-iron gate; guided tours can be arranged.)

CSORNA (31.5 km southwest of Győr on Rd. 85): Standing next to the **Baroque church** (on Szabadság tér), the late Baroque building of the provost's residence is today a district office and the home of the local historical collection.

KAPUVÁR (17 km west of Csorna) was a fortress from the second half of the 13th century. Its castle was destroyed by the *Kuruc* forces during the Rákóczi War of Independence for fear that it would become an imperial base. A two-storied Baroque **mansion** was built in place of the fortress around 1750. Among others, the **collections of the Rákóczi Museum** have been placed here. Its exhibition of Pál Pátzay's statues can be seen at **Fő tér 1**.

SZIGETKÖZ is 450 sq.km in area. It is surrounded by two branches of the Danube, and the 24 communities that are hidden between small backwaters and tiny islands can be reached by taking the northwest road between Győr and Mosonmagyaróvár.

ÁSVÁNYRÁRÓ (18 km northwest of Győr) is a well-known **fishing centre** provided with a camp for anglers. The **church** was built in 1398, reconstructed in 1658, and enlarged to include three naves in 1820.

HÉDERVÁR (3 km from Ásványráró) has a three-storied **fortified castle,** the corners of which are occupied by sturdy towers. It was constructed from the remains of a medieval fortress in the 17th to 19th centuries. A 15th-century **cemetery chapel** and a Baroque **Catholic church** from 1755 are the other two historic buildings of the community.

LÉBÉNYMIKLÓS (14 km from Győr on Rd. 1 to Öttevény and from there a further 8.5 km to the west) has a former **Benedictine Abbey Church** with two towers and three naves, which is one of the most important historic monuments of Romanesque architecture in Hungary and is well worth seeing. The church was built in 1208, but was seriously damaged and rebuilt many times during the ensuing centuries; it was restored between 1850 and 1879 to its original form and beauty. The semicircular gate on the main façade as well as the typically Romanesque south gate adorned with a statue of an angel are especially striking.

Mosonmagyaróvár

38 km from Győr on Rd. 1, 158 km from Budapest, 177 km by rail.

In the 1st century A.D., a Roman camp called Ad-flexum stood where the community of Mosonmagyaróvár is now situated. After the founding of the Hungarian State, two settlements came into existence here: Moson and Magyaróvár. First Moson and then Magyaróvár became the county capital, and at the foot of the castle of Magyaróvár an urban settlement developed. Beginning in the 14th to 15th centuries, Magyaróvár played an important part in cattle trade with Vienna. Magyaróvár again became economically important when industrialization started in the 19th century. In 1939 Magyaróvár united with Moson and has since then been called Mosonmagyaróvár (aluminium factory and a factory manufacturing knitted goods, agricultural machine works).

Several branches of the Lajta river wind through the inner city and unite with the Moson branch of the Danube. Seventeen bridges of various sizes span the rivers within the town.

A road leads from **November 7. tér** across one of these bridges to the town's most important historic monument, the ancient **castle** standing on Lajta Island. In the barrel-vaulted, tunnel-like entrance to the castle, which was built in the second half of the 13th century (its gate is from the 15th century), one catches sight of four Gothic *sedilia*. The castle received its Renaissance exterior in 1630 following the brief Turkish occupation. A division of the Keszthely University of Agricultural Sciences has been accommodated in the three-storied castle building, which has four corner towers. The system of corridors underneath the castle building is open to the public. (In 1818, the College of Economics was established in Mosonmagyaróvár; between 1822 and 1823 the poet Nikolaus Lenau was a student there.) The town has had a secondary school since 1739, and at the middle of the 16th century one of the country's first printing presses was established here.

Several 18th-century **peasant Baroque houses** as well as a small Baroque **chapel** from 1713 can be found not far from the castle in **Lucsony utca**. The three-storied castle-like Baroque building complex of the former **Salt Depot**, built at the end of the 1600s, stands in **48-as tér**. At **Lenin út 47** stands the Lenau House where the poet lived from 1822 to 1823. In the 17th century a beerhouse and restaurant already operated in the building of the present **Fekete Sas** (Black Eagle) **Hotel** at **No. 55.** On October 23, 1847 Lajos Kossuth spoke to a crowd of people from the balcony of the Baroque, 16th-century Habsburg mansion at **No. 82** which has two courtyards and numerous arcades. (Today it is an elementary school dormitory.) The **Hanság Museum**, situated at **No. 135**, is one of Hungary's oldest museums in the provinces; the collection of the museum was established in 1882. The rich material of the collection showing the peasant life of the area is particularly interesting.

HEGYESHALOM (10 km from Mosonmagyaróvár on Rd. 1): railway and road **border crossing between Hungary and Austria.** Its **Catholic church,** which received its present appearance in 1850, dates from the 15th century.

Rajka (16 km from Mosonmagyaróvár on Rd. 15 [E75]) is a road crossing between Hungary and Czechoslovakia. The 14th-century Gothic **Catholic church** as well as a Baroque **mansion** from the end of the 18th century have interest as historic monuments.

WESTERN TRANSDANUBIA

Western Transdanubia can be reached from Budapest by taking the M1–1 (E75, E60) and turning off onto Rd. 85 after Győr or the M7 as far as Székesfehérvár and from there on Rd. 8. The southern parts of Western Transdanubia can be reached by taking Rds. 71 and 75, or Rd. 7 (E71). These roads, for the most part, run parallel with the Budapest–Győr–Vienna, Budapest–Székesfehérvár–Veszprém–Szombathely, and Budapest–Nagykanizsa–Murakeresztúr railway lines. The traffic routes running from north to south are Rds. 82, 83, 84, 86, 87 and 74.

A large part of the area is subalpine in character, because the foothills of the Alps lie along the Austrian border; in fact, the **Sopron** and **Kőszeg Mountains** have been called the "Hungarian Alps". The slopes of the Sopron Mountains (highest point 558 m) extending down as far as the city of Sopron are holiday resorts. The highest point in Transdanubia, the 883 m high **Írottkő,** is situated in the Kőszeg mountains (close to the frontier). The volcanically-formed **Ság** and **Kis-Somló Mountains** (around 300 m high) rise in the eastern part of the uplands. Wine-production on the slopes of these mountains is traditional, just as it is on 433 m high Somló Hill. The terrain of the Zala Hills is wooded and abounds in quiet chestnut groves.

A considerable amount of Hungarian crude oil is brought to the surface in the Zala Hills. There is, however, little sign of the barrenness usually seen in oilfields and around oil wells and drilling towers, because the surroundings are thick with vegetation.

The 82 sq.km part of Lake Fertő (known in German as the Neusiedler See) belonging to Hungary lies near Sopron.

Sopron, Kőszeg, and **Szombathely** are virtual treasure-houses of valuable historic monuments. The miniature villages of the **Őrség** in the southern part of Western Transdanubia have preserved traditions of folk architecture as well as many characteristics of peasant life up until today. The **Göcsej** area is also ethnographically interesting.

Administratively, the following areas belong to Western Transdanubia: Sopron and its vicinity (part of Győr-Sopron County), Vas County (county town: Szombathely), and Zala County (county town: Zalaegerszeg).

Sopron

210 km from Budapest on Rds. M1 and 85 and 84, 227 km by rail.

Sopron is situated at the foot of the Lövér Mountains and is the only Hungarian city whose old buildings have remained in almost perfect condition (115 historical monuments and 240 buildings of historic interest).

Sopron's past can be traced back to the Celts. Called Scarbantia under the Romans, the city, by virtue of its favourable location, was a natural junction of the intercontinental north-south trade route and the trade route towards the west used by Byzantine merchants. As early as 1277, the set- tlement was raised to the rank of a city. The city escaped the Mongol invasion and the Turks did not reach its immediate vicinity either, so the medieval buildings, for the most part, have remained intact; furthermore, the Baroque buildings have blended in with them harmoniously.

Sopron is rich in cultural tradition. Its first secondary school, a Lutheran lyceum, was established in 1557. Texts accompanying Haydn's works were printed on a printing press set up here in 1722.

Since 1769 the city has had its own permanent theatre (Károly Goldmark's career as a composer began here), eight secondary schools, a teacher's training college for nursery school teachers, and a university of forestry (the latter is located in the middle of a beautiful botanical garden).

The **Liszt Ferenc Museum** is one of the richest museums in Hungary outside Budapest; the **Museum of Mining** is also interesting. During the summer, **Sopron Festival Weeks** (Soproni Ünnepi Hetek) offer a rich and varied programme.

Besides cotton, cloth, and carpet factories, wine production is also important (Soproni Kékfrankos).

Sopron's natural environment is also most attractive. A section of the eastern Alpine foothills, the Lövér mountains, stretch as far as the town's outskirts. A holiday area for walking, swimming and health resorts has been established in the Lövér, together with an outdoor swimming-pool and several sports establishments. The **Castle Tower** and its protective building known as the **Fire Tower** are the symbols of the town. The lower part of the 61 m high structure was built in the Middle Ages in the Romanesque style by making use of the remains of the city gate built during the Roman age. (The first written evidence of the structure dates from 1409.) The middle part, which is characteristically Renaissance, dates

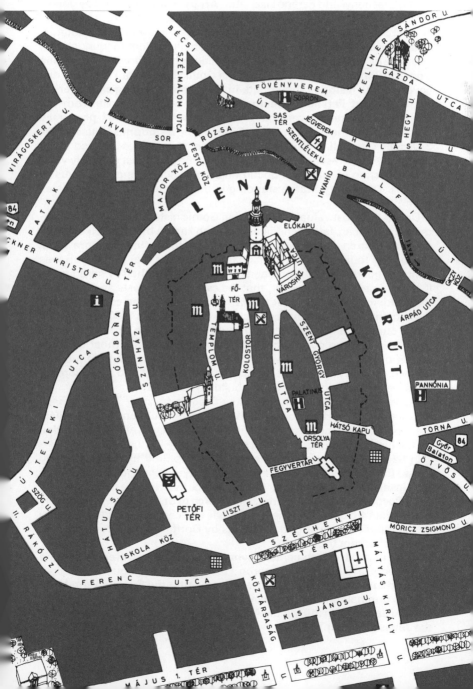

from the 16th century; and the Baroque upper part was built between 1680 and 1682. A splendid view of the city and its surroundings can be seen (and photographed) from the balcony of the tower. The so-called **Gate of Loyalty,** at the base of the tower, was erected to commemorate the event whereby the inhabitants of the city decided by a popular vote, taken in 1921, in favour of belonging to Hungary and not Austria. (Sopron has been given the designation *civitas fidelissima* for the devotion it has shown to Hungary several times throughout its history.)

The road leads through the Gate of Loyalty to **Fő tér,** where most of the houses date from the 15th century. The palace-like late Renaissance corner building at **No. 8,** the **Storno House,** was built in the 1400s. As the memorial plaque on the house testifies, King Matthias stayed here, as did István Széchenyi and Ferenc Liszt later. **Art treasures** collected by generations of the Storno family can be seen here. These include old furniture, stoves, chandeliers, handmade objects, statues, and valuable paintings. The Baroque **Fabricius House** at **No. 6** was built on Roman foundations, and several of its valuable medieval sections have survived. (Remains from the Roman age were found in the Gothic basement.) After the discovery of the historic monuments in 1962, the **archeological** materials from the **Liszt Ferenc Museum** as well as some of those from the **Stonework Museum** were placed here. There is a small **pharmacy museum** in the medieval house at **Fő tér 2.** The **Gambrinus House at No. 3** was the **City Hall** in the 15th century. The city archives situated in the building of the present **City Hall,** also in Fő tér, can boast of a truly valuable collection of medieval documents, royal edicts, and fragments of codices. The **Trinity Statue** standing in the middle of the square dates from 1701.

One of the most valuable Hungarian Gothic historical buildings, a formerly Franciscan, later Benedictine, church known by the popular name of **Goat Church** (Kecske-templom), can be found in **Templom utca.** (According to legend, it owes its name to the fact that the church was built by a goatherd on the proceeds of the gold unearthed by his animals. It is more probable, however, that the carved goat crests appearing on the building formed the coat of arms of the family who commissioned the church.) The three-naved church was built between 1280 and 1300, its tower during the first quarter of the 14th century. The small tabernacle from 1491 and the pulpit from the 15th century are the most valuable pieces of the furnishings, which are for the most part Baroque and Rococo. In the 17th century, five sessions of the Diet and three coronations were held in the early Gothic building.

Heavy bombing in 1945 in the tiny **Orsolya tér** near Templom utca uncovered the remains of an 18th-century **house standing on pillars** (Lábas-ház). The house has since been reconstructed, and an **exhibition on the history of guilds** has been set up inside.

In **Szent György utca** one's attention is captured by the **Eggenberg House (No. 12)** because of its beautiful courtyard and loggias. Also situated in this street is the former **Erdődy Palace (No. 16),** the most beautiful early Rococo building in Sopron. The **Church of St. George** was originally built in the 14th century in the Gothic style as a chapel. In the 17th century it was rebuilt and enlarged. Paintings by Dorffmeister, Altomonte and others ornament the church.

At **Új utca 11** a 14th-century **synagogue** was uncovered. When the Jews were expelled from Sopron (1526), the synagogue was reconstructed into a private residence, and only after the Second World War was its original function rediscovered. (The **New Synagogue** at **Új utca 22,** also dating from the Middle Ages, houses a collection connected with the Jewish religion.)

Kolostor utca, Sopron

In **Hátsó kapu** (Rear Gate) **utca,** a short street leading from the medieval heart of the town (the "horseshoe" of the inner city) to Lenin körút, is situated the **Caesar House (No. 2),** the window-frames of which bear witness to the building's ancient past. The courtyard with its bastions as well as the wine cellar are also interesting. **Várkerület** is Sopron's busiest thoroughfare. Since the 1700s, the "Golden Eagle" (Arany Sas) Pharmacy has been operating in the Baroque **Pharmacy House** at **No. 29.** The house at **No. 55** was the building of the former **White Horse Inn,** in which the great composer Joseph Haydn stayed. A complete row of medieval, Baroque and Rococo style historic buildings have survived intact in the northern part of Várkerület.

Ikva-híd utca with its arches crosses over the Ikva Stream, and leads from Várkerület to the northern part of the city, intersecting **Balfi utca** in which there are numerous buildings of historic interest. One of the most outstanding of these—mainly because of its collection of weapon, porcelain, faience, and paintings—is the house at **No. 11** with the private **Zettl-Langer collection.** Left of Ikva-híd utca begins **Szentlélek utca,** the most important historic building of which is the **Church of the Holy Ghost** (Szentlélek-templom) built at the end of the 14th century and rebuilt in 1782. The Gothic tower of the church dates from the beginning of the 15th century, and the interior is decorated with frescoes by István Dorffmeister (1725–1797). The oldest parts of the Gothic **Church of St. Michael**

Michael (Szent Mihály-templom) in **Pozsonyi utca** originate from the 13th century, a large part of it having been built in the 14th century. The construction of the church, however, was finished only in the first half of the 16th century. Although the interior furnishings are for the most part Baroque, the building as a whole still emanates a genuine medieval atmosphere. Among the Gothic relics of the church, there is a wooden statue of the Madonna from 1460 and a sacristy built in 1482. In the cemetery behind the church stands the oldest architectural monument of Sopron, the **St. James Chapel,** erected in a style midway between Romanesque and Gothic. The chapel was renovated in 1960. The **House of the Two Moors** at **Pozsonyi utca 9,** which received its name from the fact that a Moorish stone figure stands on each of the two spiral columns of the gate, is one of the outstanding monuments of the peasant Baroque architecture.

Ruins of an amphitheatre dating back to the Roman age were found on Vienna Hill, which closes off this part of the city from the north. It is worthwhile climbing the hill not only to visit the ruins, but also to enjoy the beautiful view.

The eclectic building of the **Liszt Ferenc Museum** stands in **Deák tér,** in the middle of a beautiful park. There are rich collections of local historical, archeological and ethnographic interest, as well as of fine arts and handicrafts in the halls and the circular gallery of the museum.

Other items of interest to be seen in Sopron: the Gothic **Church of St. John,** Bécsi utca; the Baroque **Zichy Palace,** which faces **Kolostor utca:** the Baroque **former Dominican church** (Széchenyi tér); and the neo-Classical building of the **former County Hall** (Fő tér).

Finally we must mention the town's recreation area. It is worth going up to the look-out tower on **Károly Heights,** from which Lake Fertő as well as the Alpine foothills can be seen.

EXCURSIONS

SOPRONBÁNFALVA (on the outskirts of Sopron, about 8 km from the heart of the town): The originally Romanesque nave of the **Church of Mary Magdalene** dates from the 12th century. The Gothic tower is from the first half of the 14th century, and the choir dates back to 1427. Eighty-one steps lead up to the church on the hill. Its monastery dates from the 15th century.

FERTŐRÁKOS (9 km from the centre of Sopron): In the **stone quarry** dating back to Roman times, but no longer in operation after many centuries of stone mining, halls resembling large Egyptian temples cut in rock have formed. A cave theatre has been created which—during the Sopron Festival Weeks—is the scene, every summer, of concerts and theatrical performances. The former Rococo **Bishop's Palace,** built in the middle of the 18th century, the medieval–Baroque **Parish Church** and its tower, and a pillory from the 17th century are also historical monuments.

BALF (9 km from Fertőrákos): The first bathing facilities were built hundreds of years ago over sulphuric thermal springs discovered by the Romans. Today it functions as a spa and its medicinal waters are used in the treatment of rheumatic disorders. The **Catholic church** dates from the 14th century but was later rebuilt in the Baroque style. Frescoes by István Dorffmeister adorn the **Spa Chapel** built in 1773.

FERTŐBOZ (4.4 km from Balf): The late Baroque **Gloriette** erected in 1801 on the outskirts offers a beautiful view of **Lake Fertő.**

HIDEGSÉG (2 km from Fertőboz): The apse of its **Catholic church** is decorated by a 12th-century figural wall-painting, the earliest of its kind in Hungary.

FERTŐD (known earlier as Eszterháza; 27 km from Sopron): The 126-room former **Esterházy Palace** was built in the 1760s in the Baroque style, though with some Rococo and Louis XVI stylistic tendencies. (Large-scale renovation work has restored the building from the devastation it suffered during the Second World War, and it is now open to the general public.) During the final decades of

The Fertőrákos stone quarry

the 18th century the palace, which was referred to in its own time as the "Hungarian Versailles", was full of the grandeur about which Goethe wrote in his "Dichtung und Wahrheit". Musical life in the palace was particularly brilliant; Joseph Haydn was court musician here to the Esterházy family for almost thirty years. The wooden flooring in the Sala Terrena reception hall is covered with Carrara marble, and the initials of the builder's name, F.N.E. (Fürst Nicolaus Esterházy)—fashioned in garlands of flowers—can be read on the wall-paintings on the ceiling. Each summer concerts are given in the three-story high concert hall. Facing the park is the largest hall in the palace, the ceremonial hall; the theme of the large fresco on its ceiling is Apollo's triumph. The allegorical statues of the Four Seasons stand in the four corners of the room.

The wings of the horseshoe-shaped palace are surrounded by a grand courtyard with a Rococo wrought-iron gate. (There is a hotel in the eastern wing.)

A restaurant and café are open to the public in the auxiliary buildings—the **Grenadier House** (Gránátos ház) and the **Groom's House** (Udvaros-ház). The Baroque **inn** and the Baroque-styled **Music House,** where Haydn once lived, are also interesting. There is a Haydn memorial plaque on the wall of the Music House (Jenő Bory, 1932). The **French Park** behind the palace was largely destroyed in the Second World War but it is gradually being replanted.

NAGYCENK (13.5 km southeast of Sopron at the junction of Rds. 84 and 85): **mansion** belonging to the Széchenyi family and built at the end of the 18th cen-

The former Esterházy palace, Fertőd

tury (enlarged around 1838) stands here. István Széchenyi, the great Hungarian statesman and publicist (1791–1860), worked here for a long time and was buried in the Széchenyi family's mausoleum, which stands in the middle of the parish cemetery. The mansion was burned down during the Second World War, but the main building has now been restored and the **Széchenyi Memorial Museum** as well as a **transport museum** have been established in it. Its 2.6 km long avenue lined with lime-trees was created in 1754. At the end of the row of limes under the sarcophagus-like tomb rest a member of the family and his wife. Also worth seeing is the statue of István Széchenyi (Alajos Stróbl, 1897) standing in front of the Romantic-style church that was designed by Miklós Ybl and built in 1861–64.

Taking a trip on the narrow-gauge **Széchenyi Museum Railway** is an interesting experience. The old steam-engine and signal-equipment are regarded as museum pieces. The train is driven and operated by student pioneers in uniform. This little railway runs along a 3,600 m track between Nagycenk and Fertőboz.

NEMESKÉR (17.5 km southeast of Nagycenk on Rd. 84): Its **Lutheran church** was built in 1732. The **National Lutheran Museum** has a permanent exhibit on the history of the Reformation in Transdanubia and local history.

SOPRONHORPÁCS (5 km west of Nemeskér) has a Romanesque-style **church** dating from the 12th to 13th centuries. The seven gates of the church with their paired columns show a similarity to the entrance of the Western Transdanubian churches of Ják and Lébény. The parish is also known for the Research Institute for Beet Cultivation and the **arboretum** belonging to it, to be found in the Széchenyi Mansion.

Kőszeg

50 km south of Sopron, 244 km from Budapest on the M7, then on Rds. 8 and 87 from Székesfehérvár; 254 km via Veszprém by rail, 277 km via Győr.

Kőszeg, situated at the foot of the Kőszeg mountains (270 m), is rich in historical monuments. The town's medieval castle, which for a long time served as a focal point for battles fought between Hungarian kings and Austrian counts, became an important border fortress during the Turkish occupation. In 1532 a handful of garrison troops under the leadership of Captain Miklós Jurisich heroically resisted a Turkish military force 200,000 strong and thus stopped them from advancing towards Vienna.

Kőszeg's present appearance was essentially achieved in the 18th century, but there are also a few Renaissance houses of exceptional beauty. Cultural traditions: a secondary school existed here as early as the 16th century and a musical society and music school were established in the middle of the last century.

Kőszeg's subalpine climate, the possibilities for excursions offered by its surroundings, and the green belt areas with their well-cared-for parks make Kőszeg a pleasant holiday resort.

The heart of the small town is **Jurisich tér,** which can be reached from Köztársaság tér by going through the so-called **Hero's Gate.** The gate was built in 1932 on the four hundredth anniversary of the heroic defence of the castle. **The Church of St. James** (15th c.), in the middle of Jurisich tér, is one of the most valuable monuments of Gothic art in Hungary. (It has 17th to 18th-century Baroque additions.) Frescoes from the 15th century have remained on one of the walls. The **Church of St. Emerich** also stands in Jurisich tér. It was built at the beginning of the 17th century in the early Baroque style. Certain sections of the building are characteristically Gothic and Renaissance. The small windows on the north wall of the 18th-century building of the **Town Hall (No. 8)** provide evidence of its Gothic origin (the windows can be seen from the gate of **No. 10).** The so-called **General's House (No. 6)** on the other side of the Town Hall was built in the 17th century by joining two medieval houses. The two wings of the house were built on the castle wall. House **No. 7** is **adorned with**

Kőszeg

sgraffiti; there are also sgraffiti from around 1570 in the courtyard as well as on the loggia of the **Szovják House (No. 14).** In the middle of the square stands the **town well** completed in the style of Louis XVI in 1766. The **statue of the Virgin Mary,** standing where a medieval pillory once stood, was finished in 1739.

There are also beautiful Baroque residences in **Chernel utca.** The **Chernel House (No. 10),** built in 1809, is where Eugène Beauharnais, viceroy to Napoleon, stayed. The wrought-iron gate on the **Tallián Huse (No. 12)** as well as the Baroque **Sigray House** are also worth seeing.

The houses along **Rájnis utca** near the entrance to the castle were built beside one another in a so-called saw-toothed manner. This manner of building was practised quite frequently in the Middle Ages for defensive purposes, since it insured excellent possibilities for firing at the enemy.

The castle can be entered through an alley leading from Chernel utca to the moat. Today towers stand on the north and south corners of the irregular rectangular building complex. The castle was built in the 14th century; the late Gothic, Renaissance, and Baroque parts are the results of reconstructions and restorations that took place throughout the centuries. The castle was rebuilt between 1958 and 1962 and became the home of the Jurisich Museum (old certificates, weapons, furniture, etc.), which illustrates the history of the town as well as that of the castle. A cultural centre, a tourist hostel and guest-houses are also located here.

Jurisich Castle, Kőszeg

A few historic buildings are worth visiting on **Várkör** (Castle Circle), which runs along the castle walls: the Baroque historical building at **No. 13,** the neo-Classical building at **No. 15,** that at **No. 27,** and the Rococo building at **No. 55,** as well as the Baroque **Trinity Statue** erected in memory of the plaque epidemic of 1712; and in addition **a former orphanage (No. 39,** today a school) built in 1749, utilizing one of the round bastions of the city wall. The Baroque residential building **Nos. 9–11 Schätzel Frigyes utca** was the **Ball House** in the 19th century. Ferenc Liszt gave a concert here in September 1846.

Note the outstanding 15th-century Gothic monstrance as well as a chasuble made from a piece of Turkish velvet embroidered with real pearls in the neo-Gothic **Church of the Sacred Heart** on **Köztársaság tér.**

The **Chernel Grove** (an arboretum) and the **Chernel Memorial Museum,** both in **Hunyadi utca,** are worth seeing. (Kálmán Chernel was an eminent historian; his son István was a biologist.) A beautiful view of the city and its surroundings can be seen from the Baroque **chapel** on Calvary Hill rising at the end of **Kálvária utca.**

A bus line goes up nearby **Szabó mountain,** where a tourist hostel and a hotel are situated.

Szombathely

The M7 from Budapest, then Rd. 8 from Székesfehérvár and Rd. 87 from Kám; 187 km from Budapest; 259 km by rail via Győr and 137 km via Székesfehérvár.

Szombathely, the largest town of Western Transdanubia, lies on the intersection of traffic routes which converge where the flat and mountainous regions meet.

Savaria, the predecessor of present-day Szombathely, was founded by the Roman Emperor Claudius in A.D. 43., and became the capital of Upper Pannonia province in A.D. 107. Since that time important trade routes have led through the town, for example, the Amber Route connecting Italy with the Baltic Sea. In the 8th century the city fell under the rule of the Franks, from which period its German name, Steinamanger, originates. The town was burned down in 1241 by the Mongol forces, was later frequently inflicted with grave disaster, gaining its new appearance in the 18th century when it became the Episcopal See. Today it is a flourishing industrial town with a timber plant, a shoe factory, a cotton plant, a carpet factory, a railway rolling-stock repair establishment, works manufacturing farm machinery, etc. The town has a teachers' training college and seven secondary schools.

The traffic centre of the town is **Köztársaság tér,** while the historical centre is the harmonious group of buildings on **Berzsenyi Dániel tér,** the construction of which is the work of the architect Menyhért Hefele. The three-story **Episcopal Palace** at **No. 3** (1779–83) is one of the most beautiful monuments of Hungarian late Baroque architecture. Next door **(No. 1)** is the 18th-century, three-story building of the **County Hall.** The neo-Classical, so-called **Small Town Hall** is located to the left. The neo-Classical, late Baroque **Cathedral** (1791–1815), with its two towers, is on nearby **Templom tér.**

Ruins of Roman and medieval structures discovered since 1938 can be seen in the **Garden of Ruins** (Romkert), the town's outdoor museum lying next to the Cathedral. Among the most interesting are ruins of former Pannonia's largest Christian church, the **Basilica of St. Quirinus,** with its beautiful floor mosaics; remains of a former Roman road, as well as remains of the medieval castle of Szombathely. The most valuable part of the **Savaria Museum** at **Kisaludy Sándor utca 9** is the Roman collection of stonework finds. Besides Aquincum and Gorsium (see pp. ...., ...), the most valuable and important historic monuments in Hungary from the Roman age are in Szombathely. A number of historic houses can also be seen not far from Köztársaság tér at **Rákóczi utca 2,** where the remains of the **Sanctuary of Isis,** the Iseum, built at the end of the 2nd century, lie. This extremely significant find was unearthed at the end of the 1950s and was restored during the early 1960s. Rákóczi utca 2 also houses the new Szombathely Gallery.

The former **Franciscan church and monastery** stand in **Aréna utca.** The church was built in the Gothic style (second half of the 14th c.) and was rebuilt in the Baroque style. The originally Baroque building of the monastery was heightened by the addition of an upper storey.

Alkotmány utca, which lies north of Berzsenyi tér, is virtually a live exhibition of historic buildings. **No. 1** is a former **ecclesiastical seminary** (today a student hostel) built at the end of the 18th century by Hefele. It has 16 codices and almost 100 manuscripts in its 60,000-volume **library.** The so-called **Eölbey House** at **No. 2** was built between 1796 and 1800, and was also designed by Hefele in a neo-Classical and late Baroque style. (Today it houses temporary exhibitions.) The houses at **Nos. 3, 4, 5, 17** and **18** are neo-Classical. According to the Latin date on the two-storey house at **No. 25,** it was built when the French were fighting here. (In 1809 the city was held by the French for 110 days.) It is also worthwhile visiting the former **Dominican church (Tolbuhin út 2)** built around 1670. Situated on the northern outskirts of the town is **Csónakázó tó,** a boating lake (Hotel Claudius, outdoor swimming-baths, camp site, horseback-riding) and the **open-air folk museum.**

The **Kámoni Arboretum** is situated in the northwestern part of the town. With its 2,000 different kinds of trees and shrubs, it is one of the richest herbaria in the country.

Roads leading out of Szombathely: No. 86 to the southeast and south; no. 87 to the north; the various branches of these.

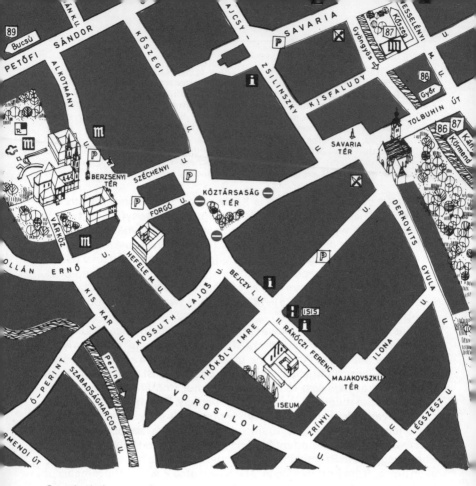

Szombathely

EXCURSIONS

JÁK (11.5 km south of Szombathely) is on no account to be missed. Here can be found an outstanding Hungarian architectural creation dating from the age of the Árpáds, a monumental building with two towers built in the Romanesque style in the middle of the 13th century. Throughout the centuries this beautiful historic monument has many times been seriously damaged; between 1896 and 1904 it was restored to its former late Romanesque beauty. The exterior of the abbey building is richly embellished; the figural ornamentation on the door, which is situated between the two towers, and also the decorative sculptures on the exterior wall of the sanctuary, are especially remarkable. The monastery was founded by Márton Nagy, who was of the Ják clan. The western façade is the most highly decorated. The door, built seven layers deep into the façade, and the adornments of the nave, indicate Norman-French influence. The niches in the upper part of the portal contain statues depicting Christ and the twelve Apostles. The well-balanced proportions of the building as well as the exquisitely carved and painted adornments have made the interior of the church an exceptional work of art. On the west side of the Church of St. George stands the **Chapel of St. James** with its onion-shaped tower, which at one time was the parish church. (A guided tour of the church can be arranged in the pavilion next door.)

BÜKFÜRDŐ (31 km northeast of Szombathely by way of Vát and Acsád) is worthwhile visiting because it has thermal baths which have one of the richest water sources in all Central Europe. The 58 °C alkaline waters are mainly used for curing locomotor disorders and gynaecological diseases, as well as diseases of the stomach and the intestinal tract. It also has an outdoor swimming-pool (26 °C). The Baroque **palace** of the settlement is today a hotel (indoor swimming-pool, outdoor thermal pool, and a pool for children).

SÁRVÁR (27 km east of Szombathely on Rds. 86 and 88) looks back on a rich past. The **castle** of Sárvár is first mentioned in 12th-century documents, but it was not until the 16th century that the present Renaissance pentagonal structure

Sanctuary of Isis, Szombathely

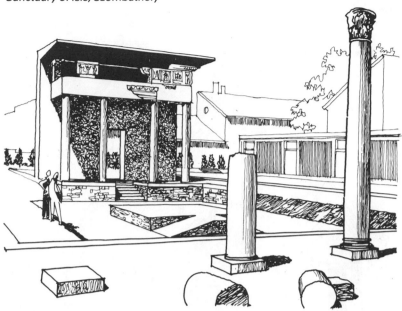

emerged. The castle became an important cultural centre during the Reformation and it was frequently visited by Sebestyén Tinódi Lantos (1505–1556), a famous 16th-century minstrel, who died here. The first book printed in Hungary in the Hungarian language, a Latin–Hungarian Grammar, came off the Sárvár printing press (1539) as did the first Hungarian translation of the New Testament (1541). The castle halls, which are adorned with frescoes painted by István Dorffmeister, today house the **Tinódi Memorial Exhibition** and valuable collections of the **Nádasdy Museum.** The **castle gardens** are at the same time an arboretum, with the country's only experimental station for pines. There are other beautiful historic buildings to be seen on the streets of this small town with its archaic atmosphere. (There is a bathing beach and hotel on the banks of the river Rába.)

Main road 8 is 22 km from here along Rd. 84, or it can be reached from the southwest by a public road which, after 17 km, runs into Rd. 87 at Rum.

KÁM (4.7 km from Rum on Rd. 87): The **Ambrózy-kert** arboretum, named after its founder, offers a beautiful sight, especially at the end of May, when the nearly 60 kinds of rhododendrons grown here burst into flower.

A village in Göcsej

Romanesque church and chapel, Ják

Main road 8 running west of Székesfehérvár is 1.2 km from Kám. It reaches the Austrian border 53 km from here.

VASVÁR (9.3 km from Kám on Rd. 8 and then 1 km to the south on Rd. 74): Valuable monuments from the Roman age. The settlement, known once as Castrum Ferrarum, was an important fortification of the Roman Empire, for a military route ran through here to Aquincum. **Remains of an iron smelting furnace** and **central heating system** both dating from Roman times have also been discovered here. (Vasvár apparently received both its Latin and Hungarian names from the iron smelting that once took place here.) A former **Dominican monastery and church** of medieval origin but rebuilt at the end of the 17th century in the Baroque style are important historical buildings.

Rd. 74 leads through Vasvár, to the southern part of Western Transdanubia, Zalaegerszeg and Nagykanizsa (see pp. 131–132).

KÖRMEND (18 km west of Vasvár on Rd. 8, or 25 km south of Szombathely on Rd. 86): around the former **Batthyány Palace,** partly of medieval origin but largely built in the Baroque and neo-Classical styles, there is a large arboretum with beautiful old trees and rare plants. The 16th-century **Catholic church** was later reconstructed in the Baroque style. In the **museum** there are local historical, ethnographical, and anthropological exhibitions.
RÁBAFÜZES (27 km west of Körmend on Rd. 8): An Austrian–Hungarian border crossing.
SZENTGOTTHÁRD (251 km from Budapest, 4.5 km south of Rábafüzes): A Turkish military force numerically twice as strong suffered a decisive defeat nearby in 1664 at the hand of the Imperial armies under the leadership of Montecuccoli. The **Cistercian church and monastery** were built in the 18th century. Both buildings are adorned with frescoes by István Dorffmeister. The furnishings are Baroque. The furnishings of the scythe factory founded in 1351 (at Mondsee, in Austria) and later transferred to Szentgotthárd are historic relics associated with industry. (Today agricultural implements are made here. Rapiers and swords are also manufactured and exported.)

The **ŐRSÉG** (south of Szentgotthárd), together with its characteristic villages, is a distinctive ethnographic area (224 km from Budapest on the M7–7 (E 96) Balaton Motorway and then on Rd. 76, or on Rd. 8 from Székesfehérvár and then south through Vasvár on Rd. 7).

ŐRISZENTPÉTER (21 km south of Szentgotthárd) is the centre of the Őrség region. It has a 13th-century **Romanesque church**. A characteristic manner of settlement can be observed here: the groups of houses are situated at great distances from each other. Many houses were built from wooden beams and put together without iron nails. The national costume of the Őrség region has numerous unique features. (Private accommodation at Körmend and Őriszentpéter.)

VELEMÉR (17 km south of Őriszentpéter): **Early Gothic church** with 14th-century frescoes.

GÖCSEJ, another characteristically distinct region, lies to the east of Őriszentpéter in the Zala Hills. Its villages, almost without exception, are situated on hills. The area is extremely rich in natural springs (as many as 40 to 50 springs are to be found near some of the villages), and in the past it was possible to avoid swamps only by building on higher ground. Because of the marshy land, it used to be extremely difficult to reach the different settlements, and interesting ethnographic differences therefore arose between them. Today the area is covered with a network of asphalt roads, but the characteristic folk architecture of the villages has nevertheless survived: houses decorated with hand-carved rafters, barge-boards, and adorned with wooden belfries. A few exquisite examples of this type of building can be seen in the villages of **ZALALÖVŐ,** and **FELSŐBAGOD.** (Tourist office: **NOVA,** 38 km from Zalaegerszeg on road 75.)

Zalaegerszeg

224 km from Budapest on the M7—7 (E71) Balaton Motorway and then on Rd. 76 (or on Rd. 8 from Székesfehérvár and then south through Vasvár on Rd. 7), 252 km by rail.

The settlement, built on the bank of the Zala River, is mentioned as being a market town as early as the 13th century. During the period of Turkish occupation, the castle of Zalaegerszeg became a border fortress of Royal (Western) Hungary, while the town itself became the capital of the county. 19th-century railway construction bypassed the city; only oil production, which began in the 1930s, provided it with impetus for development. A large part of the industrial plants situated here have come into existence since 1945; today the town has its own oil refinery. Concurrently with industrial development, the profile of the town has also been modernized. The number of houses with more than one storey has increased almost tenfold since 1949.

The centre of the town is **Széchenyi tér, Kovács Károly tér,** and the surrounding streets. The public building at Széchenyi tér 1 was built in 1765–1767 in the Baroque style. One of the halls is adorned with a painting by Dorffmeister. The archaic building complex of the "Arany Bárány" Hotel as well as the Baroque **Catholic church,** built between 1750 and 1760 and adorned in the interior with beautiful frescoes by Cymbal, are both situated in this square. The history of Zala County is on exhibition in the **Göcsej Museum** in **Marx tér** (next to Széchenyi tér). (The Museum also has a permanent exhibit of the works of the sculptor Zsigmond Kisfaludi Strobl, who was a holder of the Kossuth Prize and an honorary freeman of the city.) The **County Hall** was erected in what is now Szabadság tér in 1730–1732 where the former castle once stood. A Baroque **Calvary chapel** of 1756 stands on **Kálvária tér** (in the southern part of the town).

A small street beginning at the intersection of **Lenin út** and **Vörös Hadsereg útja,** in the modern western part of the town, leads to the **Village Museum** which was the first outdoor folk museum in the country, and which exhibits the most beautiful examples of the traditional architecture of the region, moved here from their original location.

Fortified castle, Egervár

EGERVÁR (10 km to the west of Zalaegerszeg on Rd. 10): In the 13th century a fortress stood near here. A Renaissance castle was built in the 16th century on the foundations of the fortress mentioned above, and it was from this that the palace (now a tourist hostel) later took shape in 1712–1713.
RÁDIHÁZA (next to Gutorfölde, 30 km southwest of Zalaegerszeg by first Rd. 74, then 75, and finally a minor road): A community traditionally known for horse breeding. It has a riding school where horse-shows are held every summer.
LENTI (to the west on Rd. 74, then on Rd. 75 from Bak; 42 km to the southwest of Zalaegerszeg): district seat with medieval **castle ruins.**
RÉDICS (6 km from Lenti) is a frontier crossing between Hungary and Yugoslavia.

Nagykanizsa

208 km from Budapest on the M7 and Rd. 7; 221 km by train.

Nagykanizsa has been a flourishing settlement ever since the Hungarian state was founded. Its castle was an important fortification, especially during the time of the Turkish wars. Beginning in 1600, and lasting for almost a century, the settlement was the seat of a Turkish vilayet (district). The rail-way from Budapest to the Adriatic has run through Nagykanizsa since it was built in the second half of the 19th century. Chiefly owing to the exploitation of the Zala oil fields, the town has since become strongly industrialized. Today it is the administrative centre of the oil industry in Zala.

There are no traces of the former border castle, but ruins of the so-called **"Corrupt Castle"** (Romlott-vár), once an establishment for the entertainment of Turkish military officers, can still be seen on a mountainside planted with vineyards (southeast of the town).

The former **Franciscan church** in **Zetkin Klára utca** not far from Szabadság tér, as well as a **statue of the Trinity** (1758) in **Kossuth Lajos tér** were built at the beginning of the 18th century.

Local collections of the **Thury György Museum** have been housed in a neo-Classical building on **Szabadság tér,** the main square of the town **(No. 11).** (György Thury was a courageous captain of the castle during the Turkish period.) A **picture gallery** belonging to the museum is situated in the 18th-century Baroque house at **Lenin út 5–7,** a street running into Szabadság tér from the south. Opposite is a neo-Classical **synagogue** from the early 19th century **(No. 6).** Like the **Inkey Sepulchral Chapel** (1768), standing north of the city beside the main road, the **church** situated on **Deák Ferenc tér** is also a Baroque building.

ZALAKAROS (18 km north of Nagykanizsa): Known for its warm-water thermal baths (hotel, restaurant, camping site for motorists).
MURAKERESZTÚR (17 km south of Nagykanizsa): A railway frontier post with Yugoslavia.

CENTRAL TRANSDANUBIA

Central Transdanubia can be reached from Budapest by taking the M7–7 (E71) and Rd. 8 from Székesfehérvár; by rail in the direction of Szombathely or Nagykanizsa.

The most important part of Central Transdanubia is the area around Lake Balaton, discussed in a separate section (see pp. 155). The Vértes Mountains are in the northern section of the area, while the Velence Mountains (351 m), with Lake Velence at their feet, are situated towards the south. In the west, more distant mountains are connected to the romantic Magas-Bakony mountains lying north of Veszprém and the Southern Bakony Mountains, which become gradually lower as they approach the Balaton. The whole Bakony area abounds in natural beauty.

The **Cuha River Valley** is an example of a romantic canyon valley formed by a small river. Bauxite production as well as manganese, coal and basalt mining are carried out in the mountains. Many kinds of factories ranging from bauxite-processing plants and power-plants to large chemical, machine, and light industrial plants operate here. The two traditional branches of agriculture are wine production, which has a long history, and horse breeding.

Administratively, both Fejér County (capital at Székesfehérvár) and Veszprém County (capital at Veszprém) belong to this region.

ÉRD (21 km from Budapest on Rd. 70): There is a 15th-century **Catholic church**, later rebuilt in the Baroque style, and the still remaining lower section of a **Mohammedan mosque** built in the middle of the 16th century. (A restaurant, café, hotel, camping site with log cabins, and beach are all situated in the resort area of **ÉRDLIGET**.)

MARTONVÁSÁR (32 km from Budapest on Rd. 70): Famous for its 18th-century **castle** (rebuilt at the end of the 19th century in an English neo-Gothic style), which was formerly the **home of the Brunswick family**. It was Teréz Brunswick who founded the country's first nursery school. Ludwig van Beethoven stayed here when he visited the Brunswick family on several occasions as a personal friend of Count Ferenc. It has been said that Josephine Brunswick was the "immortal beloved" to whom the great composer addressed his love letters, which were written without either salutations or dates. Tradition has it that many of Beethoven's works were inspired by his visits to Martonvásár, for example, the "Appassionata Sonata" which he dedicated to the Brunswick family. The "Moonlight Sonata" was also reputedly composed in Martonvásár. The small **Beethoven Museum** (open only on Saturday and Sunday) in the castle recalls memories of the composer's stay here. (Hotel, campsite, tourist accommodation on the M7 road to Balaton.) Since 1958, outdoor **Beethoven concerts** have been given each summer in the small, carefully-tended park where a bust of the great composer stands on the small, picturesque island in the lake. (The larger section of the castle is today occupied by the Agricultural Research Institute and the Experimental Farm Centre, both belonging to the Hungarian Academy of Sciences.) The Baroque **Catholic church** next to the castle is adorned with frescoes by Johann Cymbal. Teréz Brunswick rests in the crypt of the church.

LAKE VELENCE (Velencei-tó): The south shore begins 46 km from Budapest on Rd. 70. (Its northern shore can be reached from the M7.) Its surface comprises 26 sq.km, but half of it is covered by reeds. As a result of this, a natural game preserve for birds covering 420 hectares has been created in the southwestern part of the lake. Some 25,000 to 30,000 birds belonging to 28 different species, including the rare egret, nest in the vast expanse of reeds. The average depth of the lake is only between 1 and 3 m, while the average temperature of the water in the summer ranges between 19° and 26° C. Rowing and sailing on the lake are popular sports (water carnivals are also held); and being rich in fish, the waters are also ideal for angling. A traditional resort area has been created on the southern shores of the lake, where the principal settlements are **VELENCEFÜRDŐ, GÁRDONY** and **AGÁRD**. (In Gárdony there are restaurants, a beach and a confectioner's; in Agárd there is a bathing beach, a campsite and a tourist hostel provided with wooden cabins for two. The Agárd Motel operates here throughout the year. There are bathing beaches on the shores of the lake, and in Agárd there is also a ferryberth from which boats travel to the far side of the lake.)

AGÁRDPUSZTA is the birthplace of Géza Gárdonyi, a writer mainly known for his historical novels "The Stars of Eger" and "The Invisible Man".

VELENCE (situated on the northern shores of the lake, 40 km from Budapest on the M7) was one of the settlements lying on the Aquincum–Savaria (Óbuda–Szombathely) military route used by the Romans. The Turkish *hodja* Molla Sadik, a travelling companion of the world-famous Hungarian orientalist and

Asian scholar, Ármin Vámbéry (1832–1913), is buried in the parish cemetery. (Hotel, campsite, tourist accommodation on the M7 road to Balaton.) **PÁKOZD** (10 km west of Velence) is an old fishing settlement. The **Szúnyog csárda** (Mosquito Inn) is not only worth visiting for its fish soup, but because of its **exhibition** of old fishing tackle. The **stone obelisk** on Mészeg Mountain, which lies on the outskirts of the parish, commemorates the first victorious battle fought here during the War of Independence on September 29, 1848. A beautiful view of the lake and the Velence mountains can be seen from the monument.

Székesfehérvár

60 km from Budapest on Rd. 70; 67 km by rail.

The Székesfehérvár area was inhabited very early by the Celts, and during the Roman age an important settlement existed here. Tradition has it that the Magyar conqueror Prince Árpád pitched camp where present-day Székesfehérvár is situated and took possession of the area for the princely tribe. This is why the town is considered to be the oldest in Hungary. The founder of the Hungarian state, King Stephen I, made Székesfehérvár the capital of the country and a chapter seat as well. He also had a magnificent basilica built here and surrounded it with walls. The town was the scene of coronations and an ecclesiastical centre for almost three hundred years. The former royal castle was built on an elevated part of a marshy area and for that reason remained impregnable for a long time. Even the Mongols were unable to take possession of it. In 1543 the city fell into the hands of the Turks, who not only ravaged the royal tombs but had the coronation church blown up as well, so that all that remained after they left in 1688 was a deserted heap of ruins. The town was rebuilt in the 18th century, when it became an Episcopal See. In the 19th century the town expanded even further after the marshes drained and the Sárvíz River had been diverted. After recovering from the heavy damage it suffered in the Second World War, Székesfehérvár entered a new age characterized by great industrialization.

Among the beautiful old buildings of **István tér,** the neo-Classical seat of the **County Hall,** built between 1807 and 1812 and designed by Mihály Pollack, is particularly worthy of attention. **Arany János utca** leads from the west side of the square to the Baroque **Cathedral,** which was erected in the middle of the 18th century by using the remains of a church originally built in the Romanesque style. The sanctuary and main altar represent the work of Franz Anton Hillebrandt, while the frescoes on the ceiling were painted by Johann Cymbal. Near the Cathedral stands the city's most beautiful Gothic monument, **St. Anne's Chapel** built around 1470. József Budenz, the 19th-century pioneer of Finno-Ugrian linguistics, lived for two years in the house, built in the style of Louis XVI, at **Arany János utca 12. A historical exhibition of the city** is situated in the basement of the building; items from the legacy of a native son, the architect Miklós Ybl, are exhibited upstairs.

The complex of the **City Hall** consisting of two buildings, stands on the southern side of **Szabadság tér,** the city's main square. The two-story wing on the right-hand side was built in 1690, and the façade was restored in 1790 in the style of Louis XVI. The three-storey wing on the left, the **former Zichy Palace,** was also built at the end of the 18th century, together with the ornamented, Baroque gate facing Kossuth Lajos utca. The **Bishop's Palace,** situated at **Szabadság tér 10,** was built in the style of Louis XVI between 1790 and 1801. Valuable codices and almost 500 incunabula are preserved in the 4,000-volume library of the palace. A relief made in 1938 by the sculptor Ferenc Medgyessy on the wall of the former Baroque **Franciscan church** situated nearby recalls the expulsion of the Turks. The beautiful historic building standing on the corner of Szabadság tér and Jókai utca was at one time the **city magistrate's**

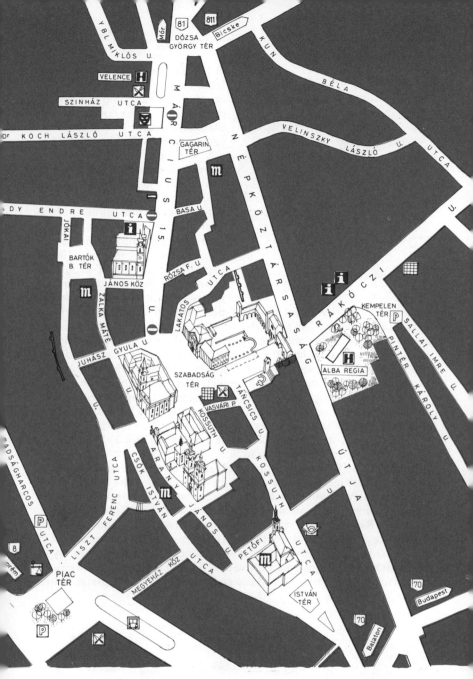

Székesfehérvár

house; it was reconstructed in the Baroque and Rococo styles in the 18th
century, and today is a parsonage. The road leads from the square to the
Garden of Ruins (Romkert) behind the Bishop's Palace. The carefully
excavated remains of the 11th-century Basilica and the royal **Coronation
Church** are preserved in the beautiful outdoor museum. 38 Hungarian
kings were crowned here and 18 kings were buried in the crypt. After the
Turkish withdrawal, the Basilica stood for some time in a seriously damaged condition, then at the end of the 18th century stones from its walls
were used to construct the Bishop's Palace. 11th to 15th-century carvings
have been placed on exhibit at the collection of stonework finds situated

Saint Anne's Chapel, Székesfehérvár

in the Garden of Ruins. Also exhibited is the stone coffin of St. Stephen (or according to more recent views, the coffin of St. Stephen's son, St. Emerich) carved from a Roman sarcophagus. Not far from the Garden of Ruins an almost 90 m long section of the old medieval city wall as well as the remains of a bastion dating back to the beginning of the 17th century can be seen.

One of the country's oldest pharmacies, the "Fekete Sas" (Black Eagle), established in 1758 and known for its splendid Rococo furnishings, is situated in **Március 15. utca.** In the same street **(No. 6)** stands a **church** with Rococo furnishings, built between 1745 and 1755. It originally belonged to the Jesuits and later to the Cistercians. The stairway, library, and dining room in the former **monastery** (at **No. 8**) adjoining the church are all adorned with magnificent Rococo stucco-work. The **King Stephen Museum** (István Király Múzeum) at **Gagarin tér 3** exhibits valuable archeological, local historical, and ethnographic materials. Outstanding creations of the 19th to 20th-century Hungarian art can be seen in the **Csók István Art Gallery** at **Bartók Béla tér 1.** An **ecclesiastical museum** can be visited in the Baroque building of the former **Carmelite monastery** (today a home for elderly priests) in **Petőfi Sándor utca.**

The Baroque **Carmelite church** next door, on the corner of **Kossuth Lajos utca,** was built in the middle of the 18th century. The interior of the church is adorned with frescoes by Maulbertsch (the most beautiful one being on the oratory alongside the sanctuary). The **Greek Orthodox church** in **Rác utca,** with its Byzantine wallpaintings, also dates back to the 18th century. At the end of the 18th century and during the first half of the 19th, strolling players gave performances in the Baroque **Győri House** at **Kossuth Lajos utca 15.** The poet Sándor Petőfi, who was a strolling player at that time, also made an appearance on the stage of this house.

Garden of Ruins, Székesfehérvár

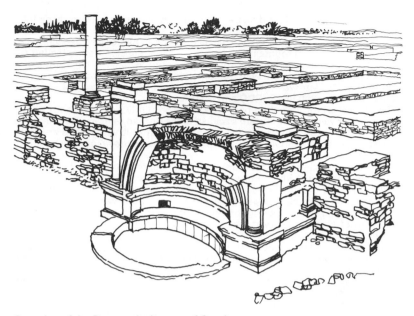

Remains of the Roman settlement of Gorsium

A few minutes from Marx tér, the **Bory Castle** is a veritable museum of architecture. At the beginning of the century the sculptor, painter, and architect Jenő Bory designed and built it in various architectural styles: Romanesque, Gothic, Baroque and even in the style of Scottish castles.

EXCURSIONS

Rd. 81, leading to Győr, gives an idea of what the Vértes Mountains can offer the visitor.

CSÓKAKŐ (20.5 km southwest of Székesfehérvár and then by a side road to the southeast): Remains of a 13th-century **castle,** already ruined during the Turkish occupation, stand on the outskirts (298 m; beautiful view).
BODAJK (2 km on a public road in a southwest direction from the Csókakő turn-off): There is a neo-Classical **palace** (today a tourist hostel) standing in a 9.12-hectare park. The historic building of the **parish council hall** is also neo-Classical. A Baroque **Calvary** (1737) stands on Kálvária Hill.
MÓR (27 km from Székesfehérvár on Rd. 81) is the centre for walks into the southwestern section of the Vértes mountains. Points of interest: the former **Lamberg Castle** (today a cultural centre) built between 1762 and 1766 by Jakab Fellner in **Lenin tér;** the former **Láncos** (Chain) **Castle** at **Lenin tér 6** (it derived its present name from the chain fence in front); the former **Capuchin church** in **Marx Károly tér,** dating from the beginning of the 18th century.
    The area around Mór is a well-known vine-growing region, the best vintages being preserved in the community's **Wine Museum,** a row of wine-cellars for sampling wines. The "Vértes" tourist hostel can be found opposite the Wine Museum. Several old wine-cellars in the village bear witness to the rich history that wine production has had here.
SZABADBATTYÁN (12 km southwest of Székesfehérvár on Rd. 70): The late Gothic **Kula Tower** nearby was used in the Middle Ages to guard a road that ran through the marshy region around Székesfehérvár. Today it houses an exhibition of weapons and implements from the era of the Turkish occupation.
TÁC (5 km south of Szabadbattyán): Archeologists discovered the ruins of **Gorsium,** a Roman settlement in Fövénypuszta on its outskirts. The settlement had 7,000 to 8,000 inhabitants and was given the rank of a city by Emperor Hadrian. It was destroyed many times in successive wars, and completely ruined after the Romans had left. Most of the stones were used in the Middle Ages for building

Székesfehérvár. Scientific and methodical excavation began as recently as 1958 and is still being carried on. An outdoor museum shows remains that have been uncovered so far (an early Christian basilica, a capital, part of a street, villas, columns and ornamental fountains). Each spring a Floralia celebration lasting several days is held here, and in the summer the dramas of classical authors are staged. (There is a restaurant with Roman-style furnishings nearby.)

VÁRPALOTA (22 km west of Székesfehérvár) is a young town, united some twenty years ago with **PÉTFÜRDŐ** and **INOTA**.

The older town of Várpalota became known primarily as a centre for lignite mining. Inota was once important because of the Roman military route that ran beside it. A 300 m long Roman stone structure almost 1800 years old, a weir consisting of gigantic stones which in certain places reaches the height of a building, can be seen near Pétfürdő.

Of the three settlements, old Várpalota has been mentioned by Hungarian chronicles since the 13th century. Known by the name Bátorkő (Courageous Rock), it was then that the first castle in the town was built. A new **fortified castle** was erected on its ruins between 1439 and 1445, and this was one of the most important border castles during the time of the Turkish occupation. Under the leadership of György Thury it was for a long time able to resist all Turkish assaults. A large section of the castle is built in the late Gothic style, but features of other styles are also evident. The castle building with its four corner towers was recently restored and a **museum of chemistry** as well as a cultural centre have been established here.

Since the unification of the three former communities, the present town centre, old Várpalota, has seen great changes due to the modern construction that has taken place there (a hotel, restaurants, residential and public buildings). The former **Zichy Castle** built in 1725, housing an **Artillery Museum** (open daily except Monday from 10 to 6), can be seen here as well as the **chapel** built ten years earlier, both constructed in the Baroque style.

ÖSKÜ (9 km west of Várpalota on Rd. 8): There is an 11th-century, semicircular **chapel** with a round nave, a sanctuary, and a mushroom-shaped cupola on its outskirts which, with the exception of the 15th-century sanctuary and the roof, has survived in its original state.

Veszprém

110 km from Budapest on the M7, then on Rd. 8 from Székesfehérvár; 112 km by rail.

Veszprém is the unofficial capital of the Bakony mountains. In addition to serving as the county capital of Veszprém County, it is also the centre of cultural life in the North Balaton region.

The vicinity of the five hills on which the town was built was inhabited by Stone Age man. As numerous findings indicate, the Romans did not settle in the area occupied by the present town, but just outside it.

Southeast of Veszprém, for example, one of the largest groups of Roman buildings from the former province of Pannonia was discovered in **BALÁCAPUSZTA**. The centre of this group of buildings was a 32-room **villa** dating back to the 1st century. Two **mosaic floors,** one 60 and the other 33 sq.m in size, have been discovered intact. A few fragments of wall-paintings have also been found. Today's Veszprém was also the centre of the easternmost province (bounded by the Danube and the Drava rivers) of the Frankovian Empire.

During the age of Prince Géza, one of the first bishoprics in Hungary was established in Veszprém. A cathedral and a royal palace were built in the walled-in castle area on the town's highest rocky hill. During later centuries, the court, especially the queen's household, lived in the palace, but the prebendal school—it would be called a college today—also added importance to the palace. As a result of the Turkish wars, wars of independence and fires, most of the town was destroyed. The present appearance of its historic core was essentially created during the time of Baroque reconstruction.

Since 1949 the town has acquired a chemical technical university as well as two chemical research institutes and has become the intellectual and administrative centre of the Bakony industrial area.

Veszprém's tourist attraction lies, first of all, in its large number of historical points of interest. The historic buildings of the town, built in Baroque, Louis XVI, or other styles, fill the rows of winding streets. The town itself is all hills and valleys with splendid rock masses, streams, bridges.

The more important streets lead from the hills to the squares of the old town centre, situated no more than a few steps from one another.

Veszprém

The **Town Hall,** built in the style of Louis XVI, is on **Szabadság tér.** As one continues towards the Castle, another beautiful building in the style of Louis XVI can be seen at **Vörös Hadsereg tér 3.** The **Fire Tower** rises at the foot of the hill on which the Castle stands. The lower part of the tower dates from the Middle Ages, while the upper stories and the dome were built during the Baroque period and the last century respectively. A beautiful view of the area surrounded by the Bakony mountains can be seen from the circular balcony of the tower, which can be reached from the Castle. The castle area can be entered through the so-called **Gate of Heroes** (Hősök kapuja) situated above the town centre and erected in 1936 from stones from the 15th-century castle gate. Inside the gate there is a small **exhibition dealing with the history of the town** as well as a **collection of stonework finds.** (Next to the Cathedral there is a steep lane passable only on foot.)

Detail of a street in the Castle, Veszprém

The only street in the castle area is **Vár utca,** which widens into a small square in front of the **Bishop's Palace** and the **Cathedral.** (Outdoor concerts are held here every summer.) Almost every house in Vár utca is either a historic building or otherwise of architectural interest. The building in the style of Louis XVI at **No. 19** is the old **County Hall** (today the seat of judicial institutions). The former **Piarist church** (1828–1833) and **monastery** at **No. 10** (the ground floor was built between 1750 and 1778, and the upper part between 1783 and 1821) has in its rear courtyard ruins of the old city wall. It is also a neo-Classical building. A piece of stonework, **a dated Renaissance altar stone** (1467) with the coat of arms of Bishop Vetési, can be seen in front of house **No. 27.** The town's oldest and most beautiful historic monuments are in the square created by the widening of the street, on which there stands a **statue of the Trinity** (1750). The **Cathedral** or Church of St. Michael, originally a Romanesque building, was first reconstructed in the Gothic style, then in the Baroque style, and, finally, at the beginning of the 20th century, in the neo-Romanesque style. The Baroque and neo-Classical altars are indeed beautiful, and the sacristy preserves valuable collections of the goldsmith's art and vestments. The **crypt** under the Cathedral is also worth seeing. Almost two decades ago ruins of the 10th-century **Chapel of St. George,** rebuilt in the 12th and 13th centuries in the Romanesque style, were discovered next to the Church of St. Michael. In the course of the excavations, remains of the earliest, medieval city walls were also found. On the other side of the Cathedral we find the **Gizella Chapel,** a rather beautiful early Gothic monument which originally consisted of two stories. The walls of the chapel are adorned with 13th-century frescoes.

The **Bishop's Palace** standing next door was built in 1765–1776 by Jakab Fellner with stones from the medieval royal palace. A **museum of ecclesiastical art** has been established in the halls of the palace, which are adorned with beautiful frescoes, including works by Cymbal. The **former Franciscan church** at **Vár utca 21** was built around 1730. There is a beautiful Baroque stucco decoration in the dining room of the **former monastery** adjoining the church. Tolbuhin út continues on to a terrace erected on the north stairway of the castle, where next to the **modern statues** of **St. Stephen** and **Gizella** a magnificent panorama of the old sections of the town unfolds: the **concrete, double-arched viaduct** (150 m long and 4 m wide) over Betekints Valley, and the picturesque surroundings.

It is worthwhile paying a visit to the **Bakony Museum** in Lenin Park, which—in addition to having a rich archeological, local historical, and art collection—contains ethnographic material and display folk art from the Bakony region as well as objects once in the possession of highwaymen and shepherds. The so-called **Bakony House** next door to the museum exhibits characteristic types of old folk architecture from the surrounding area and items of village furniture. The steep **Bajcsy-Zsilinszky út** leads to **Budapest utca**. The city's new centre, with a 17-storey high-rise building, modern shops, public and residential buildings, was created in the area bounded by Münnich Ferenc tér, Kossuth Lajos utca and Budapest utca. In another part of the city, situated higher up, the university district as well as another new residential district have been developed.

Many points of interest are also offered by the valleys of the city, including the old **water-mills** (which are reserved as historical monuments), and the picturesque ruins of two **medieval convents**. A **zoo** and an **amusement park** provided with a small railway can be visited in **Fejes** and **Betekints Valley**.

EXCURSIONS

The Balaton is 10 km distant from Veszprém, from which any one of the three roads can be taken to the lake's northern shores. However, only excursions into the Bakony Mountains will be considered here.
NEMESVÁMOS (5 km west of Veszprém): The two-storey Baroque house of the **Vámosi csárda,** on the outskirts of the town, standing in a courtyard surrounded by a stone wall, displays an architectural style characteristic of the Bakony region. The inn was built at the end of the 18th century. The date 1831 on the façade of the house recalls the year in which the stairway was completed. At the end of the 19th century, the most notorious highwayman of the Bakony region, Jóska Savanyú, claimed the inn as one of his homes. The tap-room with its receptacles

The csárda-inn of Nemesvámos

for catching wine dripping from the casks, the cellar with its tables and seats made out of felled tree-trunks, and the furnishings of the tap-room upstairs are all typically Hungarian.
ZIRC (23 km north of Veszprém on Rd. 82): Its **Cistercian Abbey** was founded in 1182. Although the medieval church and monastery belonging to Zirc have long since fallen into ruin, a Baroque **abbey church** built between 1739–1753 as well as a former **monastery** several years older are nevertheless still standing in **Népköztársaság útja** in the middle of the town. Altar pieces painted by F. A. Maulbertsch, as well as the beautifully carved furnishings, all contribute to making the church an important historic monument. A library valuable for its scientific collection is situated today in the abbey's **Library Hall,** which was created in the middle of the last century in a neo-Classical style. The most interesting items to be seen in the **museum,** also situated in the building, are the folk art material from the Bakony region. A beautiful **arboretum** adjoins the abbey buildings. The arboretum, together with its multitude of plants and trees, was established where a medieval game preserve was once located in the middle of the 18th century. The **Cuha Stream,** over which there is a **stone bridge** dating from 1759, runs through the middle of the arboretum. There is also a smaller, Baroque **church** in the town, a stone crucifix (1721) and the statue of St. John of Nepomuk (1729) nearby.
    A whole series of well-signposted roads begins at Zirc. A railway as well as a number of public roads lead to areas surrounding the Magas-Bakony, and from there the whole region can easily be visited.
CSESZNEK (13 km north of Zirc on Rd. 82): Its castle was built in the 13th century on the summit of a steep hill. In the mid-15th century it was enlarged in the Gothic style. (It is at present being restored.) A beautiful view of the romantic surroundings can be seen from the ruins.
BAKONYBÉL (17 km west of Zirc) lies at the foot of Kőris Mountain. In 1018 a monastery was established here deep in the valley, but today the only historic buildings to be seen are a **former Benedictine monastery** (now a home for the elderly), built in the middle of the 18th century, and the **church** belonging to it. A two-hour walk leads from the village (trade-union rest home, tourist hostel) to Kőris mountain (713 m). A railway built in 1896 runs from Veszprém to Győr via Zirc through the Cuha Valley, between cliffs, over bridges, and through tunnels. (Pannonhalma [See p. 115] also lies on this railway.)
HEREND (15 km west of Veszprém on Rd. 8) has become world famous because of its porcelain factory founded in 1839. The factory makes profitable use of the moulding and decorating talent developed by generations of the local population. Almost since its establishment, it has done work for fastidious domestic and foreign customers (monarchs and other heads of state), frequently winning prizes at international exhibitions. The most valuable pieces produced by the plant so far are exhibited in the **factory museum.**
FARKASGYEPŰ (7.5 km west of Herend on Rd. 8, and then a further 7 km to the north on Rd. 83) is one of the main centres of tourism of the western Bakony region, with a well-situated campsite, a tavern and the Nimród restaurant.

Pápa

161 km from Budapest on the M7, then on Rd. 8 and finally on Rd. 83; 189 km by rail (or 45 km south of Győr).

As early as the period immediately following the founding of the Hungarian state, Pápa was mentioned as being an important trading and market town, for the defence of which a castle was built. Its streets follow the contours of the former fortress system.

The effect produced by the city wall can be felt in the crowded historical centre of the town. Pápa's Baroque atmosphere came into being during 18th-century reconstruction work that took place after the Turkish occupation (1594–1683) and the fires.

In 1531 a Protestant college was founded in Pápa, and somewhat later a printing-house was established. Two prominent figures of 19th-century literature, Sándor Petőfi and Mór Jókai, were students in the town's **Protestant College;** the building itself, completed in 1797, is late Baroque and stands at **Petőfi Sándor utca 3.**

Rocks from the medieval fortified castle of Pápa were used to build the former **Esterházy Palace** which, having been completed in 1783–1784 in late Baroque style, stands in the centre of the town on **Fő tér 1**. The palace is the work of Jakab Fellner and József Grossmann. (Today it is the home of cultural and educational institutions.) One of the frescoes in the palace chapel is the work of F. A. Maulbertsch. Otto Nicolai, when he was a guest of Károly Esterházy, composed a considerable part of his opera "The Merry Wives of Windsor" here. The Baroque **Catholic Parish Church** standing in **Fő tér** was designed by Jakab Fellner and built between 1774 and 1785. A whole row of frescoes by Maulbertsch adorns the church. The **Zichy House** built in the style of Louis XVI at **No. 21** as well as the Baroque house standing at **No. 23** also deserve attention. (At **No. 12,** a Baroque house, there is a tourist office.)

A **Calvinist church,** built without towers in the second half of the 18th century, stands together with its beautiful Rococo pulpits and ecclesiastical art collection in the courtyard of the house at **Fő utca 6**. Also in Fő utca, at **No. 10** is the former Paulite and later **Benedictine church,** with its carved main altar, pulpits, and benches, built between 1737 and 1742. Today, the **Town Hall** is situated in an 18th-century, former **monastery** next door. The present façade of the Renaissance building at **Corvin utca 9,** the Corvin House, was fashioned in the 18th century. A former Baroque **Franciscan church,** built in 1721 and 1722, as well as the former **monastery building** (1715) adjoining it are historic buildings standing in **Szelestey János utca.** A rare historical monument can be found in the courtyard of the house at **Március 15. tér 12:** the **18th-century Kluge factory** for blue-dyeing cloth, with its complete furnishings. Today an interesting collection of the **Rába Blue-dyeing Museum** (Kékfestő Múzeum) is on display here.

EXCURSIONS

AJKA (36 km south of Pápa and west of Rd. 8, and then by a minor road for 5 km) is an important industrial centre. Manganese and bauxite are mined nearby, and brown coal is mined in the immediate vicinity. The town has a power-plant, a glass factory, and an aluminium factory and foundry.
DEVECSER (10 km west on Rd. 8) was already fortified at the time of the Turkish battles. The **fortified castle** of Devecser was built between 1532 and 1537, it acquired most of its present form at the end of the 18th century. Some of the peasant homes of the area are from the beginning of the last century.
SOMLÓVÁSÁRHELY (6 km from Devecser on Rd. 8), situated at the foot of the 435 m high Somló Mountain is known for its traditional grape culture and fine wine. At one time a **castle** stood on the mountain, a few **remains** of which can still be seen today on one of the small basalt cones to the north. In clear weather the highest mountain of the Bakony Range, the 713 m high Kőris Mountain, the mountains belonging to the Balaton area, and even certain peaks of the Austrian Alps can be seen from the four-storey high **Petőfi Look-out Tower,** which is built out of dark igneous rock.

EASTERN AND SOUTHERN TRANSDANUBIA

Eastern and Southern Transdanubia can be reached by taking Rd. 6 from Budapest towards the south and southwest, or by the Budapest–Pusztaszabolcs–Sárbogárd–Dombóvár–Pécs railway, or by taking roads branching off from the main Balaton and Pécs roads.

Under the present heading we shall discuss the area averaging about 50 km in width along the Danube from Budapest as far as the Yugoslav border, and the area lying between Road 61, which branches off at Dunaföldvár towards Kaposvár–Nagykanizsa, and the southern border. The northern part of this region includes a narrow strip along the Danube, the triangular area lying between Lake Velence, Budapest, and Paks (the eastern range of the so-called **Mezőföld**). The southern part of the region widens out and includes three Transdanubian counties (Tolna, Baranya and Somogy, with county towns Szekszárd, Pécs and Kaposvár respectively). South of Mezőföld lies the damp, marshy area of the **Sárköz**, the 250–280 m-high ridge of hills belonging to the **Hegyhát** (with valleys, ravines, and deep lying roads) surrounded on the west by the river Kapos and the Sió Canal, as well as the hills of Szekszárd and the so-called **Völgység** (Region of Valleys). Afterwards comes the almost 50 km long chain of mountains averaging 10–20 km in width which belong to the **Mecsek Mountains,** the highest point of which is Zengő Mountain (683 m). Romantic valleys and rocky hills offering beautiful views of the area follow one another, while natural springs, mountain streams, and caves can be found at every step of the way. The Mecsek mountains as well as the **Villány Mountains** (442 m) lying to the south of it have been known from time immemorial as famous wine-producing areas. The climate of the whole region is Mediterranean in character (early springs and long autumns).

The industrial centres of the Eastern Transdanubian territory (Százhalombatta, Dunaújváros, Pécs, Komló) are some of the most important bases of heavy industry in the country, although the smaller industrial units are also significant (the enamel-ware factory at Bonyhád, the silk mill at Tolna, the leather factory at Simontornya, the Pécs glove factory, the Paks canning factory, etc.).

History has left its marks on the appearance of Pécs, Szekszárd, Szigetvár, and Mohács, where the forces of throbbing modern life, the beauties of nature, as well as historical and cultural monuments blend harmoniously.

A number of valleys and streams (Sió, Koppány, Kapos) add colour to the Somogy Hills which spread over almost 100 km from the southern shores of the Balaton almost to the Yugoslav border. The Zselic wine-and fruit-producing area nestles between two such valleys (near Kaposvár).

Industry here takes second place to agriculture; nevertheless there are textile and clothing factories as well as plants manufacturing agricultural products. As far as tourism is concerned, the Somogy district rules the southern shores of the Balaton.

ÉRD is the first community on Rd. 6 from Budapest (Rd. 6 here crosses Rd. 70, which continues on towards Lake Velence and the Balaton.

ADONY is the realm of fishing camps. Historical monuments include the former Baroque **Zichy Palace** and a Baroque **church** built in 1772–1776. (There is a regular ferry from here to Csepel Island.)

Dunaújváros

68 km from Budapest on Rd. 6; 80 km by train.

Dunaújváros was founded in 1950 next to the village of Dunapentele. Its purpose was to serve as a settlement for a new and highly important base of heavy industry. The city's past, however, extends much further back in history, for **Dunapentele** is an ancient settlement. The Romans erected a fortification here known as Intercisa, whose purpose was to protect the provincial borders. The first Hugarian settlement appeared in the 11th to 12th centuries. Construction work uncovered the ancient remains, and archeological excavations followed.

Dunaújváros's largest industrial plant is the Danube Ironworks.

Most of the tourists who come to Dunaújváros visit the **Intercisa Museum** at **Lenin tér 10.** to inspect its collection on local history, which is particularly rich in materials excavated from the Bronze and Roman ages. The museum also exhibits documents on the construction of the town. A Baroque **Serbian church** (1748) stands in the former village of Dunapentele on **Vörös Hadsereg útja.** The city also has a pleasant outdoor swimming-pool, and indoor swimming-pool, an amusement park, a children's railway, botanical gardens, an area reserved for water sports, and a campsite.

DUNAFÖLDVÁR (20 km south of Dunaújváros on Rd. 6) is an old Danube crossing, for the protection of which a castle was built in the 16th century. The square, stocky **tower of the castle** can still be seen just off Rd. 6. A **museum of local history** has been established in the tower. Rd. 52, which connects the cent-

ral areas of the Great Plain with Transdanubia, crosses the Danube here by a bridge and is continued by Rd. 61, which crosses the southern portion of Transdanubia on its way towards Dombóvár, Kaposvár, and Nagykanizsa.
SIMONTORNYA (33.5 km west of Dunaföldvár on Rd. 61) lies where the Tolna and Somogy Hills meet. The **castle** of Simontornya, which was originally built in the 13th century and consisted only of a keep, was later enlarged in the Gothic style, and enriched with beautiful Renaissance additions. The castle houses a museum and a collection of stonework finds.
In **OZORA** (12 km west of Simontornya) the three-storey **fortified castle** was built on a square ground-plain in the early 15th century; in the 18th century the Esterházy family had the castle rebuilt in the Baroque style. (It is at present under restoration.)
PAKS (20 km south of Dunaföldvár on Rd. 6): There are two ferry crossings situated nearby. The country's first nuclear power-station is being built on the outskirts of the town. (There is an inn on the outskirts of the city next to the main road from which there is a beautiful view.)
At **DUNAKÖMLŐD,** a few kilometres north of Paks, the fishermen's inn is a favourite resting place on the main road.

Szekszárd

144 km from Budapest on Rd. 6; 148 km by rail.

Szekszárd is a typical small, Transdanubian town built partly on hills near the banks of the Sió River. One settlement after another has established itself in this area ever since the Stone Age, and during Roman times the Aquincum military route ran through here. A settlement called Alisca also stood here at that time. King Béla I founded a Benedictine monastery in Szekszárd (1601), on the ruins of which the County Hall was built much later. The Turks made it a fortified area surrounded by a series of stockades. In the 18th century Germans settled in the deserted town, and life was again revitalized, mainly through wine production. (Since the last century, red wine from Szekszárd has been appreciated throughout Europe, but wine production was already highly developed as long ago as the Roman period.)

Besides the traditional branches of industry (timber-processing, milk and meat industries), Szekszárd also produces instruments and machines as well as textiles. Wine production has naturally maintained its earlier importance.

One of the most beautiful buildings of Szekszárd is the **old County Hall** built by Mihály Pollack between 1828 and 1833. On **Castle Hill (I. Béla tér)** stands the impressive building complex of the columned neo-Classical **palace. Remains of an abbey church** from the age of Árpád as well as the **foundation wall of an early Christian sepulchral chapel** were found not long ago in the courtyard of the palace. The **Catholic Church** standing on the other side of the square is from the early 1800s. The birthplace of the poet and writer Mihály Babits is situated in **Babits Mihály utca,** which

Babits Mihály Cultural Centre, Szekszárd

begins from the square. It has today been converted into a **memorial museum**. Ferenc Liszt was a frequent guest of the former proprietors of the **Augusz House**, located at **Széchenyi utca 18,** where the great musician once gave a concert. A statue of the town's other great poet and native son, János Garay, can be seen on **Garay tér,** in the busiest part of the town (with a hotel and restaurant). (It was János Garay who created the figure of János Háry that was to become the symbol of boastfulness and that was to inspire Zoltán Kodály to compose his well-known musical drama.) The neo-Renaissance building standing on Felszabadulás tér is the **Béri Balogh Ádám Museum.** The museum's archeological collection, which is particularly rich in findings from the Stone Age and Roman age, as well as the ethnographic and local historical collections are certainly worth seeing. (The museum received its name from a *kuruc* general who was captured on the outskirts of Szekszárd by the imperial Austrian forces during the Rákóczi freedom struggle.)

A beautiful view of the surroundings opens up from **Calvary Mountain** lying to the west of the town.

EXCURSIONS

There are five communities lying in the 600 sq.km territory of the **Sárköz** (south of Szekszárd on Rd. 56 and then on a minor road to the east): **ÓCSÉNY, DECS, SÁRPILIS, ALSÓNYÉK** and **BÁTA.** Apart from their geographical proximity and the common natural endowments they share as settlements, these communities are also held together by a similar way of life as well as by an ethnographic unity resulting from the isolation they shared in the past. The characteristic national dress of the five Sárköz villages is highly colourful, with two pieces of clothing hardly ever having the same colour combination. The handwoven material and the painted furniture are also famous. Folk art has become a domestic industry in the area with many hundreds of women from the five communities being employed by the Sárköz Folk Art Co-operative whose products are in great demand both at home and abroad. A small **home museum** located in the centre of Decs provides examples of Sárköz's folk-art forms which are particularly rich in flower motifs.

The **forest of Gemenc,** the country's most beautiful and largest game-preserve, is situated south of where the Danube and Sió Canal meet in an area 30 km long by 5 to 6 km wide. This area represents the central section of forested land (almost 20 thousand hectares) lying in the basin along the Danube, which has remained in its wild, natural state and where deer, wild boar, different kinds of aquatic animals and plants indigenous to the basin live undisturbed. Old-fashioned trains leaving from the entrance take visitors around the forest.

FADD-DOMBORI (20 km northeast of Szekszárd) is a holiday resort along the 7 km long, 400 m wide backwater of the Danube with a beach, hotel, camping site and restaurant.

BONYHÁD (20 km southwest of Szekszárd on Rd. 6): A Baroque **Catholic church** built in 1769–1782 stands on the main square. A Louis-XVI-style **synagogue** (1780), as well as a **mansion** formerly belonging to the Perczel family, built in a late Baroque Louis XVI style around 1780, where Mór Perczel, a general in the 1848–1849 War of Independence was born and died, are the main attractions.

MECSEKNÁDASD (10 km south of Bonyhád on Rd. 6): 13th-century **chapel** and a Baroque **mansion** (today a school and library) from 1770. The community also has an artificial lake (an outdoor swimming-pool), a *halászcsárda* or fishermen's inn; nearby a **viaduct** spans the valley and a scenic widing road meanders over the mountain side.

PÉCSVÁRAD (11 km south of Mecseknádasd on Rd. 6) is situated at the foot of **Zengő Mountain** (682 m). The castle-like building of a former **Benedictine abbey,** founded around 1015, was completed during the 14th and 15th centuries; its lower floor is from the 11th century. (There is an exhibition as well as a tourist hostel situated in the building.) The 12th-century **cemetery chapel,** enlarged in the 15th century, is of historical interest. Pécsvárad is also a centre for tourism, for it is much easier to reach the best-known destinations of the Mecsek (Zengővár, Vöröspart, Dobogó-csúcs, etc.) from here. A lake nestling among the beautiful surroundings of Tó-völgy, 2 km from the community, is ideal for rowing.

Pécs

198 km from Budapest on Rd. 6; 229 km by train.

Pécs, one of the oldest cities in Transdanubia, was originally a Celtic settlement. At the end of the 3rd century the area now occupied by the city of Pécs and known at that time as Sopianae became the seat of the civil regent who ruled over the Roman province of Pannonia Valeria. During the 9th century, when Pécs belonged to the principality of Moravia, there were five Christian churches or chapels already standing in the city. King Stephen I made the city, which developed on the southern slope of the Mecsek, an episcopal see; and after the Mongol Invasion it was reinforced with a city wall. In 1367 the first university in Hungary (the fifth in Europe) was opened in Pécs; its activities can only be followed, with any degree of certainty, for a few years. From 1459 to 1472 the bishop of Pécs was Janus Pannonius, the internationally-known Hungarian humanist poet who wrote his poetry in Latin.

One and a half centuries of Turkish rule turned Pécs into a bustling commercial city with an oriental appearance and a lively Turkish intellectual life. (A literary trend that developed here, inspired by the activities of the "Pécs Circle", forms a separate chapter in the history of Turkish literature.) Pécs continued to remain a cultural centre, as is exemplified by the presence of the 300,000-volume University Library which houses numerous codices, incunabula, and documents relating to the Turkish age. (Its predecessor, the Klimó Collection founded in 1774, was the country's first public library.) In 1930 the Hungarian University of Arts and Sciences of Pozsony (Bratislava) was moved to Pécs. The Law and Medical Schools belonging to this university developed into an independent university in 1950. The theatre at Pécs existed as early as 1839; today it is part of the National Theatre of Pécs (Pécsi Nemzeti Színház). It is one of the country's leading theatres, whose ballet company is known throughout Europe. The collections belonging to the Janus Pannonius Museum occupy five buildings.

Industry likewise developed early in this historic city. In addition to a number of other smaller-type plants, a series of mills powered by waterfalls in the karst spring streams of Tettye were set up in the 14th century. Towards the end of the last century, heavy industrial plants as well as certain industries manufacturing luxuries (glove, porcelain, and organ factories, etc.) started to develop.

The original inner city, and its nucleus, **Széchenyi tér,** form the centre of the city on the southern slope of the Mecsek Mountains. From Széchenyi tér the various streets radiate outwards. The most interesting building in the square is the **former mosque** belonging to Gazi Kasim Pasha, which today serves as the inner city's **Catholic church.** This domed structure is Hungary's largest architectural monument from the Turkish age. It was built during the 1580s from stones of the medieval Church of St. Bartholomew. Certain features of the building, such as the prayer niche *(mihrab)* facing Mecca near the main entrance, offer clear evidence that it was originally built as a Muslim place of worship.

The other characteristic feature of Széchenyi tér is a colourful **eosinglazed well** made in the Zsolnay Porcelain Factory and erected in 1892 where a Turkish well once stood. The **archeological collection of the Janus Pannonius Museum,** also situated in this square, exhibits findings uncovered during excavations in Pécs and the surrounding areas from the Stone Age to the Magyar Conquest.

Janus Pannonius utca, in which the house at **No. 11,** the **Csontváry Museum,** exhibits works by Tivadar Csontváry Kosztka, laid out in a sawtoothed manner on the even numbered side of the square (several Baroque buildings stand here), leads towards the northwest to a veritable outdoor museum, **Dóm tér.** In the middle of the square stands one of Hungary's most important medieval historic buildings, the **Cathedral,** covering 70 m by 27 m, with four corner towers. The oldest parts of the Cathedral are a sanctuary built in the 11th century, the crypt underneath the

Dóm tér, Pécs

Cathedral, the western part of the nave, and the two western towers. The passage-ways leading to the crypts, as well as the two eastern towers, were built in the 12th century, while the series of chapels opening from the side aisles was constructed in the 14th century. The Cathedral was later rebuilt several times. Large-scale reconstruction was completed at the beginning of the last century under the direction of Mihály Pollack. The Cathedral's present appearance, which bears a strong resemblance to a building from the Romanesque period, is the result of plans inaugurated by the architect Friedrich von Schmidt between 1882 and 1891. The Renaissance, red-marble altar belonging to the **Corpus Christi Chapel,** as well as a number of frescoes and statues by notable Hungarian artists all situated inside the Cathedral, are well worth seeing. Behind the Cathedral stands the **Berényi Well** adorned with grill-work from 1739. A **collection of stonework finds** (its material is from the Cathedral), which preserves the rich Romanesque finds of the **Janus Pannonius Museum,** has been placed in a building completed to resemble a Roman house on the eastern side of the Cathedral. Opposite the southwest tower is an exceptionally valuable early Christian historic monument, the remains of a so-called **trefoil chapel** (cella trichora—4th century) adorned with frescoes. An early 4th-century Christian burial vault covered with wall paintings which resemble those found in the Roman catacombs was discovered in the eastern part of the square.

The **Bishop's Palace** on the western side of Dóm tér dates originally from the 12th century but was later rebuilt between 1752 and 1770 in the Baroque style. Its present eclectic appearance is the result of restoration that took place during the last century.

The south side of Dóm tér is occupied by Szent István tér. A round bastion (barbican) at **Esze Tamás utca 4—6,** a street beginning at Szent István

The barbican, Pécs

tér, is all that remains of the old city walls. Other historic monuments in the area are the Roman **burial vaults** (two of which are painted) situated at **Geisler Eta utca 8**.

The city's oldest two-storey residential house, of medieval origin, rebuilt in the Renaissance style during the early 16th century and enlarged with a Baroque wing in the middle of the 18th, can be seen in **Káptalan utca 2**. Today, the **Zsolnay Museum,** which forms part of the Department of Art History of the Janus Pannonius Museum, and exhibits the finest creations produced by the famous Pécs Zsolnay porcelain factory, has been given a home here. The house at **No. 3**, the birthplace of Victor Vasarely, is today the **Vasarely Museum,** where the works presented by the famous artist to his home town are exhibited.

Kulich Gyula utca, a continuation of Káptalan utca, is noted for the houses standing on the odd side of the street that were constructed along the 13th to 14th-century crenellated city wall. Remains of the wall can be seen in the courtyards of these houses. The house at **No. 5,** a Baroque building from 1731–32 with a sculptured, escutcheoned main gate, is one of these. **All Saints' Church** (Mindenszentek temploma) standing on a nearby hill in **Mindszent utca** was originally built in the middle of the 13th century but was later rebuilt in the Gothic and Baroque style in the 15th and 18th centuries respectively. During the Turkish period this building was the city's only Christian church; it was used by three different denominations and divided by partitions into three sections.

By going south from here it is possible to return to the city's main street, **Kossuth Lajos utca,** where several historic buildings are situated. The **Baroque building at No. 44** is the so-called **Lyceum Church** built in the 18th century. (Its furnishings are partly in the Rococo style.) The former **Franciscan church** standing at **Sallay utca 35,** which forms a continuation of Kossuth Lajos utca, is also for the most part from this same period. (The former monastery next door is today the Hotel Minaret.)

The 16th-century **mosque of Pasha Hassan Yakovali** at **Rákóczi út 2**, is an extraordinary historical building from the Turkish period. Preserved in an almost completely intact condition, this historic building is the only remaining Muslim place of worship in Hungary with its minaret still standing. (An exhibition displaying Turkish *objets d'art* has been placed in the mosque.)

Standing on the western outskirts of the city, the octagonal **sepulchral chapel** (türbe) of **Idris Baba** built in 1591 of natural stone and situated today in the courtyard of a children's hospital at **Nyár utca 8,** is also a Turkish monument. (There is an exhibition in the building depicting history as well as showing historic relics connected with Turkish death rites.) The city's only **well** dating from Turkish times which has remained intact is situated nearby.

Újmecsekalja is one of Pécs's most important, newer districts. It has been given the name Uranium City by the inhabitants of Pécs, since the majority of those living there are uranium miners.

Several **walks** can be taken in the immediate vicinity of the city. It is only an hour's walk from Széchenyi tér to the **Tettye Plateau** with its park, from which the whole city can be seen. Ruins of a Renaissance **summer palace,** built around 1510 and once used by the Turks as a dervish monastery, can be seen on Tettye tér. A road with yellow tourist waymarks leads from the **Dömörkapu Tourist Hostel** situated on the Mecsek to Misina Peak (543 m). The road here, which is fairly steep in places, can also be covered by bus in 30 to 40 minutes. It is certainly worth the effort: the TV-tower on the summit offers a magnificent panorama of not only the whole Mecsek, but of the mountains beyond the Drava as well. A lift in the TV-tower runs up to the look-out section above;

The minaret and mosque in Pécs

here there is also a café. (A zoo, amusement park and a camping site are situated on the way.)

EXCURSIONS

ABALIGET (20 km northwest of Pécs): There is a stalactite cave with several passages. Its entrance is situated 220 m above sea level and its main passageway is 466 m long. A small stream runs at the bottom of the cave. The climate of the cave has a healing effect due to the steady temperature, the high humidity and salt content of the steadily dripping, eroding water. (A tourist hostel, campsite, and restaurant are situated not far from the entrance to the cave. In the neighbouring community of **ORFŰ** there is a group of lakes providing opportunities for camping, rowing, swimming, and fishing.)

SZIGETVÁR (33 km west of Pécs on Rd. 6) was a fortress as early as the Middle Ages because of its strategic position. At the end of the 14th century a characteristic marsh castle was built on an island in a stream. The castle was strengthened at the beginning of the 16th century and in the summer of 1566, a Turkish army 100,000 strong, led by Sultan Suleyman, besieged the castle. A garrison consisting of barely 2,400 men led by Miklós Zrínyi managed to hold off the Turks for 33 days. Then as soon as the fortress was no longer capable of further resistance, the small garrison broke out with heroic resolution and fought in bloody hand-to-hand combat until almost the last man had fallen. (A greatgrandson of the heroic commander who was killed in the battle, the poet and general Miklós Zrínyi, immortalized the memory of the event in an epic poem.) The castle is a structure with four towers and is surrounded by stocky walls. Although it was rebuilt by the Turks, the castle nevertheless underwent centuries of neglect. (It was completely restored between 1960 and 1966.) There is a **museum of local history** located in an adjacent building, a **mosque** belonging to the castle built in 1566 (its minaret is in ruins). There is a tourist hostel in the casemates of the castle.

A **historic monument** named after Miklós Zrínyi, the castle's defender, stands in **Zrínyi tér.** Szigetvár's other mosque is also situated here. Originally built with two minarets in 1568–69, this Turkish edifice was reconstructed at the end of the 18th century and turned into a Baroque Catholic church. Several residential buildings stand around the church in the square.

BARCS is situated 31 km from Szigetvár on Rd. 6 and is a frontier crossing into Yugoslavia. (Hotel.)

HARKÁNY (26 km south of Pécs on Rd. 58) is a famous thermal spa resort lying at the southern tip of the Villány mountains. The 62–63 °C warm waters of the baths, as well as the mud containing sulphur and fluoride, are particularly useful in the treatment of articular diseases, neuritis, and chronic women's diseases. The value of the baths was discovered a century-and-a-half ago. Hotels, modern camping facilities, restaurant, and a café can be found near the bathing establishment.

Ruins of the castle of Szigetvár

For those interested in ethnography, we suggest a trip to the **Ormánság** region. The manner in which the area west of Harkány was settled as well as its architecture, way of life and dialect, have all contributed to shaping the villages along the region of the Drava (**SELLYE, VAJSZLÓ** and others) into a separate ethnic unity. The homes for the most part are constructed of wooden frames, and beautifully-painted wooden ceilings can be found in certain churches (**KÓRÓS, DRÁVAIVÁNYI**). The decorative folk art is colourful and varied.

SIKLÓS (6 km east of Harkány on a minor road) was at one time a significant Roman settlement called Seres, probably provided with a *castrum*. The **castle** was built at the turn of the 15th century; at the beginning of the 16th century it was enlarged and reinforced. For 143 years the castle was in the hands of the Turks. It acquired its present appearance at the beginning of the 18th century, and it was completely restored between 1954 and 1969. It is one of the country's few medieval fortresses that have remained almost completely intact, and has been continually inhabited ever since its construction. The quadrangular shaped castle (hotel, restaurant, tourist accommodation) houses a prison museum. The gigantic bastions, protective towers (a beautiful view of the surroundings can be seen from the bastion promenade), the gate of the barbican, and the casemates are all truly magnificent. Special attention should be paid to the **chapel** built in the first half of the 15th century. Its curtain-arched windows, fragments of old frescoes and Renaissance stone carvings make it a masterpiece of Gothic architecture. The community of Siklós has a medieval **Catholic church,** remodelled later in the Baroque style, as well as an 18th-century **Orthodox church** built in the Baroque Louis XVI style.

VILLÁNY (13 km east of Siklós) is a historical wine-producing area lying at the foot of the conical Mount Szársomlyó (422 m) where wine production flourished almost 2,000 years ago and where excellent red wines are still produced. A park of statues which is continually growing, as a result of the activities undertaken by the artists' summer camp, is an interesting sight.

The castle of Siklós

Mohács

40 km east of Pécs on Rd. 57; 60 km by rail or 190 km from Budapest on Rd. 6, then Rd. 56 (from Szekszárd); 289 km by rail from Budapest.

Busó masks from Mohács

On August 29, 1526 the armies of the Hungarian King Louis II were annihilated near Mohács by Turkish forces. This bloody battle marked the beginning of one and a half centuries of Turkish rule in Hungary. Mohács had already had a distinguished past: a Roman settlement once stood here, and following the Magyar Conquest, Mohács became an important market town. After the Turkish occupation, the population of Mohács was increased by settlements of Serbians and Germans. The town later grew in importance for transport and trade with the coming of steam shipping (one of the country's largest river harbours was built here); numerous industrial plants were also erected.

Several historic sites to be seen in Mohács recall the former battle with the Turks: a **votive church** erected on the 400th anniversary of the tragic event, in Széchenyi tér, a **memorial chapel** in Északi út, and on the outskirts of the town, a **historic monument of Louis II** who fell as he was fleeing from the battlefield. In August 1976 the **Mohács Memorial Site** (Mohácsi Történelmi Emlékhely) was established in Sátorhelyi út on the 450th anniversary of the battle. There are also several Baroque **churches** as well as the former **Bishop's Palace** (today a secondary school) which are classed as historic buildings. The school on the corner of Szabadság út and Ságvári utca is likewise a historic monument, the foundations of which were laid by the Romans. It was later used by the Turks as a bath. The **Town Museum, Szerb utca 2,** exhibits the rich findings of the large-scale excavations of the last decade which unearthed mass graves on the Mohács battlefield, as well as very interesting ethnographic materials. The Carnival Sunday Procession *(busójárás),* a popular tradition dating back many centuries, is still alive in Mohács today.

Rd. 66, running in a north–northwesterly direction, leads from Pécs to Rd. 61, which cuts across the southern part of Transdanubia.

MÁNFA (about 13 km north of Pécs on Rd. 66), Melegmányi Valley, Mély Valley, and a natural game preserve belonging to the Körlyuk and its surroundings in the immediate vicinity, are nature conservation areas. A 12th-century Romanesque **church,** rebuilt in the Gothic style, is worth seeing (outside the community about 1 km to the west).
KOMLÓ (67 km east of Mánfa): Bituminous coal was already mined in its vicinity at the end of the last century, but large-scale production began only after 1950. Today a mining city with a population of 30,000 and consisting of modern residential quarters stands next to the ancient community. Worthy of interest are the ruins of a 14th-century **Gothic church** near Kossuth tér, a geological, mineralogical and local historical exhibition belonging to the **Zrínyi Ilona Cultural Centre** in Kossuth Lajos utca. An **exhibition** on the history of the 13th-century reconstructed **Castle of Máré** has been set up among the ruins of one of the peaks along nearby **Máré Valley.** (An inn and an outdoor swimming-pool are situated near the beginning of the valley.)
DOMBÓVÁR (about 47.5 km north of Pécs, first on Rd. 66 and then on Rd. 61): Once the earthwork of an ancient settlement stood here. The **castle** of Dombóvár, which has a keep, was built after the Mongol Invasion. Today the town is a railway junction with industrial plants.

GYULAJ (25 km northeast of Dombóvár): Its forests, like those of Gemenc, are well known abroad. The paddle-shaped antlered fallow deer lives and breeds here in undisturbed solitude, and hunters come from distant lands for their sake. The world record-holder fallow deer trophy also originates from the forest of Gyulaj. On the Tamási side of the forest there is a thermal bath, a hotel, a restaurant and a boating-lake.

Kaposvár

188 km from Budapest first on Rd M7, then Rd. 7, and from Balatonlelle on Rd. 67; 194 km by rail (30 km east of Dombóvár).

Almost 80% of the residential buildings of the city of Kaposvár, which lies in the Kapos Valley, have been built since the turn of the century, thus giving the town a modern appearance. Kaposvár is nevertheless not as new as it seems, for its castle was built in the Middle Ages, and the town was the constant scene of battles during the Turkish period. Development accelerated in the 18th century when Kaposvár became the county town, and in the 19th century when the town was connected to the network of Hungarian main railway lines.

Its main thoroughfare is **Május 1. utca,** where we find the neo-Classical building of the **County Hall** (No. 10), and the so-called **Dorottya House** (No. 1) built in the late Baroque style at the end of the 18th century. (It owes its name to the fact that Mihály Csokonai Vitéz, an eminent lyrical poet at the turn of the 19th century, who spent a lot of time in Somogy, chose this house as the scene of his comic epic entitled "Dorottya".)

From the town's main square, **Kossuth Lajos tér, Ady Endre utca** leads to the old market place, where ruins of the former **Kapos Castle** can be seen. The part of the castle built during the 14th century and held by the Turks for 131 years was destroyed by the Austrian Command in the 18th century after the Rákóczi War of Independence.

The town **museum** named after a famous son, the painter József Rippl-Rónai, stands on **Rippl-Rónai tér** behind the County Hall. The picture gallery and archeological collection, an exhibition of tools and implements used by Dráva fishermen and Somogy shepherds, as well as examples of hand carved and decorative art are especially interesting.

EXCURSIONS

LAKE BALÁTA (61 km west of Kaposvár first on Rd. 61 and then on a minor road): Vegetation covering its 171-hectare surface has remained in the same state since the Ice Age. The area is for this reason a natural game preserve. (Previous permission must be obtained before visiting.)
IGAL (24 km northeast of Kaposvár) has outdoor and indoor warm-water thermal baths.
SZENNA (8.5 km south of Kaposvár): Open-air museum of folk architecture and folk-art exhibition; village church with painted coffered ceiling.

Lake Balaton

*Lake Balaton can be reached by taking the M7 from Budapest. The nor-
thern shores of the lake can be approached by taking Rd. 71 from
Balatonakarattya; the southern shores of the lake can be approached by
taking the M7 as far as Zamárdi and then taking Rd. 7 (E71).*

*By rail: the northern shores can be reached by taking the Tapolca railway
line from the Southern (Déli) Railway Station in Budapest, the southern
shores by taking the Nagykanizsa line from the same station.*

Lake Balaton lies in the middle of Transdanubia. The northern shore and the
eastern tip of the lake belong to Veszprém County while the southern shore
belong to Somogy and its western end to Zala County. The surface of the water
covers an area of 596 sq.km. The only other European lakes surpassing it in size
are those lying in the Soviet Union and Scandinavia. At its longest point the lake
stretches for 77 km; its coastline is 197 km long. The lake is 14 km wide at its
widest point, and 1.5 km at its narrowest point (between Tihany and Szántód); its
average width is 8 km. The water reaches an average depth of 2–3 m, though at
Tihany it is 12 m 40 cm deep. Since the water of the lake warms up rapidly, it is
often possible to swim there from spring until late autumn. The water of the
southern shore being much shallower than that of the northern shore, sometimes reaches a temperature of 25 °C, and for that reason is a real paradise for
children; the sands there have a velvety texture. 50 to 100 m out, the water of
the northern shore becomes colder, and the bottom of the lake is no longer
covered with very fine sand. This is why the more popular—and better-main-
tained—resort areas are more numerous along the southern shore.
The origin of the lake goes back to the Tertiary Period, a time when the area of
present Hungary was covered by sea. The remainder of this sea, Lake Pannon,
gradually became filled up with alluvial deposits of waters feeding into the lake,
and later red-hot magma broke to the surface through fissures in the rocks
underneath. As it cooled, the lava turned into basalt; and in those places where
the basalt caps that were formed protected the layers underneath, neither wind,
rainwater, nor streams on their way down could form channels in the deposits
which were to become 300–400 m high mountains later on.
After volcanic activity in the area ceased, boiling waters gushed out of the fissures, and this is, for example, how the warm-water lake of Hévíz was formed.
Effervescent springs finally appeared of which there are about twenty still in existence.
The lake bed came into existence while the depressions were being formed
about 22,000 years ago. Lake Balaton is therefore a relatively recent lake. The
lake bed was gradually filled by water from precipitation and inflowing streams,
but at that time the lake was much larger than it is today and the surface of the
water was 12 m higher.
The water along the northern shore is provided by streams and on the southern shore mainly by man-made canals. The Zala River provides the lake with the
largest quantity of water. Today the volume of the lake is 1,800 million cubic
metres, an amount which experts are trying to maintain. At Siófok, for example,
the water level, which should be maintained at 104 m 57 cm above the level of
the Adriatic, is regulated by a lock.
The Balaton's soft, mildly alkaline water combines the effects of effervescent
baths as well as those of sun-bathing and pelotherapy. Waves—relatively short
(7–10 m) but strong and therefore dangerous—roll in rather rapidly during
windy weather and storms (the highest wave so far measured reached 1.8 m).
Storm approach is signalled by yellow or red flares; on seeing a red flare, swim-
mers and persons on water vehicles must leave the water immediately. In winter
the lake is mostly frozen over and is suitable for winter sports as soon as the
thickness of the ice reaches 15 cm. (The average thickness of the ice is between
25–30 cm; the thickest ice measured since the turn of the century was 75 cm.)
Physical phenomena appearing on the Balaton after it is frozen over are as follows: **cracking** (when narrow gaps appear in the ice along with immense cracking activity), **accumulation** (when the ice piles up along the cracks), **crevassing**
(when melting activity begins and white streaks full of water spread out along
the cracks over the entire surface of the lake. Walking on the ice is not recommended at this time.)
Vast expanses of reeds covering certain areas along the shores are characteristic of the type of vegetation found on the Balaton. When the lake is frozen
over, the reeds are harvested with sharp push-scythes and used for building

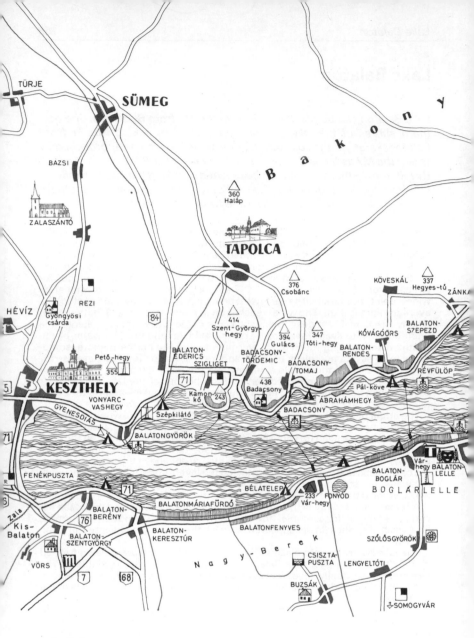

Lake Balaton

material as was the custom in the past. Seaweed, another characteristic form of vegetation, forms veritable fields in certain places.

There are 42 different kinds of fish in the lake, the tastiest being the giant pike-perch *(fogas)*. A predatory fish living there is the European wels. The common eel has been introduced there only recently. The lake abounds in carp, razor-fish and bream.

The climate at the Balaton is agreeable, the number of summer days surpassing 25 °C averaging about 70, while the water temperature in the summer is from 22 ° to 25 °C. The peak season in the summer lasts from June to the end of August. Solar radiation reflected from the surface of the water greatly increases the effects of sunlight and one should therefore exercise considerable caution when sunbathing.

The sporting season on the Balaton begins around the middle of May with the festivities at Balatonfüred, with the launching of a sail-boat race. Sailing on the Balaton is more than 100 years old. Today there are almost 1,500 sail-boats from the smallest dinghy to large ships with sails covering 54 sq.m. The largest sporting event held every two years involves circumnavigating the lake for the Balaton Blue Ribbon. International sporting events are also held, especially in the

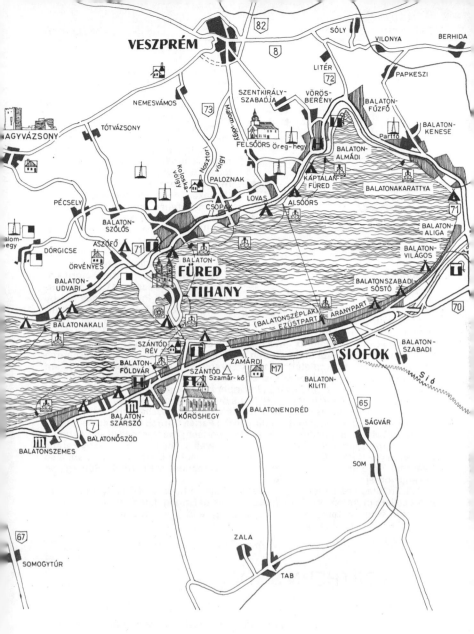

star ship and Dutch ship division. Schools for sailing and other water sports are situated in Balatonfüred, Siófok, and Tihany. (Motorboats are not allowed on the lake.) Besides rowing and fishing, there are also possibilities for horse-riding. Horses can be rented at the Tihany, Keszthely, Siófok, Nagyvázsony, Zamárdi, and Szántód riding schools, and riding trips lasting several days can be taken. During the winter season skating, and other winter sports are popular on the Balaton.

A historical sketch: Evidence of ancient settlements is provided by a 40,000-year-old mine from which dyes were extracted, as well as one used about 6,000 years ago for gathering flint found on the outskirts of the communities of **LOVAS** and **SÜMEG** respectively. Tools and vessels belonging to Stone, Copper, and Bronze Age man can be seen in the museums of the area, and implements from the Iron Age are preserved by the earthwork in Tihany and Balatonföldvár.

The fortified city of Valcum (next to Keszthely in **FENÉKPUSZTA**) was the largest Roman settlement of the area. After the Romans left, the settlement became a centre first for the Huns and later the Visigoths; and according to research, King Theodoric the Great, conqueror of Italy, was born here. Lombards and Avars followed the Goths, and finally the Slavs moved into the area (the pre-

Balaton

sent village of **ZALAVÁR,** for example, was a centre for the Slav principality). The name Balaton is attributed to the Slavs (the word "blatno" meaning stagnant, swampy water).

Following the Magyar Conquest of the country (A.D. 896) and the founding of the Hungarian state, monasteries, churches, and almost 200 villages (of which only 54 have remained) were built in the vicinity of the lake. The Balaton served as an excellent defence line for a long time, and the Turks were not able to gain a foothold on the northern shores. Remains of the border castles (Tihany, Nagyvázsony, Szigliget, Fonyód) testify to the battles fought here.

The *kuruc* soldiers won victories at Kenese and the castle of Csobánc during the War of Independence led by Ferenc Rákóczi II. After the War of Independence was defeated, the Habsburg regime destroyed most of the castles. At the end of World War II, the last line of defence for the German fascist armies in Hungary extended along the Balaton.

More **historic monuments** have remained on the northern shore than on the southern side. The crypt of the church of Tihany, the church of Hévíz, the church that has remained completely intact at Egregy, as well as the one at Türje are Romanesque. The church of Kőröshegy on the southern shores of the lake, the churches in Balatonszemes and Balatonberény, the partly renovated castle of Nagyvázsony, the church of Kinizsi, ruins of a Paulite monastery in Salföld, and the Parish Church of Keszthely, with its 15th-century frescoes, are Gothic.

The most beautiful Baroque building is the **Parish Church of Sümeg** decorated by the valuable wall-paintings of F. A. Maulbertsch; the frescoes of an unknown master in the church of Balatonkeresztúr, as well as the ones painted by Ferenc Bucher in the Roman Catholic church of Vörösberény (Balatonalmádi) are also beautiful. Among the mansions worth a visit are those at Keszthely, Sümeg and Lesencetomaj.

Folk architecture is represented by the peasant houses of Tihany, the row of wine cellars in Aszófő-Vörösmál, the houses of Szigliget, the regional home in Zamárdi, Nagyvázsony, Balatonszentgyörgy and Vörs, and the wine cellars along the northern shores.

THE NORTHERN SHORE

The northern shore is spread out along the Balaton from Balatonakarattya to Keszthely (Rd. 71).

Balatonakarattya

About 100 km from Budapest on the M7 (or on Rd. 70) and then on Rd. 71.

The bathing resort of Balatonakarattya has merged with **Balatonkenese,** to which it also belongs administratively. The community consists of two sections: the old Akarattya and the growing week-end settlement belonging to what is called Gáspár-telep. As early as 1109 a small community by the name Terra Akaratia is mentioned by a document. It was completely destroyed by the Turks, and only since 1817 has it regained its old name.

For 400 years an elm tree stood in **Rákóczi tér** that the people named Rákóczi Tree because of the belief that the prince actually tied his horse to it. Ferenc Rákóczi II, however, never came this way, only his soldiers who, under the leadership of Ádám Béri Balogh, beat the *labanc* here in 1707. Only the trunk of the famous tree exists today and it is preserved as a natural historic landmark.

Balatonkenese

4 km from Balatonakarattya on Rd. 71.

The community of Balatonkenese began to develop in 1910 after the railway line had been constructed. The tower of the community's Baroque **Calvinist church,** built between 1658 and 1660 and remodelled in the 19th century, was originally Gothic. Houses of historic character and houses displaying the features of folk architecture can be found in **Bajcsy-Zsilinszky utca 42** and **51, Fő utca 32** and **36, Kossuth Lajos utca 6, 16, 40** and **Ságvári utca 16** and **Táncsics Mihály utca 25.** The school beside the Calvinist church houses a collection of local history.

A yellow waymark points the way from the railway station to a high point called **Partfő,** which offers a beautiful view of the lake all the way to Tihany. The *tátorján (Crambe tataria),* admired by nature-lovers because of its white grape-shaped flowers, blooms here in May. The flower is also called "Tartar bread" since according to popular tradition, the stake-like roots of the flower were roasted and eaten in place of bread during the time of the Tartar or Mongol Invasion of 1241–42.

The two openings that appear so dark on the high clay banks are the so-called **Turkish Holes** or **Tartar Holes.** Tradition has it that persons fleeing from the Tartars and Turks during the invasions hollowed out crevices for themselves here. But it is not merely a popular belief, for it is confirmed by an official report of 1670. Poverty-stricken persons lived here until the end of the last century. Today, the town has a modern beach.

Balatonfűzfő

8 km from Balatonkenese on Rd. 71.

The industrial settlement of Balatonfűzfő (nitro-chemical plant) is the only community on the Balaton which is not a holiday resort. In the 11th century it was an ecclesiastical estate. **Ruins** of a small, former **church** built in the Romanesque style stand in **Jókai Mór utca 39.** Renovated in 1964, this church is representative of the simplest type of village church. The interior, which is built from hard lime-stone, consists of a nave with a rectangular ground plan and a square sanctuary. The sanctuary walls stand at almost their original height with a tympanum over the triumphal arch. Also standing at almost their original height are sections of the nave's northern and southern walls with the traces of two windows.

Steps beginning at the small church pass through a park and lead down to the centre of the community, the railway station, to the east of which the beach is situated.

The first **amateur observatory club** to be established in the Balaton region can be found in Balatonfűzfő; the club's domed building can be seen from the main road. The only **rifle range** of the lake region (reached from Rd. 72), also used for clay pigeon shooting, is situated here. Sporting guns can be rented and ammunition can be bought on the spot at the well-equipped shooting range. There is also a large Olympic-size swimming-pool.

EXCURSIONS

LITÉR (4 km north of Balatonfűzfő on Rd. 72): The arched southern gate of the **Calvinist church** originally built in the 13th century, rebuilt at the end of the 18th century in the Baroque style is of unique value. Each pillar on the outside of the gate rests on a reclining lion and the statue of an apostle stands on each of the pair of pillars on the inside.

VILONYA (6 km east of Litér): The Romanesque sanctuary of its ancient church surrounded by a stone wall was built in the 13th century; its southern gate is late Gothic. Beside the church is a 15th-century presbytery and the vaulted basement constructed from stone is from the 15th century. A wide panorama is visible from the top of **Sukoró Mountain** (253 m).

The ancient villages belonging to the region around Veszprém can be easily reached on Rd. 72.

SÓLY (4.5 km east of Rd. 72 on main Rd. 8) is the oldest of these communities. It is already mentioned in a document dating from 1009. A chapel built at that time is today a **Calvinist church.** (The former ceiling with its painted coffers can be seen today in the Museum of Applied Arts, in Budapest.)

Balatonalmádi

112 km from Budapest on the M7 and then on Rd. 71; 117 km by rail.

The soil of this region originates from the residue of red Permian sandstone. The red sandstone extracted from the soil serves as excellent building material. Good grape yields also result from the valuable soil.

The settlement is first mentioned by a manuscript in 1488 as Kisberény. In Turkish times the community was almost destroyed; however, in the beginning of the 17th century, it was annexed to Vörösberény. The situation, however, was reversed during the past one hundred years when the development of Balatonalmádi started to overshadow that of Vörösberény and as a consequence, the latter finally merged into the former. Balatonalmádi's development into a bathing resort started in 1877. The well-known Kneipp-Rikli treatment was first introduced here. The wooden houses once used for treatment are still standing today and are used as holiday cabins.

A point of interest in Balatonalmádi is the **Catholic church** built in 1930, to which was added the Chapel of the Holy Right Hand (of Stephen I, the first king of the country), following its removal from the Fortress of Buda. The mosaic wall was designed by Károly Lotz.

The **railway station** forms the **centre** of this bathing community. The square in front is occupied by the **Auróra** Hotel and Restaurant, a department store, a pastry shop, a hotel, and a bus station. A motel is situated west of the beach, followed by a playground and a first-class camping area.

The **Kék Balaton Inn** stands east of Marx tér. On the other side of the railway station are **water sports establishments** and the **beaches** of Budatava (there is a restaurant as well).

Budai Nagy Antal utca leads to the so-called **Öreg-hegy** (Old Mountain), on the top of which stands a **look-out tower.** A beautiful view in the direction of Balatonkenese and Tihany can be had from the balcony.

Little summer cottages surrounded by pine trees and oaks stand in the small forest of **KÁPTALANFÜRED,** an isolated summer resort area. A yellow waymark leads from Káptalanfüred to the **Szabadság Look-out Tower.**
VÖRÖSBERÉNY, which has merged with Balatonalmádi, is mentioned for the first time by a manuscript in 1109 under the name Szárberény. Its present name, which is obviously connected with the reddish soil of the area (vörös=red) has been known since the 16th century.

Historical monuments: a splendid red, white and grey Baroque **Catholic church** and a former **Jesuit monastery** (1777–79) standing beside it. The valuable frescoes of the church (G. Buffleur, around 1770) were recently restored.

A **Calvinist church** dating back to the Middle Ages stands on a small rise in the centre of the community. Surrounded by a 13th-century stone wall, it is the only fortified church of the lake region. The original church was enlarged in the Middle Ages by a side-aisle situated on the south end, and a stocky tower was built in front. Between 1612 and 1614 the church was rebuilt by the Protestants, and in 1789 it was again reconstructed.

The house standing at **Malomvölgyi út 14** (1825) is an interesting example of folk architecture.

SZENTKIRÁLYSZABADJA also belongs administratively to Balatonalmádi. A medieval **Catholic church** built of red stone stands on the eastern outskirts of the community on a small elevation. The tower of the church is Gothic, while the nave was rebuilt in 1789 and 1914 in a Baroque and neo-Romanesque style respectively. A beautiful part of the church is the entrance dating back to the Middle Ages. Above the entrance can be seen the coat of arms belonging to the Rátold family, who founded the church.

There are two **manor houses** in the community: one of them was built in the 18th century in the Baroque style, while the other was built at the beginning of the 20th century in the neo-Gothic style.

It was in Szentkirályszabadja that Miklós Radnóti wrote his last poem. Miklós Radnóti was a great lyric poet who, at the end of the Second World War, was driven through here on a forced march towards the west, together with his companions, by the fascists. He was shot in the community of Abda in Győr County. When his body was exhumed, a notebook, known as the "Bori Notebook", which contained his last poems, was found in his pocket. A **memorial plaque** on the house at **Kossuth Lajos utca 20,** the building housing the community library, commemorates the tragic event.

By following a yellow waymark leading from Szentkirályszabadja, it is an hour's walk to the **Garden of Ruins** (Romkert), where building remains dating back to Roman times can be found.

FELSŐÖRS (6 km from Balatonalmádi) lies on the stony terrain above Malomvölgy. The community's main point of interest is a stocky-towered **medieval church** built at the middle of the 13th century of local red stone. It is situated where an 11th-century church once stood. A new church with one nave was first built onto the tower of the older church followed by a church with three naves. In 1552 the church was burnt down by the Turks and was not rebuilt until the 18th century. Restorations completed in 1968 gave back the church its original beauty.

The most valuable part of the church, the gateway to the tower, is lined on both sides by beautifully carved, 14th-century pillars and columns. A carved edge rounds above the pointed ridge of the roof, and above that are three semicircular windows separated from one another by knotted pairs of columns, so-called "Hercules knots" which indicates medieval origin. The tower, which has a square base, becomes octagonal above the windows and is crowned with a decorative dome. The coupled windows, found during restoration, provide the aisle with light. Upon entering the church through the gateway, we reach a small vestibule where a covered sepulchre is supported by three splendidly carved stones. A triumphal arch built out of red stone is the first item one catches sight of in the main nave and this is followed by the ceiling of the sanctuary. The pillars are Baroque, and the pews date from the 18th century. The beautiful pulpit is an outstanding creation of peasant Baroque (1743). In the sanctuary is the decorative stall of the provost. The picture on the main altar depicts the church's patron saint, Mary Magdalene.

The year 1748 can be read above the gateway to the building opposite the church, once the seat of the provost.

A walk from Felsőörs, from the plateau in front of the church, leads to **Malomvölgy** (Mill Valley.) The walk leads to **Királykúti-völgy** (Valley of the Royal Well), and a road takes one to the Királykúti springs. (According to popular tradition, King Matthias once watered his horse here while hunting, hence its name.)

The red sandstone seen all over Felsőörs and Alsóörs is used to build homes, fences, small bridges above the ditches along roads, ditch banks, and the brims of wells.

ALSÓÖRS (9.5 km from Balatonalmádi on Rd. 71) is mentioned for the first time in 1290 in a manuscript as property belonging to the queen. It was here that her treasurers lived and took care of the red-stone mines, the stone of which was carved into the highly important mill stones. The mines at the foot of Cser Mountain still offer an interesting sight.

The street running through the bathing area is **Vörös Hadsereg útja. Endrődi Sándor utca,** a road leading into the community, branches off from the above-mentioned road. It is named after a pioneer of sailing on the Balaton, who used to spend his summers here. A park stretches below the road all the way to the Balaton (first-class camping grounds with a beach are situated to the east, followed by a cinema, a self-service restaurant, a row of shops, and a general department store). A memorial to the Soviet pilots who died here in 1945 as well as one commemorating steamship navigation on the Balaton (1846) stand in the park situated in front of the pier.

The **Calvinist Church** standing on the side of **Somló Mountain** dates back to the Middle Ages (first mentioned in a manuscript dated 1318). Its entrance dates from the 15th century, while the painted wooden ceiling of the choir is from 1720–23. The church has received its present shape since 1788.

On a small rise at **Petőfi köz 7** stands a building called the **"house of the Turkish tax collectors"** which is so named after the turban-like end of the chimney. The house was built around 1500 and represents a rare example of a Gothic manor house. A large basement and a carved archway built in the late Gothic style extend underneath.

The **Szabadság Look-out Tower** rises above the community, on the top of Cserelak Mountain (283 m). By following a blue waymark one is able to reach it after an hour's leisurely walk. A beautiful view of the whole region opens from the balcony of the 8 m high red-stone tower.

The basement shelters with carved doors and frontal decorations on the mountain planted with vineyards are beautiful examples of folk architecture.

LOVAS (1.5 km from Alsóörs) is known by archeologists because of the discovery of one of the world's oldest mines here. While mining operations were being carried out in this area for dolomite graves, bone implements came to light in one of the mines in the tracks left by a shovel. It was established that these implements were used for working the mine and are at least 35,000 to 40,000 years old. Early man moulded the reddish material he mined here with fat into globules and used them for body ornamentation as well as for other cultic purposes. The tools, mining implements, hewers, chisels and horns used for holding paints were constructed out of the bones of animals that lived at the end of the Ice Age but disappeared soon after.

PALOZNAK (2.3 km from Lovas) has a **Catholic church** originally built in the 13th century but rebuilt several times since. (There is a large open-air pool with parking facilities, and a campsite.)

CSOPAK (2 km from Paloznak) lies at the opening of a beautiful valley. Because of its good bathing facilities and carbonic waters, the community is receiving more and more visitors. The railway station forms the centre of the town, with the new buildings belonging to the bathing establishment extending to the south. The older section of the community is located to the north. **Ruins of the medieval church** belonging to the community of **Kövesd** can be seen in the courtyard of **Kossuth Lajos utca 19**. The door of the square-ended stone fence has remained intact.

The **Calvinist church** is late Baroque, while what is called the **Ranolder-villa** is built in the Romantic style (today the central office of the county **plant-protecting station**). In front stand a neo-Classical **wine-cellar** and **tavern**. Mentioned for the first time in 1266, the tower of the **Church of St. Stephen** stands in its remodelled state in front of the community's town hall. Opposite the tower on the far side of the valley, the waters of the **Nosztori Stream** propel the wheel of a **water-mill**. Earlier a water-mill and *csárda* once stood where the **Malom csárda**, furnished with folk motifs, is now standing at the entrance to the valley. Wine presses with stucco ornamentations can be seen on the vineyard-dotted mountain-side which grows the splendid wines of Csopak (Olaszrizling, Furmint).

Fürdő utca leads from the railway station to the beach (restaurant, summer cinema), where carbonic waters flow from a well next to the enclosure. A cellar dating back to the Roman age as well as Roman sepulchre-chests were found above the beach on what is called **Stone Sarcophagus Hill**. The look-out tower on **Csákány Mountain** above Road 71 offers a beautiful view of the area.

Balatonfüred

126 km from Budapest on the M7 (70) and then on Rd. 71; 132 km by rail.

People have come to Balatonfüred for medicinal treatments and bathing for almost 250 years. As early as the 18th century the mineral waters coming from the carbonic springs were employed against stomach ailments, and then—by mixing it with the whey produced from goat's milk—the water was used for curing lung diseases. It is during the present century that the waters have effectively been applied to the treatment of cardiac and circulatory diseases.

Foundations of Roman villas are constantly being unearthed, but there is no evidence as to whether or not the

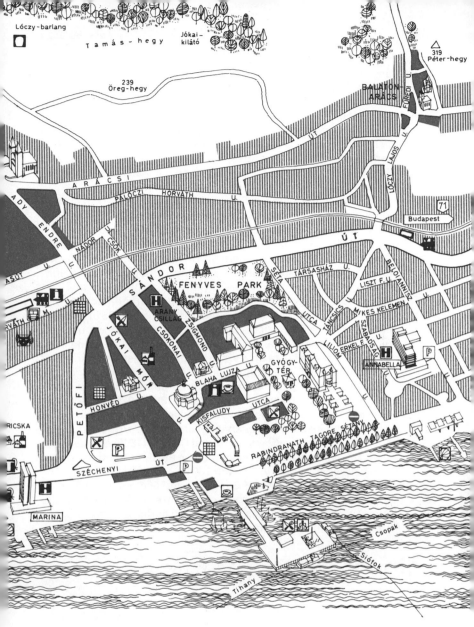

Balatonfüred

Romans actually made use of the mineral waters. In 1772 the waters from the springs were analysed and the area was made into a thermal bathing establishment with its own physician.

In 1945, the private sanatorium that existed here became a state hospital, and a whole series of new sanatorium buildings and summer rest homes have been built.

Between 1825 and 1848 political and cultural leaders of the movement for independence regularly met in Balatonfüred, and in 1846 the first steamship ever to travel on the Balaton set out from here.

The most important buildings are located on **Gyógy tér,** the central part of the square being occupied by a **well room** built in 1800 and later named after Lajos Kossuth. Five springs flow here, four of them serving the hospital, and the Kossuth Spring, which is open to the general public between May 1 and September 30. Almost 10,000 patients are treated in the **State Hospital** each year, and every day 500 to 600 patients are cared for in the baths adjoining the hospital.

The large building-complex of the SZOT (National Council of Trade Unions) Sanatorium, closed off on the north by a square, provides follow-up treatments for patients suffering from cardiac diseases. "Anna Balls" and various kinds of cultural events are held today in its large hall. The first Anna Ball was celebrated in 1825, and it has since become the social event of the year; it is held on Anna Day in July. Memorial plaques to Hungarian and foreign celebrities, scholars, writers, musicians, and others who have stayed here are displayed on the walls of the **Balaton Pantheon** in the building's arched, circular promenade.

A statue by Zsigmond Kisfaludi Strobl adorns the small park in front of the building. It was here that the first permanent Hungarian-language theatre in Transdanubia was erected in 1831. In 1878 the theatre was torn down and in its place another was built in the Kiserdő (Small Forest). Six columns from the original theatre, standing in their original location, pay tribute to the theatrical pioneers involved in the introduction of the Hungarian language on stage.

The square is closed off on the south by the **Horváth House.** The Szentgyörgyi-Horváth family had the building erected in 1798 in the style of Louis XVI and in the first half of the 19th century it became a place of resort for the country's outstanding political and cultural personalities.

All the houses in **Blaha Lujza utca** are of historic interest. On the right of the Sanatorium of the Trade Union Council stands a **pharmacy** established in 1782. The neo-Classical style **summer home** of the "sweetest song-bird of the land", the actress **Lujza Blaha** (1850–1925) is also a historic monument. The building housing the **Kedves confectioner's,** which has a modern décor inside but preserves its original form on the outside, dates back to 1795. The neo-Classical **Round Church** (1846) stands at the end of the street. The picture on the side altar on the right-hand side of the church was painted by János Vaszary in 1891.

The large park situated south of Gyógy tér and laid out in 1865 on an embankment is bordered by four rows of plane trees. (At the end of the rows of trees is situated the large **town beach,** and across from it, the **Hotel Annabella.**) In the park is the statue entitled **"Girl Playing a Lute"** by

Drinking-well of the Kossuth medicinal spring, Balatonfüred

Ferenc Medgyessy (1957), one of **István Széchenyi** (by János Andrássy Kurta, 1941), **a memorial bench to Lujza Blaha, the bronze statue of the poet Sándor Kisfaludy** (1772–1844) and **the statue of Rabindranath Tagore** (the Nobel Prize-winner Indian poet), are especially noteworthy. Tagore came to Balatonfüred in 1926 for treatment, and in memory of his stay he planted a lime tree and wrote a poem here. On his initiative, treeplanting has become a tradition and a **memorial grove** has already taken shape.

Hotel Marina, Balatonfüred

The other large hotel in Balatonfüred, the **Hotel Marina,** as well as the **Baricska** and **Hordó csárda** can be found past the glass-fronted exhibition hall of the **Balaton Gallery** and the sailing club houses in Széchenyi út west of the harbour. Beyond the hotel is the campsite where the 27th World Reunion of the F.I.C.C. ("Fédération Internationale des Clubs de Camping") was held in 1966. The **Hotel Margaréta** is also located in Széchenyi út.

The great novelist **Mór Jókai** (1825–1904) spent 22 summers in the **villa** he once owned opposite the Round Church on the corner of Jókai Mór utca, a street leading up to the town. Jókai's personal belongings, and documents related to his life and literary activities, can be seen here.

Jókai Mór and Horváth Mihály utca (outdoor theatre) continue past the railway crossing as **Ady Endre utca.** (The house at **No. 13** was built in 1785 and was formerly owned by the poet Ádám Pálóczi Horváth. (The **Catholic church** with its two towers at the beginning of Kossuth Lajos utca is of interest because it was built of the red stone characteristic of the area.

The **Calvinist church,** built in the style of Louis XVI (1829) as well as most of the houses situated around it are historic monuments. **Siske utca,** the oldest street in Balatonfüred, begins at the church and contains monuments of folk architecture **(Nos. 21, 29/a, 40, 45,** and **49).** A house standing on the corner of Siske utca and **Vázsonyi utca 1** is also a folk monument. (This area was once the centre of the town.)

Two beautiful buildings can be seen in the eastern part of Balatonfüred (towards the former Balatonarács) in **Arácsi út:** the Baroque **Gombás Mansion** at **No. 94** and the building at the end of the street, today a technical institute for horticulture, built in 1782 by Ferenc Széchényi, the founder of the Hungarian National Museum.

The **Balatonarács Catholic** and **Calvinist churches** are both protected monuments dating from the 18th century. The most beautiful house of the community is perhaps the one at **Lóczy Lajos utca 68,** which is adorned with a porch supported by pillars. The edelweiss which the world traveller Aurél Stein sent from the Himalayas for the grave of Lajos Lóczy (1849–1920), a pioneer of research on the Balaton, can be seen underneath a glass plate on Lóczy's red **gravestone** in the old cemetery of Arács.

EXCURSIONS

The valleys in the vicinity of Balatonfüred: the Siske, Kéki, Koloska, and Nosztur, offer wonderful opportunities for excursions. The 120 m long **Lóczy Caves**, which are electrically lit, lie in Kéki Valley. By following a green waymark from the Lóczy Caves, it is about three hours' walk to the **Noszlopy Look-out Tower** on Recsek Mountain (430 m). From here there is a splendid view of the Bakony mountains and Lake Balaton.

Koloska Valley, a nature conservation area, is wide at its entrance but narrows on reaching the **Koloska csárda;** a path through the shady forest leads to the most beautiful part of the valley, a small clearing at **Koloska Springs,** below high precipices. A red waymark points the way along a road leading from the fresh, cold-water springs (rain shelters, tables, benches, and places for barbecues) to the **Noszlopy Look-out Tower** (2.5 hours).

The **Jókai Mór Look-out Tower** on top of **Tamás Hill** (317 m), which rises above the town, can be reached in an hour by following a blue waymark from Arácsi út. From here the eastern basin of Lake Balaton can be seen.

Nagyvázsony

20 km northwest of Balatonfüred or 21 km southwest of Veszprém, along the main road.

At the beginning of the 15th century, a certain Vezsenyi family, who owned the area, built the nucleus of the castle, the keep. In 1462 the castle passed as a gift from King Matthias into the ownership of Pál Kinizsi, who, starting as a local miller's assistant, became a famous military leader. The fortress, which owes its present form to him, became a border castle in the 16th and 17th centuries, and survived the wars which followed in a relatively good condition. The castle's keep was used from the middle of the 18th century as a prison. During the 19th century it gradually began to deteriorate, and it was not until the years between 1952 and 1960 that excavations and restoration work began.

The inner courtyard can be reached by crossing the bridge lying over the moat that once existed here. The keep, 28 m high, is situated in the inner courtyard. The former prison can be seen at the base of the keep. The upper rooms—restored and furnished in accordance with their former purposes—now serve as **the historic museum of the castle.** A magnificent view opens up from the uppermost balcony.

The remains of the red marble **tomb monument of Pál Kinizsi** is in the middle of the restored building of the **fortress chapel.** A few objects once belonging to Kinizsi as well as some documents connected with the history of his time can also be seen in the chapel.

An **equestrian statue** of Pál Kinizsi (by Iván Szabó) stands in the square in front of the castle. A number of historic buildings in traditional style are situated around the castle. A **tourist hostel** has been established in one of them, while another houses a **post-office museum** in memory of the time when post-horses were once changed in Nagyvázsony. The peasant house and estate built in 1825 at **Bercsényi utca 21,** today serves as an **outdoor village museum.** A small **Lutheran church** (built in 1796) stands south of the castle. Ruins of a **Pauline monastery** and **church** established by Kinizsi have been discovered and preserved on the outskirts of the community. The monastery, built in the 1480s, where a series of valuable codices were written (4 have remained), was blown up in 1552. During Kinizsi's time there was also a carver's workshop in Nagyvázsony, works from which are preserved in a number of churches in the area.

A **mansion** (today a hotel) built at the end of the 19th century stands in the park (tournaments, jumping contests) located on the other side of **Séd Stream** which runs below the castle. Guests interested in the riding-school or who come to see the colourful tournaments organized here on the first week-end in August are accommodated in the school or in the hotel.

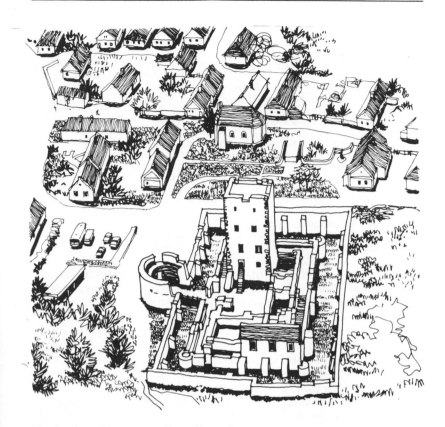

The Castle and its surroundings, Nagyvázsony

The **Church of St. Stephen** that Pál Kinizsi had built (1481) where a smaller 14th-century church formerly stood, is situated at a bend in the main road. The church was rebuilt in the Baroque style during the 1740s. Its reticulated vaulting and pointed tracery windows are original. An interesting contrast is presented by the excellent Baroque altars.

Tihany

11 km from Balatonfüred; no railway station; reached by bus or by boat and motor-ferry connections from the southern shore at Szántód.

The Tihany peninsula, stretching far into the Balaton, can be seen from a considerable distance. The ancient community of Tihany lies on a prominent point of this peninsula. The peninsula itself is joined to the hilly region by marshy meadows, and centuries ago there was only one narrow road leading into the area which could for this reason be easily protected. As it was secluded for so long and is particularly rich in natural endowments, the region has preserved its appeal.

In 1952, the peninsula was declared a national park and the first natural conservation zone in Hungary was developed here.

Interesting facts about the history of Tihany, the inhabitants, the land itself, its animal and plant life have already been compiled in works that would fill a library, but nevertheless new discoveries are constantly being made. Besides its splendid situation, Tihany owes its appeal to its other natural endowments. The basalt tuff covering the hills of the peninsula was formed from volcanic dust, from the rubble of volcanoes that erupted in the Tihany area. Warm-water springs later burst out and it is from the deposits and mineral matter left by these that the more than 160 cones belonging to the hot-water springs originate. Wind and rain formed two lake basins, the Inner (Belső) Lake and the Outer (Külső) Lake, which still exist in the middle of the peninsula. (Both are nature conservation areas.)

The peninsula was inhabited as long ago as the early Iron Age. An earth-work has remained from this period. Later Roman villas were built here.

The first written mention of the community of Tihany dates from 1055. It was at that time that King Andrew I founded a Benedictine abbey here. (The king himself was buried in the crypt of the Abbey Church in 1060. It is the only royal grave of the House of Árpád which stands in its original place.) Almost 100 Hungarian words occur in the Latin text of the deed of foundation (see p. 115, Pannonhalma). Andrew I was responsible for bringing Russian monks into the area. The cells which they hollowed out in the rocky walls of the Old Castle (Óvár) can still be seen. Near the cells are springs which people have named the *Russian Well* (Oroszkút) in memory of these Russian monks. In 1267 a fortress was built around the Abbey Church, and this fortress became an important border castle in the wars against the Turks. The fortress was demolished by the Habsburg forces in 1702. Towards the end of the 1848–49 War of Independence the Hungarian government began to strengthen the fortress, but soon afterwards this had to be interrupted. Traces of a conduit begun at that time can still be seen.

Tihany has three main points of interest, the Central (Belső) harbour and its surroundings, the Abbey Church, and the ferry port. On warm summer days the Central harbour situated on the east side of the peninsula is the scene of heavy traffic. The Sport Restaurant is situated next to the harbour, and behind this domed building there is a semicircular row of shops. Research in the Balaton's animal world is carried on in the **Biological Institute of the Hungarian Academy of Sciences**. The winding **Kvassay Promenade** leads from the harbour to an 80 m high plateau where the church stands with its two towers. The winding road ends at **Pisky István Promenade,** which leads to the church past 100 to 150-year-old peasant houses. The promenade offers a breathtaking view of the lake and its northern shore.

At one time there was to hear an echo of up to 16 syllables produced from **Echo Hill** which rises to the right of where the winding road ends. Today the echo produced here is weak, which can be explained partly by the considerable building activity, partly by the ever increasing density of the vegetation, but mainly by the noise produced by motor vehicles.

The **House of the Fishermen's Guild,** one of the peasant houses standing along Pisky Promenade, is a museum of old fishing implements and mementoes. (There were at one time many fishermen in the village.) The complete furnishings of a Tihany farmer's house, along with his personal belongings and tools, can be seen in the white peasant house next to the museum. (Folklore performances are held in the courtyard on an outdoor stage.) A woman potter's works are on display in the third house. (In September her work is sold in the courtyard.) Exhibitions are also held in the fourth house.

The **Abbey Church** with its two towers was built between 1719 and 1754. Its oldest section is the Romanesque crypt supported by stocky columns dating from 1055, with the white marble-covered grave of King Andrew I.

The main points of interest inside the Baroque church are the specially carved furnishings (pulpits, altars, the screen on the organ loft, the furniture in the sacristy), which the wood-carver Sebestyén Stulhoff made between 1753 and 1765. After the early death of his fiancée, Stulhoff lived and worked as a lay brother in Tihany monastery until his death. (According to local tradition, he preserved the memory of his fiancée's features in the face of the angel kneeling on the right side of the first altar on the left, the "Altar of the Virgin Mary".) While the church was being remodelled at the end of the 19th century, some of the most outstanding artists of that period, Bertalan Székely, Károly Lotz and Lajos Deák-Ébner, adorned the

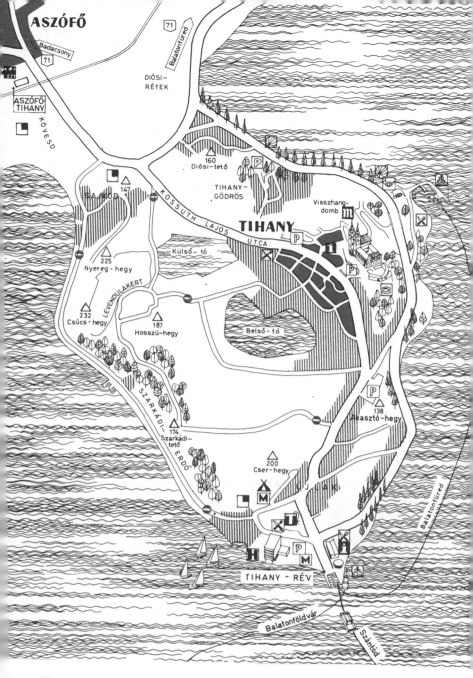

Tihany

interior with their frescoes. During the months of June, July, and August organ concerts are held in the church every Tuesday and Wednesday. Each evening the church and its towers are flood-lit.

The **former abbey building** adjoining the church is now a **museum,** whose object is to introduce the Balaton region. Photographic exhibitions are staged on the ground floor. The rooms on the first floor house temporary exhibitions. A beautiful view of the lake can be seen from the east windows of the first floor corridor. Residents of Tihany claim that whoever looks down from here for the first time and sighs deeply will have his wish come true.

The Abbey Church, Tihany

A collection of stonework finds, consisting mainly of Roman and medieval materials, can be found in the basement.

A statue by Amerigo Tot entitled "His Majesty the Kilowatt" (1970) stands in front of the building, and a statue by Imre Varga entitled "The Founder" (1972), made of basalt and aluminium, dedicated to the memory of King Andrew I, stands at a turn in the road.

The servants' quarters and stables belonging to the abbey are today occupied by the **Rege Confectioner's**. (A marvellous panorama can be seen from its balconies.)

Mineral material condensed and deposited by the boiling hot water a long time ago litters in various colours on the walls of the **Cave of Springs** located in the Csokonai Grove next to the church.

Houses built in the traditional style of the region are mainly to be found in **Csokonai utca** and **Petőfi utca**. The walls of these houses were built out of the grey basalt tuff extracted on the peninsula. The doors and windows are outlined in white, while the porches are decorated with beautifully carved columns. A **csárda** has been opened in the house at **Kossuth Lajos utca 13**, while a **travel agency** can be found at **No. 20**. The old houses are being restored and what is now being built is adapted to the earlier style by making much use of basalt tuff.

The **Inner Lake** (Belső-tó), situated on the outskirts of the community, is 25 m above the level of the Balaton. It has no outlet whatever, and rainwater and ground water running down the hillsides feed the lake. The lake is extremely rich in fish, especially large carp, pickerel, and eels. There is also another lake called the **Outer Lake**

*The Romanesque crypt
of the Abbey Church, Tihany*

(Külső-tó, 20 hectares), which was drained in 1809; since 1975 it has been gradually filling up and has been declared a conservation area to protect the birds returning to its shore.

The **Golden House** (Aranyház) geyser cone rising to the south of the lake consists of a number of gigantic rocks lying on top of one another; they were formed from the limestone deposited by the hot water bursting out here at one time. A channel formed by the hot water is still clearly to be seen. Geyser cones follow each other all the way to the ferry port, each of them a protected natural treasure.

The third centre of tourist interest is the area around the **ferry port** (rév), which at one time consisted of pasture land. The end jutting out into the water is a harbour. Until as recently as 1927, a single wooden rowing-boat, propelled by six muscular young men and taking one and a half hours to cross, carried passengers across the Balaton. Today the trip takes only seven minutes, and each ferry can transport up to 20 cars and more than 300 passengers between the two shores. A restaurant accommodating up to 1,000 persons, a hotel, and a bathing beach are situated close to the terminal.

Footpaths for tourists facilitate access to the peninsula. By following a path marked with green waymarks, it is an hour's walk from the central harbour to the **Russian Well** and the **dwellings of the Russian monks** hollowed out of the basalt tuff.

A beautiful view of the two basins which make up Lake Balaton can be seen from **Csúcs Mountain** (235 m) which can be reached on foot in about an hour and a half by following the red waymarks. The peak itself was formed out of the gigantic deposits left by the hot water that burst forth here. The funnel formed by the hot water can still be seen in the small cave in the side of the mountain.

By following the yellow waymarks along the path from the ferry terminal, walkers can reach the sediment cones of the **geyser field**. From here they can go on to Csúcs Mountain, and descend to the **ruins of a medieval church** belonging to the community of **Apáti** which is located among the basalt tuff rocks and geyser sediments lying above them, and finally back to Rd. 71 and Aszófő.

ASZÓFŐ (7.5 km from Balatonfüred) has an important Baroque church. On the vine-covered hillside, there are rows of 19th-century wine-cellars called the **Vörösmáli wine-cellars.** (Campsite on the outskirts of the settlement.)

The so-called "farewell to winter" (Franthis hiemalis), a very rare plant and precursor of spring, blooms in great quantities in the forests east of Aszófő. Its protected yellow flower frequently appears as early as February. A small road lined by trees leads from Aszófő's former railway-station to the **ruins of the church** of the one-time community of **KÖVESD.** This single-nave church was built around 1260–70, and then became a victim of Turkish destruction. A pyx belonging to the church, unearthed in 1957, can be seen among the collection of stonework finds housed in the museum at Tihany. The ruins were restored in 1958.

ÖRVÉNYES (2 km from Aszófő): Operated by the water of Pécsely Stream, which gushes down from a considerable height, the only watermill in operation in the Balaton region is to be found here. **Remains of a Romanesque style sanctuary** of the medieval church of the village of Örvényes stand on the hill above the mill.

BALATONUDVARI (1.5 km from Örvényes on Rd. 71): Its 13th-century **Catholic church** was rebuilt in the 19th century in the neo-Classical style; the **Calvinist church** dates from the 18th century. Fifty **heart-shaped gravestones** carved out of white limestone in the early 19th century have been preserved in the community's old cemetery, which has now been declared a national shrine and where burials no longer take place.

KILIÁNTELEP (on the western outskirts of Balatonudvari) has two campsites, a motel and restaurant.

BALATONAKALI (6 km from Balatonudvari): There is a **Catholic church** built in 1827 from the ruins of a Romanesque church which was erected over the Roman buildings once standing there (boat harbour, two campsites). The area around

*Heart-shaped gravestones
at Balatonudvari*

Balatonakali is a famous wine-producing region ("Akali muskotály"; wine-tasting at the Mandula csárda), but there are also a number of medieval remains. The best known are the remains of the **medieval church of DÖR-GICSE,** where a double church with two naves and two sanctuaries once stood. The double church was probably covered by a single gabled roof; the two sanctuaries, however, were probably covered separately. The northern and southern parts of the church were probably built in the 11th and 13th centuries respectively.

Kű Valley, with its limestone cliffs resembling towers, is a mere 10 minutes' walk along the road leading past the church. A Baroque-style stone bridge can be reached from the valley. (Its pointed arch suggests medieval origin.) Ruins of a small, Romanesque-style church can be seen from the bridge.

A look-out tower stands on top of **Halom Mountain** (339 m), which rises above Dörgicse. From the look-out tower the Bakony Mountains can be seen towards the north, while towards the south the Balaton can be seen as far as Badacsony.

ZÁNKA (5 km from Balatonakali on Rd. 71) lies at the entrance to Káli Valley. Traces of a stone wall belonging to an 11th to 14th-century fortress from the age of the Árpáds can be seen underneath the peak **Hegyestű** (Pointed Needle, 338 m). Zánka's most beautiful historic monument is a **Calvinist church** dating from the Middle Ages, completely rebuilt in 1786. The windows of the church were built in the Romanesque style; two of the pedestals of the columns supporting the pulpits are inverted capitals dating from Roman times. Several houses built in traditional style can also be seen in the community (Kossuth u. 2, etc.). The beach and the Rétes csárda are below the railway crossing.

An international Pioneer camp for schoolchildren has been erected on the outskirts of Zánka. The camp has its own boat harbour and railway station, and as many as 2,500 young people can spend their holidays at one time in the comfortable buildings of the camp.

Balatonszepezd

3 km from Zánka on Rd. 71.

Both the railway and the road run close to the lake at this point. The community itself lies on rather higher ground.

The **Catholic church,** situated on a small hill above the road and reinforced by a red stone buttress, is of medieval origin. The door leading from the open tower into the church has a pointed arch and is framed in stone. The semicircular sanctuary is Romanesque; the sacristy is likewise of medieval origin.

The railway-station forms the centre of the bathing resort; the small Sellő Restaurant and wine cellar are situated just behind. A camping site lies to the east of the railway-station. The **fortress-like building** standing to the west is today a coal-miners' holiday home.

Révfülöp

4 km from Balatonszepezd on Rd. 71.

The present-day centre of Révfülöp was inhabited by the Romans. (Excavations have brought to light a number of monuments dating back to the Roman age.) The community constituted an important link with the harbour of Balatonboglár lying on the other side of the lake.

The name of the settlement occurs as Filip in the Tihany endowment deed dating from 1055. The Turks almost entirely destroyed the settlement along with its Romanesque-style 13th-century single-naved church built out of red sandstone. The **church ruin** excavated in 1953 stands opposite the new railway halt.

The harbour (regular boat service to the southern shores, beach, campsite) forms the centre of the bathing area.

Balatonrendes

5.4 km from Révfülöp on Rd. 71.

Pleasant-tasting mineral water flows out at the foot of the hill bordering the community. The bathing area lies next to the **springs.** Endre Bajcsy-Zsilinszky, a leader of the Hungarian anti-fascist movement, had a summer cottage here, and during his visits wrote a number of his more important articles in this house. The cottage, consisting of one room and a kitchen, is today a **memorial museum.**

The **Catholic church** dates from the 18th century, but it was renovated in the 20th. The house at **Fő utca 31** is an interesting example of folk architecture.

ÁBRAHÁMHEGY lies in the winding, canyon-like valley of the Burnót Stream. The community has recently started to develop as a bathing area. An almost 6 km public road marked with red waymarks leads from here to the ruins of a 13th-century **Pauline monastery.**

This monastery is mentioned for the first time in a manuscript of 1263; the **Gothic church** is mentioned in 1307. The walls of the church stand almost as high as the roof-line, so that it was possible to restore the Gothic windows.

From Ábrahámhegy a footpath lined with rocks leads to the **arboretum.** Almost 100 different kinds of pine trees and cypresses are represented in the collection which was begun in 1910.

Badacsony

164 km from Budapest on the M7 and then on Rd. 71; 170 km by rail.

The Badacsony nestles in the Tapolca Basin. Fourteen cone- and coffin-shaped basalt mountains stand behind one another around the Badacsony; vine is cultivated on the mountain slopes, and the wines produced here are excellent. The most impressive of the mountains that were formed as a result of volcanic activity is the Badacsony (438 m) itself. The beautiful panorama seen from the top of the mountain, which appears to rise abruptly out of the lake, attracts many visitors. There are four towns in the vicinity: Badacsonytomaj (with the resort called Badacsonyfürdő in its southern part), Badacsonyörs, Badacsony-lábdihegy and Badacsonytördemic (with the Szigliget railway-station).

Archeologists are able to trace the history of the region as far back as the Bronze Age, but the majority of finds discovered here originate from Roman times.

In the Middle Ages, the communities of the Badacsony are mentioned only in connection with their wine production. There was no bathing here until the beginning of this century.

Thousands of tourists arrive daily during the summer season at the Badacsony railway and boat-stations. Today a café as well as a bathing beach are situated next to the harbour. (There are also a row of shops, a car park and a petrol station in the area.) The former house and workshop of **József Egry** (1883–1951), a painter admired for his paintings of Balaton area, stand on the edge of the park behind the railway-station. There is a **memorial exhibition** in his house today.

The **statue** of a fish (by Miklós Borsos) stands in front of the Hableány Restaurant. The connecting road, which is covered by basalt slabs, ends at what is called **Római út** (according to tradition, the Romans built the road). The basalt road leads up to the mountain. Water from the **Kisfaludy Springs** flows down alongside the road.

The old porched houses on both sides of the **street** named after **Sándor Kisfaludy** (1772–1844), who sang the praises of Badacsony in his poems, today belong to the **Research Institute for Viticulture,** where experiments are conducted on new types of grapes. The Szürkebarát, Kéknyelű, Zöldszilváni and Olaszrizling are the most popular wines produced on the south slopes of the mountain, and have won countless gold medals. Today two state-owned winecellars store the wine produced here: 1,5 million litres are kept at Badacsonylábdihegy, and 700,000 litres in the cellars at Badacsonyörs.

The road divides at the bottom of the slope. Turning left, the road leads towards the west, to the **Wine Museum.** The museum building, constructed out of basalt, consists of a single large hall. The finest wines produced in the whole country can be tasted and bought here, among them very old wines.

Returning to Kisaludy út, it is only a few steps to the **wine-press and dwelling-house** which at one time belonged to Sándor Kisaludy's wife, Róza Szegedy. An exhibition consisting of implements and tools formerly used of the vintage occupies the ground floor of the two-storied, arcaded building. The first floor is occupied by a **literary museum** where Sándor Kisfaludy's personal belongings as well as his furniture can be seen in the first room. In the second room are an assortment of items connected with other writers living at the time, as well as some relics of Kisfaludy's literary activities; and finally, works of modern writers concerned with the Balaton are exhibited in the last room.

The crystal clear waters of Kisfaludy Springs bubble forth opposite Róza Szegedy's house. The **Kisfaludy House,** which served during the last century as the poet's wine-press, rises above the springs. Today the house, which is furnished in Hungarian peasant style, is an inn with gypsy music. A magnificent view of the lake can be seen from the terrace.

The volcanic mountains of Badacsony and its environs

Róza Szegedy's house at Badacsony

On the road leading past the Kisfaludy House there is a gigantic block of basalt standing under the shady trees. Its name, **Rózsakő** (Rose Stone), is engraved on it. There is a superstition that if a young man and woman sit on the stone with their backs towards the Balaton and think about each other, they will be married the same year; and there are still many who make use of the opportunity.

The road continues upwards from the Rose Stone where it becomes steps. Upon reaching a **look-out tower** called the **Páholy** (Theatre Box), a steep ascent leads to the top of the mountain, which is a nature conservation area. Paths marked by signs lead in every direction from here. By following the blue waymarks, it is possible to reach the **Kisfaludy Sándor Look-out Tower,** the balcony of which offers a beautiful panorama of the basalt mountains situated in the Tapolca Basin interspersed by the ruins of old fortresses. Also seen from here are the ancient volcanoes as well as Lake Balaton itself. After following the yellow waymarks leading towards the west, a gigantic **stone cross** erected in 1857 soon comes into view. It took 40 teams of oxen to haul the individual pieces of the cross up the mountainside. At the end of the road a beautiful view unfolds of another volcano rising opposite, St. George Mountain (Szent György-hegy).

A road marked by red waymarks leads from Badacsonytomaj railway-station to a **basalt church with two towers,** the only church of its kind in Europe. The road then leads to the **Egry József Tourist Hostel** and to the fresh-water **Monastery Well Springs** (Klastromkút-forrás), and from there to the so-called **Stone Gate Cliffs** (Kőkapu Sziklái), where the traces of destruction left by wind, rain, snow and frost are clearly discernible on the shattered basalt shafts. 464 separate steps forming what is called **Exiles' Stairs** (Bujdosók lépcsője) lead down to the former **Rodostó Hos-**

tel, which today is a company owned holiday home. (The steps and house preserve the memory of Ferenc Rákóczi II and his companions, who all fled with him to Rodostó, Turkey. Another plaque on the wall of the house preserves the names of those who struggled by their speeches and their writings to save Badacsony until they finally managed to stop the destructive mining operations taking place on both sides of the mountain. The large quarries were filled with earth and trees were planted. In a few decades the site once occupied by the quarries will be feast of green.)

Beginning at the holiday home, a road waymarked with red crosses for tourists leads below the basalt cliffs all around the mountain. In certain places, including the area near the house, huge landslides can be seen, which show where stone cliffs have collapsed. An unusual world of stone can also be observed quite near at the Exiles's Stairs. Green waymarks lead back to the **harbour**. Red waymarks lead to the Badacsonylábdihegy railway-halt. (Camping site in Badacsonyörs.)

SZIGLIGET (11 km from Badacsonytomaj on Rd. 71; 25 minutes by boat) was at one time an island. Today the community is surrounded by water on only one side and two sides are encircled by reeds. The hills in the area are covered by a basalt tuff much softer than ordinary basalt. The region has been inhabited ever since the Stone Age and, following the Mongol invasion, in 1260–1262 a fortress belonging to Pannonhalma Abbey was built here. In 1702 the Vienna Council of War ordered the fortress to be blown up.

Ruins of a 12th-century **church** preserved in 1958–1959 stand at the branch leading off Road 71 to the village. The most interesting part of the church is the tower which is square below but octagonal above.

The **castle** standing on the north side of the main square, today a **rest-home for writers,** was built around 1780; the neo-Classical façade, however, was added later. The fast-flowing Tapolca Stream borders the park.

Paths running along the part of the village below the fortress link houses that have been sited above one another and of which a good many are historic landmarks. A small church was built in 1721 on the highest spot in the village, while a **former mansion** belonging to the Tóti-Lengyel family stands next to it. The family coat of arms adorning the gate of the Baroque building, built in 1782 and remodelled in 1968, dates from the 18th century and was found in the fortress. (There is a restaurant in the building.)

A short walk along the road beginning behind the church takes one to the lower fortress; the round tower on the east side has survived in the best condition. The reservoir belonging to the upper fortress was found in the courtyard of the fortress, and a large number of old vessels that probably fell into the cistern as time passed were found on the lead-covered bottom.

Arriving by boat it appears as if the vineyards, fruit orchards, summer homes, and wine cellars were lying in a giant shell. This is the so-called Golden Shell Valley. Above, the Kamonko cliffs complete the picture. A small chapel standing on the top of a hill towards the east rises above the cliffs; while the ancient structures on the top of the crinoline-shaped **Queen's Skirt** Hill towards the west are most probably the remains of the fortress's outer defences.

BALATONEDERICS (5 km from Szigliget on Rd. 71) is not only worth mentioning on account of its beautiful bathing beach, but also because it is here that Rd. 84, which goes towards Western Transdanubia (Sárvár), turns off Rd. 71.

Tapolca

3 km from Balatonederics on Rd. 84 and then to the east on a side road.

The community of Tapolca was formerly called the city of wine because of the wines produced by the vineyards on the nearby mountains. Today it is nicknamed the bauxite city because it forms the centre of the bauxite mines of the region. It was not until the 18th century that Tapolca developed into a place of importance. Up to 1981 the **Tavas Caves** were the town's chief attraction. However, owing to mining work in the area, their water has dried up.

The town has several **neo-Classical houses** and two bronze statues of János Batsányi, a revolutionary 18th-century poet, and his wife Gabriella Baumberg, an Austrian poet, after whom the Hotel Gabriella in Batsányi tér in the town is named.

The **Catholic church** was built in the 15th century and was enlarged in the Baroque style in 1757; the sanctuary, however, has remained in its original Gothic form.

Sümeg

21 km northwest of Tapolca on Rd. 84.

Sümeg lies in the valley between the western foothills of the Bakony and the Keszthely mountain ranges and was inhabited as early as the prehistoric period. A cemetery from the Bronze Age was found here, and the foundation walls of an early Christian basilica are monuments from the Roman age. The first written mention of Sümeg is from 1301; the fortress dates back to 1318. In the 18th century the bishops of Veszprém lived in Sümeg and enriched the community by having many beautiful Baroque buildings constructed.

The **Parish Church** (Deák Ferenc tér), built in 1756–59, is a valuable historical monument. The splendid frescoes (1757–58) are considered by many to be the greatest works of Franz Anton Maulbertsch.

In **Szent István tér,** the birthplace and residence of Sándor Kisfaludy, the poet of the Balaton, is today a **memorial museum.** Mansions of the nobility dating back to the end of the 18th century border the square. Reconstructed remains of the former town wall can be seen in their gardens.

The magnificent Baroque mansion in Szent István tér was at one time the **Bishop's Palace** (today it is a students' hostel). Built between 1748 and 1753, the palace is adorned with balconies, an ornamental portal, and several statues; one section consists of only one floor, while the middle and west wings are multi-storied. The wrought-iron screen of the two outer chapels of the Baroque **Franciscan church and monastery** (1652–1657) dates from 1733. The church's principal embellishments are the main altar, richly adorned with carvings, and the wooden Pietà from 1653.

Past the Hotel Tourist in **Vak Bottyán utca** are the 18th-century Baroque stables in which the stallions of four counties are now kept, they are a notable historic monument. A harness and saddle exhibition can be seen in the eastern part of the building.

The **fortress of Sümeg** stands on top of 270 m high Castle Mountain (Várhegy). Limestone material from the Cretaceous period makes the mountain a natural curiosity and because of this, and also because of the peculiar vegetation growing there, the mountain has been declared a natural conservation area. The southern part of the fortress, the **citadel,** was built in the second half of the 13th century, enclosed by a wall during the second half of the 15th century, and strengthened in 1537. The Turks were unable to penetrate the fortress, but in 1714 it was burned down and later fell into ruins. Between 1959

View of the Castle, Sümeg

and 1964 it was restored. The **exhibition** set up in the Old Tower of the castle presents its history and shows the results of the excavations that have taken place there.

In one of the 19th-century graves of the cemetery of Sümeg rest Sándor Kisfaludy and his wife.

TÜRJE (15 km west of Sümeg) has a 13th-century **church** originally built in the Romanesque style but remodelled in the Baroque style during the 18th century. It contains a large number of frescoes by István Dorffmeister, from the 1760s.

Returning from Sümeg to the shores of the Balaton, take Rd. 71 again.

BALATONGYÖRÖK (5 km from Balatonederics on Rd. 71; 30 min. by boat from Szigliget) is a settlement of villas, the most popular tourist attraction being a small hill called **Szépkilátó,** which offers one of the most beautiful panoramas of the Balaton. The dormant volcanoes of the region, including St. George Mountain, the Csobánc and Szigliget crowned by fortresses, the cone-shaped Gulács, and the coffin-shaped Badacsony all rise to the north. The twin-peaked Castle Mountain (Vár-hegy) of Fonyód on the other side of the Balaton completes the panorama.

Directly beneath Szépkilátó is situated the **Roman Spring** (Római-forrás). (There is a youth camp nearby.)

From Balatongyörök pleasant walks can be taken into the Keszthely Mountains. (On the road to Gyenesdiás there are several look-out towers.)

Situated on top of **Szent Mihály Hill,** which appears white from the distance and which lies between Balatongyörök and Vonyarcvashegy, there is a small chapel built in the 18th century out of a medieval structure in memory of 40 fishermen who were rescued from drifting ice in the Balaton. (An anglers' camping site with wooden cabins, restaurant.)

By following the red waymarks along the pine forests from **VONYARC-VASHEGY** (3 km from Balatongyörök) we reach the **look-out tower** on top of Pető Mountain (335 m) in about 70 minutes. (Bathing facilities, restaurant.)

GYENESDIÁS (2.5 km from Vonyarcvashegy) is a scattered settlement below the pine-covered hills. (Two public beaches.)

Historic monuments include: the neo-Classical **Chapel of St. Helen** (1826) standing in the cemetery; the statue of **St. John of Nepomuk** at János springs; and a road-side cross, the so-called **Cross of Courage,** erected in 1807.

Keszthely

192 km from Budapest on Rd. 71; 209 km by rail.

Keszthely lies on a low sand-hill where there has been a road since Roman times. The present main road running through Keszthely, **Kossuth Lajos utca,** follows the path of this ancient road. Excavations conducted in the area have brought to light graves of Bronze and early Iron Age man as well as articles for personal use. The Roman fortification of Valcum once stood where Fenékpuszta, a community lying 7.6 km south of Keszthely, is now situated. The first written mention of Keszthely dates from 1247. The church of Keszthely as well as the monastery next to it were fortified in the 16th century. (The Turks laid siege to these buildings on several occasions, but they were never able to penetrate them.)

The town and its surroundings were the property of the Festetics family from the beginning of the 18th century until 1945. Keszthely was connected to the railway built in 1866 on the southern shores of the Balaton only by a small branch line. This is why Keszthely is more of a school town and bathing resort than a commercial town in character. Today Keszthely has a university, a developing industry, and prospers as a bathing resort.

The most important historic monument to be seen in Keszthely is the former **Festetics Palace** standing at the end of **Kossuth Lajos utca** and flanked by Szabadság utca and Soproni utca. The Baroque south wing of the building was constructed in 1745. The palace received its present form between 1883 and 1887. The statues adorning the façade facing the

Keszthely

courtyard are suggestive of the family's horse breeding, agricultural, and boat building activities. The town's main attraction is the **Helikon Library**, which was founded in the 18th century. It contains 52,000 volumes, among them codices and a large number of rare editions. The neo-Classical furnishings in the library are the work of János Kerbi (1801), a master joiner from Keszthely. The other rooms are arranged with furniture from the palace. Evenings of chamber music are held in the renovated ballroom of the palace, and during the summer, orchestral concerts are given in the park outside.

A statue of the family's greatest son, Count György Festetics (1755–1819), stands in front of the palace. In 1797 Count Festetics founded Europe's first agricultural institute, the **Georgikon** (today a University of Agricultural Sciences), and started the so-called Helikon Fes-

The Festetics Palace, Keszthely

tivities at which the best progressive writers and poets from Trans-danubia used to meet.

The row of houses on the east of **Szabadság utca,** which leads to the palace, has preserved the community's Baroque street image. A **memorial plaque** on the wall of **No. 5** indicates that this was the birthplace of Sándor Asbóth (1811–1868), who was Lajos Kossuth's adjutant during the 1848–1849 War of Independence and afterwards became one of the military leaders fighting on Lincoln's side in the American Civil War. The **Hotel Amazon** at the end of the street was built in the 18th century.

Kossuth Lajos utca is lined by houses in Baroque, Louis XVI, and Romantic styles. It was in the house at **No. 22** that Károly Goldmark (1830–1915), the composer of the opera "Queen of Sheba", was born. (A **bust** in the palace park stands in his memory.)

The **Trinity Statue** standing in front of the town Hall, built in the style of Louis XVI around 1790 on **Fő tér,** the city's main square, dates from 1770. A Gothic **Catholic church,** built in the 14th century from the walls of an older chapel and probably with stones from the Roman *castrum* at Fenékpuszta, closes off the square to the east. Recent restorations uncovered 14th- and 15th-century frescoes in the sanctuary. The red marble tombstone (1397) of the church's founder, the Palatine István Lackffy, and Kristóf Festetics's tomb opposite, constructed in the style of Louis XVI, can both be seen here. György Festetics lies buried in the crypt of the church (1819).

Széchenyi utca, a street beginning opposite the church, leads to the building of the **University of Agricultural Sciences** located on the corner of Deák Ferenc utca. The precursor of the university, the **Georgikon,** built in the style of Louis XVI, can be found at **Georgikon utca 20,** which begins at the end of Deák Ferenc utca.

(From **Bercsényi Miklós utca** it is possible to gain access to the **Farm Museum** where much 18th-century farming equipment is on exhibition.)

The rich material found in the **Balaton Museum** (Múzeum u. 2) gives a broad view of the origin of the Balaton region. The material also provides information about the Hungarian way of life in the Balaton region; it displays objects that have been found in the graves of peoples once living on the shores of the lake (including maquettes of border castles); it also illustrates the history of bathing in the Balaton. The large diorama

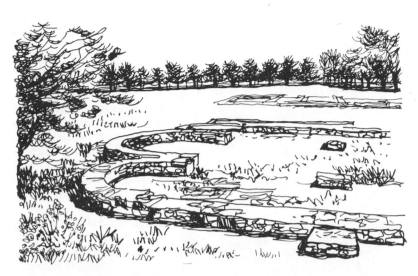

Roman ruins of Valcum, Fenékpuszta

depicting the world of the **Little Balaton** (see p. 192) marshes, a natural conservation area, is indeed beautiful.

There are interesting tombstones in the town **cemetery** not far from the museum. The sepulchral vault of the Festetics family is in the style of a Greek temple.

Festetics György út, which is lined by a row of wild chestnut trees, leads to the university hostel, which adjoins the new botanical gardens. Behind the hostel there is a riding school in the old manorial farmhouse (today the Szendrey colony).

The centre of bathing life, the lakeside promenade, is flanked on the east by the L-shaped **Hotel Helikon.** A pier juts out into the lake in the middle of the promenade, which ends at **Szigetfürdő** (Island Beach) to the west.

The 15-hectare **Helikon park** is situated behind two hotels on the lakeside promenade. The paths running through the park are lined with statues and monuments. The other large bathing area is **Helikon Beach,** with an adjoining camping site for 600 people.

EXCURSIONS

FENÉKPUSZTA (7.6 km from Keszthely): Three buildings among the ruins of Valcum have been discovered so far: an **early Christian basilica** with three naves, the foundations of a **storehouse,** and the southern gate with a section of the **castle wall.**

Neo-Classical stables and reception-centres preserve the memory of the Festetics family's horse-breeding colony.

REZI (8 km northwest of Keszthely) has a single-naved **Catholic church** which dates from the 14th century, but it was rebuilt in the middle of the 18th in the Baroque style. By following a path marked with blue waymarks, you can reach the ruins of the **castle** on the north slope of Meleg Mountain in about an hour.

Romanesque church near Hévíz,
at Egregy

Hévíz

6.6 km from Keszthely on a minor road.

Hévíz is Europe's largest warm-water lake with a surface area of 4.4 hectares. The steaming lake creates an unusual exotic impression, especially during slightly cold weather. The crater springs of the lake are 39 m deep, while the warm water along the sides flows from a depth of 2.5 m below the surface. (60–80 million litres of warm water gush from the springs daily, which means that the water of the lake is completely changed every 28 hours.) The temperature of the water at the bottom of the lake is 35–36 °C, while that on the surface averages from 28 to 30 °C.

Cemeteries dating back to Roman times and the Period of Migration have been found near the lake. The first written mention of Hévíz dates from 1328.

The waters of Lake Hévíz are radioactive and are particularly effective in curing locomotor, rheumatic, inflammatory, and articular diseases (the water is not suitable for cardiac diseases). The greyish-brown-grained mud covering the bottom of the lake is especially therapeutic. It is used for mud-packs, and is dried and exported.

Warm-water lake, Hévíz

As the water of the lake is continually steaming, one cannot catch cold. (There is a beach on the northern part of the lake.)

The centre of Hévíz comprises the lake itself, the park created around it, the **State Hospital,** the **Hotel Thermal** (and the new **Hotel Aqua** both with medicinal baths), the winter baths opened in 1968, and a **sanatorium** belonging to the trade unions.

East of Hévíz lies the former community of **EGREGY** where a **church** still remains from the Romanesque period. Nearby (Egregyi u. 10) a Roman sepulchre, still in good condition, can be seen.

EXCURSIONS

The **Gyöngyösi csárda,** built in 1728, lies 6 km from Hévíz beside the road leading to Sümeg. The inn is still standing in its original state, and in its courtyard there is a well and a covered car-park. Weapons belonging to the highwaymen who used to frequent the inn as well as warrants for their arrest can be seen in the large hall. Nearby are the graves of two outlaws executed in 1862.

ZALASZÁNTÓ (15 km from Hévíz towards Sümeg): Its 13th-century restored **Gothic church** is an important historic building.

THE SOUTHERN SHORE

The main attraction of the southern shore of Lake Balaton lies in its excellent bathing facilities. The nearly 70 km long shore is almost one single huge, warm, shallow beach.

The plan of the communities lying along the southern shore is almost the same everywhere. The bathing facilities are nearly always situated between the shore and the railway station: the community itself, consisting of residential and summer homes, usually lies between the railway and the main road, and finally, the old houses of the community can generally be found beyond the main road.

Hotels, company-owned and private apartments, and family vacation homes are situated near the beaches. Life here is at its gayest during the bathing season. The shopping service section is in the second zone.

Bathing activity on the southern shore started to grow after the opening of the Southern Railway (1861), and by the end of the century the larger bathing resorts had already developed.

BALATONVILÁGOS (98 km from Budapest on the M7; 107 km by rail): Its eastern section was once the independent community of **BALATONALIGA.** A traveller going by train catches his first sight of the Balaton just after passing the Aliga railway station.

The centre of the community is situated above the railway. The most interesting part, however, runs along the lakeshore, where every building site has its own beach (public beach, restaurants, cafés, bazaars).

It is possible to see both shores of the Balaton from the memorial column to Géza Mészöly (1844–1887), an outstanding painter of the Balaton. The memorial stands on the most beautiful spot of Felső-telep above the railway station (restaurant).

Siófok

106 km from Budapest on the M7; 115 km by rail.

Siófok, the largest community on the southern shore of Lake Balaton, today embraces an almost 16 km section of the shoreline.

In A. D. 292 the Emperor Galerius built the first canal in the area of present-day Siófok (remains of a sluice and soldiers' garrison were found during the construction of the town's water-supply system). After 1541 the Turks built a strong water fortress at the mount of the Sió Canal. The Turkish fleet on the Balaton, which was capable of transporting a thousand men at a time, was stationed here until 1686. Between 1705 and 1707 General Vak Bottyán, a commander serving under Ferenc Rákóczi, had a fort built against the attacks of the Habsburg forces.

Row of hotels along Lake Balaton, Siófok

Siófok's bathing-resort area can be divided into three sections: the **older bathing district** with its large beach and hotels adjoining it forms the centre of Siófok; **Golden Beach** (Aranypart) stretches to the east of the centre. Siófok's third area, **Silver Beach** (Ezüstpart), stretches behind the older bathing area from the west bank of the Sió Canal. This coastal stretch, also under development, is already dotted with multi-storied trade-union and company-owned vacation homes and resorts as well as smaller summer houses. Siófok's principal attraction is its bustling and colourful bathing life.

An exhibition showing the history, the present and future of water-supply management on the Danube and on Lake Balaton has been set up in the **Beszédes József Museum** standing by the Sió Bridge. (The museum is named after the hydraulic engineer, József Beszédes.) The memorial exhibition of the world-famous operetta composer, Imre Kálmán, who was born in Siófok, can also be seen here.

The single-towered **church** was built in 1749, and was reconstructed in 1904 in a neo-Romanesque style. The former Hotel Fogas, standing in front of the Sió Bridge, as well as the hotel's inner courtyard section with its porticoes and wine-cellar known as the **Borharapó,** which preserves the memories of a former roadhouse, are both historic monuments.

The harbour situated at the end of **Mártírok útja** in the western part of the town serves as the centre of navigation on the Balaton and is at the same time the winter harbour for the lake's boats. The **Rose Gardens** next to the harbour contain a statue by Tibor Vilt called "Balaton Girl".

The green pyro-granite tower of the **Balaton Meteorological Research Station** located on the western side of the Sió Canal provides a view in all directions and gives warning of approaching thunderstorms.

Beyond the Rose Garden, under the shady trees of **Dimitrov Park,** stands the **memorial monument** of the martyrs executed in 1919 ("Martyr Mourner", the work of István Bors).

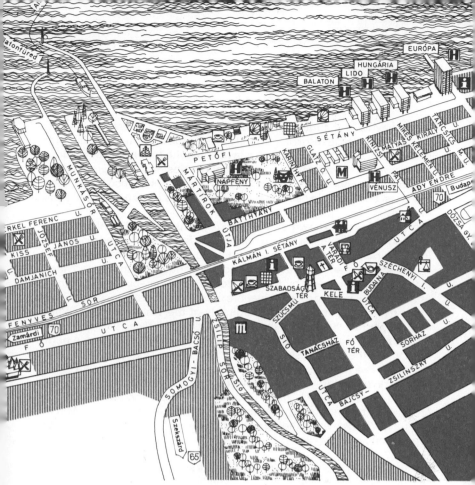

Siófok

The north side of **Petőfi sétány,** beginning at Dimitrov Park, is completely occupied by a large beach which can accommodate more than 20,000 vacationers. Next door is a group of hotels consisting of three 7-storey and one 13-storey hotel buildings (restaurant, café, bar). **Aranypart** (Golden Beach), with its free public beach, lies behind the 7 m long dike that immediately follows.

Beyond the Sió Bridge lies **Balatonújhely,** which merged with Siófok in 1949, followed by **Balatonszéplak** (now Ezüstpart), where the hotel of the International Association of Journalists and trade union resort are located.

The **Tourist Hostel** and the **Piroska csárda** stand next to the main road at Balatonszéplak.

EXCURSIONS

SÁGVÁR (9 km south of Siófok on Rd. 65): Houses built in the traditional folk style and the remains of walls belonging to a Roman fortress can be seen here.
SOM (13 km from Siófok on Rd. 65): Its **church** was built in 1758. The Baroque altar and organ chest inside the church are the work of a simple wood carver.
TAB (14 km from Som and west of Rd. 65): Baroque **church** with beautiful furnishings and frescoes by István Dorffmeister.
ZALA (4 km northwest of Tab) is the birthplace of an important 19th-century Hungarian painter, Mihály Zichy. The artist's **collection of paintings** can be seen in his former family mansion.

Zamárdi—Szántód

9 and 15 km from Siófok respectively on Rd. 7.

Motorway M7 runs into Rd. 7 at Zamárdi, which almost merges into Siófok. The bathing resort community of Szántód is a virtual continuation of Zamárdi. Zamárdi is above all a favourite with families with children. There are several holiday homes, two tourist hostels and a camping site.

Its Baroque **church** was built in 1771–1774 and has Rococo furnishings. The most beautiful old peasant house at **Fő utca 83** was turned into a folk museum.

A gigantic rock known as **Szamárkő** (Donkey Rock), which can be reached on foot in about fifteen minutes by following the red waymarks from the railway station, was, according to popular legend, a sacrificial site used by the ancient Magyars. Another variation of the legend has it that a hoof-print made by Christ's donkey can be seen on the stone. Archeologists believe that a signal fire was lighted on the rock during the Iron Age in order to help the inhabitants of the Tihany Earthwork find their way, while the name of the settlement can be traced back to the cultic customs of the Pechenegs. The busiest part of Szántód is the perth from which the ferry crosses to Tihany (see under Tihany).

The old **Rév csárda** stands at the beginning of the road leading to the ferry. (Travellers formerly had to wait for hours, sometimes for days, to cross to the other side.) The inn was built in 1839, and the interior still preserves its original appearance. A memorial plaque to Mihály Csokonai Vitéz, an outstanding poet of the Age of Enlightenment, can be seen on one of the walls.

SZÁNTÓDPUSZTA (on Rd. 7, between Zamárdi and Balatonföldvár): An 18th to 19th-century farm building complex, belonging at one time to the Benedictine Abbey of Tihany, has remained in almost perfect condition. Its first building was

Church, Kőröshegy

constructed in 1741; this was followed by a huge arched wine-cellar large enough for a cart to pass through, then followed the house of the overseer, the inn, the stables, barns, etc. The group of buildings ends with the Baroque **Kristóf Chapel** which overlooks the entire *puszta* area. (Accommodations, exhibitions, riding-school, cultural centre, restaurants.)

Balatonföldvár

122 km from Budapest on Rd. 7; 129 km by rail.

Partitioning and construction of bathing facilities was begun here at the end of the last century. Contemporary manuscripts claim that only an inn (*csárda*) stood in the area now occupied by the community of Balatonföldvár, and at night the howling of the wolves from the nearby reeds could be heard. Today the resort community is provided with beautiful parks, a network of shops (also a dozen trade-union, company, and collectively-owned holiday homes), an outdoor theatre and cinema, a clubhouse, a confectioner's, a hostel, a camping site, a beach, and the "Express" youth camp.

A 4 km long path from Balatonföldvár (there is a bus service as well) leads to the **Kőröshegy Catholic church** which was built in the late Gothic style during the second half of the 15th century. Organ, vocal and chamber music concerts are held each summer in the church, which was restored in 1968–1969.

Balatonszárszó

4.5 km from Balatonföldvár on Rd. 7.

Balatonszárszó, a small bathing community, developed around its railway station. The first written mention of this old village lying on the hillside dates from 1082.

A **memorial museum** dedicated to Attila József, a revolutionary poet of the 20th century, has been opened at **József Attila utca 7**. It was in this house that the poet spent his last days before throwing himself under the wheels of a freight train on December 3, 1937. A statue of the poet was erected on Latinca Sándor tér.

Balatonszemes

6 km from Balatonszárszó on Rd. 7.

The name of this community was mentioned in the Papal tithe registers for the years 1332–1337. During the time of the Turks it was called Bolondvár (Jester's Castle), and its fortress was destroyed at the end of the 17th century. Construction work turning the small community into a summer resort began in the middle of the last century and is still in progress. (The vacation spot known as "Vadvirág" [Wild Flower] is provided with wooden cabins and is situated next to the largest camping site along the southern shore, along with the Lido Motel.)

The **building** at the corner of **Gárdonyi Géza utca** (today an elementary school) with arched porches dates from the 18th century. The granary next door is also a historical monument.

Bajcsy-Zsilinszky utca 36 was once a station where horses of the mail service were changed. Today it is a **post-office museum** with an interest-

ing display showing the history of the mail service as well as the history
of postage stamps. Old vehicles once used by the mail service can be
seen in the courtyard. The museum also has its own post office which
stamps the mail with special postmarks.

Built in the 15th century in the Gothic style, the **Parish Church (Fő u. 23)**
was later remodelled in the middle of the 18th century. Restoration work
that took place in 1970 uncovered the church's architectural history. The
church's tracery windows as well as the Renaissance pyx from 1517 are
all particularly beautiful.

Situated on the hillside, the **Bagolyvár** (Owl Fortress) was built where
the former Bolondvár (Jester's Castle) once stood; but even though the
ramparts can still be seen on three sides, the building with its romantic
appeal has nothing in common with the old fortress. A **Roman sepulchre,**
engraved with four figures and placed on a stone wall next to the restaurant at **Árnyas sor 1,** is one of the few Roman historic monuments that
have survived in the district.

Boglárlelle—Balatonlelle

136 km from Budapest on Rd. 7; 145 km by rail.

The centre of Balatonlelle, a bathing resort stretching many kilometres
along the Balaton, has developed from an older community lying across
Rd. 7. It has merged with the town of Balatonboglár and the two are
known as Boglárlelle.

The centre of the bathing-resort community is occupied by a promenade which lies between the harbour and the railway station and is provided with beautiful shady trees, carefully-planted parks on both sides,
and parking places for cars. The main shopping centre of the community
includes shops of all kinds, services, and a department-store building (it
lies near the railway station).

The peristyled **mansion** once belonging to a member of the nobility
and built in 1838 in the neo-Classical style stands on a small hill at the
beginning of Rd. 67 **(Kossuth Lajos u. 2)** which leads to Kaposvár. Today
the mansion serves as a small cultural centre with its own outdoor
theatre. Each year an exhibition of folk art as well as carving contests are
held here. The bronze bust depicts Antal Kapoli (1867–1957), famous for

Cultural centre, Balatonlelle

his wood carving. (There is a library with books in foreign languages and a reading room in the park of the cultural centre.)

The **school in Petőfi Sándor utca** was originally built as a mansion for the nobility, and dates back to 1812.

An old **blacksmith's shop** provided with typical old village furnishings can be seen at **Szabadság utca 52,** near the school.

The area now occupied by the red stone **church** was once the site of an 11th-century church that was destroyed during the Turkish period. The most interesting piece of furnishing inside the church is the Pietà (1600), which also adorned the previous church.

Red waymarks lead to a vine-covered hill called Kis-hegy (Small Mountain) on which an 18th-century Baroque **chapel** stands. (There is an old wine-press nearby.)

Boglárlelle—Balatonboglár

3.5 km from Balatonlelle on Rd. 7.

Three hills, formed of basalt tuff, just like the mountains of Szigliget opposite them on the northern shore, provide Balatonboglár with its special character. **Chapel Hill** (Kápolnadomb) is a small, symmetrically-shaped volcano. Ramparts easily distinguishable even today extend over the top of **Castle Hill**. Personal articles used in prehistoric daily life are frequently unearthed on the mountain. Presumably the earthwork at Balatonboglár were constructed during the early Iron Age.

The ferry at Balatonboglár, which crosses over to the community of Révfülöp on the other side of the lake, was mentioned for the first time in 1211. This ferry-crossing was used until the beginning of the 20th century, but with the development of steam navigation it soon discontinued operations.

Bathing activities in the small community began in the 1890s. At the same time summer homes were erected; restaurants, dining halls, and a café were built.

A **harbour,** a large **pier,** and the small **Szúnyog** (Mosquito) **Island** that was developed in 1913 and where there is a campsite, form the centre of the bathing community. Heavy boat traffic connects Balatonboglár with Révfülöp on the opposite side as well as with other harbours on the Balaton. The bathing area with its many summer homes, its holiday centres, and its beach extends to the right and left of the harbour.

The historic monument at **Szabadság utca 4** is a former mansion built in 1834 in the neo-Classical style. Today it serves as a State Farm centre.

A small **cultural centre** with an outdoor theatre constructed in the courtyard, stands in **Árpád utca.** The cultural centre was named after Béla Vikár (1859–1945), an outstanding Hungarian ethnographer, who translated the "Kalevala", the famous Finnish epic. A memorial plaque written in both Hungarian and Polish hanging next to the entrance proclaims that it was in this building that a group of Poles fleeing from their country after the 1939 Nazi onslaught on Poland continued their studies. (During the war, this was the only secondary school on the continent where all subjects were taught in Polish.)

A spherically shaped **look-out tower** on top of **Castle Hill** offers a beautiful view of the opposite shores from Keszthely all the way to Tihany. Two small **chapels** (Lutheran and Catholic) stand on **Temető Hill.** (Each summer art exhibitions are held in them.)

EXCURSIONS

SZŐLŐSGYÖRÖK (8.5 km south of Balatonboglár): A manor house built in the neo-Classical style around 1820 stands in the middle of a 21-hectare park. Almost a hundred different kinds of trees and shrubs can be seen in the park. **BUZSÁK** (20 km southwest of Balatonboglár) is known for its folk art. Embroidered pillows and tablecloths from Buzsák are exported to many parts of the world. The community's **Parish Church** dates from the 18th century. The **folk museum** and the village hall are worth a visit for the furniture painted with local motifs and the fine needlework and embroidery (Tanács tér 6). **SOMOGYVÁR** (24 km south of Balatonboglár) was the capital of Somogy County for 600 years. In 1091 King Ladislas I was instrumental in bringing a group of Benedictine monks here from the Saint-Gilles Abbey near Arles in southern France. The king also had a magnificent church and monastery built for the monks; but in the 16th century these buildings were converted into a fortress that was soon taken over by the Turks. Excavations on the former church and monastery are now in progress. The foundations have already been unearthed and it can now be seen just how gigantic the structure once was. The foundations of the monastery and other buildings, as well as 40,000 objects have also been unearthed. (The stone carvings that have been discovered so far can be seen in the Rippl-Rónai Museum in Kaposvár.)

Fonyód

150 km from Budapest on Rd. 7; 157 km by rail.

Fonyód lies at the foot of a hill rising almost directly from the shores of Lake Balaton. It comprises five formerly independent settlements: Fonyódliget, Sándorliget, Fonyód, Bélatelep and Alsóbélatelep.

The twin-peaked **Fonyód Hill** (Sipos Mountain and Sándor Mountain, 207 and 233 m high) is of volcanic origin as are the mountains lying in the Tapolca Basin opposite. The hilltop is covered by a layer of basalt; and today only a few basalt blocks lying scattered in the area testify to the hill's volcanic origin. The water of the lake has undermined the northern side of the hill, and this is how, from layers of sandstone which slid down from the hill and spread at its foot, the 7 km long slope, over which the lakeside resort has developed, came into being.

During the years following the Magyar Conquest, a small village stood at the end of the present **Szent István utca**. It was around the **church** of this village that a border-fortress was built in 1547. Fonyód itself lies in a pass between the two hills, but it is now scattered over the neighbouring slope as well.

The railway station forms the centre of the community and nearby are shops and restaurants, as well as a harbour and a bathing beach.

The ancient border-castle standing at the end of **Szent István utca** in an area surrounded by a 10 m wide moat is 100 × 100 m in size. **Foundation-walls belonging to an earlier church** that once stood there can be seen inside the newly-dug circular network of trenches in the middle of the castle. At one time drawbridges led across the moat to the interior of the fortress, and a mace-tower likewise situated there at the time made easy the surveillance of the rippling reed forest and water in front. This swampy area was the most important natural fortification held by the Castle of Fonyód, which was built in 1547.

A reed-covered, village **wine-press** and a **carriage entrance** with a tympanum and 4 columns are protected examples of folk architecture. They stand above the castle at **Lenke utca 11**. Today a **restaurant**, furnished in Hungarian folk style, operates here. A beautiful view of the shores on the other side of the lake can be seen from the winding road leading to Bélatelep. Relics from the time spent here by Jenő Huszka (1875–1960), the popular operetta composer, have been collected in one of the rooms belonging to the composer's former summer house in this road.

It is possible to reach **Castle Hill** at Fonyód in about an hour and fifteen minutes by following a forest road marked with red waymarks from the railway station. The wide trenches on the hilltop were probably parts of early Iron Age earthworks later used as an observation post in the battles fought against the Turks. There is also a small observation post in the interior of the former earthworks. A panorama of almost the entire shore in the other side of Lake Balaton can be enjoyed from the flat roof of the observation post, as well as a magnificent view of the beautifully-cultivated plains, which at one time were swamps, and of the sand ridges in the far distance.

Balatonfenyves

5.5 km from Fonyód on Rd. 7.

A line of summer homes built among the pine groves along the edge of the shore forms an unbroken chain all the way to Balatonmáriafürdő.

Balatonfenyves is the centre of the Nagyberek State Farm, which has utilized the marshy land here. The almost 10,000-hectare area has been provided with canals since 1950, which help to carry surplus water to the Balaton and which convey water from the lake to the arable land in times of drought. Protective belts of wooded land have also been built here, and today nearly 10,260 hectares are being farmed. The entire area is served by a small agricultural railway station. The small railway also leads to **Csisztapuszta** where, as a result of oil drilling (1956), warm water (42 °C) has come to the surface from a depth of 600 m. The warm water found here is effective in treating rheumatic diseases.

Balatonmáriafürdő

5 km from Balatonfenyves on Rd. 7.

One of the most recent bathing resorts on the Balaton, Balatonmáriafürdő was built on an almost 10 km long sand embankment; it did not become a separate community until 1927. Actual development of the bathing resort community began in 1967. (Recently joined administratively to Balatonkeresztúr.) The centre of the community is formed by the modern bathing area next to which stands the **Tourist Hostel** at a bend in the highway. The **Delta Restaurant** and a group of shops are situated opposite the hostel.

Balatonmáriafürdő has regularly-scheduled boat connections to Balatongyörök.

BALATONKERESZTÚR (166 km from Budapest on Rd. 7.): Its name has appeared in documents since the 15th century. Balatonmáriafürdő is also part of this administrative unit.

The Baroque **Parish Church,** built between 1753 and 1758, is a historical monument. The 18th-century frescoes on the walls inside the church were painted by an anonymous master who was probably well acquainted with the Maulbertsch frescoes of the church of Sümeg.

The former **manor house** of the Festetics family **(Ady Endre u. 26.)** which is surrounded by a park with an area of 1.14 hectares, is today a tourist hotel.

Rd. 76 joins Rd. 7 2.5 km south of Balatonkeresztúr and then continues in the southern direction as Rd. 68 towards Barcs, a border crossing. Rd. 7 (E71), however, turns southwest and after passing through Nagykanizsa goes on to Letenye and to the Yugoslav border.

Balatonberény

5.5 km northeast of Balatonkeresztúr, on Rd. 71.

Balatonberény is the last coastal settlement on the southern shores of the Balaton (beach, camping site).
The **Parish Church** standing at **Kossuth Lajos u. 58** was built in the 14th and 15th centuries in the Gothic style. During the Turkish period the church was destroyed, only to be restored again in 1733 in the Baroque style. Gothic *sedilia* can be seen in the sanctuary, which is supported by buttresses.
After Balatonberény reeds stretch all the way to the mouth of the Zala.

BALATONSZENTGYÖRGY (5.5 km from Balatonberény on Rd. 76) is no longer situated on the shore of the lake. The community itself has no bathing facilities, and the lake shore here is entirely covered with reeds.
The **peasant house** at **Csillagvár utca 60** was built in 1836, and it is the only historic monument which shows the characteristic folk architecture of the region. At present the peasant house is a folk museum, the first room of which contains works of folk art from the Balaton region. The other parts of the house have been arranged just as if the former owners were still living there.
The **Star Fortress** (Csillagvár) is situated in the Bari Forest 1.5 km beyond the end of the community. It was long believed that the star-shaped structure was originally a border-fortress, but closer examination has disclosed that it was built during the 1820s as a hunting-lodge and that it had been modelled on old fortresses. The building has the atmosphere of a 16th to 17th-century border-castle and provides a picture of how border-castle warriors once lived.
VÖRS (4 km south of Balatonszentgyörgy): Entry to the road leading to the Kis- (Little) Balaton with a **look-out tower** with a view of the lake. Old Haban pottery is on view at the **folk museum at Dózsa György utca 17.**

THE LITTLE BALATON

The Little Balaton (Kis-Balaton), an area whose special birdlife has for a long time attracted natural scientists and nature lovers alike, lies west of Balatonszentgyörgy in an area enclosed by ridges of hills extending behind one another.

The Little Balaton was at one time a separate gulf forming part of Lake Balaton and had a surface area of almost 60 sq.km. Gradually, sand and clay brought in by the Zala River filled up the gulf, and the vegetation which at one time covered it turned to peat.

This is why only a few open places have remained on what was once part of the lake; most of the area is now covered by reeds.

Hundreds of rare birds, including the egret, nest here undisturbed, while a large number of birds pass this way as they migrate to other parts of the world.

In order to ensure that the scientific work at the reservation can proceed undisturbed, visits to the area can be made only with permission from the NYU–KÖVIZIG H–9700 Szombathely, Vörösmarty utca 2.

The Great Plain

The region lying between the Danube and Tisza rivers can be reached by taking Rd. 4 (E60) from Budapest to Szolnok, Rd. 5 (E75). The chief railway lines are the following: Budapest–Szolnok–Debrecen–Nyíregyháza, Budapest–Kecskemét–Szeged,Budapest–Cegléd–Szolnok–Békéscsaba, Budapest–Kiskőrös–Kalocsa.

The Great Plain is an enormous stretch of lowland lying to the southeast of the capital. It occupies the largest part of the country. The Great Plain is bordered on the west by the Danube, on the south by the Hungarian–Yugoslav border, on the southeast and east by the Hungarian–Rumanian border, on the northeast by the Hungarian–Soviet border, and on the north by the southern foothills of the Northern Mountain Range.

Before large-scale work was begun to regulate water routes and build new roads, the area was dotted with a confused mass of winding rivers and was difficult of access. A rich plant and animal world flourished here, and the rivers abounded in fish. But since the difficult traffic conditions made transport expensive, the most profitable occupation on the vast expanses of meadow land was the breeding of animals. Another reason for the development of agriculture in the area was the Turkish occupation that lasted one and a half centuries. The invaders made a great effort to deplete the territory they had occupied, and even destroyed the forests; most of the population residing in the villages retired to the towns, where their safety could be guaranteed; in this way uncultivated land and wastes took the place of deserted villages. Later the plains became the scene of horse-breeding, cattle-and sheep-farming, and the romantic and exotic colours of the area were enjoyed by fishermen and outlaws fleeing from justice. Today the famous Hungarian prairie is only a memory, as is the American Wild West. Nevertheless, efforts at nature conservation are taking place in two areas—Bugac and Hortobágy—and have preserved part of the earlier character of the region as well as some of the animals that were once bred here. (Bugac is situated between the Danube and the Tisza; the Hortobágy is to the west of the Tisza.) On the whole, however, the Great Plain does not present a romantic picture. From a car or bus the area appears monotonous; the larger communities are distant from one another; and, at best, a few scattered farms can be seen here and there along the highway. The towns lying on the Great Plain are very different from other Hungarian towns; but perhaps it is for this very reason that the city-dweller can find so much of interest in them. Crowded market-places can be seen where a vast variety of merchandise is sold and where, occasionally, women still dress in folk costumes. Characteristic folk art, ethnographical and archeological features of the region are also to be seen. There are far fewer historic monuments in the area than in other parts of the country, a result of the very nature of the Great Plain. Not only were the Mongols able to occupy and ravage the area without restraint, but in the 16th century the advancing Turkish forces had no difficulty in bringing the Great Plain under their control. During the one hundred and fifty years of Turkish occupation, nothing new was built on the Great Plain, and the public buildings, churches, and private homes that did exist were all destroyed.

The Great Plain is not uniform in character: the area between the Danube and Tisza is different from the areas lying beyond, just as it is different in the Hajdúság in the east or in the Nyírség (a district in northeast Hungary).

THE REGION BETWEEN THE DANUBE AND THE TISZA

The Great Plain can be reached from Budapest by taking Rds. 4(E60), 5(E75), 31 and 51 as well as the roads branching off from them via Kecskemét to Szeged, or Rd. 51 from Budapest via Kalocsa and Baja to Hercegszántó. The other towns can be reached by taking various minor roads branching off from the above-mentioned major highways. Railway lines run parallel to the main roads.

A hypothetical line running from Budapest through Jászberény to the Tisza can be said to border the area on the north. In the west the area is bounded by the Danube, in the east by the Tisza, and in the south by the Hungarian–Yugoslav

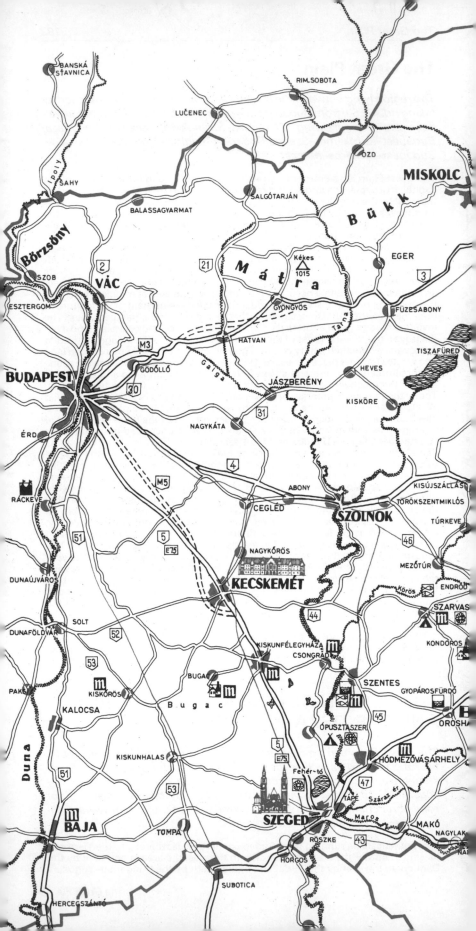

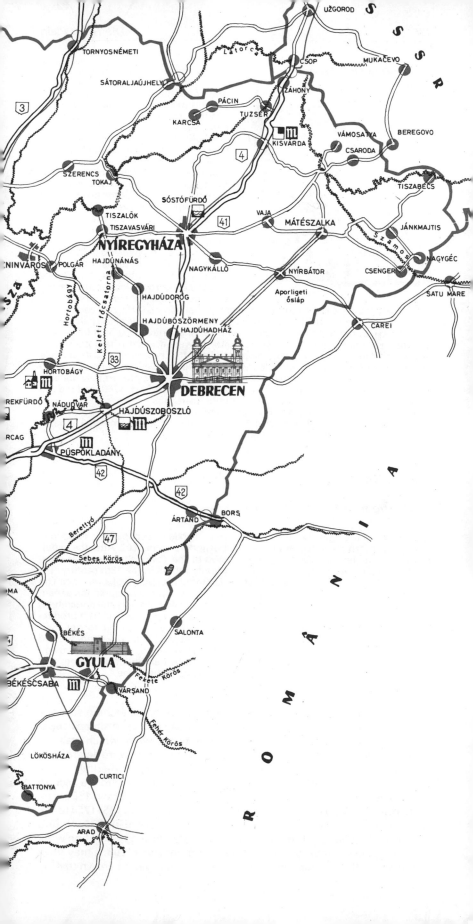

Serbian Orthodox church,
Ráckeve

border. It was at one time covered by sand-drifts; but today these sand-drifts or sandhills can hardly be seen, for human effort and skill have changed the appearance of the region completely.

RÁCKEVE (46 km south of Budapest, reached by taking Rd. 51, or in an hour by taking the express suburban train that begins at the Soroksári út in Budapest on the southern outskirts of the city) lies at the south end of Csepel Island, where it serves as the fishing centre for the Soroksár branch of the Danube, which abounds in fish. The magnificent Baroque **palace** standing next to the main road was built in 1702 according to the plans of Johann Lucas von Hildebrandt for Prince Eugene of Savoy, a leader of the army that drove out the Turks. The richest section of the palace is the monumental octagonal portico facing the ceremonial courtyard. Statues embellish the domed parapet in the middle of the palace. The Gothic style **Serbian Orthodox church** with its single nave was built in 1440 by a group of Serbian settlers. Two Baroque stories were added to the Gothic tower in 1758, and the tower clock was completed in 1776. The church and its chapels are filled with late Byzantine-styled wall-paintings depicting scenes from the Bible. Although they date from the 18th century, they were presumably done by repainting the originals. The Baroque iconostasis dates from 1768, and the red marble sepulchral monument in the vestibule from 1528.

From Rd. 51 running south of Budapest, and towards Baja, two roads branch out to the east at **SOLT** (85.5 km): Rd. 53 in the direction of Kiskőrös–Kiskunhalas towards Tompa and Rd. 52 to Kecskemét (see pp. 199)

Kalocsa

118 km from Budapest on Rd. 51.

Kalocsa, which originally lay on the banks of the Danube, is today situated 6 km from the river as a result of an alteration in the river-bed. Kalocsa was founded in the 11th century by the first Hungarian king, Stephen, who also established here an episcopal (later an archiepiscopal) see as well as a cathedral building. During later centuries Kalocsa became fortified, its protection being made easier by the surrounding water and swamps. The city enjoyed its golden age in the 15th century, but it soon became a victim of the Turkish occupation and was burned down in 1602. After the expulsion of the Turks, the town was completely rebuilt in the 18th century. Today industrial plants of all sizes can be found here, but the population's main source of livelihood is still agriculture, especially vegetable and fruit production, notably the cultivation of their excellent paprika. The land around Kalocsa devoted to paprika-growing includes 32 neighbouring villages and covers 3,500 hectares.

Two buildings representative of the rich heritage of the archiepiscopacy in the town stand on the main square, **Szabadság tér:** the **Archiepiscopal Palace** and the Baroque **Cathedral** with its two towers, which was the fourth cathedral to be built on this spot (the other three were destroyed). Foundation walls of the 11th- and 13th-century cathedrals were unearthed in 1908–1912, but the Gothic cathedral erected in the second half of the 14th century was completely destroyed by a fire in 1602. The cathedral standing here today was completed between 1735–1754 to the plans of András Mayerhoffer. Its interior was completed in 1770. Among the old **archiepiscopal tombs** found in the crypt during restoration work in 1910 was a red marble sepulchral monument from 1203. It may have belonged to the archbishop who brought the Hungarian crown to King

Stephen I from Rome. The three-storied Baroque **Archbishop's Palace** was built between 1770–76 by Gáspár Oswald, a Piarist brother. Frescoes done by F. A. Maulbertsch around 1780 adorn the hall and the chapel on the first floor. The achiepiscopal library holds a valuable collection on its beautifully-carved shelves.

In front of the cathedral is a **statue of the Trinity** completed in 1786; a statue of **Pál Tomory,** Archbishop of Kalocsa and the leader of the Battle of Mohács (1526), stands in the square next to the church. A light mobile sculpted by Nicolas Schöffer, who was born in Kalocsa, has also been erected here recently.

A "painting woman" of Kalocsa

István király utca, the main street of the city, begins at Szabadság tér. Along the street are a few beautiful Baroque and neo-Classical buildings, among which is a three-storied Baroque **seminary** built in 1760. Today it houses a **cultural centre.** The **Viski Károly Museum** at **No. 25** has a collection of folk art. In addition to folk costume, furniture and ceramics, the working tools of handicraftsmen, slipper-makers, shoe-makers and weavers may also be seen here.

A reed-thatched peasant house with a porch stands at **Tompa Mihály utca 1.** It has been furnished with richly coloured **folk art** from Kalocsa and the surrounding area, including embroideries, furniture, and painted walls. The women painters of Kalocsa are well known for their wall-painting.

Baja

160 km from Budapest on Rd. 51; 243 km by rail.

Baja was built on the banks of the so-called Kamarás-Danube. The many islands lying in the vicinity, the small branch of the Danube, and the wooded landscape have made Baja a popular summer resort area and a favourite with campers. (There is a beach as well as a camping site on Petőfi Island, opposite the main square of the city.)

Baja was a centre of commerce in the Middle Ages, and under the Turkish occupation it became an important fortified town (although it was only a stockade castle reinforced with timbers) and a centre of the Moslem religion. After being freed from Turkish rule, Baja became an important Danube post; in addition to being an industrial and cultural centre, it still retains its commercial importance.

Béke tér, encircled on three sides by beautiful, protected buildings, forms the centre of Baja; the fourth side of the square is bordered by the Kamarás-Danube, otherwise known as the Sugovica. The most important structure in the square is the neo-Classical building of the **Türr István Museum** standing on the corner of Deák Ferenc utca. (Türr, who was born in Baja in 1825 and took part in the preparation of the construction of the Panama and Corinth Canals, also drew up the plans for the construction of the irrigation canals in the Great Plain.) The museum has a rich

Sándor Petőfi's birthplace, Kiskőrös

collection of archeology, folklore and fine arts. The Baroque **Parish Church** in **Tóth Kálmán tér** was built in 1765; the Baroque **Franciscan church (Bartók Béla u. 4)** was built in 1728. It is also worth visiting the late Baroque **Serbian Orthodox churches** at **Táncsics Mihály utca 21** and **Szabadság útja 6** respectively. A beautiful late 18th-century iconostasis can be seen in the latter.

The neo-Classical synagogue at **Munkácsy Mihály utca 7–9** was erected in 1845. At present it is being converted into a library. Founded in 1946, the **artists' colony** of Baja was given a home in the neo-Classical (former Vojnich) mansion at **Arany János utca.** (It is interesting to note that the capitals are adorned with the Hungarian coats of arms; this is the result of a movement, started at the beginning of the last century, to create a "national" style of architecture to replace the traditional style.) A **statue of** the adventurous 18th-century world traveller, native of Baja, **András Jelky,** was erected in **Április 4. tér** (Ferenc Medgyessy, 1936).

Next to the modern hospital in Petőfi Sándor utca lie the Déry-gardens with their beds of roses. A memorial to the men who fell in World War I also stands here. It consists of a gigantic 15 m high stone prism, the only decoration on it being a sword in relief. A memorial to the liberating Soviet army has been erected behind the stone prism. It is also worth visiting the city **Observatory** (Csillagvizsgáló Intézet).

West of Baja, at **BÁTASZÉK** (20 km), Rd. 55 runs into Rd. 56 leading from Budapest to Mohács, and leads to Szeged in the east (see p. 204).

The first small community on Rd. 53, which turns off Rd. 51 at **SOLT** (see p. 196) towards Szeged, is Kiskőrös.

KISKŐRÖS (31 km from Solt): Its attraction is a reed-thatched, single-storied peasant house. It was in this house that the great poet and national hero Sándor Petőfi was born on January 1, 1823. The other building in the garden is today a museum. The restored house at **Szent István utca 23** is also well worth a visit. The building, which is a monument of folk art, now houses a Slovak folklore centre.

Kiskunhalas

145 from Budapest first on Rd. 51 and then turning off onto Rd. 53.

The multi-storied, neo-Classical **former Town Hall** was built in 1833–1834 by the Kecskemét architect Ágoston Fischer. Another historic monument to be seen is the 18th-century **Calvinist Parsonage** with its columned façade standing in **Hősök tere. A windmill** built around 1850 is still standing in **Kölcsey utca.** (At the turn of the century, 87 windmills were working in Kiskunhalas and its neighbourhood.) The rich collection housed in the **museum,** consists of paintings by **János Thorma,** a native of Kiskunhalas. The archeological collection housed here is also important. What Kiskunhalas is really famous for, however, is its **lacework.** This finely hand-sewn needle lacework, which has since conquered the world, started to develop in 1902, on the initiative of Árpád Dékáni, a fine arts and drawing teacher, and Mária Markovits. In the **Lace House** the making of exquisite pieces of lacework can be watched, finished pieces bought, or old pieces admired in the small museum.

Kecskemét

85 km from Budapest on Rd. 5; 106 km by rail.

On the way to Kecskemét, one of the most important towns lying between the Danube and Tisza rivers, the road passes through **DABAS.** Dabas was formerly an important community, and even today a large number of neo-Classical mansions with porches, at one time belonging to the nobility, can be found in the small community. The neo-Classical building formerly housing a casino today serves as a **library.**

Like most of the cities found on the Great Plain, Kecskemét is surrounded by a rural belt consisting mainly of farms.

Archeological discoveries show that the Kecskemét area was inhabited as early as the 1st century. The conquering Hungarians also established a settlement here, which in the 14th century became a provincial market town. Kecskemét was ravaged when the Mongols overran the area, and this was soon followed by a period of Turkish destruction. Under the Turks, Kecskemét was governed directly by the Sultan, and as a result of being granted this status, it enjoyed some protection. The town started to prosper towards the middle of the last century, when wine and fruit production began in large areas of sandy soil on the outskirts of the city.

The rich archeological material on exhibition in the **Katona József Museum** is not the only point of interest worth seeing on **Katona József sétány** in front of the railway station; the promenade with the statues of the town's famous citizens should also be visited. A memorial plaque on the main building of the station states that **Zoltán Kodály,** the great Hungarian composer, was born in the house. It was not long ago that the

Kodály Zoltán Institute of Music Teaching, Kecskemét

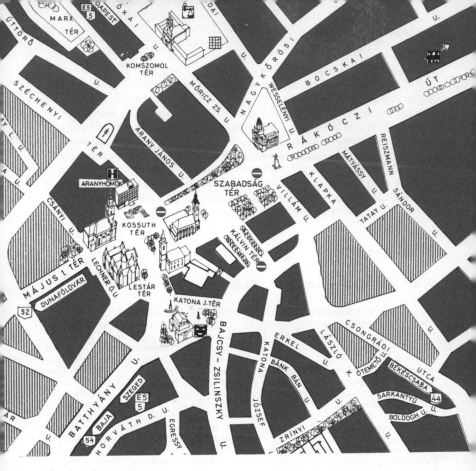

Kecskemét

Kodály Zoltán Institute (Kodály Zoltán Zenepedagógiai Intézet) was opened in a recently restored Baroque convent building (Kéttemplom köz).

Four squares running irregularly into one another form the heart of the town. The Moresque building of a **former synagogue** standing in **Szabadság tér** (1862, János Zitterbarth) is today the home of the House of Technology. Szabadság tér also includes the Hungarian *art nouveau*-style **Cifra** (Ornamental) **Palace**. The modern **Aranyhomok Hotel** is at the end of Széchenyi tér. Three churches stand on adjoining **Kossuth Lajos tér**: a former Franciscan church, built at the turn of the 14th century and remodelled during the Baroque period (it includes Gothic and Renaissance sections); a **Calvinist church** from 1680–1684, which has been rebuilt several times; and a **Catholic church** known as the Old Church, which was built between 1774 and 1806 by Gáspár Oswald, a Piarist brother. The most famous building in Kossuth Lajos tér is the three-storied **Town Hall** built between 1893 and 1896 by Ödön Lechner and Géza Pártos. It was one of the first experiments with a uniquely Hungarian style of architecture. Adorning the ceremonial hall are frescoes painted by Bertalan Székely in 1896–1897.

On a **natural stone block**, which has been split into two in the gardens in front of the Town Hall, is written: "One of Kecskemét's greatest sons broke his heart here." This unusual memorial stone marks the spot where **József Katona,** the father of Hungarian historical drama, and the creator of "Bánk bán", died of a heart attack in 1830. The **Museum of Hungarian Naïve Artists** is located in a renovated house at **Gáspár András utca 11.**

Shepherd and sheep-pen at Bugac-puszta

The southern façade of the Town Hall faces a third, smaller square, **Lestár tér,** which in its turn ends at **Katona József tér** with its neat park. A **theatre** named after József Katona, as well as a **statue of the Trinity** erected in 1742 and standing by a bronze statue of the dramatist, are also worth mentioning.

The **artists' colony** (Műkert) lying in the southeastern part of the city was founded in 1912; **Béla Iványi Grünwald** was its first director, and he was followed by **Imre Révész** in 1920. Many famous artists received their training here. (Like other colonies, this one is supported today by the Fine Arts Foundation.) The **Bozsó Collection (Klapka u. 34)** houses the work of a local painter.

EXCURSION

Bugac-puszta (40 km south of Kecskemét) was at one time an area where sand-hills, salt lakes, and small forests full of groves alternated with one another, and all-the-year-round animal breeding was common. The Bugac-puszta at one time consisted of almost 17,000 hectares; today more than a third of the area is covered with flourishing fruit-orchards and forests. Part of the puszta has been preserved to exhibit the former pastoral life of the area. In addition to herds of grey cattle, horse-breeding and other traditions native to the life on the puszta, there is also a **Museum of Pastoral Life** (Pásztormúzeum) which contains an interesting collection. The **Bugac csárda** is especially attractive with its special dishes and atmosphere.

During the Turkish occupation, Kecskemét and two towns lying to the northeast, Cegléd and Nagykőrös, constituted a special kind of community. Delegates from the three towns deliberated on important matters and acted as one single corporate body. As a result of this strange legal situation they appeared under the joint name of "the three towns", administered justice, and made decisions collectively. (Cegléd will be discussed on p. 209)

Nagykőrös

16 km north of Kecskemét on Rd. 441, or 15 km south of Cegléd.

Nagykőrös became a market-town 500 years ago. During the last century, when the sands of the Great Plains were being prepared for human habitation, Nagykőrös became Kecskemét's chief competitor. Today it is one of the country's best-known vegetable and fruit producing centres. Besides the canned-food industry, other industries are in the process of being developed here.

In **Szabadság tér** is the two-storey ornate, Baroque **Town Hall** built about 1810 with a fire tower rising above the gable (the structures at the sides date from the 19th century). The **Calvinist church** in the same square was built in the 15th century in the Gothic style and was later enlarged in the 16th and 19th centuries (the treasury is rich in Hungarian goldsmiths' works). The **Catholic church**, built between 1782 and 1788, is a beautiful example of architecture in the style of Louis XVI. From 1851 to 1860 the great Hungarian poet **János Arany** was a teacher at the Nagykőrös grammar school. A bust and a small museum in the grammar school preserve his memory. The poet's home was at **Arany János utca 28** (today a school). The **Arany János Museum** is housed in a neo-Classical building with a central projection supported by Doric columns at **Ceglédi út 19.** At one time the museum building was part of a stud farm; it later became an army barracks. Not far from here is situated the **Cifrakert,** formerly an abode of outlaws. Today it is one of the town's favourite places of recreation.

Kiskunfélegyháza

27 km southeast of Kecskemét on Rd. 5.

Kiskunfélegyháza was occupied by the Cumanians in the Middle Ages, completely destroyed during the Turkish period, and later settled by the Jazygians in 1743. (The Cumanians and Jazygians, nomadic people from the east, migrated here in the 13th century.) The new settlers worked the area hard, so that Kiskunfélegyháza soon became one of the most prosperous towns on the Great Plain.

The single-storied **inn and meat-market** at **Szabadság tér 9** was built in 1819 by János Mayerhoffer, and the poet **Sándor Petőfi's father,** István Petrovics, leased it for some time. The former home of the Petrovics family is located nearby in a small side street. The birthplace of another great figure of Hungarian literature, the novelist **Ferenc Móra** (1879–1934), is in **Móra Ferenc utca.** The single-naved **Parish Church** on Béke tér was built in 1744–1752 (and enlarged and remodelled in 1803 and 1904 respectively); the pulpit and statues on the side altars are in Rococo style.

The former **Cumanian Captain's House** at **Vörös Hadsereg útja 9,** built in 1753 and enlarged with an upper storey in 1794, is today the home of the **Little Cumania Museum** (Kiskun Múzeum). An interesting exhibition on the history of prisons can be seen in the two-storey former prison standing in the courtyard. An old **windmill** has been erected in the museum's courtyard.

CSONGRÁD (25 km east of Kiskunfélegyháza on Rd. 451) lies on the right bank of the Tisza. This typically Great Plain town was the county capital in the 10th to 13th centuries. The thatched peasant houses of the inner town are protected

architectural monuments. The **museum** has a good archeological collection (recreation area, beach, campsite and restaurant on the bank of the Tisza and at the mouth of the Körös River; facilities for fishing in the Holt-Tisza branch; thermal baths in the town centre).
ÓPUSZTASZER (34 km from Csongrád towards Szeged): **National Historical Memorial Park.** Behind an impressive entrance building, the Conquest Memorial commemorates the first assembly of the 7 conquering Magyar tribal chiefs. Excavations have uncovered the remains of a medieval monastery and a rich settlement; these may be seen in the garden of ruins. A little further away an

Windmill at Kiskunfélegyháza

open-air museum presents the architecture and way of life of the Hungarian agricultural town and homestead. On 20th August each year celebrations are held with a rich programme of folklore.

Szentes (12.5 km from Csongrád on Rd. 451) lies beyond the Tisza. The town will nevertheless be discussed here, because it is easier to approach it from Csongrád.

Szentes

37.5 km from Kiskunfélegyháza on Rd. 451.

Szentes is an agricultural community lying on the left bank of the Tisza. Like the other communities on the Great Plain, it was rebuilt and populated in the two hundred years or so following the destruction that took place during the period of Turkish occupation.

Points of interest: the neo-Classical **Catholic church** with its Baroque tower in **Köztársaság tér** (1843–1847), the Baroque **Greek Orthodox church** (1786) and its iconostasis (now restored) at **Kossuth Lajos utca 4;** and the **Calvinist church** (1808–1826) in **Kossuth tér.** Other public buildings, such as the **Town Hall** and the old eclectic **County Hall** also stand in Kossuth tér, but the tone of the square is better set by the trees and flowers growing there.

The houses of the pleasant small town, with their columns and porches, testify to considerable wealth and do not accurately reflect the former hard life of the agricultural workers. This is better shown by Zoltán Kovács's "Labourer", a statue erected in **Széchenyi Park** with its large number of rare trees. The neo-Classical building of the **Koszta József Museum,** built around 1840 **(Széchenyi liget 187),** contains an extremely rich collection of findings dating back to the Age of Migrations, as well as local historical and ethnographical materials. The famous black cooking ware with its metallic lustre made by the potters of Szentes are specially noticeable among items of the collection of folk art. Paintings by József Koszta are also exhibited here. (József Koszta, 1861–1949, a painter who depicted on canvas the peasant life of the area, lived most of his life and created his work on a farmstead near Szentes.)

Szeged

170 km from Budapest on Rd. 5; 191 km by rail.

Szeged is the most important economic and cultural centre of the southern part of the Great Plain. Five thousand years ago a people who formed the so-called "Kőrös Culture" inhabited the area now occupied by Szeged, which is situated on the banks of the Tisza and at the mouth of the Maros rivers. The area was inhabited by the Illyrians from the 8th to the 7th centuries B.C., and they were followed later by the Celts, the Jazygians from the east, and then by the Huns in the 5th century. Following the death of Attila and the collapse of the Hunnish Empire, the Gepids and then the Avars appeared on the scene. During the first years following the founding of the Hungarian state, Szeged became an unloading and distributing centre for salt shipments arriving on the Maros from Transylvania (a document written by King Béla III [1183] refers to Szeged in connection with the salt shipments arriving there). The city's development was interrupted by the Mongol invasion (1241–1242). Following the withdrawal of the Mongol forces, King Béla IV had a fortress built in Szeged. After the defeat at Mohács (1526), the Turks ravaged and plundered the city, taking it in 1543 and holding it until 1686. Thus, Szeged became the centre of the Sultan's lands. Almost a century passed after the Turks had been driven from the country before economic and cultural life started to develop to any signifi-cant degree. In March 1879 destruction caused by the flooding of the Tisza river reduced almost six thousand homes to ruins, leaving only about three hundred still habitable. In gratitude for the help they received from abroad for the reconstruction of their city, the citizens of Szeged named certain stretches of the Great Boulevard (Nagykörút) after the cities that came to their aid (Vienna, London, Paris, Berlin, Brussels, Rome). The streets still bear these names. The period of rapid development, which followed the reconstruction efforts, gave the city of Szeged the appearance it has today. Development gained even greater momentum after 1945 when a number of new residential estates were built. Industrial development was boosted by the fields near Szeged which produce most of the country's hydrocarbon output. A significant industrial settlement developed around the city (house construction factory, rubber factory, cable works, etc.). Today Szeged enjoys a highly developed agricultural (paprika and fruit production), and an important and up-to-date food industry (salami, and canned-foods production, paprika-processing, etc.), many textile factories and many other industries. Szeged is one of Hungary's most important university cities; the Open-air Theatre Festival held each summer enjoys an international reputation.

Széchenyi tér, a square covering more than 50,000 sq.m, forms the centre of Szeged's inner city. The square's harmonious buildings, its four rows of plane trees, and the statues erected in the gardens all contribute to making Széchenyi tér one of the country's most beautiful public squares. The most important building in the square is the **City Hall,** which was originally built in the Baroque style in 1799, but later enlarged and remodelled in an eclectic-Baroque style after the floods of 1879.

The city's "promenade" **Kárász utca** begins at Széchenyi tér and runs towards the south. It passes **Klauzál tér,** a square with a neo-Classical atmosphere in the middle of which stands a statue of **Lajos Kossuth.** It was here, from the balcony of the neo-Classical **Kárász House,** that on July 12, 1849 Kossuth delivered the last speech he was to give in Hungary before he went into exile.

On the south end of Kárász utca, at **Dugonics tér,** a statue of the first Hungarian novelist, a native of Szeged, András Dugonics, stands in the park. The most prominent building in the square is the **main building of the University,** in front of which is a statue of Attila József (by Imre Varga). Attila József began his studies in Szeged, but because of a revolutionary poem which he wrote, he was expelled from the university. In the middle of the square stands a modern fountain fashioned into the shape of an amphitheatre, with automatically-controlled water, sound and light effects.

Szeged

In the middle of **Aradi vértanúk tere** (the Martyrs of Arad were thirteen generals of the 1848–49 Hungarian War of Independence executed by a summary court-martial under Habsburg absolutism) stands the equestrian **statue of Ferenc Rákóczi II** (by György Vastagh). **Április 4. útja,** which runs from the south, ends at the square where the **Heroes' Gate** (1936) stands. From the Heroes' Gate there is a fine view of the chromium steel "waves" of the **Flood Memorial** on the bank of the Tisza (György Segesdi, 1979). Bordering the square on the east is the early eclectic building of the **university's Faculty of Natural Sciences.** A replica of the **equestrian statue of St. George,** a great creation of the Hungarian medieval sculptors Márton and György Kolozsvári (1373), stands on **Rerrich Béla tér,** the eastern extension of Aradi vértanúk tere. (The original is in the Hradčany in Prague.)

A triumphal gate and arcade lead from Aradi vértanúk tere into **Dóm tér,** on the north side of which stands Szeged's most monumental building, the neo-Romanesque **Votive Church** with its two towers. Following the floods of 1879, the city fathers made a vow that they would erect a memorial church. Construction work on the church began in 1913 and was completed in 1930. The length of the church on the outside is 81 m, its width is 51 m; the spires are 93 m high, and the height of the chapel on the outside is 54 m. The façade is adorned with mosaics of the twelve apostles, and in the middle there is a 3 m high white marble statue of Our Lady of Hungary. The church's huge organ has 9,040 pipes housed in the main works of the organ loft, in the dome and on the choir just above the sanctuary oratory. (The pipes range in size from 1.2 cm to 5 m.)

The Medieval **Tower of St. Demetrius** stands on the square in front of the church. The square-shaped lower half of the Romanesque, three-storey monument is from the 12th century, while the octagonal upper section was built in the 13th century. It was moved from the Baroque tower (reconstructed in 1731) of the inner city Parish Church in 1925. The interior of the church is adorned with wall-paintings by Vilmos Aba Novák (1894–1941).

A row of arcades forming a circle on the ground floors in the buildings around the square is where the **National Memorial Hall** was established in 1931. A number of great figures of Hungarian literature, art, science, and history have been immortalized in statues, reliefs and memorial plaques in the wall.

Each summer the **Szeged Open-air Theatre Festival** (Szegedi Szabadtéri Játékok) is held in a part of the square closed off by the arcaded buildings. The first performance was held here in 1933 ("The Tragedy of Man", a drama by Imre Madách, [1823–1864]). The festivities were interrupted by World War II and were not revived until 1959; but since then

Dóm tér with the Dömötör Tower, Szeged

View of the bank of the Tisza from Újszeged, Szeged

they have continued to attract growing international interest. The seating capacity of the theatre is 6,100 and the stage is 600 sq.m in size.

A **Serbian Orthodox church** (1773–1778) with a tower in the style of Louis XVI stands behind the Votive Church. The iconostasis dates from the middle of the 18th century. A new building adjoining the Dome is a later addition to the building complex encircling the square. It houses the **Somogyi Library.**

The **University Clinic** is situated between Dóm tér and the Tisza River. **Oskola utca,** a street beginning at the square and running in a northeast direction, is extremely old. The neo-Classical house at **No. 20** (1867–1868) was originally a hotel; today it is the main office of the Szeged committee of the Hungarian Academy of Sciences.

Oskola utca ends at **Roosevelt tér,** where a new bridge, built in 1948 in place of the old bridge that was blown up by the Germans, spans the Tisza. The **Palace of Education and Culture** standing in the square houses the **Móra Ferenc Museum.** The building was completed in 1896. The neo-Classical façade is adorned with Corinthian columns. **Statues** of two writers from Szeged, Ferenc Móra and István Tömörkény, who were also directors of the museum, and the poet Gyula Juhász stand on the square in front of the museum buildings.

The **Móra Ferenc Museum** contains, in addition to rich material on local history, fine arts, history, biology and ethnography, and the rich archeological materials amassed by Ferenc Móra, an outstanding writer and director of the museum between 1917 and 1934.

A few **ruins of the former castle** can be seen on the promenade behind the museum building. Work was started on the castle in the 13th century and continued throughout the following centuries. The castle, at one time strategically significant, was, after the expulsion of the Turks, used as a prison until the 18th century. Following the floods of 1879, the castle was torn down with only a section of the 18th-century casemates remaining. It is in these remains that an exhibition of local history and a collection of stonework finds have been set up.

The eclectic building of the **National Theatre of Szeged** (Szegedi Nemzeti Színház), which has a seating capacity of 1,000, stands almost opposite the castle, with its back towards the park. On the promenade opposite the theatre stands a monument to the Hungarian Republic of Councils (Tanácsköztársaság emlékmű, 1960, by György Segesdi and János Dávid).

József Attila sugárút is an avenue which leads north towards the **Upper City** where the **former Minorite church and monastery** (1754–67) in **Szent György tér** are worth visiting.

Hunyadi János sugárút is an avenue which begins at Aradi vértanúk tere and leads to the **Lower City**, a part of Szeged still preserving the atmosphere of a village. Here, in **Mátyás király tér** stands an important historic building, the **former Franciscan church**. The 60 m long Gothic church, originally built without a tower, contains a stellar-vaulted sanctuary completed in 1498. The nave of the church with its reticulated vaulting was constructed in 1503; and the tower was added in 1772. The Baroque furnishings in the interior, the altars, the pulpit, and the richly carved furnishings of the sacristy date from the 18th century. The **former Franciscan monastery** building is also Baroque. There are several traditional **peasant houses** with the beautiful ornamentation characteristic of Szeged near Mátyás király tér.

The so-called **Rókus** (Roch) **section** of the city lies northwest of the inner city. The most worthwhile points of interest here can be reached by taking **Kígyó utca**, which begins at **Klauzál tér**. Kígyó utca ends at **Hajnóczy utca** where there is an old neo-Classical **synagogue**, built in 1843. Almost next door stands a **new synagogue** built between 1900 and 1903 with a gigantic 48 mg high dome. The interior furnishings consist of valuable handmade pieces.

The **Star Prison,** so named because of the shape of its ground-plan, is situated in square-shaped **Marx tér**.

The part of the city lying on the left bank of the Tisza is called **Újszeged** (New Szeged). Separated from the inner city only by the river, Újszeged nevertheless offers a completely different picture. (Left of the bridgehead are situated the Tisza public beach and a swimming-pool. Several thermal-water pools and four pools which can also be used in winter are located nearby.) Szeged's largest park, the **People's Park** (Népliget), lies on both sides of **Rózsa Ferenc sugárút,** which runs towards the east beyond the bridge. In the park is an outdoor theatre with seating for 1,500 people. One of the main points of interest in Újszeged, where new residential sections are being built, is the 18-hectare **University Botanical Gardens** (Füvészkert). The Gardens contain more than 2,000 kinds of domestic plants as well as around 1,500 tropical plants.

Residents of Szeged as well as visitors enjoy walking or driving along the **banks of the Tisza.** On the right bank of the river, almost adjoining the city, are a number of fishermen's inns where the visitor can have his choice of a real Szeged fish dish such as the Szegedi *halászlé*, a fish soup popular throughout Hungary, or the *halpaprikás*, a combination of fish seasoned with paprika, fried carp or catfish, all prepared under the watchful eye of the visitor, as well as excellent wines grown on the sandy soil. A 3 km walk along the left bank of the Tisza towards the north leads to the area surrounding the mouth of the Maros, a real painter's paradise.

TÁPÉ (on the outskirts of Szeged, 3 km to the east) is a fishing community on the right bank of the Tisza. The inhabitants of Tápé have preserved their old songs and dances, and occasionally an inhabitant dressed in national costume can be seen. Bulrush-weaving is a characteristic form of handicraft among the people of Tápé. (**Ethnographical collection**: Vártó utca 4.) The **church** built in the 13th century but rebuilt in the 14th and 18th centuries was enlarged during reconstruction work in 1939 to such an extent that the original Gothic nave has become the transept, but the original Gothic sanctuary with its 14th-century frescoes has remained unaltered.

A large part of **Fehér-tó** (White Lake, 5 km on Rd. 5 from the outskirts of the city) comprises a fish hatchery, while another part, 350 hectares in size, is a natural conservation area where large numbers of rare, aquatic birds nest. (Many of the birds are found nowhere else in the country.) The area also serves as a resting place for giant flocks of birds migrating to other parts of the world. Ornithologists have observed almost 250 different kinds of migrating birds here. Since it is a nature conservation area, Fehér-tó may be observed only from the look-out tower which can be approached from the Szatymaz cemetery hill.

Cegléd

70 km from Budapest on Rd. 4 (E60); 73 km by rail.

The community of Cegléd, mentioned earlier in connection with Kecskemét, has been inhabited ever since the Migration Period. A rural market-town as early as 1444, Cegléd was the scene in 1514 of a speech given by György Dózsa, the leader of the peasant revolt, calling the whole nation to war.

Owing to its status as a "sultanate" town, Cegléd suffered relatively little damage during the Turkish occupation. It was here that Lajos Kossuth, in September 1848, summoned the inhabitants of the Great Plain to battle against Habsburg autocracy. Both the large statue and the rich historical material on exhibition in the **Kossuth Museum** (corner of Rákóczi út and Marx Károly utca) preserve the memory of this event.

The neo-Classical **Calvinist church** with two towers and a domed antevestibule supported by columns (Szabadság tér; built between 1836 and 1881) was planned by József Hild. The **Catholic Parish Church,** built between 1822 and 1825 and located in **Kossuth tér,** is also a historic monument. The **Dózsa statue** standing in Kossuth tér was erected in memory of the historic speech that György Dózsa made here.

Jászberény

79 km from Budapest on Rd. 31; 93 km by rail (or 50 km north of Szolnok on Rd. 32 and by rail).

Jászberény was the centre of the former province of Jászság (Jazygia). The Jazygians were a nomadic people, descendants of the Alans, who settled along the Zagyva River during King Béla IV's rule in the first half of the 13th century. Today the territory called the Jászság no longer differs in either landscape or ethnography from the rest of the area. In 1876 Jazygian autonomy ended, and since then Jászberény has been the most important town of the district. At the beginning of the 18th century, following the expulsion of the Turks, it already enjoyed the status of the country's sixth most populous city. Later decline set in. Jászberény began to develop again after 1945.

A **former Franciscan church,** built in the Gothic style in the middle of the 15th century, stands on an island surrounded by branches of the Zagyva River in **Hatvani utca,** a road leading from the heart of the town to the Zagyva River. The church was destroyed by the Turks in 1560; it was restored in the 18th century in the Baroque style. At the entrance to the island stands the **statue of Mrs. Déry,** otherwise Róza Széppataki, a 19th-century pioneer of the Hungarian theatre, an actress and a native of the city (Károly Vasas, 1965). A row of Baroque and neo-Classical historical buildings, including the Baroque **Jászkun Centre,** stand in **Lehel vezér tér,** a square forming the centre of the town. The **Jász** (Jazygian) **Museum** is housed at **Táncsics Mihály utca 5.** It was constructed in 1782 in the style of Louis XVI, but was remodelled at the beginning of the 19th century. Another part of the museum is in the courtyard of the **Town Hall** by Mihály Pollack (1838–39). The museum contains archeological material, finds dating back to the Age of Migrations, objects associated with the various guilds, and ethnographic items, but its most valuable treasure is the Lehel Horn, an 8th-century Byzantine work carved out of ivory. Tradition has it that in 955 A.D., after the defeat at the Battle of Augsburg, and before he was executed, Lehel, one of the leaders of the attack, struck the emperor a blow in the head with this horn. There is no historical basis to this story, but in any case the horn has carefully been preserved in Jászberény since 1642.

Szolnok

98 km from Budapest on Rd. 4 (E60); 100 km by rail.

Szolnok lies between the Danube and the Tisza and is the gateway to the region beyond the Tisza (the Tiszántúl). The castle of Szolnok, founded in 1076, was considered for centuries to be one of the country's most important fortresses. From 1552 it was a Turkish administrative centre for more than 130 years. Because it supported the Rákóczi War of Independence, the Habsburgs had the castle blown up.

On September 1, 1847 the Pest–Szolnok railway line opened, after which the town's first industrial plants came into existence. During World War II the city was almost completely destroyed. Since its rebuilding, Szolnok has become not only the county capital, a transport and agricultural centre, but also the most advanced industrial centre in the Great Plain.

Kossuth Lajos tér forms the centre of the town. In the square is the **Town Hall,** which was built during the second half of the 19th century, as well as the **Damjanich János Museum** housed in a late neo-Classical, former hotel built in 1860. The museum is named after the general of almost legendary fame who fought in the 1848–49 War of Independence and who was put to death in Arad (Rumania) following the defeat. Prehistoric materials, materials dating back to the Age of Migrations, archeological finds, materials connected with the history of the town and the Turkish period, as well as an ethnographic collection and paintings and statues by local masters living in the local artists' colony are on display in the museum. The **former Franciscan church (Koltói Anna u. 8)** built between 1723 and 1727 is a beautiful Baroque edifice. The town's old wooden-gabled **peasant houses** are very interesting; the majority of them can be found in the part of the town called the Tabán on the west bank of the Zagyva River **(Tabán u. 7, 8, 11, 19, 51, 63),** but there are also such houses at **Jókai utca 25, Kazinczy utca 3** and **Úttörő utca 5** and **18.**

Szolnok is also noted for its **artists' colony** built between the Zagyva and Tisza rivers, where the castle once stood. Founded at the beginning of the 1900s, the artists' colony has provided a workplace for a number of important Hungarian artists, such as László Mednyánszky (1852–1919) and Adolf Fényes (1867–1945). After being forced to close in World War II, the artists' colony is again the home of a number of well-known painters. A **marble memorial** to the leader of the victorious Battle of Szolnok (March 5, 1849), General János Damjanich (1804–1849), stands in the park. (The promenade along the Tisza provides a pleasant walk, while Marx Park nearby has a swimming-pool, a hotel and thermal baths.)

Szolnok

Thermal water (56 °C) used for curing rheumatism, inflammation, and women's diseases gushes forth in the bathing establishment next to the **Hotel Tisza.** Next door to the hotel is the **Szigligeti Theatre.**

A new recreation area called the **Tisza Park** is situated on the other end of the Tisza bridge. This contains camping facilities, wooden cabins, a hotel, thermal baths, public swimming facilities and a restaurant.

THE REGION BEYOND THE TISZA

The section of the country beyond the Tisza, the Tiszántúl, consists of all the Great Plain lying east of the Tisza with the exception of the northeastern corner of the plain.

With a low annual rainfall and frequently suffering from drought, it is even less varied than the country between the Danube and the Tisza. The settlements lie at great distances from one another and, before 1945, a significant proportion of the population earned their living from agriculture or from poorly-paid occasional work. The area was settled in a series of farms, and families lived an iso-

View of Szolnok

lated life remote from one another and unconnected with any village or town. By establishing small farming centres the government is trying to ensure that those still living on the farms are provided with economic and cultural opportunities. Industrial centres have also been established and agriculture has been advanced by the construction of irrigation systems. Each of the towns, which are rural in appearance but are fast becoming modernized, has its own individual atmosphere. However, with the exception of Gyula and Debrecen, not one of them can boast of any great historical monuments; but the historical traditions of these towns, findings dating back to the Age of Migrations, as well as their folklore, are all significant. The larger ethnic units of the Tiszántúl are: Nagykunság, Viharsarok and Hajdúság.

The southernmost sections beyond the Tisza can best be reached from Szeged, while its northeastern sections can be approached through Szolnok.

Makó

30 km from Szeged on Rd. 43.

Makó is not a typical town of the Great Plain, for at least half of the population is employed in industry (agricultural machinery plant, food processing). Makó's European reputation, however, can be chiefly attributed to one of its agricultural products, the onion, which it has been exporting in large quantities ever since the 19th century.

The strikingly-busy and lively small town existed as a settlement as early as the Age of Árpád. The name Makó was given to it in the 13th century when King Endre II (1205–1235) bestowed two neighbouring villages, where the town now stands, on one of his soldiers named Makó. It was almost completely destroyed by the Turks, and then in 1821 the flooding of the Maros River brought such destruc-

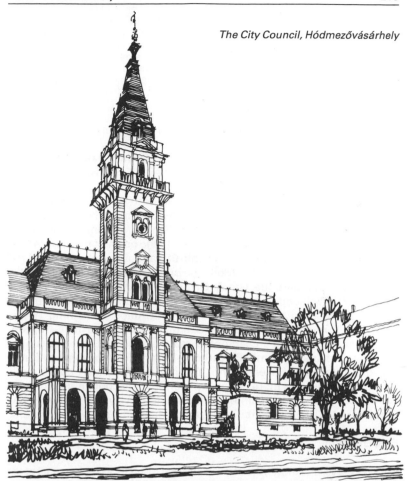

The City Council, Hódmezővásárhely

tion to the town that only a few homes remained intact. Makó's present appearance is therefore largely the result of the development of the past one and a half centuries. A large proportion of the town's historic buildings were constructed in the neo-Classical style.

The **bishop's residence at Szabadság tér 2,** and the **chapel** adjoining it were built in 1826. Serving today as the **Town Hall** the former county hall **(Lenin tér 22)** built in 1780 was later remodelled and enlarged in 1836 in the neo-Classical style. The Baroque **Calvinist church** in **Kálvin tér** was built in 1776–88 from a medieval structure that once existed there. The **Catholic church** was built between 1765 and 1772. (Thermal baths in the centre of the town.)

EXCURSION

KISZOMBOR (5 km south of Makó): **Parish Church** with 12th-century Roman stone chapel and 14th-century wall-paintings.

Hódmezővásárhely

25 km from Szeged on Rd. 47; 175 km from Budapest on Rds. 5, 451, and 45; 222 km from Budapest by rail.

In the 14th and 15th centuries numerous communities stood within the boundaries of the present-day town. The little town grew again after the

Turkish withdrawal, and since the end of the last century right up to the Liberation, it fulfilled an important role in agrarian proletarian movements. Folk art in Hódmezővásárhely has a rich tradition. Furniture-painters, embroiders and potters working in the market-place are mainly responsible for giving the city its reputation. A 70-year-old **majolica factory,** which is becoming better and better known, is continuing the reputation already established by Hódmezővásárhely's artists.

The most important buildings are situated in the centre of the city in **Kossuth Lajos tér**: the **Old Calvinist Church** surrounded by a fence and built in 1713; the two-storey, neo-Classical **former County Hall** (built in 1723, its present shape dating from 1882); the eclectic **Town Hall** designed by Miklós Ybl (1895). **Three statues** adorn the square: a statue of Kossuth by Ede Kallós, a Hussar memorial and the "Girl with a Jug", both by János Pásztor. The enormous late Baroque **New Calvinist Church** stands on **November 7. tér** (1792–1799). The town's new residential district has been built around Tanácsköztársaság tér, to the north of the square. The Baroque **Catholic Parish Church** in **Lenin út** was built between 1752–1758 and enlarged by Miklós Ybl in 1860. The principal works of importance in the 18th-century Baroque **Greek Orthodox church** at **Szántó Kovács János út 7,** which begins at Kossuth tér and runs towards the north, are the rich iconostasis and an icon from Mount Athos, containing 16 pictures. The **Tornyai János Museum (Szántó Kovács János út 16–18)** contains important ancient archeological materials, as well as the outstanding, so-called **Kökénydomb** (Blackthorn) **Hill** find, and the famous statue called the Venus of Kökénydomb. The museum's folk art collection is also well known, and there is also a picture-gallery containing works by János Tornyai and other painters of the artists' colony. The **Csucsi House (Rákóczi u. 101)** has an exhibition of the products of local master potters.

EXCURSION

MÁRTÉLY (10 km to the northwest) is a pleasant resort by a dead channel of the Tisza with wooden cabins in a campsite, a *csárda* and boats for hire.

Orosháza

34 km from Hódmezővásárhely on Rd. 47; 30 km by rail.

Points of interest to be seen in Orosháza: a **Lutheran church** built in 1780; the **Sarmatian Discoveries** and a rich **ethnographic collection** of the **Szántó Kovács János Museum (Dózsa György út 19).**

GYOPÁROSFÜRDŐ (4 km from the town) is a favourite resort of residents of Orosháza and visitors alike. It is situated near Gyopáros Lake, whose water is rich in mineral salts and other curative materials. The bathing facilities are situated close to the lake, whose water is used to fill some of the pools; but there is also a warm-water pool which is filled with thermal water (39 °C) flowing from a well.

Békéscsaba

208 km from Budapest first on Rd. 4, then, from Törökszentmiklós, on Rd. 46 and 47; 196 km by rail (35 km east of Orosháza on Rd. 47).

Békéscsaba, the capital of Békés county, was the largest town included in the former so-called Viharsarok (Stormy Corner). (The area extending east of the Tisza and south of the Körös rivers as far as the border was so called because it was the "stormy centre" of the agrarian socialist movements that took place in Hungary. It was here that the national struggle to improve the future of farm workers and poor peasants began.) As it had a fortress and the beginnings of a town, Békéscsaba was an important settlement as early as the 14th century. There was a significant decrease in population during the Turkish occupation; and after the withdrawal of the Turks, the area became unstable owing to frequent hostile attacks. Its development was hindered by natural disasters: several fires and earthquakes devastated the area, and in 1738 the plague, in 1838 a cholera epidemic took its toll of the population. It was only in the 18th century when Slovak settlers came in, that life in the city began again.

The small Baroque **Lutheran church** in **Rózsa Ferenc tér** with its stocky, galleried tower was built in 1745. The three-storey eclectic **secondary-school** building was built in 1899 by Ignác Alpár. The large Lutheran church in **Kossuth tér,** completed in 1824, is neo-Classical. The huge neo-Classical **ale-house (Kórház u. 4),** built about 1840 with a central projection and tympanum, is also interesting. A few **old peasant homes** in **Szigetvári utca (Nos. 41 and 43)** and **Kinizsi út (No. 20)** are protected buildings.

Mihály Munkácsy, a world-famous Hungarian painter, served as a joiner's apprentice in Békéscsaba. The **museum,** which bears the name of the great painter **(Széchenyi út 9)** contains a separate Munkácsy Memorial Room arranged with a few of his works and personal belongings. The museum building is also neo-Classical, and contains a collection dating back to the Bronze Age as well as ethnographic material.

Gyula

15 km from Békéscsaba on Rd 44; a Hungarian–Rumanian border crossing.

The small community of Gyula, a town which developed in the Middle Ages, was named in all probability after the grandson of one of the chiefs of the age of the Magyar Conquest. A brick fortress, Italian in appearance, was built here at the end of the 14th century. This important strategic point was taken by the Turks in 1566 and held until 1694. After the defeat of the War of Independence led by Rákóczi, the Harruckern family acquired Gyula and its surroundings from the Court of Vienna; but the fortress outside the city was demolished. Today it is an important centre of vegetable production, and is also known for its meat products (Gyulai sausage).

The Castle of Gyula

The **fortress** of Gyula, restored between 1954 and 1960, is a large Gothic brick building, an imposing sight with its 3 m thick walls and embrasures on top, and the gate tower on the south side. Among the vaulted rooms inside is the former castle chapel, now a **castle museum**. Though renovations have taken place almost every century, the Gothic features of the castle are still evident. The 16th-century round tower on the south-west corner which was once used for storing gunpowder (according to some views, it was a cannon-tower) houses a café. Each summer outdoor performances, the **Castle Performances**, are held in the castle.

There are almost twenty neo-Classical, one and two-storey houses in Gyula; and in addition, there are eighteen other kinds of houses and public buildings, seven chapels and a church, all of which are historical monuments. The house at **Apor Vilmos tér 7** is the birthplace of Ferenc Erkel, the composer who wrote the music for the Hungarian National Anthem and who was responsible for establishing the Hungarian National Opera. The **memorial plaque** on the front of the house now serving as the **Erkel Memorial Museum (Dürer Albert utca)** informs the reader that the house of the family from which Albrecht Dürer is descended stood here in the 16th century.

The **Catholic Parish Church** in **Szabadság tér** is an outstanding example of an ecclesiastical protected building. The furnishings inside the Baroque church, built in 1775, are spectacular.

A large park lies near the castle, which contains the town's second largest attraction, the **bathing area**. The thermal baths found here are considered one of the country's most attractive public pools. The **pool** is fed by thermal water (70 °C) which contains sodium and a number of alkaline-hydrogen carbonates and is therefore very effective as medicinal water. A former indoor ménage built in 1833 was converted into the **indoor swimming-pool**. A visit to the **former Almássy Mansion** built between 1798 and 1803 in a late Baroque style is well worth while. Large square, flat-roofed towers rise on the corners of the mansion. The tower on the right, which is provided with a Gothic gate, at one time formed part of the castle.

EXCURSION

BÉKÉS (10.5 km northeast of Békéscsaba on Rd. 47, or 21 km northwest of Gyula) was the site of a fortress during the age of the Conquest; the fortress was reinforced with stone walls at the beginning of the 14th century. It was destroyed without trace during the Turkish period. Today the visitor to Békés can see a number of historic monuments displaying traditional architectural features, for example the beautiful **old peasant houses** in **Babilon sor, Damjanich, Gorkij, Jancsik** and **Kispince utca**. The Baroque **Greek Orthodox church** in **Kossuth utca**, as well as the **Calvinist church** also standing here, built in 1775 and enlarged several times since then, are all protected buildings. The iodized radiferous thermal waters of the Békés Medicinal Baths (38–40°C) are used treating locomotor and women's diseases.

Szarvas

162 km from Budapest on Rd. 44; 161 km by rail; 46 km northwest of Békéscsaba on Rd. 44.

The old settlement which stood where Szarvas now stands had developed into a rural market town by the time the Turkish forces moved into the country. The Turks soon reduced the small town to ashes, and the population was almost completely wiped out. It was not until the beginning of the 18th century when resettlement began (mainly Slovak settlers) that the town came to life again. Sámuel Tessedik (1742–1820), the learned Lutheran

minister who, soon after arriving in
the recently-reborn village, urged the
solution of economic problems, played an important role in Szarvas's
growth. In 1770 Tessedik established
one of Europe's first agricultural institutes; he also wrote textbooks on agriculture, especially the cultivation of
alkaline soil.

Though present-day Szarvas is
a relatively young settlement,
there are a number of historical
monuments.
*The statue of a stag (szarvas) at
Szarvas*

The old **Bolza Man-
sion** built in 1780 and standing on the bank of the Körös River is Baroque
and so is the **Tessedik Sámuel School of Economics** built in 1790 and
situated in **Vajda Péter utca**. In the same street is a Baroque **Lutheran
church** (1786–88) as well as the **Tessedik farmhouse**, built around 1780.
A cultural institution is today housed in the neo-Classical building of the
former Vitrovszky mansion at **Szabadság utca 30**. There are a number of
neo-Classical residences in **Kossuth Lajos utca**; but the ones in **Arany
János, Jókai,** and **Vajda Péter utca** are regarded as historic monuments.
The construction and ornamentation of the **peasant houses** built in the
last century are especially interesting. The **Tessedik Sámuel Museum** at
Szabadság utca 34 was established in 1951; in addition to local historical
materials, it contains archeological and ethnographic collections. The
horse-driven mill at **Ady Endre utca 111** dating back to 1836 is a museum
piece. The furnishings of the mill have remained completely intact. (It is
the only such historic monument of folk industry in the country.) On the
main square **in front of the former Town Hall** stands a statue by György
Vastagh, a **bronze stag** which has become the symbol of the city.
A memorial plaque on an old acacia tree a few metres from the statue
informs the reader that it was Sámuel Tessedik who planted this tree.
A 19th-century **bronze well** depicting Ceres, the goddess of agriculture
and plenty, stands in **Kossuth tér**. In the courtyard of the **former Bolza
Mansion** (today a Research Institute for Irrigation and Rice Cultivation)
a bronze statue of Romulus and Remus proclaims the Italian origin of the
Bolza family. The 85-hectare **arboretum** is a sight unique on the bare
Great Plain.

It was Count Pál Bolza, a former landowner, who began to lay out the arboretum
at the end of the 18th century; but most of the credit for developing the
arboretum must go to his son, József. The arboretum is particularly rich in different types of pine trees (138 species and varieties), but deciduous trees are also
abundantly represented. Altogether, the number of species and varieties growing in the arboretum is 1,092 while the number of individual plants is approximately thirty thousand. Almost all the countries of the world except Australia are
represented in the Gardens. The most valuable species are a mammoth pine,
a gingko, Spanish pine, swamp-cypress, Chinese cedar, a cork-oak found along
the Amor River, a liquidambar, and a white oak.

EXCURSIONS

GYOMA (25 km northeast of Szarvas
on Rd. 443) is a small community of
ten thousand inhabitants. Founded
here in 1882, the **Kner Printing House**
soon became an internationally-fam-
ous institution for the publication of
Hungarian limited editions.

Rd. 46 which joins Rd. 4 at **TÖRÖKSZENTMIKLÓS** going towards Debrecen passes through Gyoma. Rd. 46 has a branch at Mezőtúr which ends at Kisújszállás.
MEZŐTÚR (19 km northwest of Gyoma on Rd. 46) is primarily known for its potters. Basing themselves on traditions extending back several centuries, the Mezőtúr potters make (mostly in co-operatives) jugs, flasks, jars, dishes and mugs, which are well known both in Hungary and abroad. (Folk art exhibition at the **Badár Museum**.) In addition to a few neo-Classical mansions and residences, Mezőtúr has a **Calvinist church (Kossuth tér)** and a **synagogue (Damjanich utca)** both built in neo-Classical style. Outside the town are six tumuli (burial mounds) that have remained intact.
TÚRKEVE (16 km northeast of Mezőtúr): **Two windmills** can be seen on the outskirts. The fittings on one of the windmills have remained in perfect condition. Interesting sculpture collection and folk art exhibition at the **Finta Museum (Attila utca 1)**. (Thermal baths.)
KISÚJSZÁLLÁS (14 km north of Túrkeve) lies on Rd. 4 leading to Debrecen. The next town on Rd. 4 is Karcag, 18 km from Kisújszállás.

Karcag

154 km from Budapest on Rd. 4; 162 km by rail.

The oldest historic monument of the small town, the **ruins of a 16th-century chapel**, is situated on **Chapel Hill**. A Baroque **Calvinist church** built between 1745 and 1755 with a tower dating back to 1789 stands in **Szabadság tér**. At **Horváth Ferenc utca 7** stands the **Györffy István Museum** with its rich collection of folk art, which reflects Karcag's former status as the folk art centre of the area. The Baroque **Greek Orthodox church** in **Horváth Ferenc utca**, built around 1780, as well as several **peasant houses** supported by pillars and provided with porches **(Dózsa György u. 62, Honvéd u. 3, Szondi u. 9** and **21)** are all worth visiting. The **windmill** at **Vágóhíd utca 22**, with its wide base and two windboards, was constructed in 1955. Another point of interest is the **stone bridge** built with four piers on the outskirts of the town.
     Central Europe's largest **rice-hulling mill** (with a daily output of 2,000 quintals of rice) has been in operation in Karcag since 1953.
     BEREKFÜRDŐ, situated 12 km from the centre of the town, also belongs to Karcag. The baths contain thermal waters and public swimming-pools.

The main road divides into two at **PÜSPÖKLADÁNY** (14 km east of Karcag). Rd. 4 continues northeast towards Debrecen, and Rd. 42 (E15) goes southeast through Berettyóújfalu towards the Rumanian–Hungarian border. A small road (13 km north of Püspökladány) leads to **NÁDUDVAR**, where masters working on folk pottery make the famous unglazed "smoky" black Nádudvar earthenware. The dishes are baked in smoky ovens and the bright patterns are created by rubbing. The home of István Fazekas, a master potter and the Master of Folk Art, is a **museum**. The two **churches** of the community are both protected monuments.

The Hajdúság

Used ever since the 16th century, the appellation **hajdú** (Heyduck) does not designate the name of a people but the members of a community brought into existence by means of social and political ties. Some of the Heyducks were the descendants of drovers involved in medieval cattle trade, and some were descendants of Southern Slav outlaws who arrived during the battles fought against the Turks. The peasants who were made homeless during the battles also became part of this group. These Heyducks were hardened and reckless fighters. They fought against the Habsburgs in the armies of the Prince of Transylvania, István Bocskai (1557–1606), and helped him gain a decisive victory over the Habsburgs in 1604. The prince in turn provided the scattered Heyducks with land and they settled down in communities such as Nánás, Dorog, Böszörmény, Szoboszló and Hadház. The word *"hajdú"* was attached to the names of these settlements as a prefix. The newly settled Heyducks were raised as a group to the rank of the nobility and the *hajdú* district, an independent administrative unit, was created. (The *hajdú* district ceased to exist officially only in 1876.)

Hajdúszoboszló

204 km from Budapest on Rd. 4; 202 km by rail.

A document dating back to 1255 mentions the Castle of Szoboszló, but during the period of Turkish occupation this fortress as well as the surrounding communities were considerably reduced in population. The town as it exists today can look back on a history of three and a half centuries.

Hajdúszoboszló was once an agricultural market-town with little industry, which made its living chiefly through animal husbandry. In 1925, however, warm-water springs were discovered during drilling activities for oil and natural gas. Initial drillings produced water of 73 ° C from a depth of 1,090 m, and it was not long before the first small baths sprung up. The modern up-to-date spa has since been developing at an increasing rate; today almost a million bathers visit Hajdúszoboszló each year.

The warm mineral waters of the baths contain salt, alkaline, iodine and bromine, the salt content being five times greater than that of ocean water. The spa covers an area of about 23 hectares; it has two large swimming-pools, effervescent baths, a pool with artificial waves, a swimming-pool for competitions and a children's swimming-pool. The new indoor thermal baths, which include several pools, tub baths, sauna and medical facilities, are at the disposal in both winter and summer of those desiring treatment. The waters (32 ° and 38 °C) are recommended for rheumatic diseases, articulatory inflammations, forms of neuritis, muscular pain, certain skin diseases, women's diseases, varicose veins, and in certain cases of vasoconstriction. The drinking cure method is recommended for the treatment of digestive and respiratory diseases.

Hajdószoboszló's most interesting architectural monument consists of a 20 m stretch of the 15th-century **fortress wall** consisting of eight embrasures, and one of the remaining round towers of the fortress. The present **Calvinist church** was built in the 15th century, later (1711–17) remodelled by the Heyducks, and finally enlarged in 1818. Located in a fine new building in Bocskai utca, the **Bocskai Museum** contains mainly historical and ethnographic materials and materials connected with baths. The museum also preserves the green silk embroidered flag which Prince István Bocskai presented to the Heyduck cavalry as well as the deed of gift concerning Szoboszló by which he presented the town to its inhabitants.

Medicinal baths, Hajdúszoboszló

Debrecen

226 km from Budapest on Rd. 4 (E60); 221 km by rail.

Debrecen is the third largest city in Hungary after Budapest and Miskolc. The area now occupied by Debrecen was inhabited in prehistoric times and later settled by the Hungarians who entered the Carpathian Basin at the time of the Conquest. In the 12th century a village which became a rural market-town at the end of the 14th century stood here. Debrecen's early development can be attributed to the guilds (the charter of the Debrecen furriers, one of the oldest authentic Hungarian charters of incorporation, dates from 1394). Concurrently with the development of the guild industry, the city gained a large estate, and trade also started to develop with increased vigour; at the end of the 15th century, eight annual fairs were held in Debrecen. Turkish forces took possession of the town in June 1555, and it was soon declared a sultanate holding. The inhabitants of Debrecen were able to remain largely independent of the Turks and even increased in population. Debrecen, which lay on the "border of three countries"—where the territories occupied by the Turks and the parts of the country under the domination of the Transylvanian Principality and that of the Habsburg met—enjoyed a relative degree of independence at a heavy cost in taxation. Debrecen developed into an international trade centre and gradually became one of Hungary's wealthiest cities.

Even before the Turkish occupation, the inhabitants of the city were converted to Protestantism. This conversion took place in 1540, and Debrecen became a "Calvinist Rome" to such an extent that in 1552, when the local Catholic church was closed, it was enacted that only Calvinists would be allowed to settle in the city. Through its Calvinist College it soon became a cultural centre as well and its attraction extended to distant areas. The new school established in 1538 became an institution of higher education by the end of the 17th century. Today Debrecen has three universities and three academies.

The freedom-loving city of Debrecen sustained a considerable amount of damage in the 17th- and 18th-century struggles for independence against the Habsburgs; the Emperors's forces more than once plundered and burned the city. During the 1848–49 War of Independence, the Kossuth government had its headquarters temporarily transferred to Debrecen (at the beginning of 1849) after the capital had been lost, and it was also here that the deposition of the House of Habsburg was proclaimed on April 14, 1849. The city sustained serious damage during World War II, but was finally liberated on October 19, 1944. The Provisional National Government was set up here.

The city of Debrecen is characterized by a street running almost in a straight north-south direction from the railway station to the so-called Large Forest, and by the side streets running perpendicular to this thoroughfare. **Vörös Hadsereg útja,** an unusually wide street, connects **Petőfi tér,** a square situated in front of the railway station, with the asymmetrical **Kossuth tér** in the centre of the city. Several interesting and beautiful buildings can be seen along this long street: **No. 54,** which is adorned with a copper-crested turret and a Zsolnay majolica, and the old County Hall built in an *art nouveau* style in 1912 (today an office building). The huge reception-hall of the last building has stained-glass windows by Károly Kernstok (1870–1940). In **Béke útja,** a street turning off to the right just after the County Hall, is the Baroque **Church of St. Anne** built between 1721 and 1746 and designed by Giovanni Battista Carlone (1682–1747), as well as several beautiful neo-Classical residential houses. The two towers of the church date back to 1834. A small Baroque **Calvinist church,** built between 1720 and 1726 and remodelled in 1876, stands at the beginning of **Széchenyi utca.** The church's onion-shaped dome was struck down by a storm in 1907, and the lower part that remained was afterwards rebuilt in the form of a bastion. Included among the few beautiful residential houses in Széchenyi utca, a street, running to the left of the small church, is the oldest house in Debrecen:

the so-called **Diószegi House,** at **No. 6.** Dating back to the end of the 17th century but considerably reconstructed since, this house was where the Swedish king Charles XII spent the night on his way home from Turkey in 1714. The Romantic-eclectic building of the **Csokonai Theatre** stands in **Kossuth Lajos utca,** a street beginning on the other side of Széchenyi utca. One of the oldest and most beautiful houses in the street is the garret-roofed, two-storied Baroque **Balogh House (No. 18).** Standing on the corner of Vörös Hadsereg útja and Kossuth Lajos utca, the **City Hall** is one of Debrecen's most beautiful neo-Classical buildings. Constructed by the architects József Rachauer and Ferenc Povolny, the building has a central projection provided with five windows and divided off by Corinthian pilasters. On the tympanum is the town's coat of arms. At the south end of Kossuth Lajos tér stands the famous old **Aranybika Hotel.** One of the innkeepers had a sign erected in memory of the former owner, János Bika, a sign consisting of a guilded bull. Hence the name Aranybika (Golden Bull). (The hotel acquired its present appearance in 1915.) The new **market** (vásárcsarnok) is located at the beginning of **Csapó utca,** which was at one time Debrecen's most characteristic street. Widening into **Kálvin tér, Vörös Hadsereg útja** is closed on the north by the imposing building of the **Great Church** (1805–23). The façade of the neo-Classical church with its two towers is adorned by a colonnade, on top of which is a tympanum. Cast by György Rákóczi I from cannons seized during the Thirty Years' War, the country's largest bell (56 quintals), the so-called Rákóczi Bell, hangs in the left-hand tower. With a seating capacity of 5,000, the church is the largest Calvinist church in the country. It was in the Great Church that two joint sessions of Parliament announced on April 14, 1849 the deposition of the House of Habsburg. (Kossuth's reverently-preserved armchair stands behind the railing surrounding the communion table.) In front of the church stands a statue of Kossuth (1913).

The neo-Classical building of the **Calvinist College** (Református Kollégium), built between 1803 and 1816, stands behind the Great Church. The side wings of the college were built between 1870 and 1874. This huge square-shaped, three-storied building has a side projection adorned with two large Corinthian columns arranged on the main façade. In the spring of 1849 a session of Parliament met in the oratory of this building and in December 1944 the Provisional National Assembly likewise held meetings here. The college's most valuable treasure is the almost 500,000-volume library which includes 125 incunabula.

West of the Great Church in **Múzeum utca** is **Déri tér,** the location of **Déri Museum.** Built between 1926 and 1928, this museum houses collections of rich Eastern Asian materials, important ancient (Etruscan) items as well as other archeological and ethnographical objects, such as a splendid series of embroidered shepherd's coats made of felt and worn on the Hortobágy. The museum's principal attraction is its art gallery, where 19th- and 20th-century works are exhibited, including the famous painting by Mihály Munkácsy, "Ecce Homo". Four statues by Ferenc Medgyessy symbolizing Science, Art, Archeology and Ethnography stand in front of the museum building. (The **Kölcsey Ferenc Cultural Centre** is located nearby, at Hunyadi u. 1–3.)

A number of beautiful Baroque and neo-Classical town houses are situated along **Péterfia utca.** At No. 28 stands the **Medgyessy Ferenc Memorial Museum.** The street runs into **Bem tér** and continues along **Simonyi út** towards the city's famous 2,300-hectare park, the **Large Forest** (Nagyerdő). The first part of the park nearest the city is one large garden. This also contains Debrecen's **Public Pool and the Thermal Baths** (the waters of which are rich in minerals and are effective in treating several diseases), the **zoo,** and a small lake for rowing.

The Great Church, Debrecen

Situated just beyond the baths and recreation area in the university quarter is the **Kossuth Lajos University** and the **Medical School** (Orvostudományi Egyetem).

The Hortobágy

Rd. 33 leads from Debrecen in a westerly direction. After crossing the bridge over the Eastern Main Canal 26 km from the city, the traveller finds himself entering the area of the Hortobágy puszta, a vast stretch of land consisting of more than 100,000 hectares.

In the Middle Ages there were 52 communities lying in the Hortobágy, some of which were destroyed in 1241 during the Mongol invasion. Most of them, however, were annihilated during the Turkish occupation, but Debrecen and the Heyduck towns soon took possession of these depopulated areas. The Hortobágy, however, was not repopulated after the Turkish withdrawal; instead, it was leased as pasture-land to cowboys, herdsmen, shepherds, and swineherds, who grazed their large herds of horses, cattle, sheep and pigs here. Until the 1830s, that is to say, before the Tisza River had been regulated, the Hortobágy consisted of damp pasture land rich in grass. But ever since the waters of the Tisza were forced to run in a definite channel, the river has no longer flooded the Hortobágy, nor has it been able to bring its rich fertilizing mud onto the land. The *puszta* consequently dried up and a large section of it became alkaline.

The last few decades have been instrumental in bringing about a decisive change in the life of the Hortobágy. Through the construction of the large Eastern Main Canal, water has again been brought to the *puszta*. Today an important part of the Hortobágy has developed into arable land.

A Hungarian peasant room in the Déri Museum

The Hortobágy is today a **national park,** and as such, it preserves the ancient traditions of the area. Each summer so-called **bridge fairs** (hídi vásár) are held around the Nine-holed Bridge (see below) in memory of the older large-scale stock markets. The fairs are combined with **horse shows** and other traditional events reminiscent of the old life of the *puszta.* The Hortobágy International Horse Show is held each year in June.

The Hortobágy also serves today as a resting place for migrating birds, especially the large white-fronted goose. There are so many flocks of birds migrating here each year that the *puszta* has become an attractive area for sportsmen, particularly during the autumn migrations.

The famous **Nagycsárda** (36 km from Debrecen) is today the centre of the Hortobágy. The inn, originally built in 1699 and then remodelled in 1781 and 1815, consists of a wide vaulted portico and guest-rooms furnished in traditional style. The **Shepherd Museum,** recalling the former life of the *puszta,* has been accommodated in a cart shed built in 1780 and situated opposite the inn. An exhibition of the **Hortobágy National Park** is located nearby. Next to the csárda-inn stands the **Hortobágy Gallery,** which houses an exhibition of paintings of the *puszta* and the Great Plain. A huge stone bridge spans the Hortobágy River next to the romantic inn. This famous bridge, which is called the **Nine-holed Bridge** by the shepherds living on the Hortobágy, was built between 1827 and 1833 and is believed to be the longest stone bridge in Hungary. (It is 92 m long;

Watering horses on the Hortobágy

including the approaches its overall length is 167.3 m.) Guests can admire not only the inn and the bridge, but also the cattle and the horses; and if they are lucky, they can even witness the famous Hortobágy mirage, the Fata Morgana.

TISZAFÜRED (36 km from Hortobágy on Rd. 33) is a rail and regular road-crossing over the Tisza. In the near future it will become a lakeside town on the shore of the Kisköre Reservoir, which is connected to the Tisza's second water-barrage.

HAJDÚBÖSZÖRMÉNY (19 km northwest of Debrecen on Rd. 35) is the most interesting of the former Heyduck towns, for it was the former headquarters of the one-time Heyduck captains. Today Hajdúböszörmény (population 30,000) is a characteristic example of a **Heyduck settlement:** the outlying streets as well as the rows of houses built somewhat later are arranged virtually symmetrically and concentrically around the core of the town, which is surrounded by the old town wall. The courtyard of the former Baroque Heyduck headquarters, with its arcades, has retained its original 17th-century appearance; the façade, however, dates from the 18th century. This is where the **Hajdúság Museum** is housed, showing the history of the Hajdúság as well as the way in which the Heyducks lived. The **Calvinist church** next to the Heyduck headquarters was a 15th-century Gothic building that was completely remodelled at the end of the last century.

HAJDÚDOROG (16 km north of Hajdúböszörmény by road) is the country's only Greek Catholic episcopal see. The **Greek Catholic church** was built in its present form in the 18th century with a part of its bastion remaining from the crenellated wall of its medieval predecessor.

The Nyírség

The Nyírség, which occupies an area of around 5,000 sq.km north of the land once inhabited by the Heyduck forces as far as the Tisza River and east as far as the border, lies somewhat higher than the rest of the Great Plain because winds blowing from a north–northeast direction brought with them tons of sand from the Tisza flood basin and deposited it here in thick layers. The wind-blown sands generally settled into ridges of hills running in a north–south direction, and it was from these hills that the completely-enclosed depressions were formed in which the birch forests grew up alongside the stagnant water rising from below the surface of the ground. The drainage projects of the past century have turned the old depressions with their stagnant underground water into agricultural land. The region is dotted with numerous groves of trees and large orchards. The Nyírség is the country's most important apple-orchard (Jonathan apples are exported from here to distant countries). Excellent potatoes and tobacco are also produced here. With the exception of the immediate vicinity of Nyíregyháza, there are fewer farms and more villages here. The area is densely populated, which can be explained by the fact that the Turks did not penetrate as far as this owing to the large swamps which once bordered the area to the south. There are a number of small village churches that have remained in their original Romanesque or Gothic forms.

Nyíregyháza

243 km from Budapest on Rd. 3 (M3—E71), then from Nyékládháza on Rds. 35 and 36; 270 km by rail.

The first written mention of Nyíregyháza, the capital of the Nyírség, dates from 1219, when it was referred to under the name of Nyírfalva. One part of the Nyírség was owned by the Báthori family from the beginning of the 14th century to 1627; Nyíregyháza itself became the property of István Bocskai, the Prince of Transylvania, in 1605, and many of the prince's Heyducks made their home here. Quarrels frequently broke out between the county and the town during the sec-

ond half of the 17th century, quarrels which now and then led to armed conflicts. The town was depopulated as a result of these conflicts, so that only fifty families were still living there at the beginning of the 18th century. It was then that the new owner of the town brought in new settlers, mainly Slovaks. Development was greatly speeded up in the second half of the 19th century, but this did not affect the town's agricultural character.

In addition to the eclectic **County Hall** standing on **Tanácsköztársaság tér,** the town centre of Nyíregyháza, and a few Romantic and eclectic residential homes, the **Town Hall (Kossuth tér),** originally built in a late neo-Classical style but later remodelled, is also worthy of attention. Another interesting historical monument is the Baroque **Lutheran church (Felszabadulás tér)** built between 1784–1789 and remodelled between 1850–1860. There is a set of chimes in the tower of the church. The **Jósa András Museum** at **Benczúr Gyula tér 21** preserves rich archeological material, some dating back to the time of the Hungarian Conquest (haversacks, unique round figured breastplates). The museum also has an important ethnographic collection. A number of the works of Gyula Benczúr (1844–1920), a painter who was born in Nyíregyháza, can be seen in the picture gallery. A modern **cultural centre,** built in 1981, stands in **Szabadság tér.**

It is only about 6 km from the centre of the town to **SÓSTÓ-FÜRDŐ.** In the last century there were two connected alkaline-sodic lakes occupying about 14 hectares where the bathing area is now situated. About 100 years ago it was realized that the area could be developed as a resort, and the therapeutic value of the water was soon discovered. In 1948 two new wells, with a water temperature of 49 °C and 51 °C, were drilled; today thermal and cold-water public swimming-pools, tub baths, etc., await

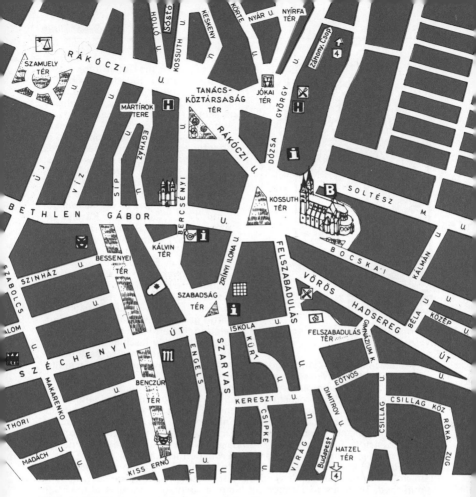

Nyíregyháza

guests. (The thermal baths are mostly used for the treatment of locomotor diseases.) Sóstó-Fürdő is surrounded by woods covering 500 hectares, and in addition to taking the waters it is also possible to go rowing on the lake. The surrounding woods also offer pleasant possibilities for walking. There is also a game-park. The folk architecture of the region is presented by an **outdoor folk museum.**

EXCURSIONS

NAGYKÁLLÓ (12 km southeast of Nyíregyháza) was the county capital until 1876. There was also a Heyduck fortress here, but in 1769 it was destroyed. The small community has a few beautiful historic buildings: the **old countyhall** built in 1769 (today a hospital); a 15th-century **Calvinist church** without a tower, remodelled between 1710 and 1740, and a bell tower from the same period (remodelled around 1780 in the style of Louis XVI); a 15th-century **Catholic church** which has been considerably rebuilt; as well as a few neo-Classical public buildings and houses.

NYÍRBÁTOR (36.5 km southeast of Nyíregyháza) is undoubtedly worth visiting, because one of Hungary's most beautiful late Gothic architectural wonders is situated here, a **Calvinist church** built between 1484 and 1511 by István Báthori, which fell into Calvinist ownership at the end of the 16th century, and was finally restored in 1958. It is the scene of the "Nyírbátor Musical Days", concerts staged here every August. The spatial effect of the building with its reticulated vaulting and single nave is fascinating; the lancet windows are late Gothic, while its *sedilia* and main gate are Renaissance. As the church was originally built to serve as a family burial church, it still preserves a number of beautiful tombs.

*Interior of the Calvinist church,
Nyírbátor*

One of them is the Gothic tomb (1490) of the church's founder, István Báthori; another is a Renaissance tomb from the beginning of the 17th century erected for someone called István, who translated psalms. A **bell tower** dating back to 1640 and consisting of four turrets and a shingled roof stands next to the church. It is also worth visiting the **Minorite** (formerly Franciscan) **church** which was built by Báthori around 1480. In 1587 the Turks plundered this church and it was not until 1717 that Sándor Károlyi restored it in the Baroque style. The church's altars and pulpit were made around 1730 in the workshop of a sculptor at Eperjes (now Prešov in Czechoslovakia) in a style perhaps rather provincial, but nevertheless containing attractive Baroque features. The **Altar of the Passion** and large groups of wooden statues situated in the left-hand side of the nave are particularly fascinating. The altar is frequently referred to as the **Krucsay** Altar, since it was commissioned by a János Krucsay in memory of his wife.

The **Báthori István Museum** is housed in the former Minorite monastery built on medieval foundations around 1720. The material to be found in the museum is mainly connected with local history, especially that of the Báthori family. The most beautiful piece is one end of a splendid Renaissance stall taken from the furnishings that once existed in the Calvinist church. The museum also shows something of the plant and animal world that survived the Ice Age at **Bátorliget ősláp** (Prehistoric Swamp) 15 km southeast of Nyírbátor. (Bátorliget is a nature conservation area and can only be visited with permission.)

KISVÁRDA (46 km from Nyíregyháza on Rd. 4): Its castle assigned it an important role during the Turkish occupation; later its significance gradually diminished. There are two important historic buildings: the **ruins of the huge castle** that once existed here and a **Catholic church** from the Middle Ages. The first written mention of the fortress, a portion of which was constructed in the 16th century, dates from the beginning of the 15th century. An **open-air theatre** has been set up in the castle, and a **museum** exhibiting local historical items has been established in the restored corner tower. (Thermal baths and riding-school nearby.) The **Catholic church,** built during the 15th century in a Gothic style, was later remodelled into the Baroque structure with only the sanctuary remaining in its original form. The tower and nave of the church date from 1806.

For those interested in enchanting small medieval village churches, old belfries and old castles, and are willing to travel on poor roads in order to see them, here are a few small villages:

VAJA (36 km east of Nyíregyháza on Rd. 41 and then on Rd. 49): 15th-century **Calvinist church** (reconstructed in 1821), and 16th-century castle with **Kuruc museum.**

MÁTÉSZALKA (15.5 km southeast of Vaja on Rd. 49.) The **Szatmár Museum** and the **thermal baths** are certainly worth visiting.

At **CSENGER** (33 km southeast of Mátészalka), a village lying on the Rumanian border, there is a **Calvinist church** built in the 14th century but remodelled several times since, as well as a number of interesting houses built in a traditional folk style.

JÁNKMAJTIS (12 km northwest of Csengersima): **Catholic church** originally built in a Gothic style (its present appearance dates from the 19th century), and a Baroque **manor-house** parts of which date from the 16th century.

TÁKOS (29 km north of Mátészalka and then east of Vásárosnamény on Rd. 41): The centre of Bereg **folk embroidery**. The **Calvinist church** with painted wooden ceiling is a fine example of folk Renaissance.

CSARODA (2.5 km east of Tákos): Its **small church,** restored between 1971 and 1973, is Romanesque in style. The church was built around 1250, the frescoes in the sanctuary are from the 14th century, and the wooden painted ceiling of the nave was done in 1777. The three-storey tower, built in a Romanesque style, has a wooden spire with a gallery.

VÁMOSATYA (8 km north of Csaroda): 13th-century **Calvinist church** with beautiful early Gothic sections. The bell tower and gallery were added in 1691.

Northern Hungary

Northern Hungary can be reached from Budapest by taking Rds. 2, M3 and 3 (E71), as well Rd. 22, which branches off from Rd. 2; on Rd. 23 branching off from Rd. 21, and on Rds. 21, 24, 25, 26, 32, 33, 35, 37 branching off Rd. 3; also by rail and bus.

Northern Hungary includes the region extending in a west–east direction from the Danube Bend to Sátoraljaújhely and the region lying between the Great Plain and the Hungarian–Czechoslovak border. (Northern Hungary lies 120 to 1,015 m above sea level.) The mountain chains (the Börzsöny, Cserhát, Mátra, Bükk, Aggtelek, and Zemplén Mountains) running through Northern Hungary provide the area with its special characteristics. The Bükk and the Mátra are the country's highest mountain ranges. There are many grottoes and caves to be found among the mountains, and springs provide thermal and warm water. The mountains and hills found in Northern Hungary are covered with extensive woods and forests, in the midst of which valleys and basins of various sizes are to be found.

Deep within the mountains are hidden large quantities of iron-ore (the country's only iron-ore quarry is located here), coal, lignite, bentonite and perlite rocks, etc. Largely as a result of this, Northern Hungary has for centuries been a relatively well-developed industrial region. The Bükk Mountain Range was the "cradle" of the Hungarian metallurgical industry (Miskolc–Diósgyőr is today still one of the bases of Hungarian iron and steel production), and there are numerous industrial centres (Salgótarján, Ózd, Kazincbarcika, Leninváros, etc.) operating all over Northern Hungary. Two of the most important branches of agriculture practised in the area are forestry and viniculture. The vine-growing regions of Northern Hungary (Tokaj, Eger, Gyöngyös) produce world-famous wines.

Mountains covered with forests, romantic valleys and grottoes (including the world-famous Aggtelek Stalactite Caves), thermal baths, and opportunities for winter sports are among the natural wonders of Northern Hungary that are particularly attractive to Hungarians and tourists alike. The numerous historical and architectural relics found in the region, ancient fortresses and castle ruins, great houses, Romanesque, Gothic, Renaissance and Baroque buildings of all kinds testify to a rich historical and cultural past. For example, the minaret at Eger, representing the northernmost historic monument of Ottoman-Turkish architecture in Europe, is unique in its class. Folk art offers a particularly rich and varied picture of the region. (For example, folk art produced by the *Matyós* living in or near Mezőkövesd is known throughout Europe for its richly-coloured patterns.)

THE CSERHÁT MOUNTAIN RANGE

The Cserhát Mountain Range, situated between the Börzsöny (see the Danube Bend, pp. 83–84) and the Mátra, should perhaps be thought of more as hill country, because only a few mountains rise here and there among the gentle slopes. Tiny villages lie hidden in almost every small valley formed by the hills and the mountains.

Balassagyarmat

80 km from Budapest first on Rd. 2 and then on Rd. 22; 104 km by rail.

In the area now occupied by Balassagyarmat there was a settlement as early as the end of the 9th century, even before the Magyar Conquest of the Carpathian Basin. In the Middle Ages a rapidly-developing market town grew up here (a small fortress was standing here as early as 1290); but like many other Hungarian towns, the development at Balassagyarmat came to a standstill during the one and a half centuries of Turkish occupa-tion. The fortress changed hands several times during the fighting. The small town itself suffered greatly as a result of the endless warfare and was finally deserted by the popula-tion. It was only near the end of the 17th century that it again started to grow out of the ruins. In 1790 Balassagyarmat became the capital of Nóg-rád County but it still remained a quiet market-town.

Northern Hungary

Balassagyarmat proudly refers to itself as the "capital of the *Palóc*", one of the country's most interesting ethnic groups. As most of them lived in rather closed communities, they were able to preserve their old traditions until recently: the multicoloured clothing worn by the women, the ancient customs, and the strange dialect. A decisive change has taken place, however, in the lives of the Palóc during the past few decades. Their way of life has become more in keeping with recent developments: earlier customs and architectural styles are disappearing as a result of a rise in the standard of living; and the colourful folk-costumes once worn by most of the inhabitants every day of the week can now be seen only on holidays. But the richly-coloured ornamentation used on the objects—both useful and purely ornamental—made by groups of older women in cooperatives is an attempt at keeping alive earlier traditions.

Balassagyarmat's most beautiful group of buildings is the **cultural and educational centre** standing in **Köztársaság tér** (formerly the county hall), built in the neo-Classical style in 1835. Two marble plaques on the wall state that it was here that two famous Hungarians worked: Imre Madách (1823–1864), the author of the dramatic poem "The Tragedy of Man", and Kálmán Mikszáth (1847–1910), one of Hungary's outstanding novelists. (The circular former prison standing in the courtyard is also worthy of attention.) It is also worth seeing the furnishings inside the nearby **Catholic church** (1740) as well as the Baroque and neo-Classical residential houses on **Rákóczi út (Nos. 11, 39, 41).**

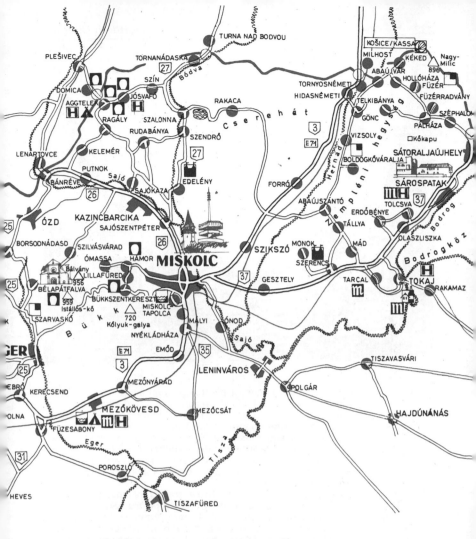

The **Palóc Museum (Palóc liget 1)** contained a rich historical and ethnographic collection before World War II, but in 1945 almost all the material was destroyed. After the end of the war the museum started to replace what had previously been lost, and today visitors to the museum have the opportunity of again seeing rich ethnographical material as well as the **Madách and Mikszáth memorial rooms.** The **Palóc Regional House** standing in the courtyard of the museum gives a lifelike picture of early folk architecture employed in the Palóc country as well as the way of life once enjoyed by the inhabitants. The small town also has a public swimming-pool with camping grounds located next to it.

EXCURSIONS

SZÉCSÉNY (18 km east of Balassagyarmat on Rd. 22): Its former fortress (early 15th century), of which only two corner bulwarks remain, is where the Hungarian Diet elected Ferenc Rákóczi II ruling prince in September 1705 and declared the unification of the motherland and Transylvania. Historical buildings to be seen in Szécsény are the **former Franciscan church and monastery** (the church's Gothic sanctuary and sacristy date from the 14th century) and the **former Forgách Castle.** In the 18th century one of the bastion walls and towers belonging to the fortress was incorporated into the castle. (Today it houses a **museum** with valuable archeological, historical, natural-historical and hunting collections.)
IPOLYTARNÓC (26 km northeast of Szécsény on the Hungarian–Czechoslovak

Main street of Hollókő

border): Internationally-known traces of plants and prehistoric animals have been found in the area of **Csapás Valley,** which can be reached by travelling for about an hour in a southeasterly direction. The most important find is a **petrified pine tree** from the Miocene Age. Pieces of the tree have been presented to a number of Hungarian and foreign museums. The remaining portion of the tree, which is now 8.5 m in length, is preserved under a shelter. Footprints of prehistoric animals encased in and preserved by volcanic ash as well as petrified impressions of leaves of exotic plants from the past have been discovered nearby, and are also preserved under cover.

HOLLÓKŐ (17 km southeast of Szécsény): The centre of this small picturesque *Palóc* village consists of several **houses with traditional protruding roofs** as well as a **small church with a wooden tower,** all of them protected buildings. Colourful folk attire is now worn less and less and can generally be seen only at folklore festivals. The **Folk Museum (Kossuth u. 82)** presents the home-making, lifestyle and utilitarian objects of the *Palóc* people. The **ruins** of a 13th-century **fortress** can be seen on the mountain (365 m).

Both the Budapest–Miskolc railway line, which leads from the capital into the "heart" of Northern Hungary, and Rd. 3 go into the interior of the Cserhát Mountain Range and to the Karancs-Medves Hills.

14th-century church of Mátraverebély

GÖDÖLLŐ (30 km northeast of Budapest on Rd. 30 or M3 [E71]) was the Hungarian summer residence of the Habsburgs; today it is one of the centres of the agricultural sciences (University of Agricultural Sciences, agricultural research institutes, experimental stations). The **Grassalkovich Palace** built during the 1740s is one of the country's most beautiful Baroque buildings. (Antal Grassalkovich, who was a personal and trusted friend of Empress Maria Theresa, acquired huge estates of land in Hungary in the middle of the 18th century, and had a number of magnificent mansions built.) The palace at Gödöllő was built by András Mayerhoffer and remodelled by Miklós Ybl after 1867. The **Máriabesnyő**

Church of Gödöllő as well as the **former monastery** next door are both protected Baroque buildings.
ASZÓD (12 km from Gödöllő on Rd. 30 or M3 [E71]): **Lutheran church** built in the 15th century but later remodelled in the Baroque style in the 18th century and the former Baroque **Podmaniczky Palace.**

Proceeding from Aszód in a northern direction along the **Galga Valley,** both the railway and a road running parallel to it lead into the interior of the Cserhát and eventually to the communities lying along the Galga River, famous for their folk art **(GALGAGYÖRK, GALGAHÉVÍZ, TURA, GALGAMÁCSA).** The national dress can be seen only seldom today (mainly in **ZSÁMBOK,** 22 km east of Gödöllő), but the beautiful embroidery work (seen on blouses and pillows) is on sale at shops where folk art is sold and is popularized by books on the subject. Local folk songs are still sung by choirs.
BUJÁK (34 km northeast of Aszód by main road, or on Rd. 21 from Hatvan): The native dress once commonly worn by the inhabitants of the community as well as the traditional furniture, pillows, etc., can generally be seen today only in a few old *Palóc* homes or ethnographic museums. The **former castle** of Buják was built between the 13th and 14th centuries on top of a 340 m high cliff north of the village. Only its ruins stand today.
HATVAN (57 km from Budapest on Rd. 30 or M3) became a market-town 800 years ago. Today it is an important railway junction and centre for the food industry (sugar and tinned foods factory). Its historic monuments are the former Baroque **Grassalkovich Palace** (today a hospital) and the **Catholic church** standing in the main square, believed to be the work of András Mayerhoffer (1751–57). (Thermal baths.)

Rd. 21 as well as a railway line branching off of the main Miskolc line towards the north both lead to Salgótarján, the centre of the Karancs-Medves hills which are abundant in brown coal. (For communities lying along the way, Pásztó, Hasznos, etc. see below.)

PÁSZTÓ (29 km from Hatvan on Rd. 21; 30 km by rail): The historic building belonging to this lively community is a **church,** originally built in a Romanesque style in the 13th century, then remodelled in the 14th century with Gothic features, and finally rebuilt as a Baroqe church in the 18th century. (The church's side-chapel remained Gothic; special attention should be paid to the traceries of the windows facing east.) Between the church and the former Cistercian 18th-century monastery stands a recently-uncovered garden of ruins with the remains of a late 11th-century church and monastery. Pásztó is also very popular as a starting point for trips taken into the western part of the Mátra. (At the Pásztó junction of Rd. 21 is the Cserhát Restaurant which offers a fine panoramic view of the surrounding area.)
HASZNOS (2.5 km northwest of Pásztó): 18th-century Baroque **church.** A half hour's walk from Hasznos towards the interior of the Mátra Mountain Range leads to the ruins of the **Cserter Castle.** The castle was built at the beginning of the 14th century; a large part of it was destroyed during Turkish rule.
MÁTRASZŐLŐS (5 km northwest of Pásztó): 14th-century **church** (reconstructed several times) with 600-year-old frescoes.
MÁTRAVEREBÉLY (12 km north of Pásztó): Gothic sections of a 14th-century **church;** interior reconstructed in the Baroque style in the 18th century. Near the settlement in **SZENTKÚTPUSZTA** stands a Baroque **devotional church** with medieval hermit caves carved into the rock behind it.
KISTERENYE (16 km north of Pásztó on Rd. 21): Restored early Baroque **castle** with four corner towers which today serves cultural purposes.

Salgótarján

112 km from Budapest on Rds. M3 and 21; 126 km by rail.

As early as the Neolithic Age dwellings were being built on the hills above Salgótarján, and in the Bronze Age a settlement already stood in the area occupied by the present town. At the beginning of the last century Salgótarján was nothing but a poor village consisting of 800 inhabitants and resembling a small feudal town. Coalmining operations began in the middle of the last century in the rich brown-coalfields of the area, as a consequence of which industrialization soon commenced at a rapid pace. The coalfields, steelworks, and plate-glass factory that have been operating here for more than one hundred years have turned Salgótarján into a centre of heavy industry. Since 1950, the town has been the county town, and it is now important for a wide variety of industries (metallurgical plants, the making of mining equipment, glass factories, enamel production, etc.)

City centre, Salgótarján

A fire that broke out in 1821 and two floods during the last 30 years of the 19th century destroyed what few historic buildings once stood in the town. Some of the modern buildings and statues in the public squares, as well as the decorations on buildings (mosaics, ceramics) are significant works of modern Hungarian architecture and sculpture. The only historic monument worthy of mention is the Baroque **Catholic church** in **Rákóczi út.**

The **Museum of Coal Mining,** housed in the shafts of an old mine, is also worth seeing. Guided tours conducted through the museum show visitors how mines are worked. (There is a large public swimming-pool as well as a campsite in the northern part of the town. The **Eresztvény** recreation area includes a motel and a hotel.)

EXCURSIONS

Mount Karancs (729 m): For mountain climbing tourists. There is a beautiful panorama, especially in clear weather, of the area all the way to the High Tátra from the **look-out tower** built on the summit.

The **Castle of Salgó** (8 km northeast of Salgótarján) was built in the 13th century on a 625-m high basalt cone. It fell into ruins after the Turkish wars. Only a few picturesque parts of the huge walls that stood here, the towers and courtyard carved out of rock, can still be seen today.

The **Castle of Somoskő** (3 km from Salgó Castle): The hill where the castle was built in the 14th century is cut in two by the Hungarian–Czechoslovak border. Ruins of the castle, together with its five towers as well as petrified cataracts of the castle hill, basalt blocks several stories high and basalt stones resembling organ pipes, lie on the Czechoslovak side and can therefore only be visited by obtaining permission from a travel office, and in the company of a special guide.

THE MÁTRA MOUNTAIN RANGE

The Mátra is Hungary's most popular holiday excursion area after the Balaton and the Danube Bend. Bordered by the Cserhát in the west and the Bükk in the east (it is separated from the former by the Zagyva River and from the latter by the Tarna River Valley), the Mátra is continuous with the Karancs–Medves area and the Borsod Basin to the north. Its southern slopes run down all the way to the

Great Plain. The average height of the volcanically formed mountain range is from 600 to 700 m, but also included in the area are Hungary's two highest peaks, the Kékestető (1,015 m) and the Galyatető (966 m). Uninterrupted forests cover the Mátra (mainly oak, with beeches in the higher regions), and it is very rich in springs and streams.

The Mátra is Hungary's most highly-developed mountain tourist area. There are a large number of holiday resort hotels, campsites, tourist hostels and look-out towers, and a well-planned system of road signs. The importance of the Mátra as a centre for tourism has greatly grown as a result of its proximity to and easy accessibility from the capital. The Budapest–Miskolc–Sátoraljaújhely main railway line as well as Rd. 3 run below the southern slopes (the Gyöngyös line branches off from the main line at Vámosgyörk and a narrow-gauge railway goes from Gyöngyös to Mátrafüred). The western part of the Mátra can be reached by taking the railway running through the Zagyva Valley (the Hatvan–Salgótarján line), or Rd. 21 (Pásztó). (Buses from Gyöngyös, and long-distance buses from Budapest, Miskolc, and the Great Plain.)

Gyöngyös

79 km from Budapest on the M3 (E71); 100 km by rail.

Lying at the foot of the Mátra, the town of Gyöngyös attained the rank of a market-town as early as the first half of the 14th century. Though it was harassed by both the Turks and the Habsburgs, Gyöngyös developed into a prosperous trading town and cultural centre during the one and a half centuries of Turkish rule. At the beginning of the 18th century, the town was a focal point for the freedom struggle led by Ferenc Rákóczi II.

Gyöngyös's handicraft and textile industries have long been famous, especially since the second half of the 17th century. Today the town has a number of modern large-scale industries (a thermal plant, a factory manufacturing machine-tools, a transistor factory, etc.). The town is important not only as the economic, cultural and transport centre of the Mátra district, but also as the centre of the Gyöngyös-Visonta vine-growing area which lies on the sunny southern slopes of the mountain range. It is known chiefly for its greenish-white and golden-yellow wines. (There is a large thermal plant at Visonta, a community lying east of Gyöngyös; there is also an open coal mine located there.)

In **Fő tér** stands the **Church of St. Bartholomew,** the country's largest Gothic church built in the middle of the 14th century but remodelled with the addition of Baroque features during the 18th century. At **Vachot utca 8** and **10,** there are two Baroque **residential houses,** one late Baroque **(No. 9)** and a residential house built in traditional peasant style **(No. 22).** The **Church of St. Urban,** which is of medieval origin but is now Baroque, stands in **Eötvös tér,** a square adjoining Vachot utca. The richly-carved pulpit demands special attention.

The **former Orczy mansion** stands in Dimitrov Park, which is connected with **Kossuth Lajos utca,** the continuation of Lenin út beginning at Szabadság tér and running to the east. The house is the home of the **Mátra Museum** which exhibits the animal and plant world, history, folk art, and vine-growing traditions of the Mátra region, and the **Bajza József Museum of Literature** which has a library containing valuable rare editions. There is an outdoor theatre in the courtyard. The 18th-century watermill at **Batthyány tér 2,** the hospital built in 1725, today serving as a school **(Április 4. körút),** as well as the **former Franciscan church (Nemecz József tér)** built about 1400 and since then frequently remodelled, are also worth visiting. The church is the burial place of General János Bottyán (Vak Bottyán) the legendary commander of the War of Independence led by Rákóczi. In Nemecz József tér stands the new **Mátra Cultural Centre.** The Finnish functionalist-style building houses a theatre and a concert hall with a seating capacity of 480. In addition to the historic buildings, the new residential areas of the town are also worthy of notice.

EXCURSIONS INTO THE MÁTRA

Rd. 24 leads from Gyöngyös into the interior of the Mátra.

MÁTRAFÜRED (6 km northeast of Gyöngyös, can be reached by taking the narrow-gauge railway from Dimitrov Park in Gyöngyös) is a resort lying 340 m above sea level. As well as the modern **Hotel Avar,** there are bungalows and private accommodation in Mátrafüred; there is also a camping site with wooden cabins and a motel, and facilities for rowing and angling on the shores of **Lake Sás** which lies 3 km from Mátrafüred at a height of 520 m. Mátrafüred offers a number of possibilities for walks and other excursions. The highest of three look-out towers in the immediate area is the **Hanák Look-out Tower** (584 m). **MÁTRAHÁZA** (8.5 km north of Mátrafüred on a road passing through forests) lies 715 m above sea level. Protected by the mountains from the severe winds, Mátraháza is suitable for summer and winter holidays alike. The small community boasts a number of beautiful resorts, but apart from the accommodation available to Hungarian workers, the **Vörösmarty Tourist Home** is the only place offering rooms. Together with the Kékestető, Mátraháza is the country's largest winter sports centre.

The 1,015 m high **Kékestető** (3 km from Mátraháza) rises 300 m above Mátraháza. There is no look-out tower on top, but it is possible to obtain special permission to climb the nine-storey tower belonging to the Research Institute for Telecommunications from where a breath-taking panorama can be seen of the Great Plain towards the south, with mountains in every other direction; under favourable weather conditions even the High Tatra can be seen. (A television relay tower also stands on Kékestető.) Different kinds of metabolic disturbances, respiratory catarrhs, as well as anaemia and nervous breakdowns are effectively treated in the **Kékes Sanatorium.**

A 2,400 m long, gently sloping **ski-run,** which has a height differential of 330 m, begins at Kékestető and runs towards Mátraháza. There is a large skijump nearby. A ski-run has also been laid out from Kékestető towards the north, but it is much steeper and therefore more difficult.

The road divides into two north of Mátraháza: one road leads to Galyatető (10 km), and the other to Parádfürdő (12 km).

GALYATETŐ (965 m) is a resort whose centre is the **Grand Hotel** (Nagyszálló), built of natural stone and provided with a swimming-pool. (Like other nearby holiday homes, the hotel, however, is only open to members of Hungarian trade unions. Private-accommodation service: Mátratourist, Gyöngyös.) A splendid panorama of the Mátra and more distant mountains can be seen from the look-out tower standing near the hotel. The country's highest observatory as well as a seismographic station both operate on **Piszkéstető** (946 m), west of Galyatető. **MÁTRASZENTIMRE** (5 km west of Galyatető, 810 m): A considerable number of private rooms can be found in the community. (Tourist hostel in the nearby Ágasvár, 879 m.) The area is a popular resort and winter-sports centre, offering many opportunities for excursions. **MÁTRASZENTISTVÁN** (760 m) and **MÁTRASZENTLÁSZLÓ** (800 m) also attract large numbers of visitors.

Sharp bends in the 10 km long road leading to **PARÁDFÜRDŐ,** north–northeast of Mátraháza, offer changing views of the romantic landscape. Four communities, each bearing the name Parád, lie on the way **(PARÁDSASVÁR, PARÁD, PARÁDHUTA, PARÁDFÜRDŐ).** (Inn and private accommodation in Parádfürdő.) The sulphurous effervescent thermal water of Parád, which enjoyed such a wide reputation at the beginning of the last century, flows from recesses deep under the ground at Parádsasvár, the first of these communities. People not only drink the thermal water as a remedy against stomach disorders and digestive disturbances, but they often mix it with wine to soothe heartburn. The glass factory at Parádsasvár, which began operations more than 250 years ago, produces artistically-polished glassware.

PARÁDFÜRDŐ (240 m) is a thermal bathing resort. Its first baths were built at the end of the 18th century. The bathing resort now comprises a park of some 72 hectares surrounded by oak and beech forests. The aluminous thermal baths are mainly effective in curing women's ailments and locomotor diseases. Healthy guests will take great delight in the public swimming-pool surrounded by huge old trees. (There is a motel near the pool.) The country's only **cart museum** is located in Parádfürdő, and in Parád one can visit a **Palóc** peasant house, the contents of which are arranged as a museum.

The neighbourhood of the four Parád communities offers countless possibilities for excursions of all kinds.

It is worth making a large detour from Parádfürdő on the return trip to Gyöngyös and taking a road that at first bears to the east, then southeast, and finally to the west. The 13th-century **castle** on top of the rocky mountain situated on the outskirts of **SIROK** was almost completely cut and carved out of rocks lying on the mountain. A beautiful view of the eastern and western ridges of the Mátra and Bükk Mountains as well as of the Slovak mountain ranges can be seen from the castle ruins.

BÜKKSZÉK (9 km north of Sirok) is a bathing resort famous for its Salvus water (39 °C), which flows from a depth of 517 m and is extremely rich in sodium, hydrogen, carbonate and other minerals. The water, by virtue of its high mineral content, is particularly effective in treating hyperacidity, trachitis, and bronchitis. Some of the mineral water is bottled, but the rest flows into a circular pool used for bathing. The medieval church has some beautiful Romanesque work.

TARNASZENTMÁRIA (8 km south of Sirok): 11th-century Romanesque **church ruins** are worth mentioning. Further south, two **churches,** one situated in **VERPELÉT** (5 km), a community famous for its tobacco factory and wine, the other in **FELDEBRŐ** (4 km south of Verpelét), both contain medieval (Romanesque and Gothic) elements. The crypt of the latter, the **Feldebrő Church,** dates from the 12th century, while Byzantine influence can be noticed on the church's frescoes, which are considered to be some of the oldest wall-paintings in Hungary. The famous "Debrői hárslevelű" wine is produced in Feldebrő.

Eger

127 km from Budapest on Rd. M3 (E71), then on Rds. 3 and 25, which branches off at Kerecsend; 142 km by rail.

Eger lies in the Eger Valley, in a hilly area between the thickly-wooded Mátra and Bükk Mountains. Because of its past history, historic buildings and world-famous wines, Eger is one of the most frequently visited of all Hungarian towns. (With its 175 historic monuments it takes third place after Budapest and Sopron.)

The area now occupied by Eger was inhabited as early as the Stone Age. The Eger Valley was settled by the first generation of Hungarians who entered the Carpathian Basin. At the beginning of the 11th century, Stephen I made it an episcopal see. In 1241 the town was burned down by the Mongol forces, who slaughtered most of the inhabitants. (Large numbers of settlers from the territories now occupied by Belgium, France, and Italy came to Eger and helped make up for the loss it suffered in population.) By the second half of the 15th century, the town was one of Hungary's main centres of Renaissance culture. It again suffered seriously during the Turkish occupation. Helped at the first siege (1552) by the women of Eger, who fought alongside the men, the 2,000 soldiers stationed in the castle managed in a heroic struggle under the leadership of István Dobó, the castle commander of legendary fame, to avert an attack by Turkish forces six times as strong as themselves. The news of the victory at Eger soon spread throughout all Europe, causing great relief and ending the legends about the invincibility of the Turks.

The victory also stopped the spread of the Ottoman Empire for some decades. At the second siege in 1596, however, a garrison consisting of foreign mercenaries gave itself up, after barely a week's struggle, to the Turkish armies led by Sultan Mohammed III. (The mercenaries could not, however, avoid their fate: they were promised their freedom, but were attacked by the Turkish janissaries who slaughtered many of them and took prisoner most of the rest.)

From 1596 up until it was freed in 1687, Eger was the seat of a newly-established Turkish province (vilayet), and many mosques were built for the population. Today there is only one minaret standing and this represents the most northerly monument of Islam. With the exploitation of the natural warm springs lying in the neighbourhood, numerous baths were established here; only fragments of these remain today.

In the second half of 1687 the relieving forces set up a rigorous blockade of the Turkish garrison of 4,000 men at Eger for four months. The Turks, both soldiers and civil residents, withdrew from the town unharmed. However, 600 Muslim residents stayed behind, became converted to Christianity, and gradually assimilated into Hungarian life.

Even so, there were only three and a half thousand people living in barely more than 400 habitable homes in 1690. In 1702 the Emperor Leopold ordered that the bastions and outer walls of the castle should be blown up, so that the Hungarian troops struggling for independence should not be able to use the castle against the Habsburg forces. In spite of this, Eger became one of the centres of the Rákóczi War of Independence.

Eger started to develop at a rapid rate in the middle of the 18th century; this was mainly due to its status as an episcopal see with a number of huge estates at its disposal. Within a few decades, Eger's still characteristically Baroque appearance developed through the construction of a large number of public buildings (chiefly churches) and private houses.

The city began to flourish economically in the 19th century, but industrial development on a large scale began only after 1945.

The principal points of interest in Eger are the following: **the Castle,** on which construction work was started in the second half of the 13th century and lasted for several decades. However, the castle had fallen into disuse by the 16th century when the Turkish siege took place. Modernization and complete rebuilding did not take place until after the famous siege of 1552 (between 1553 and 1583). The Castle's fate was sealed when it was blown up in 1702. Excavations and restoration work started between the two world wars and is still in progress.

The Castle can be approached through its main gate on the south by taking the steep, cobblestone road beginning at **Dózsa György tér.** The trapezoid-shaped bastion to the east of the gate is the only such structure on the castle built by the Turks. The structures and building remains within the castle walls include the **Dobó István Bastion** (1549) and the **Gergely Bastion** 1553), as well as the 15th-century **episcopal palace** and Gothic remains of the **cathedral** in the medieval castle. Valuable material is contained in the **historical collection and picture gallery of the Castle**

View of Eger with the Church of the Minorites

Eger

Museum inside the restored episcopal palace (the picture gallery is housed in a separate building). The casemates are also of interest. The barrack chambers, cannon chambers and shaft observation corridors inside the casemates, which have been built below one another many stories deep, have all remained in good condition.

Géza Gárdonyi (1863–1922), a great Hungarian writer who sang of the heroic defence of the castle in 1552 in his novel the "Stars of Eger", lies in a simple **grave** at the southeastern winged bastion of the Castle. In compliance with Gárdonyi's last wishes, the following words were inscribed on the stone slab covering his grave: "Only his body lies here" ("Csak a teste"). The writer's former home near the castle at **Gárdonyi Géza utca 32** is where he spent the last 25 years of his life. Today it houses the **Gárdonyi Memorial Museum.**

The road leading away from the Castle goes through **Dózsa György tér** (beside a two-storied Baroque **residential house** at **No. 6)** and the ruins of some **Turkish baths** and finally on to **Kossuth Lajos utca,** along which the houses are almost all of historic interest. The Baroque **Buttler House** at **No. 26** (today a tourist hostel) plays a role in Kálmán Mikszáth's novel "A

Strange Marriage". Today the **County Library** is housed in the late Baroque **Palace of the Grand Provost** standing at **No. 16** and built between 1774 and 1776. The **former Franciscan monastery** at **No. 14** was built between 1714 and 1749, and there is a **Franciscan church** from 1736–1776 where a Turkish mosque once stood. The most beautiful ornamentation on the imposing **County Hall** (1749–1756) is the magnificent Baroque wrought-iron gate, a masterpiece made by Henrik Fazola. It is likely that Fazola also made the iron railing on the balcony of **No. 4**. This building, which is called the **Palace of the Vice-Provost,** is a beautiful Rococo edifice.

The former **Lyceum** or archiepiscopal secondary school (today the Ho Chi-Minh Teachers' Training College) and the Cathedral stand in **Szabadság tér.** The square-shaped college was built, to the plans of the Viennese architect Joseph Gerl, by Jakab Fellner, and, following his death, was completed by József Grossmann (1765–1785). This huge edifice is 85×21 m in size and a 53 m high observatory tower rises from the middle of the eastern façade. (A museum of astronomy is housed in the eleven storey high tower.) The large square-shaped inner courtyard is surrounded by the side wings of the building and is considered to be one of the country's most beautiful enclosed architectural areas.

The library in the south wing is well worth visiting. The wall is adorned with an interesting fresco by Johann Lucas Kracker (1778) depicting the Council of Trent. The furniture is carved in Louis XVI style. The library contains 80,000 volumes and 700 manuscripts, among them fourteen codices and 87 incunabula. The ceiling of the large hall in the north wing, formerly a chapel, is adorned with one of the last frescoes of Franz Anton Maulbertsch (1793).

The neo-Classical **Cathedral** was built between 1831–39 where a medieval church once stood. Planned and supervised by József Hild, the cathedral is Hungary's largest ecclesiastical structure after the Cathedral of Esztergom. The building is 93 m long and 53 m wide, the two towers are each 54 m high; the dome in the middle has a diameter of 18 m and is 40 m high; and the six Corinthian columns forming the open colonnade on the façade are each 17 m high. (The longitudinal axis of the brightly-lit interior is 80 m, while its width is 33.5 m; the width of the transept is 41.5 m.) Four statues stand on either side of the steps leading up to the Cathedral: the Hungarian kings St. Stephen and St. Ladislas in front, and the apostles Peter and Paul at the back. The statues on the main façade as well as the reliefs on the inside are for the most part the works of Marco Casagrande, a Venetian artist (1804–1880). The large painting on the main altar, the "Martyrdom of St. John", is the work of the Viennese painter Joseph Danhauser (1834–35).

The U-shaped building of the **Archiepiscopal Palace** standing on the corner of **Szabadság tér** and Széchenyi utca dates from the 18th century; the neo-Classical sections were built between 1829 and 1846. Outstanding Baroque buildings in Széchenyi utca are the two-storied corner house at **No. 13** (built by the Italian architect Giovanni Battista Carlone in 1725), as well as the house on the other side of the street **(No. 14)** built in a Louis XVI style. A two-towered former **Jesuit church** (later a Cistercian church), built between 1731–43 by István Pethő where a mosque once stood, is situated at **No. 15.**

The three-storey Baroque building constructed in 1754 on the corner of **Csiky Sándor utca,** now housing a high school was once a **Jesuit high school** (gymnasium). The **Church of St. Anne** at **Széchenyi utca 29** was built between 1729–33 from the stones of a Turkish mosque. The covered steps behind the **Orthodox Parsonage** at **Széchenyi utca 55** lead up to an **Orthodox Church** built by János Povolny in Louis XVI style at the end

Gárdonyi Géza Theatre, Eger

of the 18th century. The church's most valuable treasure is the Baroque–Rococo style iconostasis.

Eger's old-fashioned **inner city** with its winding streets, narrow lanes and many historic buildings is situated in the part of the town bounded by Kossuth Lajos utca and Széchenyi utca. **Dobó István tér,** the centre of the inner city, was the market square of Eger as early as the Middle Ages. A statue of the castle commander István Dobó (by Alajos Stróbl) as well as a **memorial** entitled "Soldiers of the border fortress" stand in the square. The square's main point of interest is the **former Minorite church** with its two spires (each 57 m high) built between 1758–73 probably by Kilián Ignaz Dientzenhofer of Prague. The church and the decorations both outside and inside are considered to be a particularly beautiful creation of mature Baroque art. The painting on the main altar depicting the Virgin Mary and St. Anthony is the work of Johann Lucas Kracker. The **former Minorite monastery** next to the church was built between 1773–75 and has been remodelled many times since.

One of Eger's most famous historic buildings is a 40 m high, 14-sided **minaret,** the northernmost monument from the time of Turkish rule, built at the turn of the 17th century and situated only a few minutes' walk from Dobó István tér. The mosque which once stood beside the minaret was demolished in 1841.

Eger is not only a city of historic buildings, but is a well-known spa as well. Buildings housing bathing facilities stood here around 700 to 800 m deep springs as early as the 15th century. The first period in which bathing activity really flourished here was during the period of Turkish occupation. **Evlya Celebi,** the famous Turkish traveller, mentions three baths situated in Eger. The **spa district** of the city (public swimming-pool, thermal and medicinal baths, an indoor swimming-pool and a swimming-pool used for competitions) is situated south of **Petőfi tér.** (The spa water of 28–32 °C contains significant quantities of radium emanation, calcium, magnesium and sodium hydrocarbonate.)

The famous wines produced in Eger can be sampled in intimate, traditionally-furnished **wine-taverns** (Szabadság tér, Dobó István tér, etc.) and in **wine-cellars** (Szépasszony Valley, etc.). Eger's vine-growing area, comprising more than 3,700 hectares, produces the well-known Egri bikavér (Bull's Blood of Eger) which became famous in the 18th century. In addition to the dark red, slightly-acid Bikavér with its characteristic taste and bouquet (it is matured for two to three years before bottling), Medoc Noir (a dark red, strong, sweet dessert wine) as well as the honey-coloured, fragrant Egri leányka are among the wines now exported from Eger.

Romanesque church, Bélapátfalva

THE BÜKK MOUNTAIN RANGE

The Bükk Mountain Range lies in an area bordered by the Sajó River, the valley of the Eger and the Bán, and the Great Plain. Among the 800–900 m high mountains in the area, the **Istállóskő** (959 m) and the **Bálvány** (956) m) are the two most prominent.

The central part of the Bükk Mountain Range is formed by a plateau 20 km long, 5–6 km wide, and 600–950 m high; it is surrounded by steep rocky cliffs. A large part of the plateau was formed by ocean deposits (limestone, dolomite, etc.). Most of the forests of the mountainous terrain consist of beech trees. The area is also rich in springs and mountain streams, but even more characteristic is the exceedingly large number of caves. (Almost 300 caves have been discovered so far.) Some of them are well known in Europe, because they served as dwellings of Ice-Age man. The most valuable archeological finds are from the **Szeleta Caverns** near Lillafüred. 38,000 hectares of land in the Bükk Mountains (Eger, Lillafüred, Bükkszentkereszt, Bélapátfalva, Felsőtárkány, Szarvaskő, Szilvásvárad, Répáshuta and their surroundings) were made into a National Park in 1976.

The chief point of departure into the Bükk is Eger, since the western part of the mountain range can be reached most easily from there.

SZARVASKŐ (12 km from Eger): Its **castle** was built at the turn of the 14th century, but gradually fell into ruins after the expulsion of the Turks.

BÉLAPÁTFALVA (8 km north of Szarvaskő): The **abbey church** built here in 1232 by a group of Cistercian monks who settled here from France is the only Romanesque monastic church in Hungary to have remained in almost perfect condition.

MIKÓFALVA (2 km west of Bélapátfalva): In the cellar of the former lower-gentry dwelling at **Kossuth utca 25** a blacksmith's workshop has been set up and equipped with 19th-century tools.

SZILVÁSVÁRAD (8 km from Bélapátfalva) owes its popularity to its beautiful location. Until 1945 wire fencing kept tourists out of this beautiful region of the Bükk, which belonged to the family of Count Pallavicini. Today, the former manor-house on top of the hill is a trade-union home. A pleasant walk from the village takes one up the **Szalajka Valley,** an enchantingly beautiful corner of Hungary rich in mountain trout and small waterfalls. (As it is a nature conservation area, camping is not allowed.) It is about an hour's walk there and back from the Szalajka Valley to the **Istállóskő Caves** which open facing south above the source of the Szalajka stream. As a result of recent excavations, a rich collection of ancient material finds has come to light. An interesting **open-air exhibition** showing items concerned with forestry and life in the forest can be seen in **Horotna Valley** lying towards the south. A road going through this picturesque region connects Szilvásvárad with Lillafüred (see p. 247).

Two highways lead from Eger to the "capital" of the Bükk Mountain Range, Miskolc. The shorter of the two routes winds through the mountains and is 61 km long, while the longer (80 km) route leads from Eger to Kerecsend on Rd. 25 and continues from there on Rd. 3.

NOSZVAJ (12 km northeast of Eger): An enchanting historical monument is the Rococo-style **De la Motte Palace** (1774–76); another is the **museum** in the old peasant house at **Lenin utca 40.**
MEZŐKÖVESD (21 km southeast of Eger) is the centre of the so-called **Matyóföld.** The *Matyós,* an ethnic group living on the southern slopes of the Bükk Mountains, have become famous outside Hungary for their richly-decorated national dress and embroidery work. The rich colours and designs used in *Matyó* folk art can be seen in the **Matyó House** in Mezőkövesd **(Béke tér 2),** where shops and stores belonging to the handicraft and folk art cooperative can be found. The museum established in the **Cultural Centre** illustrates the rich national dress and the traditional architecture.
The 15th-century **Gothic sanctuary** of the **Catholic church** is worth seeing. Also interesting are the characteristic peasant homes along **Anna köz, Diófa utca** and **Horvát utca, Kökény köz** and **Mogyoró köz** as well as **László király utca,** such as the thatched-roofed house of Bori Kisjankó, a famous master of embroidery, who died a few years ago. The medicinal water flowing from a depth of 875 m at **Zsórifürdő** (southwest of Mezőkövesd) is used in the treatment of locomotor and rheumatic diseases.

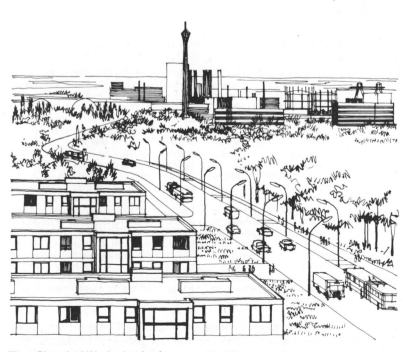

Tisza Chemical Works, Leninváros

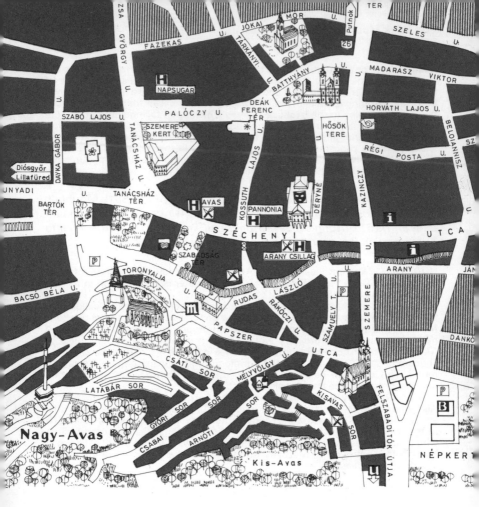

Miskolc

178 km from Budapest on Rd. 3 and M3; 182 km by rail.

Miskolc, Hungary's second largest city and at the same time the country's second most important industrial centre, is built along a long rectangular-shaped stretch of land at the eastern end of the Bükk Mountains. The site of the present inner city was already inhabited at the end of the 9th century, but Miskolc did not begin developing into a city until the end of the 14th century. In 1544 it was ravaged by the forces of the Turkish Pasha of Buda; most of its buildings were burned and plundered, and many of the inhabitants were taken captive. After the fall of Eger in 1596, Miskolc fell under Turkish jurisdiction and was not freed until 1687. The city served for a time as Rákóczi's general headquarters during the War of Independence (1703–11) which he led. For this reason Austrian Imperial forces plundered Miskolc in 1706 and afterwards reduced most of it to ashes.

Miskolc started to develop again during the 1720s. The development of its heavy industry began at the end of the last century, but Miskolc did not actually become an important industrial centre until after 1945. (There were 29 industrial plants here in 1938; today there are more than 130.) A few neighbouring communities have been joined to Miskolc since the liberation, and a whole series of new residential estates has been built around the old centre of the city. In 1949 the Polytechnic University for Heavy Industries was opened here; Miskolc thus became a university city with a large and modern university area.

There are several beautiful Baroque, neo-Classical, Romantic, and eclectic **residential houses** along the main thoroughfare of Miskolc's inner city, **Széchenyi utca 9, 12, 14, 20, 40, 46,** and **54.** The neo-Classical build-

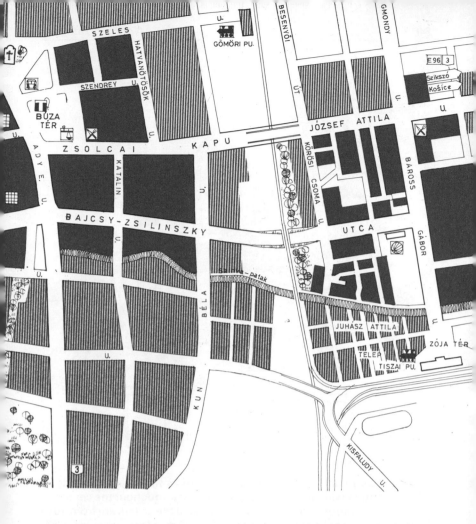

ing of the **National Theatre** on the corner of Széchenyi utca and **Déryné utca** is also worth noticing. From 1823 up to 1843, when it was destroyed by fire, the country's first theatre to produce plays in Hungarian stood near the National Theatre. The **Dark Gate** (Sötét kapu), a vaulted passageway linking Széchenyi utca with **Rákóczi utca,** is an interesting architectural monument from the 18th century, enlarged by the addition of an upper storey in the last century. The **Rákóczi House** at **Rákóczi utca 2,** probably constructed in the second half of the 17th century, was where Prince Rákóczi lived on several different occasions. The house is particularly interesting because of the first-floor arcade facing the courtyard as well as the staircase going up to it. The **County Hall** in **Tanácsház tér** originally built in the Baroque style in 1727, was remodelled during the last century in the neo-Classical style. Facing the County Hall is the eclectic **City Hall** constructed during the last century. A building which was once a school that can be traced back to 1453 but is today the home of the **Herman Ottó Museum** stands at **Papszer utca 1** on the bank of the **Szinva stream,** which divides Miskolc into two parts. The museum building was originally built in the 15th century but was remodelled twice during the 18th century. (The museum contains one of the country's most valuable collections of finds dating back to ancient times, including flint implements from the Ice Age, ceramic materials from the New Stone Age—the so-called "Bükk Culture"—and sepulchral urns with figures on them. The museum also houses a rich collection connected with the history of the city as well as an ethnographical collection.)

Church on Avas Mountain, Miskolc

It is an easy walk from the museum to **Avas Mountain,** the side of which is dotted with 800 cellars hollowed out throughout the centuries mainly for the purpose of storing wine. Most of the cellars are from 10 to 20 m deep, but some reach a depth of 50–100 m. Many are at least 300 years old, but some were carved into the mountain over 500 years ago. (There are an additional 800 cellars on the hillsides surrounding the city to the north.) A magnificent view including the city, the Bükk Mountain Range and, under favourable weather conditions even the Carpathians, can be seen from the circular café of the **look-out tower** on top of Avas Mountain. This tower is the lower section of a 52 m high radio and television tower.

A Gothic **Calvinist church** stands on Avas Mountain. A chapel built in the middle of the 13th century is the oldest part of the church. The chapel was enlarged between 1365 and 1411, and at the end of the 15th century it was converted into a three-aisled Gothic church. The church was set on fire by Turkish troops in 1544, but in the 1560s it was again rebuilt, but this time as a Calvinist church. The pews inside the church are made in a Renaissance style and date from the 18th century; the backs of the pews contain flower decorations done in an interesting combination of both folk-art and Rococo styles. A wooden Renaissance gallery encircles the roof of the bell tower (1557) standing next to the church. The cemetery surrounding the church has been used ever since the 11th century.

The **Orthodox church** situated in the courtyard of the house at **Deák Ferenc tér 7,** can be reached from Kossuth Lajos utca. Much of it is built in the style of Louis XVI. The church was originally built between 1785–1806 by the descendants of a group of Greeks fleeing here from Turks in the Balkans. The church's main points of interest are the sacred **icon of the "Black Mary of Kazan"** on the 16 m high iconostasis (the icon was given to the church by Tsarina Catherine II when she was travelling through Miskolc on her way to Vienna) and the **Cross from Mount Athos,** made in 1590, decorated with precious stones, and brought here by the first Greek settlers. A **former Minorite church** with two towers standing on **Hősök tere** and the **former monastery** (today a student hostel) adjoining it were both built in the Baroque style between 1729–1740.

The western part of Miskolc, which lies in the Bükk Mountain Range and which offers such sights as the **Castle of Diósgyőr, Lillafüred,** the **ancient foundry** of Massa, etc., can be reached either from the inner city by taking a train or a bus or from the Kilián (North) housing estate by taking the picturesque narrow-gauge railway.

One of the country's largest and most important industrial plants, the **Lenin Metallurgical Works** (the original factory started operations in the second half of the 18th century), is situated in what is called the ironworks area of the city, surrounded by modern residential quarters. The **Diósgyőr Machine Factory,** one of the chief centres of Hungarian machine industry, is also situated in this part of the city.

After leaving the ironworks area of the city, one goes through both old and new residential districts and finally reaches the oldest part of Miskolc, the former **DIÓSGYŐR.** The historic buildings here include two Gothic **churches** remodelled in the 18th century (one is a Calvinist church, the other is Catholic). The most important historic monument, however, is the **four-towered castle,** one of the most beautiful Hungarian medieval castles. Construction on the fortress began in the middle of the 13th century, and achieved its final form in the second half of the 14th century, when it became a favourite retreat of King Louis I (the Great) of the Anjou dynasty. Later the castle became the property of the queens. For this reason, it is also referred to as the "queen's castle". The castle frequently changed hands at the beginning of the 18th century during the battles for independence against the House of Habsburg, and it gradually fell into ruins. Restoration work began during the 1950s. Today a beautiful view of the surrounding area can be seen from the restored castle. Interesting dramatic productions are held each summer in the outdoor theatre situated in the courtyard.

LILLAFÜRED (reached by taking either the bus or the narrow-gauge railway) is a resort in the outskirts of Miskolc, situated 320 m above sea level at the junction of the valleys of the Szinva and Garadna streams. The centre of the resort is the **Palace Hotel,** built between 1927–1930, now a trade-union home. There are terraced hanging gardens and a large park. The resort is surrounded by a forest covering over 100 hectares, with foot-paths.

Lake Hámori, which is fed by the Garadna Stream, and the romantic **valley of the Szinva stream** are two of the most beautiful spots near Lillafüred. An artificial waterfall plunging into the depths right next to the hotel building also offers a beautiful sight. (The waterfall works only when there is enough water in the stream.)

Next to the waterfall, there is a **limestone cave** named after the poet Sándor Petőfi which is widely admired as an unparalleled natural wonder. Professional guides working in the electrically-lit cave show the visitors the fine lace-like limestone formations.

It is almost half a kilometre from the Palace Hotel along the road connecting Lillafüred and Eger to the **István Caves,** which were opened to the general public in 1931. The strangely shaped stalactite formations in the electrically-lit caverns have been given such names as "Alpine Pine", "Waterfall", "Great Horned Owl". "St. Nicholas", "Fairyland", "Jack and Jill", "Stalactite Curtain", etc.

The **Herman Ottó Memorial House** stands in **Erzsébet sétány** south of the István Caves. Ottó Herman (1835–1914) was the man who discovered dwellings

The Castle of Diósgyőr

used by ancient man in the Bükk. In addition to his archeological research, he wrote ethnographic, ornithological and other studies. Herman grew up in Lillafüred and wrote his scientific works in a villa he owned here; this house became the memorial museum. His remains lie buried in the cemetery of Felső Hámor. A **Foundry Museum** is also located in Felső Hámor, in an 18th-century building next to the church.

It is worth taking a 50 minute walk from the centre of Lillafüred to the **Szeleta Caves**. The entrance to the caves is situated on a steep cliff 95 m high and situated above the road. There was excitement among international circles when excavations at the beginning of the century stumbled upon the Ice-Age remains belonging to what is called the **"Szeleta Culture"**. Large numbers of arrow- and spear-heads shaped like bay leaves and made with splinters and flakes of grey-coloured chalcedony were among the material finds discovered in the cave. Fragments of dishes dating back to the New Stone Age as well as relics of the Bronze Age (axes) have been found in the upper layer.

A road beginning at the Palace Hotel and running west along the shore of Lake Hámori leads to an interesting historic relic, an **ancient foundry**.

Henrik Fazola, a master locksmith living in Eger who came originally from Würzburg in Bavaria, laid the foundations of what is now known as the Lenin Metallurgical Works when he set up a blast-furnace to be used for developing the deposits of iron-ore found in the northern part of the Bükk. The crude iron was then processed at Hámor. When the plant had to be expanded, his son, Frigyes Fazola, constructed the **Újmassa foundry** between 1810 and 1813, and this remained in operation for sixty years. In 1952 the plant was rebuilt and a small **museum** was established next door.

The Újmassa foundry

A road (bus route) runs through the university city to Miskolc's other holiday resort, **MISKOLC-TAPOLCA** (7 km). The same kinds of splintered-stone dishes from the Ice Age that were found in the Szeleta Caves were also found here in a niche in the rocks, along with human bones, evidence that this area was already inhabited by the prehistoric period. Remains of an Iron-Age **earthwork** can still be seen on the castle mountain above the resort.

The mildly radioactive waters of the Tapolca springs, flowing from depths of 800–900 m, were used as early as the Middle Ages for curative pur-

poses. At first, only wooden bath-
houses were erected here; the first
stone building was not constructed
until the 18th century. The spa is surrounded by a 1,200-hectare oak,
beech and pine forest that has been
made into a beautiful park. The main
establishment found here includes
the medicinal baths with two swimming-pools. One of the pools is built
directly over the springs in such a way
that the therapeutic warm water
(29°–31 °C) flows out through spaces in
the flooring. The water of the other
pools is much milder and is recommended for those who cannot tolerate
the radioactivity found in the first
pool. The therapeutic baths are particularly effective in treating diseases
of the sympathetic nervous system,
cardioneurosis, stomach and bowel
complaints arising from nervous disorders, as well as physical and mental fatigue.

Cave baths, Miskolctapolca

Established in 1959 in a rock cave formed inside the mountain by centuries of
warm flowing water, the **cave baths** can be entered from the thermal baths mentioned above. The temperature of the water, which is from 130 to 140 cm deep, is
29° to 31 °C, just like the water of the thermal baths. Expelling water in a wide
radius, the so-called "thrashing" shower provides bathers with natural mas-
sage. The air inside the cave has been proved effective against trachitis and
asthmatic conditions.

The lake baths, reconstructed in 1969, are joined to the cave and thermal baths
and can be approached from the inside. Its indoor pool is used mainly during
cooler weather. When the weather is warmer bathers prefer the crystal-clear
water of the outside pool where thermal water bubbles out from the gravel-
covered bottom.

A lake used for rowing, surrounded by giant old trees, is situated behind the
lake baths. At the end of the lake are bathing facilities which also include a swimming-pool used for competitions.

EXCURSIONS

After Lillafüred, the road connecting Miskolc with Eger traverses some beautiful
country in a south–southwest direction. One of the most popular travel destinations is the tourist hostel at **HOLLÓS-TETŐ** (510 m, 6 km from Lillafüred) from
where pleasant walks can be taken in six different directions. (There is a camping
site situated near the tourist hostel.)

A winding road branching off the main road to Eger goes from Hollós-tető to
BÜKKSZENTKERESZT (583 m, 9 km from Lillafüred), a quiet mountain resort
with clean air and a number of excellent opportunities for walking tours. The climate here is particularly recommended for treating Graves' disease. (There is
also a tourist hostel at Bükkszentkereszt, but the Hollós-tető tourist hostel and
camping site are only a forty-five-minute walk from here.)

Perhaps the most romantic road in the Bükk Mountains connects Miskolc with
JÁVORKÚT (686 m), a village lying at the southern foot of Mount Jávor. After
leaving Lillafüred, the road winds its way over an Alpine-like plateau. A whole
series of tourist routes branch off at Jávorkút, including one towards Bálvány
(956 m). A national conservation area called the Swedish Primeval Pine Forest
near Jávorkút consists of 100 to 150 year old spruces.

Kazincbarcika

21 km from Miskolc on Rd. 26; 25 km by rail.

Kazincbarcika, one of the country's
more important industrial towns,
came into existence in 1945 when
three small communities, Barcika, Sajókazinc and Berente were united. It
was not long after this that construction on two large plants, the Borsod
Thermal Power Station and the Borsod Chemical Works, began. The
country's largest coal separator,
about 900 m in length, is also at
Kazincbarcika.

When the industrial plants of the area were being constructed, a modern town developed next to the three small communities mentioned above. (Barcika and Sajókazinc have **churches** dating back to the 15th century; the **wooden belfry** at Berente is from the 18th century.)

PUTNOK (17 km northwest of Kazincbarcika on Rd. 26) became important because of its medieval **castle** during the wars that took place against the Turks and during the struggles for freedom fought against the House of Habsburg. In 1834 the neo-Classical former Serényi Castle was constructed here out of stones from the former castle, which had by that time already fallen into ruins. Two late Baroque **peasant houses (Szabadság tér 38** and **Tompa u. 100)** as well as the late Baroque **Calvinist church (Tompa u. 13)** are both worth seeing.

Ózd

19.5 km southwest of Putnok.

Ózd is one of Hungary's oldest metallurgical centres, its first plant having been founded in 1843 and operating at a high capacity by the end of the last century. During the final stages of World War II, Ózd served as one of the bases of Hungary's partisan movement.

Urban development started around 1950. A whole series of industrial plants were built in addition to the foundry (an oxygen factory, a clothing factory, etc.) and modern residential estates were constructed for the almost doubled population. Nearby, in the Uppony Pass, a large **mountain reservoir** was created.

THE AGGTELEK MOUNTAIN RANGE

Bounded by the Bükk and the Sajó River as well as the Czechoslovak border and the Hernád Valley, the Aggtelek Mountains consist of low hills with a wide variety of scenery. The highest point of the area, rising north of Jósvafő, is Nagyoldal (604 m). The mountain chain is cut in two by the Jósva Stream. The Aggtelek karst proper extends west of the Bódva on both sides of the Jósva Stream as far as the border. This karst territory is particularly known both abroad as well as in Hungary for its caves, which attract great numbers of tourists.

Besides its caves, the area is thickly covered with forests which offer a number of opportunities for pleasant excursions.

Aggtelek—Jósvafő

(The Stalactite Caves of Aggtelek)

55 km from Miskolc on Rd. 26 (from Sajókaza) and then on a minor road; 49 km by rail.

Aggtelek and Jósvafő lie at the western and eastern end respectively of one of Europe's largest and most beautiful systems of stalactite caves, the **Baradla.** The two communities are about 6 km from one another.

The points of interest to be seen above the surface at **Jósvafő** are the following: an old **fortified church** with a painted coffered ceiling and a separate bell tower; a few interesting **residential houses** built in the traditional style; an **old cemetery** containing graves with wooden memorials; and an emerald-coloured **mountain lake** lying at the foot of the hills.

The entire length of the Baradla cave passage is 22 km, of which a 7 km long section known as the Domica Cave lies on Czechoslovak territory. (Groups can also see the Domica without a passport.)

Scientific excavations conducted in the caves have uncovered bones of Stone-Age man as well as stone and bone implements, clay pottery, etc.; even bones belonging to prehistoric bears have been found here, which suggests that it was the dwelling place of prehistoric man. The caves served as a refuge for inhabitants of the surrounding area and were lighted by torches. The slowly dripping karst water covered the smoke and soot deposited on the stalactites from the torches with a thin layer of lime, preserving them almost intact. This is the reason for the dark colour of many of the stalactite formations inside the Baradla cave.

Professional guides accompany visitors to the caves and arrange group tours which vary according to distance, duration, and purpose. The short tours beginning at the **Jósvafő** and **Aggtelek entrances** take about an hour; the one commencing at the **Vörös-tó entrance** between Aggtelek and Jósvafő takes approximately two and a half hours. Groups starting at the entrance to the **main branch** of the cave, which is 7 km in length, spend five and a half hours among the stalactites. The latter tour, however, demands considerable physical effort.

The permanent **exhibition** at the entrance of the Aggtelek Cave acquaints the visitor with the history of the formation of the Baradla caves as well as the wonders of the most famous stalactites. The exhibition also gives a description of prehistoric man's environment and contains the reconstructed skeleton of a prehistoric bear. (Today 262 different species of animals live in the cave, which has a constant temperature of 10 °–11 °C.)

Inside the cave an endless row of beautiful stalactite formations greets the visitor. There are two kinds of cave deposits: **stalactites** (granular limestone deposits hanging from the ceiling of the caves) and **stalagmites** (stone candles rising from the bottom of the cave). Man's imagination has endowed these formations and various sections of the caves with extremely appropriate names, for example: "The Hall of the Giants" (one of Europe's largest cavern chambers, 120 × 30 × 40 m in size), "Concert Hall" (concerts as well as opera productions are held here regularly during the tourist season), "Chinese Pagoda", "Ghost Cave", "Slaughter House", "Leaning Tower of Pisa", "Mosque", "Fairy Castle", "Leaning Locomotive", "Frozen Waterfall", "Zeppelin", "Tortoise", "Lion's Head", etc. One of the world's largest stalagmites, the "Observatory", is 25 m high, has a diameter at the base of 9 m, and is estimated to weigh 8 tons.

A **lake,** on which one can row, almost 1.5 km long and 20–25 m wide, has been formed in one of the cave's rock chambers, one with a height of 16 m. Two streams bearing mythological names, the Styx and the Acheron, feed the lake, while battery-powered boats traverse its surface. The reflection in the water from the stalactites and the ornamental lights above the lake provide a sight fit for a fairy-tale.

Explorations conducted in 1952 discovered a cave perhaps even richer in stalactites than the Baradla. This cave system, referred to as the **Béke** (Peace) **Caves,** has not yet been completely explored. One of the most beautiful passages belonging to the cave system, a passage hundreds of metres long, was found here in 1973 while explorers were penetrating a 30 m high waterfall); but it is nevertheless possible for those interested to take short walks in the cave if accompanied by a guide and dressed in proper protective clothing. A fact that has proved to be a great asset to the Béke Caves is that artificial lighting has never been installed here. The formations appear in their natural state, producing extremely new, brilliant and vivid effects.

One of the chambers belonging to the Béke Caves is used as an **underground sanatorium.** It is extremely suitable for treating respiratory and asthmatic diseases. Every year hundreds of persons suffering from these diseases undergo a two-to three-week treatment here under strict medical supervision.

Stalactite caves, Aggtelek

EXCURSIONS

RUDABÁNYA (21.5 km from Aggtelek going back towards Miskolc and then turning off to the east) is the site of Hungary's only **iron-ore mine** still in operation. The mine must have been important as long ago as the Middle Ages, as King Louis the Great had the settlement raised to the rank of a mining town in 1378. (A modern iron-ore refinery has since been built next to the mine.) In 1967, they discovered in the mine the jawbone and teeth of a 10 million-year-old monkey, the predecessor of man, called **Rudapithecus hungaricus**. In the town the 14th to 15th-century Gothic buttressed **church** is ornamented with windows with traceries and a wooden ceiling painted in the 17th century.

The best way of penetrating the area of the Aggtelek mountains is through the **Bódva Valley**.

EDELÉNY (25 km from Miskolc on Rd. 26 and then continuing by a minor road northeast of Sajószentpéter): Four-storey **mansion,** with a corner tower, built between 1725–1730. Edelény's other historic monument is its **church,** built in its original shape around 1330 but remodelled many times since then. Gothic features are evident in the interior of the church and in the part overlooking the churchyard.

SZALONNA (19 km north of Edelény) is noted for a **church** with an angular aisle which was added, at the turn of the 12th and 13th centuries, to the semi-circular apse of an 11th-century church. There are valuable fresco remains. In the courtyard stands an 18th-century wooden belfry.

The undulating hilly area lying between Bódva and Hernád valleys, connecting the Bükk with the Zemplén mountains is called the **Cserehát**. Hungary's largest **water reservoir** was built here by harnessing the water of the **Rakaca Stream** which flows through the Cserehát. This artificial lake has an area of 259 hectares, a depth of 11 m at its deepest point, and holds over 5 million cubic metres of water.

The **valley of the Hernád River** abounds in natural beauties and at the same time forms the western boundary of the Zemplén Mountain Range. A large part of the traffic moving between Hungary and Czechoslovakia uses the Miskolc–Kassa (Košice) railway line and Road 3 (E96) running along the valley.

SZIKSZÓ (16.5 km northeast of Miskolc on Rd. 3): Soldiers fighting in Hungary's wars of independence defeated the Habsburg forces on three different occasions (1645, 1679, 1849). The Gothic sections of the community's **Calvinist church** date from the 14th century; its fortress-like wall, which is provided with embrasures, was built at the end of the 16th century.

THE ZEMPLÉN MOUNTAIN RANGE

The Zemplén Mountain Range is an area bounded by the Hernád River, the Hungarian–Czechoslovak border, the Szerencs Stream and the Tisza River, and is divided by the Bodrog River into two sharply contrasting parts, one of them mountainous and the other resembling the Great Plain. North of the river lie the actual mountains belonging to the Zemplén Range, a group of mountains of volcanic origin. The sunny slopes of the Hegyalja, a strip of land running along the southeastern and southern edges of the mountain range, produce the different kinds of grapes used for making the world-famous Tokaj-Hegyalja wines. The average height of the Zemplén Mountain Range is 600 m; its highest peak is **Nagy-Milic** (895 m), which lies on the Hungarian–Czechoslovak border.

The shortest route into the Zemplén Mountain Range (including the Hegyalja) is via Miskolc.

Szerencs

35 km from Miskolc on Rd. 37; 38 km by rail (on the Sátoraljaújhely line).

Rich findings in the area indicate that an important settlement must have existed here during the Migration Period. Later, but still before the Hungarian Conquest, an earthwork made it even more significant. Szerencs's golden era, which lasted from the end of the 16th century to the beginning of the 18th, was due to the castle which once stood there.

The **fortified castle** was built in the middle of the 16th century on the foundations of a Benedictine monastery founded in the second half of the 13th century. In 1583 it fell into the ownership of the Rákóczi family which led the struggles for independence against the Habsburgs. It was here that István Bocskai (1557–1606), one of the leading figures of the war, was first elected Prince of Transylvania and then prince of all Hungary. Two years later Zsigmond Rákóczi (1544–1608) was elected Bocskai's successor here. It was after the collapse of the War of Independence led by Ferenc Rákóczi II that the castle lost its political and military importance. Together with its surrounding estate it was confiscated by the Treasury of Vienna, which gave it to aristocrats rendering useful services to the House of Habsburg.

Today Szerencs is a transport centre; it also houses a number of important industries (chocolate and pastry factories, a sugar factory, a milk plant, etc.).

The **castle** is the town's most important historic building. A massive structure with thick walls and a square-shaped ground-plan, it was restored following the Second World War. Besides the **library** and a **theatre**, a **museum of local history** has also been established here. The collections housed in the museum preserve archeological finds as well as documents and other objects from the Rákóczi period. A **collection consisting of 500,000 picture post-cards** donated to the museum by the physician Dr. László Petrikovits is the only one of its kind in the country. The castle also houses the **Hotel Huszárvár**. The castle is surrounded by a large park with pleasant paths and an artificial lake.

The approach from the small square at the intersection of **Rákóczi út** and **Kossuth Lajos utca** leads to the city's Gothic **Calvinist church** built in the first half of the 14th century and remodelled around 1480. The church is surrounded by a medieval fortress wall and is the resting place of Prince Zsigmond Rákóczi and his wife, whose remains lie here in a red marble sarcophagus.

EXCURSIONS

MONOK (13 km northwest of Szerencs) is the birthplace of Lajos Kossuth, the leading political figure of the Hungarian struggle for independence of 1848–49. The old manor-house where Kossuth was born was built in the style of Louis XVI. Today, it is the **Kossuth Lajos Memorial Museum** containing, in addition to some Kossuth relics, 1,600 objects as well as pieces of furniture, engravings, etc., from the time of the War of Independence. The fortified castle here was built in the 14th century and was later considerably remodelled. The chapel and ceremonial hall belonging to the former 18th-century **Andrássy mansion** (today a school) are adorned with valuable wall-paintings.

BOLDOGKŐVÁRALJA (28 km north of Szerencs): Ruins of a 13th-century **castle**. Bálint Balassi, the 16th-century poet, visited the castle several times and produced some of his most famous works here. The castle finally lost its strategic importance at the end of the 17th century during the War of Independence led by Imre Thököly, and fell into ruins, the only parts remaining in a fair state of preservation today being the massive walls, bastions, and towers of the upper castle. A captivating view of the surrounding area can be seen from the castle stairs. The finely-restored castle today houses a tourist hostel. The Baroque **baronial manor-house** built in the 1760s serves as a hospital.

VIZSOLY (38 km north of Szerencs): Here, in 1590, was printed the first complete Hungarian translation of the Bible, a work which has been in use, in a slightly modernized version, ever since it was first written in vivid Hungarian by Gáspár Károli, a Calvinist priest from nearby Gönc. The community's **Calvinist church,** a historic monument from the 13th to 15th centuries, is adorned with contemporary frescoes.

GÖNC (12 km north of Vizsoly) was at one time the commercial centre for wine trading in the Tokaj-Hegyalja vine-growing district. A significant proportion of the vast amount of wine sent to Poland went through this beautifully situated village. Master coopers from Gönc and its surrounding areas made the so-called Gönc barrels which served both for storing the Tokaj wines and as a unit of measure (136 litres). The village has a **Catholic church** built in the 15th century and provided with a buttressed sanctuary and traceried windows. The nave of the church was rebuilt in the Baroque style during the 1730s.

TELKIBÁNYA (10 km east of Gönc) was famous during the Middle Ages for its gold and silver mines; today it is a tourist centre. Signs along the roads of the village show the way to a large tourist hostel. Telkibánya's Gothic **Calvinist church** with two naves and a painted wooden ceiling was built in the 15th century and remodelled at the beginning of the 17th century. The community's other attraction is a 20 m long, 5 m wide rocky ravine, the temperature of which does not rise above 5 °C even in the peak of summer. (This "ice cave" is used for storage.)

ABAÚJVÁR (10 km north of Gönc): Old castle with hardly any traces left. The community's 14th-century Gothic **church** is surrounded by a **medieval castle wall** and contains a number of old frescoes.

TOKAJ-HEGYALJA

The vine-growing region of Tokaj-Hegyalja, which stretches along the southeastern and southern edges of the Zemplén Mountain Range, and which is also the birthplace of the world-famous Tokaj wines, is made up of 28 communities (including Tokaj, Tarcal, Mád, Tállya, Tolcsva) with about 5,000 hectares of vineyards.

The first vineyards to grow on the Tokaj-Hegyalja were probably planted by the Celts several centuries before Christ. The Magyars who entered the Carpathian Basin soon engaged in vine-growing. From the 11th century onwards, particularly immediately after the Mongol invasion of 1241–42, the Hungarian kings brought in settlers from Italy and Western Europe. The Walloons, for example, are responsible for introducing Tokaji furmint.

The soil of the mountains and hills making up the vine-growing region of Tokaj-Hegyalja is composed of a mixture of rocks and loess of volcanic origin. Climatic conditions are favourable here, too, for the Carpathians act as a protective shield against the freezing northeast winds. There is also an extraordinary amount of sunshine; and what is even more important, the autumn is generally long and dry. Grapes are harvested in the other vine-growing regions of Hungary in the early autumn, but owing to the special climatic conditions, vintage does not begin in the Tokaj-Hegyalja region before the end of October and frequently lasts until the beginning of December. Thus the sun's rays help the clusters of grapes to ripen to maturity; the individual grapes begin to wither and their skins become so thin that they sometimes burst apart, as a result of which some of the juices evaporate and the sugar content increases significantly.

By ancient tradition, the vintage at Tokaj-Hegyalja is celebrated with spectacular parades, merry-making, and dancing.

HOW IS TOKAJI ASZÚ MADE?

The shrivelled grapes, the so-called Aszú grapes, are picked from bunches and placed in pails where the weight of the grapes presses out some of the juices. These are the juices which comprise the essence of Aszú. One butt (28–30 litres) of Aszú grapes yields up to one and a half litres of essence. The sugar content of Aszú essence can reach 40–60% and this is why only a minimal amount of fermentation takes place. Most of the essence is used for making Aszú. The withered Aszú grapes, which have been collected in the pails and have already started their "noble rot", are kneaded by a special procedure into paste and this paste is added to the pressed-out grape juice or wine. This whole procedure, which later results in the perfection of Aszú, takes place in 136 litre Gönc barrels. Aszú wine is classified as of two, three, four, five or six butts (*puttony*), depending on how many butts of Aszú grape paste are put into one Gönc barrel of grape juice or wine.

Tokaj

A sugar content of 30% or 45% slows down the fermentation process, which is delayed even further by the cool air found in the deep cellars; this is why it takes from four to eight years for Tokaji Aszú to mature; after that it can be stored for hundreds of years.

HOW DID TOKAJ WINE BECOME WORLD-FAMOUS?

It was during the Middle Ages and in Poland that Tokaj wine first became known and appreciated outside Hungary. According to an old Polish proverb, "The only true wine is Tokaj wine!"

In the 16th century the Tokaj market was inundated not only with Polish wine-merchants, but with Russian, Greek, German, Scandinavian and other merchants as well. Tokaj wines were transported in ever-increasing quantities to places like Cracow, Warsaw, St. Petersburg, Prague, Vienna, the Scandinavian countries, and even to England. Many men of medicine at that time believed that Tokaj wine had curative powers.

After sampling the wine from Tállya, Pope Pius IV is reputed to have said at the Council of Trent in 1562 that "Summum pontificem talia[!] vina decent" (Such wines are fit for a pope). One of Pope Pius IV's successors, Benedict XIV, after tasting Tokaj wine received from the Empress Maria Theresa, uttered the following words in the form of a prayer: "Blessed be the land that yielded thee, blessed be the lady who sent thee, and blessed be I for having tasted thee".

Tokaj wine was never lacking from the table of King Louis XIV of France (it was regularly sent to him by Prince Rákóczi); and it was listed in his menu together with the following comment: "The wine of kings—the king of wines". Tokaj wine was such a favourite of the Russian Tsar Peter the Great, that he even purchased several vineyards on Hegyalja.

Frederick the Great, king of Prussia, often drank the nectar in the company of Voltaire. The great French philosopher wrote about Tokaj wine: "Tokaj stimulates the brain-cells and kindles words of genius".

Goethe has Tokaj wine served for Faust in the Auerbach Cellar. Franz Schubert immortalized Tokaj in a song entitled "Lob des Tokayers", and it was also a favourite drink of Beethoven's. Anatole France wrote about Tokaj: "One glassful, and a feeling of sweet tranquillity begins to hover over me". The numerous attempts made to copy Tokaj wine provide further proof of the wine's great popularity.

Tokaj

233 km from Budapest first on Rds. M3 and 3, then on Rds. 37 and 38 after Miskolc; 238 km by rail.

Lying at the confluence of the Tisza and Bodrog Rivers, the small town of Tokaj is the traditional centre of the Tokaj-Hegyalja vine-growing region. This area was taken possession of by the Magyar tribes immediately after their entry into the Carpathian Basin; one of the chieftains serving under the conquering Prince Árpád had an earthwork constructed at the confluence of the two rivers. Between the 14th and 15th centuries a pentagonal-shaped **fortress** was built over the earthwork, which proved to be of vital importance for two centuries both strategically and politically. The remains that were left after Turkish forces destroyed it in 1567 were reduced to ashes by the Habsburg forces in 1604.

Tokaj became an important commercial and industrial centre as early as the Middle Ages. Greek merchants (fleeing here from the Turks between the 17th and 18th centuries) contributed to Tokaj's commercial importance. At the end of the last century a number of industrial plants were built.

Today only a few scattered remains can be seen of the former **Tokaj Castle**. The imposing bridge over the Tisza offers a remarkable panorama of the surrounding area. The former **Rákóczi–Dessewffy House,** which consists of two buildings with mansard roofs **(Bajcsy-Zsilinszky út 15–17);** the **Town Hall** built around 1790 in the style of Louis XVI **(Rákóczi út 44),** as well as the building standing at **Bem József utca 2,** which was according to tradition the hunting lodge of King John Zápolya, are among the historic monuments in the older part of the town, which lies along the bank of the Bodrog opposite the castle ruins. (There is a winepress on the ground floor of the latter building; underneath is a wine-cellar provided with two large fireplaces.)

A museum of local history containing documents and items connected with the history of Tokaj as well as the history of the whole Hegyalja grape and wine culture is housed in the Baroque **Greek Orthodox church** standing at **Bethlen Gábor utca 23.** The permanent exhibits in the winepress of a hundred-year-old tavern building and in the wine-cellar underneath consist of objects connected with vine-growing and supplement the material exhibited in the museum. (The museum's collection will shortly be transferred to a museum at Bethlen Gábor utca 6.)

The **Rákóczi Cellar,** which can be entered from the courtyard of **Kossuth tér 13,** often served as the scene of important political conferences during the struggle for independence; 20,000 hectolitres of wine are stored in the twenty-four passageways (which total 1.5 km in length) of the huge cellar labyrinth built several centuries ago. A wine-shop is attached to the cellar. (There are wine-shops located in other parts of the town as well.)

EXCURSIONS

SZABOLCS (12 km northeast of Tokaj, on the left bank of the Tisza): A 10th-century earthwork and an 11th-century restored basilica; museum of local history. **TÁLLYA** (10.5 km north of Szerencs) is the second important community of the Tokaj-Hegyalja vine-growing district, with a 16th-century former **Rákóczi man-**

sion and a **manor-house** built around 1720, as well as an 18th-century Gothic **Catholic church** and a Baroque **Lutheran church**. A painting by Franz Anton Maulbertsch adorns the Catholic church; and the Lutheran church still holds the baptistal font where Lajos Kossuth was christened.
MÁD (10 km northeast of Szerencs) is likewise a well-known Hegyalja wine-producing community. A **Catholic church** was built between 1521 and 1526, a **synagogue** was erected around 1790, and a neo-Classical **Calvinist church** was constructed in 1825.
TARCAL (12 km southeast of Szerencs): a **wine museum** is situated here in one of the corridors of the Rákóczi Cellar.
TOLCSVA (27 km northeast of Szerencs, on Rd. 37) is the home of the famous Tolcsva lime-leaf grape wine (Tolcsvai hárslevelű). Historic monuments to be found here are the former **Rákóczi Castle** as well as a **Catholic church** containing a 15th-century Gothic **chapel** and **wooden steeples** with arcades.

Sárospatak

250 km from Budapest on Rds. M3 and 3 to Miskolc, then Rd. 37; 256 km by rail (36 km from Szerencs).

The area now occupied by Sárospatak was taken possession of by the conquering Hungarians at the turn of the 10th century. From the middle of the 11th century the area enjoyed for hundreds of years the status of a royal domain. The early development of Sárospatak into a town was greatly facilitated by families of settlers arriving here and the surrounding areas from Italy in the 12th century. In 1429 the Hungarian King Sigismund of Luxembourg turned Sárospatak into a royal free city; and in 1465 King Matthias gave permission to the Pálóczi family, which had possession of Sárospatak and its surrounding area, to turn their mansion into a fortified castle. The town's golden age began in 1616 when it became the possession of the Rákóczi family. During the War of Independence led by Ferenc Rákóczi II, it was here that the Diet convened in 1708. Following the collapse of the struggle for liberation, Prince Rákóczi went into exile from here (he died in 1735 in Tekirdag, Turkey), and Sárospatak became the property of foreign aristocrats. In 1945 the Hungarian state took possession of Sárospatak, and in this way the last will and testament of Zsuzsanna Lorántffy (the wife of György Rákóczi) was fulfilled. The will provided for the fortified castle she had received as a dowry, and the estate belonging to her, to be left to the Hungarian people upon the death of the last member of the Rákóczi family.
Thanks to its **Calvinist College** founded here in 1531, Sárospatak played an important role in the educational and cultural life of the country. It was in this college that J. A. Comenius, the world-famous Czech humanist and teacher, studied for almost five years from 1650. (Comenius was a descendant of a Hungarian family that emigrated from Transylvania to Moravia.) The Rákóczi family provided him with printing facilities, and his lectures on school organization, his Latin textbooks and the first sheets of his major work written in Patak, "Orbis Pictus", were printed here.
The college had to be moved from Sárospatak during the second half of the 17th century as a result of the persecutions of the Counter-Reformation. At first it operated in Gönc, then in Kassa (Košice, now in Czechoslovakia), and was able to resume its activities in Sárospatak only after 1703. (The college's reputation was further enhanced by the fact that at the beginning of the 18th century King George II of England personally intervened to safeguard the centuries-old privileges enjoyed by the college. (A number of eminent personalities, both past and present, representing Hungarian political and cultural life, studied at the Sárospatak College, for example György Bessenyei, one of the leading figures of the Hungarian Period of Enlightenment; the poet Mihály Csokonai Vitéz; the language reformer Ferenc Kazinczy; the statesman Lajos Kossuth; two great prose writers of the present century, Géza Gárdonyi and Zsigmond Móricz, as well as a number of living writers, poets, and scholars.)

The **fortified castle** stands in the park, which extends from Kádár Kata utca to the banks of the Bodrog. The different sections of this large group of buildings were constructed throughout the centuries with various purposes in mind and in a number of different styles. The ground-plan of the castle is rectangular and consists of a **medieval keep with three corner**

towers on the uppermost level (the Red Tower), remains of the penta-gonal-shaped ramparts built around the keep with **Italian bastions,** as well as the 16th to 18th-century wings adjoining the tower and surrounding the square-shaped castle-yard. As a result of the professional reconstruction work begun in 1950, the whole castle is one of Hungary's most beautifully-restored historic monuments.

The oldest section of the castle is the six-storey **Red Tower** built at the end of the 15th or at the beginning of the 16th century. (Plaster-work still remains on parts of the Red Tower and proves that the walls were once plastered; the name that has been used since the 17th century is based on the plaster's colour.)

The wooden bridge over the moat leads to the tower entrance. The gate itself is valuable because of its rich Renaissance adornments. Flanked by *sedilia* once belonging to the garrison, the entrance-hall is surrounded by three vaulted halls. The hall opposite the entrance today houses documents connected with the management of the Rákóczi estate, while the hall on the left contains old household utensils. The hall on the right leads to the two large halls belonging to the lowermost level of the tower.

A steep stairway leads from the landing in front of the entrance to the third level. The south hall on this storey once served as a chapel; today it houses an **exhibition of ecclesiastical art.** On the fourth storey we find the "large palace", an impressive hall rich in Renaissance carvings. A narrow stairway leads from here to the uppermost storey of the castle which no longer has a roof. A beautiful view of the fortified castle, the outer fortress, the town and the varied countryside around can be seen from here.

The crenellated corridor below the large hall leads to the **loggia** which acquired its present shape in the 1640s. The loggia as well as the passageway leading to it from the courtyard below, a passageway provided with columned arcades, are two of Hungary's most beautiful examples of Renaissance architecture. The third storey of the Red Tower leads to the so-called **"Fireplace Hall"**, named after a Renaissance fireplace situated on the ground floor of the east wing. The hall contains a number of 16th and 17th-century stone carvings. About the year 1670 the councils making preparations for one of the significant conspiracies of the independence movement were held under the stucco rose *(sub rosa)* that holds the arches together in the balcony room of the northeast corner bastion. (The leaders of the conspiracy were executed.) Documents connected with the War of Independence led by Ferenc Rákóczi II are exhibited in the halls of the north wing; 16th to 17th-century interiors can be seen in the series of halls of the west wing.

Other items worth examining are the **system of cellars** belonging to the fortified castle, the pentagonal-shaped advance protective bastion around the tower (16th century), and the fortifications of the outer fortress. One of Eastern Hungary's largest **Gothic hall churches** stands in the centre of the street belonging to the outer fortress (Kádár Kata utca). The main part of the church dates from the 14th century. The church itself was first rebuilt in 1492, only to be frequently remodelled a number of times throughout the ensuing centuries. Complete reconstruction has turned this church into one of Hungary's most important Gothic historical monuments. The most beautiful of the church's furnishings is the huge Baroque main altar.

A former **Trinitarian monastery** (today the Borostyán Hotel), a 17th-century Baroque **residential house,** as well as the **Old Town Hall** built in the 18th century in **Kádár Kata utca** are all worth seeing. The group of buildings belonging to the famous **Calvinist College** stands in **Rákóczi út.** The present-day main building of the college constructed in a neo-Classi-

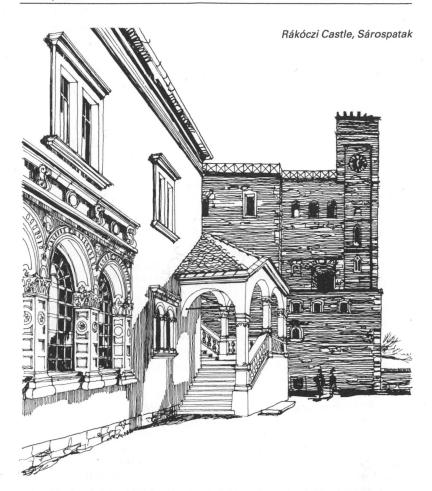

Rákóczi Castle, Sárospatak

cal style dates from the beginning of the last century. The most impressive hall of the building has decorations by Mihály Pollack, a master of Hungarian neo-Classical architecture. The hall is also the home of a **library** of 2,000 rare volumes. The last remnants of the older buildings, a **two-storey Baroque structure** erected in the 18th century, stand in the spacious courtyard which is surrounded by the wings of the college. A **collection of applied art** is housed on the first floor, while on the second floor the **Comenius exhibition,** showing the history of the college, can be seen. Statues depicting former leaders of Sárospatak and pupils of the college who later became famous line the roads of the park, the so-called School Gardens, situated opposite the college's main façade. A new **Cultural Centre,** designed by the outstanding architect Imre Makovecz (interior by Gábor Mezei) was opened in 1983.

EXCURSIONS

The ridges of the Zemplén Mountain Range north and west of Sárospatak offer a whole range of opportunities for excursions.

At **OLASZLISZKA** (14 km southwest of Sárosptak) is located the oldest **church** in the area. The Gothic sanctuary of this Catholic church is surrounded by a buttressed balcony and was built in the 14th century.

ERDŐBÉNYE (8 km northwest of Olaszliszka) is a beautifully-situated village with all the attractions of a resort. The village has a **church** remodelled in the Baroque style and provided with a Gothic tower, as well as a Baroque manor- house built in the 18th century.

KARCSA (21 km east of Sárospatak) is noted for its Dalmatian–Italian-style **church,** originally a round church. Its choir dates from *c.* 1140. The aisled nave was added to it about 1260–70.
PÁCIN (3 km east of Karcsa): Renaissance **palace** with a castle chapel built around 1581–1591.

Sátoraljaújhely

261 km from Budapest on Rds. M3 and 3 to Miskolc, then Rd. 37; 266 km by rail.

Lying on the Hungarian–Czechoslovak border, the town of Sátoraljaújhely is the centre of the Zemplén mountain district. The precursor of the present-day town developed after the attack of the Mongol forces. (Having served its purpose until 1558, the castle gradually fell into ruins and all that can be seen today are a few remains.) In 1361 King Louis the Great had Sátoraljaújhely raised to the rank of a town, and in the 17th century it came into the possession of the Rákóczi family. After this the town took part in the struggles for independence against the Habsburgs. Sátoraljaújhely was the county capital for several centuries.

The former **County Hall** of Sátoraljaújhely was originally built in the Baroque style between 1758–61 and later remodelled in the neo-Classical style (the building today serves as the **Town Hall** and is situated at **Ady tér 5).** It was within the walls of this building that Lajos Kossuth began his career as a civil servant; he also delivered his first public speech from the balcony of the building.
   The **Catholic church** standing in Széchenyi tér was built between 1768 and 1792 on medieval foundations and is one of the town's oldest buildings. Certain sections of the former **Piarist church (Deák u. 14)** are also of medieval origin (among them the tower). The former **monastery** adjoining the church was built between the 17th and 18th centuries. The house standing at **Kazinczy utca 25** once belonged to the Rákóczi family.
   An extremely beautiful panorama may be enjoyed from the 18 m high look-out tower on **Magas Mountain** (509 m). In clear weather even the High Tatra can be seen from here. A 1,800 m long ski-run is situated near the look-out tower.

EXCURSIONS

There are many picturesque areas northeast of the Zemplén Mountains (the districts lying between Sárospatak, Sátoraljaújhely and Füzérkomlós can also be reached by taking the narrow-gauge railway running through this beautiful mountain region).
SZÉPHALOM (5.5 km north of Sátoraljaújhely) was one of the centres of Hungarian literature at the turn of the 19th century, for it was here that Ferenc Kazinczy, one of the leaders of the Hungarian language reform, lived for many years and died. Kazinczy played an active role in the Jacobin movement at the end of the 18th century, for which he was sent to prison. Today a **mausoleum** (1862, Miklós Ybl), built in the style of a Greek Orthodox church, stands at the site where Kazinczy's home was once situated.
FÜZÉR (10 km north of Pálháza) with its beautiful old-fashioned **peasant houses** is a popular summer holiday retreat with tourists. On a nearby mountain peak stand the **ruins of a castle** built in the 1260s but later blown up by the Imperial high command following the defeat of the War of Independence led by Ferenc Rákóczi II. An appreciable part of the original walls, however, remains.
HOLLÓHÁZA (26 km northwest of Sátoraljaújhely) is Hungary's northernmost community. The name of the village has been made famous by the products manufactured in its porcelain factory. The porcelain produced in the factory is adorned with vivid rose-red ornamentations painted on a base of a pale colour and has already captured many foreign markets. Not far from Hollóháza a Swiss-styled **hunting lodge** stands 600 m up on the Hungarian side of Nagy-Milic.

PRACTICAL INFORMATION

For TRAVEL INFORMATION in English, German, French and Russian contact
TOURINFORM, Budapest V., Sütő utca 2.
Tel.: 1179-800

FORMALITIES

VISAS

How to obtain a visa. Visas for entry into or travelling through Hungary may be obtained, usually within 24 hours, from any consulate of the Hungarian Republic with a valid passport or other valid travel document and two passport photographs. Visa applications may also be forwarded to the consulates by mail. Visas are also available at international frontier crossings (see p. 264), as well as at Ferihegy Airport, Budapest and the International Port (Budapest V., Belgrád rakpart). It is, however, advisable to secure a visa in advance in order to avoid a possibly long queue.

If you are travelling by train it is absolutely necessary to obtain a visa in advance. **Visas are not issued on trains!**

Citizens of the following countries may enter Hungary without a visa: Austria, Bulgaria, Cuba, Czechoslovakia, China, Cyprus, Finland, the Federal Republic of Germany, the German Democratic Republic, Italy, Malta, Mongolia, Nicaragua, Poland, Rumania, Sweden, the Soviet Union and Yugoslavia.

Visas can be extended by Hungarian Consulates outside Hungary or by local police stations. Requests for an extension must be made personally 48 hours before the visa is due to expire.

CUSTOMS CONCESSIONS AND CURRENCY REGULATIONS

Printed information on customs and foreign exchange regulations may be obtained at the border crossings. A few general rules:

Articles which may not be imported:
Narcotics, arms or explosives (with the exception of hunting weapons listed on an accompanying certificate of registration).

Articles which may be exported:
Non-commercial quantities of articles purchased in INTERTOURIST, KONSUM-TOURIST and UTASTOURIST shops as well as from the Picture Gallery Enterprise (Képcsarnok Vállalat) with credit cards or with Hungarian forints originating from the conversion of hard currencies, with the exception of precious metals, stamps and works of art, which may be exported only with a special export permit. Be sure to save the purchase receipt or credit card slip, for this will have to be shown to the customs authorities on leaving.

Currency conversion, credit cards:
Cash and traveller's cheques may be exchanged and cashed only at the following official places of exchange: The National Bank of Hungary (Magyar Nemzeti Bank) and its branches, the National Savings Bank (OTP) and its branches and the exchange bureaus of travel agencies. Foreign currency is exchanged at the official rate established by the National Bank of Hungary.

Not more than 100 forints may be taken out of the country.

Foreign citizens may not use Hungarian forints to buy tickets to destinations outside Hungary.

At big hotels, restaurants and certain shops and department stores you can use your credit card, traveller's cheque or Eurocheque to settle bills. A notice at the entrance states which cards are accepted.

CAR PAPERS

Motorists from France, Greece, Iceland, Italy, Portugal, Spain, Turkey or countries outside Europe must bring with them, in addition to the usual papers and an international driving permit, the International Motor Insurance Certificate or **green card,** which certifies third-party liability insurance, otherwise they will be obliged to buy short-term insurance at the frontier. (Under international agreements cars arriving from other European countries need only the national identification plate and the registration plate.) The **blue card** issued by CASCO Vehicle Insurances insures citizens of Rumania and the Soviet Union while in Hungary. (If the car is not taken out of the country by the same person who brought it in, advance notice of this fact must be given to the nearest customs office.)

(The aforementioned obviously only partially affect cars with customs registration plates.)

HEALTH REGULATIONS

Vaccination certificate. Visitors arriving from infected areas must present the yellow **International Certificate of Vaccination** at the frontier. Pets (cats, dogs) are allowed into the country only if they are accompanied by a veterinary certificate showing that they have been vaccinated against rabies. For dogs, proof of vaccination against distemper must also be presented.

TRAVEL TO HUNGARY

ROAD DISTANCE CHART (FROM BUDAPEST)

Amsterdam	1,470 km	Lisbon	3,241 km
Athens	1,710 km	London	1,880 km
Barcelona	2,110 km	Madrid	2,665 km
Belgrade	400 km	Milan	995 km
Berlin	940 km	Moscow	1,980 km
Berne	1,038 km	Munich	705 km
Brussels	1,410 km	Oslo	1,965 km
Bucharest	805 km	Paris	1,490 km
Copenhagen	1,355 km	Prague	590 km
Frankfurt-on-Main (FRG)	1,005 km	Rome	1,365 km
Graz	329 km	Sofia	815 km
Hamburg	1,211 km	Stockholm	2,020 km
Helsinki	2,106 km	Tirana	1,048 km
Istanbul	1,860 km	Venice	814 km
Kiev	1,090 km	Vienna	270 km
Leipzig	820 km	Warsaw	695 km
Leningrad	1,680 km	Zurich	1,015 km

INTERNATIONAL ROAD FRONTIER CROSSINGS

From Austria:
(Nickelsdorf)—Hegyeshalom
(Klingenbach)—Sopron
(Deutschkreutz)—Kópháza
(Rattersdorf)—Kőszeg
(Schanchendorf)—Bucsu
(Heiligenkreutz)—Rábafüzes
From Czechoslovakia:
(Král')—Bánréve
(Rusovce)—Rajka
(Komárno)—Komárom
(Šahy)—Parassapuszta
(Slovenské Ďarmoty)—Balassagyarmat
(Fil'ákovo)—Salgótarján
(Milnost)—Tornyosnémeti
(Slovenské Nové Mesto)—Sátoraljaújhely
(Medved'ov)—Vámosszabadi
From the Soviet Union:
(Chop)—Záhony
From Rumania:
((Petea)—Csengersima
(Borş)—Ártánd
(Vărşand)—Gyula
(Nădlac)—Nagylak
From Yugoslavia:
(Hodoš)—Bajánsenye
(Dolga Vas)—Rédics
(Goričan)—Letenye
(Gola)—Berzence
(Terezino-Polje)—Barcs
(Donji Miholjac)—Drávaszabolcs
(Kneževo)—Udvar
(Bački Breg)—Hercegszántó
(Kelebia)—Tompa
(Horgoš)—Röszke

International main roads which pass through Hungary (Hungarian road numbers in parentheses).

E60 (1–M1–4): 42 (Wien) — Győr — Budapest — Szolnok — Püspökladány — Ártánd — (Oradea — Cluj — Bucuresti — Constanta)
E65 E71 (86–76–74–7): (Bratislava) — Rajka — Mosonmagyaróvár — Csorna — Szombathely — Körmend — Zalaegerszeg — Nagykanizsa — Letenye — (Zagreb — Dubrovnik — Tripoli — Chania)
E71 (3–M3–M7–7): (Košice) — Tornyosnémeti — Miskolc — Budapest — Balatonaliga — Nagykanizsa — Letenye — (Zagreb — Split)
E75 (15–1–M1–M5–5): (Bratislava) — Rajka — Győr — Budapest — Szeged — Röszke : (Beograd — Niš — Thessaloniki — Chania — Sitia)
E73 (6–56): Budapest — Szekszárd — Udvar — (Osijek — Sarajevo — Metković)
E73 (6): Budapest — Szekszárd — Pécs — Barcs
E66 (8): (Graz) — Rábafüzes — Veszprém — Székesfehérvár
E68 (43): Szeged — Nagylak — (Arad — Braşov)
E77 (2): (Zvolen) — Parassapuszta — Vác — Budapest

TRANSPORT

MOTORING

Road conditions: Single-figure main roads, eight in all, which lead directly to Budapest from the major border crossings, are in good condition. Double-figure and secondary main roads are also kept in good repair. It is advisable to drive very carefully on three-figure and unnumbered roads.

Traffic regulations: Generally speaking, the highway code in Hungary is much the same as in most other European countries:

Drive on the right is the rule of the road; consequently overtaking is on the left.

At equal intersections the general rule is to give way to traffic coming from the right, unless there are signs to the contrary.

The wearing of safety belts is compulsory. Motor cyclists must wear crash helmets. Children under ten years of age may not sit in the front seat next to the driver.

From twilight until dawn shaded lights must be used.

Speed limits: the maximum speeds for cars are as follows:
120 km/hr on motorways
90 km/hr on other main roads.

In inhabited areas (from the sign-post indicating the name of the community to the sign-post indicating its end) the speed limit is 60 km/hr. Maximum speeds for cars towing caravans (trailers), motor cycles and coaches are:
80 km/hr on motorways,
70 km/hr on other roads,
50 km/hr in inhabited areas.

Extreme caution should be taken at pedestrian "zebra" crossings where pedestrians have right of way over vehicles.

Unless there is a traffic island, cars may not overtake stationary trams, and must always give way to passengers boarding or alighting.

Unlit or inadequately lit slow-moving vehicles (cyclists, horse-drawn traffic, tractors) often present a serious hazard at night on main roads. Be particularly careful of pedestrians at night.

Parking: Parking is inexpensive in Hungary. There is metre-parking for limited periods in a number of places in Budapest.

Parking regulations are strictly enforced. Cars left in places where parking is prohibited may be towed away (Enquiries: dial 1572–811 in Budapest). In such cases, towing charges must be paid along with the fine.

It is a serious offence to drive under the influence of alcohol. If a driver is shown to have even the slightest amount of alcohol in his blood while driving, he will be fined and his licence may be confiscated; if he has caused an accident as well, he is liable to more severe penalty.

All accidents and damage to cars should be reported to the police at once, regardless of who caused it. Damaged cars may only leave the country with the permission of the police.

Following an accident or damage to the car, motorists must also notify the Hungária Insurance Company (Hungária Biztosító) at Gvadányi u. 69, Budapest XIV (tel. 1835-350). Outside Budapest, motorists should report to the county directorate of the State Insurance company.

Hit-and-run drivers are very severely punished in Hungary, and may be sent-

enced to several years' imprisonment. In such cases, drunken driving is regarded as an aggravating circumstance.
Filling stations: ÁFOR filling stations can be found in all major inhabited areas. Along the busier main roads and in several parts of Budapest there are also ÁFOR—AGIP, ÁFOR—BP and SHELL filling stations. Lead-free petrol: Budapest VIII, Kerepesi út 5–7. Service stations which sell spare parts for some of the better-known Western makes operate alongside a number of petrol stations.
Garages and service stations can be found in the larger towns. If your car breaks down and needs to be towed away the following companies will tow your car to a service station: VOLÁN, Ifjúgárda út 117, Budapest XV, tel. 1409-326,; FŐSPED, Kőér u. 3, Budapest X, tel. 1475-594.
The Hungarian Motoring Club—Magyar Autóklub (Rómer Flóris u. 4/a, Budapest II, H-1024, tel. 1152-040) operates a break-down service on the Budapest—Vienna and the Budapest—Balaton route and a week-end service only from May to September on other roads as well.
The Club's patrols drive yellow vehicles which can be alerted in Budapest day or night by calling tel. 1691-831. Members of foreign automobile clubs will be charged by the mechanic only for his travel costs and any spare parts which may be needed. Cars which cannot be repaired in Hungary will be shipped home by the Hungarian Motoring Club. The club also has service stations where the engine, headlights and brakes are seen to and other minor adjustments are carried out. (Information: 1152-865.) The Hungarian Motoring Club accepts letter of credits issued by foreign motoring clubs to cover the unforeseen expenses.

RAILWAYS

Trains are operated by the Hungarian State Railways (Magyar Államvasutak, MÁV for short). On express trains seats must be reserved in advance, preferably at least a day or two before departure. (For railway stations in Budapest see p. 276)
Timetables. For information on international trains dial 1224-052 in Budapest between 6 a.m. to 9 p.m. daily. Keleti pályaudvar (Eastern Railway Station): 1136-835, Nyugati pályaudvar (Western Railway Station): 1490-115, Déli pályaudvar (Southern Railway Station): 1558-657.
Long-distance buses are operated by **Volán**. (For bus terminals see p. 276). For information on domestic services ring 1172-966 and on services abroad 1172-562.

AIR TRAVEL

In addition to flights by **Malév** (Hungarian Airlines), Budapest's international airport at Ferihegy also handles regular flights by 17 foreign airlines. A regular bus service takes airlines passengers from the airport to Engels tér, in the centre of Budapest. Booking office: V., Roosevelt tér 2, 1051, tel. 1189-033.
Ferihegy I.: 1572-122; 1572-224
Ferihegy II.: 1577-831; 1578-406

BOATS

Boat services are run by the MAHART shipping company (Magyar Hajózási Rt.), International Port: Belgrád rakpart, Budapest V., 1056 tel.: 1181-953. A regular hydrofoil service operates on the Danube between Vienna and Budapest from May to September.
Domestic services link the capital city, Budapest, with resorts on the Danube Bend (mid April to mid October).
In summer, a regular shuttle service links the capital's southern and northern points, including Margaret Island. A ride on one of these in hot weather is a more pleasant experience than a journey by either bus or tram.
Also in summer, excursion boats depart twice daily (afternoons and evenings) as well as on Sunday mornings from the Vigadó tér pier in Budapest. Trips last from 1 ½ to 2 hours. There is a restaurant, café and dance music on board these boats.
IBUSZ office in Vienna, Kärntnerstrasse 26, 1010 Wien, tel. 56-26-86, telex: 11-3828.

PUBLIC TRANSPORT

Buses, trams, trolleys, metro

A bus service operates in the larger towns, trams run only in a few.

In Budapest public transport comprises buses, trams, trolley buses and an underground (Metro) service. Tickets for the buses (10,– Ft), for the trams, the Metro and the trolley-buses (8,– Ft) must be bought in advance from tobacconists' shops or at bus and tram terminals, Metro stations, railway stations, etc. Each ticket is valid for a single uninterrupted journey and must be validated by the passenger himself by inserting it into a ticket-punching device on the bus, tram or trolley-bus. A blue bus ticket is required for a trip on the cogwheel railway, while tickets for the Pioneer Railway (Úttörővasút), the chairlift (libegő) and the suburban railway (HÉV) as well as for the shuttle on the Danube are sold at special ticket offices.

Taxis

Taxis can be found everywhere in Budapest and the major provincial towns. A taxi is unoccupied when the TAXI sign on top of the car is lit up. In Budapest taxis can be ordered by calling FŐTAXI: 1222-222; VOLÁNTAXI: 1666-666; BUDATAXI: 1294-000; RADIOTAXI: 1767-717; INTERTAXI: 1804-040; GABRIEL: 1555-000; and CITY TAXI: 1228-855. To order at least an hour in advance, dial: 1188-888. Tipping is not compulsory, though a 10 to 15 % tip is customary.

Hiring

Travel agencies run rent-a-car services, but visitors can hire a car for personal use (with or without driver) at FŐTAXI HERTZ: 1221-471; IBUSZ AVIS: 1184-158; VOLÁN TOURIST: 1334-783; COOPTOURIST-BUDAPEST: 1181-466; CONTRAX: 1550-602.

ACCOMMODATION

In accordance with international standards, **hotels** are classified by stars (*****, ****, ***, **, *). Prices usually include breakfast. Most hotels offer pre- and off-season discounts.

Guest-houses. Small, hotel-like buildings with twin-bedded rooms, adequate bath and lavatory facilities with hot and cold running water.

Tourist hostels. Most rooms have five or more beds and are classified as A and B category accommodations. In Category A tourist hostel rooms cannot have more than eight beds (not bunks) and there must be adequate bath and lavatory facilities, with hot and cold running water.

Campsites are divided into three categories: ***, ** and * star. In every campsite there is running drinking water, at least cold water for washing, wash-basins, showers and toilets, and some sort of cooking facilities and first-aid facilities. The three-star campsites have wash-basins and showers and sinks with hot and cold running water. In accordance with international customs, campsites charge for the area occupied plus an accommodation fee for each person.

Chalets and bungalows are suitable for accommodating one or two families. Categories: apartment, first class, second class, third class. Apartments: individual building units with full amenities, fully-equipped kitchen (refrigerator), lounge, bedroom, bathroom with hot and cold running water and terrace or verandah.

The first-class chalets or bungalows are smaller, and do not always have a fully-equipped kitchen. Second and third-class category chalets and bungalows may have rooms with 3–4 beds and fewer conveniences.

Private accommodation. Flats, parts of flats and rooms can be rented through travel agencies and county tourist offices. (For list of county tourist offices and for addresses of travel agencies, see Directory, pp. 274–291)

EATING OUT

HUNGARIAN CUISINE

Over the centuries, Hungarian cooking has been influenced mainly by French, Italian, Turkish and Serbian cuisine, blending the sophisticated tastes of these with the more marked and spicier character of Hungarian cooking.

Paprika, the spice most often associated with Hungarian cuisine and the main ingredient of numerous Hungarian dishes, is by no means always as hot as most people imagine. "Exquisite delicacy" **(csemege)** and "Noblesweet" **(édesnemes)** are varieties which possess the colour and aroma of paprika, but are quite mild. Contrary to common belief, rich spicy dishes are not part and parcel of everyday Hungarian cooking. There are, however, many Hungarian dishes that are very rich owing to their high fat content.

Some Hungarian specialities: The best-known Hungarian dish is, perhaps, **gulyás** (goulash), a soup made of diced beef seasoned with paprika and cooked with potatoes, vegetables and small dumplings **(csipetke).** Cooked in a cauldron over an open fire, the thicker **bográcsgulyás** is a popular variety of gulyás soup. Fish soup, the famous **halászlé** usually made from carp, is also seasoned with paprika and onions. But the best Hungarian fish soup is made with at least 2–3 varieties of fish. A lighter, non-spicy dish is **Újházi tyúkhúsleves** (chicken broth), which is served together with the meat and vegetables cooked in it.

A popular Hungarian entrée is **hortobágyi palacsinta** (Hortobágy pancakes), thin pancakes made with eggs, fried in hot fat, filled with minced meat sautéed with onions and paprika and served with sour cream. Breaded champignon mushroom caps **(rántott gombafejek)** fried in hot fat is a light dish. **Libamáj** (goose liver) and **hideg fogas** (cold giant pike-perch) in mayonnaise are favourite cold hors-d'oeuvres.

One of the best-known Hungarian meat dishes is **pörkölt,** a stew prepared from meat cut into small cubes and stewed in lard with onions and paprika; it can be made from beef, pork, mutton or poultry and occasionally even from game. When sour cream is added to this dish, it is called **paprikás.** The most popular paprikás dish is **csirkepaprikás** (chicken paprikash). Another excellent dish made with sour cream is **töltött káposzta** (stuffed cabbage), cabbage leaves stuffed with minced meat mixed with rice and seasoned with spices and cooked together with finely-chopped sauerkraut. **Kolozsvári rakott káposzta** (Kolozsvár layered cabbage) is a dish made from shredded sauerkraut seasoned with spices and cooked together with meat.

Attractively served on a wooden platter, **fatányéros, a** Transylvanian speciality consisting of a variety of meat, roast or fried in breadcrumbs and served abundantly garnished, is a truly enticing dish. An excellent idea for outdoor cooking in the summer is **rablóhús** which is meat roasted on a skewer together with cubes of smoked bacon, potatoes and rings of onions.

Favourite **cheese delicacies** include **Pálpusztai,** a cheese which is reminiscent of Gorgonzola, **Bakony,** which resembles Camembert, and **Márványsajt,** which resembles Roquefort in taste. A special Hungarian cream cheese is **körözött** (a mixture of ewe cheese, butter, paprika, onion and caraway seeds).

The most frequently served **desserts and pastries** at Hungarian restaurants are **rétes** (strudel), wafer-thin layers of pastry filled with cottage cheese, apples, sweet and sour cherries and occasionally with cabbage; **palacsinta** (thin pancakes) filled with a variety of fillings such as nuts, jam, cottage cheese, etc.; **somlói galuska,** a sweetmeat made from sponge cake cut into small pieces covered with chocolate sauce and topped with whipped cream. Those who prefer savoury non-sweet desserts should try **túrós csusza,** flat egg-noodles boiled in water and prepared with cottage cheese and sour cream and flavoured with pork crackling, or **sonkás kocka,** noodles prepared in a similar way, but with minced ham and sour cream.

WHAT TO DRINK

Egri Bikavér (Bull's Blood of Eger) is the best-known Hungarian red wine. It is made from four different kinds of grapes and has an alcohol content of 12.5°. Other good red wines include **Medoc Noir,** also produced in Eger, and the **Szekszárdi, Villányi vörös** and **Soproni kékfrankos.** These wines are usually served at room temperature.

The finest white wines in Hungary are produced in the Tokaj region. The **Aszú** (see p. 254) and the **Szamorodni,** both heavy dessert wines, may have an alcohol content as high as 18°. The lighter wines produced in Tokaj are also excellent. The best-known are the **Furmint** and the **Tolcsvai hárslevelű,** the alcohol content of which exceeds 13°.

Some of the best table wines come from the Balaton region. Their alcohol content is around 13–14° and they are served chilled to a centigrade temperature that corresponds to their alcohol contents. The **Badacsonyi, Szentgyörgy-hegyi** and **Füredi rizling,** the **Badacsonyi kéknyelű** and the famous, semisweet **Badacsonyi szürkebarát** are all gently acidic and extremely harmonious dry wines. The **muskotály** (mouscatel), a definitely sweet wine, is also produced in Badacsony, near the Balaton, as well as in Eger, a region known primarily for its red wines. Also produced in Eger is the slightly sweet **Egri leányka**, which has an alcohol content of 12.5–13.5°; from the adjoining Gyöngyös wine region comes the famous **Debrői hárslevelű**, which has an alcohol content of 12–13° and is a well-balanced, spicy wine with very special aroma.

At home and in less expensive restaurants, Hungarians often ask for a "fröccs", two parts wine to one part soda water, or a "hosszúlépés", one part wine to two parts soda water. Hungarian **fruit brandies** are favourites with visitors. Kecskeméti barack-pálinka (Kecskemét apricot brandy), cseresznyepálinka (cherry brandy) and szil-vapálinka (plum brandy) are, perhaps, the best known; while the pusztakoktél (a special cocktail made of bitter, fruit brandy and Tokaj wine) is also recommended as an aperitif.

CSÁRDA-INNS AND TAVERNS

At one time tired travellers sought refreshment at a highway tavern or inn called a **csárda;** the wild dances of the csárda eventually became known as the csárdás. In today's csárda-inns gypsy music and peasant furniture evoke the spirit of bygone ages.

There is gypsy music in the evening in many restaurants in Hungary. Other types of music played in restaurants include schrammel music, which is Austrian popular music; at other places a single instrumentalist, a pianist, zither player or a lutist provide the music.

The **borozó** or wine-bar serves relishes—bread and dripping, toast, assorted cold cuts, etc.—with its wines.

CONFECTIONER'S

The **confectioner's** (cukrászda) serves cakes and other sweets and soft drinks, while the **café** (eszpresszó) is the place to go to for strong, Italian-style espresso coffee. Confectioner's and cafés are increasingly replacing the traditional coffee-house.

The **bisztró** (quick food restaurant), the **self-service restaurant** (önkiszolgáló étterem) and the **snack-bar** (büfé) specialize in fast food, mostly hot roasts, cold dishes, etc., which can be eaten either standing up or at a table. Prices depend on the kind of dish ordered and the category of the restaurant. Tipping is not compulsory, but a 10 to 15 per cent tip is customary. (Coats must be left in the cloak room.)

MEALTIMES AND EATING HABITS

Breakfast (7 a.m. to 10 a.m.) is usually of the Continental type and consists of coffee or tea, bread, rolls or toast, butter and jam. Larger establishments also serve a more substantial English-type breakfast.

Lunch (12 a.m. to 3 p.m.) usually consists of three courses (soup, meat dish, dessert), after which most people drink coffee. Lunch is the main meal of the day and is usually served with lager, soft drinks, wine or mineral water.

Supper (7 p.m. to 10 p.m.) is either a hot meat dish served with various garnishing, or a cold meal; cold cuts, butter, cheese, etc., are becoming increasingly popular.

SIGHTSEEING

Guided sightseeing tours are organized by local travel agencies and tourist offices. Both individual and group tours are available.

In Budapest sightseeing tours by coach (2½–3 hours) depart daily at 10 a.m. from **Roosevelt tér 5,** the Budapest Tourist and from the **Engels tér** bus terminal (IBUSZ). From 1st May to mid-October, additional sightseeing tours by bus depart at midday and in the afternoon.

Travel agencies also organize special tours to parts of the capital. For example, there are guided tours of the Parliament building and Buda Castle and, in the summer, there are trips to the Buda Hills. Similar tours are arranged to museums; there are "Budapest by Night" tours as well as folklore programmes, which include dinner followed by an evening of folk-music provided by a well-known folk ensemble.

For those vacationing at Lake Balaton there are organized daytrips, wine-sampling, boat trips to the vineyards around Lake Balaton, peasant weddings, night-time trips to local csárda-inns, night clubs, etc.

During the peak tourist season, excursions are organized daily from both Budapest and Lake Balaton to Hungary's most interesting regions: the Danube Bend, Gemenc Forest, rodeos at Bugac-puszta, Apajpuszta or Hortobágy Puszta, summer castle festivals, etc.

More detailed information can be obtained from the travel agencies and tourist offices organizing these programmes (see Appendix).

NATIONAL HOLIDAYS

1st January, 15th March, Easter Monday, 1st May, 20th August, 23rd October, 25 and 26th December.

REGULAR EVENTS

ECONOMY, INDUSTRY
Budapest International Fair, Budapest X., Dobi István út 10. Second half of May: Hungarian and foreign capital-investment goods; mid September: consumer goods.
"TRAVEL" (UTAZÁS) International Exhibition on Tourism, Budapest X., Dobi István út 10. March.
Agricultural Exhibition and Fair, Budapest X., Dobi István út 10 (once every 5 years).

SCIENCE, EDUCATION
Summer Universities: Budapest, Debrecen, Eger, Esztergom, Gyula, Kecskemét, Miskolc, Sárospatak, Pécs, Salgótarján, Sopron, Szeged and Veszprém (June–August).

MUSIC, ART
Budapest Art Weeks—concerts, theatric events, art exhibitions, premieres (September—October).
Budapest Spring Festival—concerts and other cultural events (March).
Church concerts—in Budapest church concerts are held, among other places, in the Matthias Church, the Lutheran churches at Bécsi kapu tér and Deák tér; in the Calvinist church in Kálvin tér; also in the Cathedral at Pécs, the Votive Church at Szeged, and at Debrecen, Esztergom, Eger, Győr, Kőröshegy, Tihany, Keszthely, Pannonhalma, Sopron, Nyírbátor and other historic churches (April—October).
Open-air concerts are held in the courtyard of the Zichy Palace in Óbuda, in the courtyard of the Pest County Council and in the "Dominikánus" courtyard of the Hotel Hilton (June—August).
Open-air opera performances on Margaret Island, Budapest (July—August).
Szeged Open-air Theatre Festival—Szeged, Dóm tér (Cathedral Square) 20th July—20th August.
Győr Musical Summer—opera performances, concerts of classical music in the Kisfaludy Theatre, the assembly hall of the Town Council and in the Sports Hall (June—July).
Veszprém Musical Courtyard—concerts in the courtyard of the Veszprém Academic Committee (July—August).
Diósgyőr—concerts of classical and light music and theatrical performances at the ruins of the castle.
Haydn and Mozart concerts—Eszterházy Palace, Fertőd (July—August).
Chamber music and orchestra concerts—Festetich Palace, Keszthely (July—August).
Symphony orchestra concerts in the Botanical Gardens, Vácrátót (July—August).
Beethoven memorial concerts—Garden of the Brunswick Palace, Martonvásár (June—July—August).
Debrecen Jazz Festival (July).
Sopron Spring Festival (March).

Szentendre Spring Festival (March).
Kecskemét Spring Festival (March).
Alba Regia Days—cultural, art and sport events in Székesfehérvár (May).

FOLKLORE AND OTHER EVENTS

Busójárás, masked procession on Carnival Sunday — Mohács.
Easter folk customs—Hollókő (Easter).
Sopron Festive Weeks, cultural and sport events in the old inner town, for a month (June—July).
Anna Ball—Balatonfüred (end of July).
Constitution Day celebrations, sporting events, water parade on the Danube, fire-works—Budapest, 20th August.
Launching of the summer season at Lake Balaton—Balatonfüred (late May).
Badacsony grape harvest (end of September).
Pottery fair—Veszprém (beginning of August).
Flower Carnival—Debrecen (20th August, every other year).
Hortobágy Bridge Fair—(20th August) and International Equestrian Festival—Hortobágy (July).
Equestrian Tournaments—Nagyvázsony (25th July—2nd August).
Saint James' Day fête and fair—Szántódpuszta (July).
Theatre Festival—Gyula (July).
Kiskunság Herdsmen's and Equestrian Days—Apajpuszta (July).
Fair—Vác (June).
Urban Day Wine Festival—folklore programmes, and fair in Hajós (May).
Őrség Fair—folk art exhibits in Őriszentpéter (June).
FORM 1 Hungarian Grand Prize international auto race at the Hungaroring in Mogyoród (August).

HUNTING, ANGLING, RIDING

There are excellent **hunting** grounds in Hungary. Thanks to expert game management, the forests abound in game and outstanding trophies. Visitors who wish to hunt should give 3 to 4 months advance notice to MAVAD, H–1014 Budapest, Úri u. 39. tel. 1759-611, telex 22-4967; VADEX H–1013 Budapest, Krisztina körút 41–43, tel. 1561-482, telex: 22-7653; HUNTOURS, H-1024, Budapest, Retek u. 34, tel. 1152-403, telex: 22-7800; or PEGAZUS, H-1093, Budapest, Szamuely u. 49, tel. 1171-939, telex: 22-6112. These will supply detailed information on hunting opportunities and handle specific enquiries.

Anglers can pursue their favourite pastime on Hungary's rivers and lakes, most of which abound in a wide variety of fish (carp, pike, pike-perch, giant pike-perch, sterlet, barbel, bass and catfish). Lake Balaton, the Inner Lake (Belső-tó) at Tihany and lake Velence are the largest angling waters. Other waters suitable for fishing include the lakes around Bia, Pilisvörösvár, Veresegyháza, Őrbottyán and Délegyháza, all near Budapest; also Lake Rakaca, 50 km from the town of Miskolc and Lake Szelidi, north of Kalocsa. There is excellent angling on the Danube near the north-west frontier (Szigetköz), and to the south of Budapest, in the Soroksár and Ráckeve branches of the Danube, as well as around Baja and Mohács. Also recommended are the River Tisza near Tiszalök, the mouths of the Körös rivers, which flow into the Tisza, the River Rába in Western Transdanubia (Körmend), Lake Vadász at Hegyhátszentjakab, etc. For fishing permits and information contact travel agencies and their branch offices, local angling associations of the Hungarian National Angling Association (Magyar Országos Horgász Szövetség, Budapest V., Október 6. u. 20, H–1051).

Excellent **riding** opportunities also abound. All the year round IBUSZ and Pegazus Tours organize tours to some of the most beautiful regions of Hungary —Lake Balaton, the Danube Bend, the Bükk Mountain Range, Hortobágy Puszta, the hilly region of Southern Transdanubia, etc. For those looking for lighter exercise there are riding-schools and riding-clubs at, among other places, Siófok, Szántódpuszta, Nagyvázsony, Tihany, Keszthely on Lake Balaton, and at Apajpuszta, Sarlóspuszta, Szilvásvárad and Tata, near Budapest.

Galloping and trotting races are held in Budapest every Wednesday, Saturday and Sunday. There is betting for place, odds and winner. (The race-course is situated at Budapest X., Dobi István út 2.)

SHOPPING

Business hours: Most shops in Budapest and other major towns maintain regular opening hours, between 7 a.m. to 6 or 8 p.m. Most grocery stores are open from 8 to 6 or 8 p.m.—shops selling consumer goods are open from 10 or 11 a.m. to 4 or 7 p.m.; large department stores are open until 8 p.m. on Thursdays; on Saturdays most shops close at 1 p.m. (In the provinces shops are usually closed at lunch-time.) Hair-dressers are open between 7 a.m. and 9 p.m. on weekdays and until 1 p.m. on Saturdays. (Opening hours are listed at every shop entrance and special times before public holidays are also posted well beforehand.) On Sundays only some larger supermarkets (Batthyány tér, Sugár), sweet shops, flower shops and Intertourist shops (in hotels) keep open. During the peak tourist season, at Lake Balaton, most shops keep open on Sundays. All offices and shops are closed on Sundays and on the following public holidays (see p. 270). Shops run by the **Intertourist, Utastourist** and **Konsumtourist** chains sell goods for convertible currency only. (Keep receipts, as these must be shown to the Customs on leaving the country.) Intertourist deals mainly with objects of art and folk art, souvenir items, and food and drink. Its main store is located at Budapest V., Kígyó u. 5, and there are branches in all major hotels. Utastourist operates shops at the major frontier crossings (Hegyeshalom, Letenye) and in Budapest's railway stations. Most Konsumtourist shops sell objects of art, antiques and coins; the main Konsumtourist store is at Budapest VI., Népköztársaság útja 27.

In Budapest you can buy **antiques** at the following Inner City stores:
V., Felszabadulás tér 3 (home furnishing, china, paintings)
V., Felszabadulás tér 5 (carpets)
V., Kossuth Lajos u. 1/3 (antique furniture, curios, china, pictures).

Arts and crafts shops sell objects of **folk art**—folk embroidery, embroidered blouses, pillows, table cloths, dolls dressed in national costume, folk pottery, hand-made wood carvings, bone lace, homespun cloth, hand-knotted rugs. Some folk art shops in Budapest:
V., Váci u. 14
V., Kossuth Lajos u. 2
V., Régiposta u. 12
VII., Lenin körút 5
XIII., Szent István körút 26

Works of modern fine and applied art are sold at the following galleries:
Csók István Gallery, V., Váci u. 25
Csontváry Gallery, V., Vörösmarty tér 1
Derkovits Gyula Gallery, VI., Lenin krt. 63
Dürer Gallery, V., Váci u. 16/b
Árkád Gallery, VIII., Rákóczi út 30
Mednyánszky Gallery, V., Tanács körút 26
Paál László Gallery, VIII., Rákóczi út 57/b
Poór Bertalan Gallery, VIII., József körút 70
Qualitas Gallery, V., Bécsi u. 2

There are also art galleries in every county capital.

Authentic replicas of museum pieces and archeological finds are sold at Budapest V., József nádor tér 7.

Other arts and crafts shops in Budapest:
V., Haris köz 6
V., Kecskeméti u. 4
V., Kossuth Lajos u. 14
V., Kossuth Lajos u. 17

The most famous Hungarian porcelain is hand-painted **Herend china,** noted for its folk flower motifs, and attractive eosin-glazed products of the Zsolnay Factory in Pécs with their famous metallic lustre, are also in great demand. Lately cut glass is also much sought after and can be found in many stores selling porcelain and glassware.

The bookshops listed below sell **foreign-language books,** sheet music and gramophone records:

I., Hess András tér 3
V., Kossuth Lajos u. 4
V., Kossuth Lajos u. 18
V., Martinelli tér 5 (specializes in sheet music and records)
V., Múzeum krt. 15 (chief second-hand bookshop)
V., Petőfi Sándor u. 2–4 (passageway)
V., Váci u. 22
V., Váci u. 32
V., Váci u. 33 (Russian books)
V., Vörösmarty tér 1 (records)
VII., Lenin körút 42–44
VII., Lenin körút 52 (sheet music)
VII., Rákóczi út 14 (department store for books).

POSTAL SERVICES

The cost of a 3-minute local phone call is 2 forints from a pay-phone. Public telephones are operated by 2 Ft coins. Most towns in Hungary, though not all, can be dialled directly. Direct dial calls to foreign countries can be made from Budapest, Siófok, Balatonföldvár and from all major provincial towns by dialling 00 for the international dialling tone. Hungary's code number is 36, that of Budapest is 1. International calls can also be made through the operator: just dial 01. For local trunk calls, dial 06. For information on international long-distance calls ring 1186-977. Dial 1172-200 for information in English, French, German and Russian.

Poste Restante mail should be clearly marked and bear the exact address of the post office (e.g. Budapest, 4, 1364). Always use the postal (zip) code on every type of mail—it should appear below the address. In Budapest there are two post offices open day and night: No. 62 at the Western Railway Station (Nyugati Pályaudvar — VI., Lenin körút 105) and No. 72 at the Eastern Railway Station (Keleti Pályaudvar — VIII., Verseny u. 1). The Post Office at V., Petőfi Sándor u. 17–19 (first floor) offers the following services: international calls and telegrams 7 a.m. to 9 p.m. Sundays 8 a.m. to 1 p.m. Post office hours vary in provincial towns.

NEWSPAPERS

Major foreign newspapers and journals are generally available in hotels and at newspaper stands in busy spots.

Daily News–Neueste Nachrichten is a Hungarian daily published in German and English, the **Budapester Rundschau** is a German-language weekly and the **Hungarian Digest** a bi-monthly English-language publication, while the **New Hungarian Quarterly** is a quarterly journal. **Programmes in Hungary** is a program guide in German, English and French. During the tourist season some provincial tourist offices also put out seasonal publications.

MEDICAL TREATMENT

First aid is given free to tourists. Outpatient care and, in case of emergency, hospital treatment, is also available to non-Hungarian citizens for payment as laid down by regulations.

Most medicines are available only on medical prescription; however, small quantities of such drugs as pain-killers, fever-reducing medicines, anti-spasmodics, laxatives and disinfectants can be bought freely at any chemist's. Sterile bandages and cotton wool are also available at chemist's.

INSURANCE

Insurance against accidents and damage to baggage can be taken out at the State Insurance Headquarters (Állami Biztosító Központja, Budapest VIII., Üllői út 1) and at branch offices in all major towns as well as at frontier crossings. This covers children under 14 named on a parent's travel documents.

Appendix

TOURIST DIRECTORY

The tourist offices and travel agencies listed below will also give you, at your request, addresses where private rooms are rented.
As there is a restaurant in every hotel, they are not listed under the heading "Restaurants". The majority of museums are open every day, except Monday, from 10 a.m. to 6 p.m.

AGGTELEK-JÓSVAFŐ, H-3758

Information: Borsodtourist, Aggtelek-Jósvafő, in Baradla Camping, tel. 7
Accommodation: Hotel Cseppkő*, tel. 48/12-700; Baradla camp**, bungalows and tourist hostel (seasonal), tel. 3, telex 62-273
Museum: Barlangmúzeum-Cseppkőbarlang (Museum and Stalactite Cave) tel. 48/88-031 open: 8.30 a.m. — 4 p.m.

BADACSONY, H-8261

Information: Balatontourist, Park u. 10. tel. 87/31-249; Cooptourist, Kossuth L. u. 76
Accommodation: Harsona Inn (seasonal), Szegedi Róza u. 37, tel. 87/31-379; Víg Bacchus Fogadó, Kossuth L. u. 26; Badacsonytomaj: Egry József Inn, Kisfaludy u. 2, tel. 87/31-057; Badacsonyörs: Szürkebarát Inn, tel. 87/31-298; campsite Badacsony *** (seasonal), tel. 87/31-091; Camping**, Badacsonyörs, tel. 87/31-253
Restaurants: Hableány, Park u. 12; Halászkert, Park u. 5; Tátika snackbar; Kisfaludy Ház, Szegedi Róza u. 87; Restaurant of the Wine Museum, Hegyalja u. 6
Museum: Egry József Memorial Museum, Egry sétány 12 (from May to Oct. 31).

BAJA, H-6500

Information: Pusztatourist, Béke tér 8, tel. 79/11-153, telex 28-1286; IBUSZ, Béke tér 7, tel. 79/11-161
Accommodation: Hotel Sugovica***, Petőfi sziget, tel. 79/12-988, telex 81-324; Sugovica campsite*** and bungalows (seasonal), Petőfi sziget, tel. 79/12-988, telex 81-324; Hotel Duna*, Béke tér 6, tel. 79/11-765, telex 81-220
Restaurant: Halászcsárda (fishermen's inn) Petőfi sziget
Museum: Türr István Museum, Deák F. u. 1; Bunyevác (Catholic Serbian) folklore house, Pandur u. 51/a, Nagy István Gallery, Arany J. u. 1.

BALATONALMÁDI, H-8220

Information: Balatontourist, Lenin u. 36, tel. 80/38-707, telex 32-340; Cooptourist, Bajcsy-Zsilinszky u. 15, tel. 80/38-393
Accommodation: Hotel Aurora***, Bajcsy-Zsilinszky u. 14, tel. 80/38-811, telex 32-347; Hotel Tulipán*, Marx tér 1, tel. 80/38-317; Kristóf campsite**** and bungalows (seasonal), József A. u. 2, tel. 80/38-902
Restaurants: Aranyhíd, Táncsics u. 61; Kék Balaton, József A. u. 27; Kerekes, Mátyás király út 60; Budatava, Taksony u. 1; Kulacs Inn, Hotel Auróra.

BALATONBERÉNY, H-8649

Information: Siótour, Strandépület, tel. 84/77-151; Volántourist, Botond u. 2, tel. 84/77-143
Accommodation: Kócsag inn and campsite** (seasonal), Gábor Á. u., tel. 84/77-154, telex 22-4002
Restaurant: Határ csárda, Balatoni út 1
Museum: Balatonszentgyörgy (F km), Csillagvár, Irtási dűlő.

BALATONFENYVES, H-8646

Information: Siótour, Fenyvesi út 2; Volántourist, Kölcsey u. 96, tel: 84/61-840
Accommodation: Nyaralóház park, Hámán Kató u. 12, tel. 84/61-840, (seasonal), telex 22-5416
Restaurants: Vigadó, Kölcsey u. 34; Kupa, Vörösmarty u. 187; HBH Pub, Turul u.

BALATONFÖLDVÁR, H-8623

Information: Siótour, Hősök útja 9-11, tel. 84/40-099, telex 22-7753; IBUSZ, Balatonszentgyörgyi u. 14, tel. 84/40-066; Express, József A. u. 6, tel, 84/40-303, telex 22-5084
Accommodation: Hotel Neptun*** (seasonal), Park, tel. 84/40-392, telex 22-4918; Hotel Fesztivál** (seasonal),

Rákóczi u. 35, tel. 84/40-377, telex 22-7398; Hotel Juventus*, (seasonal) József A. u. 6, tel. 84/40-379, telex 22-5084, Magyar Tenger campsite** (seasonal), tel. 84/40-240
Restaurants: Balatongyöngye, Szentgyörgyi út 1; Kukorica csárda, Budapesti út 53; Strand, Rákóczi u. 11; Önkiszolgáló (self-service) restaurant, Hősök útja 1.

BALATONFÜRED, H-8230

Information: Balatontourist, Blaha L. u. 5, tel. 86/42-822, telex 32-394; IBUSZ, Petőfi u. 4/a, tel. 86/42-337, telex 32-343; Cooptourist, Jókai u. 23, tel. 86/42-677
Accommodation: Hotel Annabella*** (seasonal), Beloiannisz u. 25, tel. 86/42-222, telex 32-282; Hotel Margareta***, Széchenyi u. 29, tel. 86/43-824, telex 32-662, Hotel Füred***, Széchenyi u. 20; tel, 86/43-033, telex 32-622; Hotel Eden***, Szabadság u. 4, tel. 86/42-111, telex 32-521; Hotel Marina*** Széchényi út 26, tel. 86/43-644, telex 32-241; Hotel Aranycsillag***, Zsigmond u. 1, tel. 86/43-466; Ring guesthouse (seasonal), Vörösmarty u. 7, tel. 86/42-884; Erdei (forest) guest-house, Koloska u. 45; Panoráma Inn, Kun Béla u. 15; "XXVII FICC Rally" campsite** and holiday houses, Tihanyi út, tel. 86/43-821, telex 32-638.
Restaurants: Halászkert, Petőfi S. u. 2; Balaton, Tagore sétány 5; Baricskacsárda, Baricska dűlő (seasonal), Hordó csárda (seasonal); Tölgyfa csárda (seasonal), Csárda u.; Önkiszolgáló (self-service) restaurant, Jókai u. 15; Napraforgó restaurant (seasonal), Beloiannisz u. 27
Museum: Jókai Memorial Museum, Honvéd u. 1.

BALATONKENESE, H-8174

Information: Balatontourist, Csizmadia u. 4, tel. 80/70-161
Accommodation: Balatonakarattya (4 km), Piroska campsite** (seasonal), Aligai út 15, tel. 80/81-121
Restaurants: Balaton, Kossuth L. u. 1; Sport restaurant.

BALATONMÁRIAFÜRDŐ, H-8647

Information: Siótour, Balatonkeresztúr, Ady E. u. 26, tel. 84/76-180
Accommodation: Hotel Mária**, Rákóczi F. u. 1, tel. 84/76-038; Balatonkeresztúr, Bél Mátyás Tourist Hotel, Ady u. 26, tel. 84/76-180
Restaurant: Delta restaurant, Rákóczi u. 1.

BALATONSZÁRSZÓ, H-8624

Information: Siótour, by the railway station, tel. 84/40-456

Accommodation: Vasmacska guesthouse (seasonal), József A. u. 17, tel. 84/40-493; Tura campsite** (seasonal), József Attila ú., tel. 94/40-254, telex 22-4002. Tourist hostel and bungalows (seasonal), Fő u. 37, tel. 84/40-492
Restaurants: Vén diófa, Kossuth L. u. 2; Balaton csárda, Szoládi út 20; Tóparti restaurant; Üdülő csárda, József A. u.
Museum: József Attila Memorial Museum, József Attila u. 7.

BALATONSZEMES, H-8636

Information: Siótour, by the railway station, tel. 84/45-057; Cooptourist, Szabadság u. 64, tel. 84/45-041
Accommodation: Lidó Inn (seasonal), Ady E. u. 53, tel. 84/45-112; Eden campsite*** (seasonal), Fő u. 2; Vadvirág summer resort (seasonal), campsite** and holiday houses, tel. 84/45-114; Lidó campsite** (seasonal), Ady E. u. 8, tel. 84/45-112; Hullám campsite**, Kasza u., tel. 84/45-116
Restaurants: Vigadó, Ady E. u. 10; Fasor, Ady E. u. 19; Kistücsök, Bajcsy-Zs. u. 7
Museum: Museum of Postal Services, Bajcsy-Zs. u. 46.

BALATONSZEPEZD, H-8252

Information: Balatontourist, Virius u. 10, tel. 87/48-048
Accommodation: Tóth Inn, Arany J. u. 10; Virius campsite** (seasonal), Halász u. 10, tel. 87/48-048
Restaurants: Sellő, Árpád u. 2; Strand (restaurant of the open-air swimming-pool).

BÉKÉSCSABA, H-5600

Information: Békés Tourist, Tanácsköztársaság u. 10, tel. 66/23-448, telex 83-408; IBUSZ, István király tér 5, tel. 66/28-428, telex 83-323; Cooptourist, Tanácsköztársaság u. 6, tel. 66/28-856
Accommodation: Hotel Körös**, Kossuth tér 2, tel. 66/21-777, telex 83-285
Restaurants: Corso, Mednyánszky u. 1; Strand, Árpád sor; Kakas, Tanácsköztársaság u. 79; Veszely csárda, 5 km of Békéscsaba on the road leading to Gyula; Halász csárda (fishermen's inn), Jókai u.; Ételbár, Tanácsköztársaság u. 50; Lencsési, Lencsési út 17
Museum: Munkácsy Mihály Museum, Széchenyi u. 9, Slovak folk house.

BOGLÁRLELLE, H-8638

Information: Siótour, Boglárlelle, Szent l. u. 1, tel. 84/51-086, telex 22-6557; Cooptourist, Móra F. u. 7, tel. 84/51-709; IBUSZ, Fonyódi u. 28; Volántourist, Rákóczi u. 60
Accommodation: Platán Inn (season-

al), Hunyadi u. 56, tel. 84/50-203; Sellő campsite** (seasonal), Landing Place, tel. 84/50-800; Aranyhíd campsite** (seasonal), Köztársaság út 53, tel. 84/50-449 **Restaurants:** Kinizsi, Vörösmarty tér 5; Hullám, Dózsa Gy. u. 61; Vöröscsillag, Köztársaság útja 4; Becsali csárda, Rákóczi u. 80; Albatros, Rákóczi u. 291; Fehér bárány csárda, Sallai u. 14; Platán, Szentmihályi u. 1 **Museum:** Blue Chapel, Red Chapel, Kápolna köz; Folklore House in Buzsák (20 km).

BUDAPEST

Railway stations: Keleti pályaudvar (Eastern Railway Station), 1087 Baross tér 10, tel. 1138-835; Nyugati pályaudvar (Western Railway Station), 1062 Lenin krt. 111, tel. 1490-115; Déli pályaudvar (Southern Railway Station), 1013 Krisztina krt. 37, tel. 1558-657 **Autobus terminals:** Central Autobus Terminal, 1051 Engels tér, tel. 1172-966; Népstadion Autobus Terminal, Kerepesi út and Hungária krt. corner, tel. 2524-496; Árpád-híd Autobus Terminal at the Pest onramp of Árpád Bridge, tel. 1291-450 **Airport:** Budapest, Ferihegy I, tel. 1572-122, 1572-224; Ferihegy II, tel. 1577-831, 1578-406; Engels tér —Ferihegy bus connection, tel. 1186-009 **Travel offices:** IBUSZ, 1075 Tanács krt 3/c (headquarters), tel. 1222-252, telex 22-5659; 1053 Felszabadulás tér 5, tel. 1186-886, telex 22-4979; 1052 Petőfi tér 3, tel. 1185-776, telex 22-4941; 1051 Vörösmarty tér 5, tel. 1172-776 (air traffic and sea-faring), telex 22-4743 BUDAPEST TOURIST, 1051 Roosevelt tér 5 (headquarters), tel. 1173-555, telex 22-5726; 1073 Lenin krt. 41, tel. 1425-521, telex 22-4107; 1087 Baross tér 3, tel. 1336-587, telex 22-4668; 1075 Klauzál tér 1, tel. 1229-286, telex 22-7420 COOPTOURIST, 1055 Kossuth L. tér 13–15 (headquarters), tel. 1121-017, telex 22-4741; 1065 Bajcsy-Zs. út 17, tel. 1117-034, telex 22-4649; 1111 Bartók B. út 4, tel. 1868-240, telex 22-4734; 1062 Marx tér, Skála-Metró Department Store, tel. 1123-621, telex 22-7561 VOLÁNTOURIST, 1051 Október 6. u. 11–13 (head-office), tel. 1123-410, telex 22-6181; 1051 Bajcsy-Zs. út 16, tel. 1172-150; 1066 Lenin krt. 96, tel. 1329-393, telex 22-6722; 1081 Üllői út 21, tel. 1382-555, telex 22-6655; 1056 Belgrád rkp. 6, tel. 1182-133, telex 22-7310; 1113 Pozsonyi út 10, tel. 1120-269, telex 22-4824 EXPRESS IFJÚSÁGI ÉS DIÁK UTAZÁSI IRODA (travel office for young people and students), 1052 Semmelweis u. 4, tel. 1176-634, telex

22-7108; 1064 Népköztársaság útja 55, tel. 1425-327, telex 22-7129; 1054 Szabadság tér 16, tel. 1317-777, telex 22-5139; DANUBIUS TRAVEL OFFICE, 1052 Martinelli tér 8, tel. 1173-652, telex 22-6342 MALÉV AIR TOURS, 1051 Roosevelt tér 2, tel. 1186-614, telex 22-6737 DUNATOURS—PEST COUNTY TOURIST OFFICE, 1065 Bajcsy-Zs. út 17, tel. 1314-533, telex 22-4271 LOKOMOTIV TOURIST, 1011 Szilágyi D. tér 1, tel. 1352-742, telex 22-7086; 1052 Türr István u. 7, tel. 1187-591, telex 22-7307 PEGAZUS TOURS, 1053 Károlyi Mihály u. 5, tel. 1171-562, telex 22-4679 OMEGA TOURIST, 1061 Paulay Ede u. 2, tel. 1421-105 OMNIBUSZ, Engels tér 5, tel. 1172-369, telex 22-5326 BLAGUSS—VOLÁNBUSZ, 1051 Engels tér 5, building B, tel. 1177-777, telex 22-3178 BALATONTOURIST, 1082 Üllői út 32/a, tel. 1836-926 SIÓTOUR, 1075 Klauzál tér 2–3, tel. 1226-080, telex 22-4520 **Other tourist agencies:** MAGYAR AUTÓKLUB (Hungarian Automobile Club), 1024 Rómer Flóris u. 4/a, International Information, tel. 1152-885, Emergency Service tel. 1691-831; MAGYAR CAMPING AND CARAVANNING CLUB, 1091 Kálvin tér 9, tel. 1177-248; MAVAD (Hungarian Cooperative Enterprise for Game Trading), 1014 Uri u. 39, tel. 1556-715; MAGYAR HORGÁSZ SZÖVETSÉG (Hungarian Anglers' Association), 1051 Október 6. u. 20, tel. 1325-315 **Hotel companies:** Book hotel accommodation in Budapest and in the country through: HUNGARHOTELS, 1053 Petőfi Sándor u. 16, tel. 1183-393, telex 22-4923; 1073 Lenin krt. 47–49, tel. 1228-668, telex 22-4923; PANNÓNIA, 1052 Kígyó u. 4–6, tel. 1183-910, telex 22-6747, 1088 Rákóczi út 9, tel. 1141-886, telex 22-7660; DANUBIUS, 1052 Martinelli tér 8, tel. 1173-652, telex 22-6342; TAVERNA, 1052 Váci u. 20 (Hotel Taverna), tel. 1187-287, telex 22-7707; 1052 Semmelweis u. 19, tel. 1181-818; HUNGAROTOURS, 1072 Akácfa u. 20, tel. 1413-889, telex 22-7575.

Hotels

*****

Atrium Hyatt, 1051 Roosevelt tér 2, tel. 1383-000, telex 22-5485; **Duna-Intercontinental,** 1052 Apáczai Csere János u. 4, tel. 1175-122, telex 22-5277; **Hilton,** 1017 Hess András tér 1–3, tel. 1751-000, telex 22-5984; **Thermal,** 1138 Margitsziget, tel. 1321-100, telex 22-5463 ****

Béke Radisson, 1067 Lenin krt. 97, tel.

1323-300, telex 22-5748; **Buda-Penta**, 1013 Krisztina krt. 41–43, tel. 1566-333, telex 22-5495; **Flamenco**, 1113 Tas vezér u. 7, tel. 1612-250, telex 22-4647; **Fórum**, 1052 Apáczai Csere J. u. 12–14, tel. 1178-088, telex 22-4178; **Gellért** 1111 Szent Gellért tér 1, tel. 1852-200, telex 22-4363; **Grand Hotel Hungária**, 1074 Rákóczi út 90, tel. 1229-050, telex 22-4987; **Korona**, 1053 Kecskeméti u. 10–12, tel. 1180-999, telex 22-4344; **Nemzeti**, 1088 József krt. 4, tel. 1339-160, telex 22-7710; **Novotel**, 1123 Alkotás u. 63–67, tel. 1869-588, telex 22-5496; **Olimpia**, 1121 Eötvös út 40, tel. 1568-011, telex 22-6368; **Panoráma**, 1121 Rege u. 21, tel. 1750-522, telex 22-5125; **Ramada Grand Hotel**, 1138 Margitsziget, tel. 1111-000, telex 22-6682; **Royal**, 1073 Lenin krt. 47–49, tel. 1533-133, telex 22-4463; **Thermal Hotel Hélia**, 1133 Kárpát u. 62–64, tel. 1121-000, telex 22-6850
***
Alba, 1011 Apor P. u. 3; **Aero**, 1091 Ferde u. 1–3, tel.1274-690, telex 22-4238; **Astoria**, 1053 Kossuth L. u. 19, tel. 1173-411, telex 22-4205; **Budapest**, 1026 Szilágyi Erzsébet fasor 47, tel. 1153-230, telex 22-5125; **Erzsébet**, 1053 Károlyi Mihály u. 11–15, tel. 1382-111, telex 22-7494; **Emke**, 1072 Akácfa u. 1–3, tel. 1229-230, telex 22-5789; **Európa**, 1021 Hárshegyi út 5–7, tel. 1767-122, telex 22-5113; **Expo**, 1101 Dobi I. u. 10, tel. 1842-130, telex 22-6300; **Liget**, 1068 Dózsa György út 106, tel. 1110-493, telex 22-3648; **Normafa**, 1121 Eötvös út 52–54, tel. 1565-373, telex 22-3673; **Orion**, 1013 Döbrentei u. 13, tel. 1755-418, telex 22-7172; **Palace**, 1088 Rákóczi út 43, tel. 1136-000, telex 22-4217; **Rege**, 1021 Pálos út 2, tel. 1767-311, telex 22-5660; **Sas-klub**, 1121 Törökbálinti út 51-53, tel. 1511-933, telex 22-3564; **Stadion**, 1148 Ifjúság u. 1–3, tel. 2512-222, telex 22-5685; **SZOT**, 1065 Benczur u. 35, tel. 1427-970, telex 22-5095; **Taverna**, 1056 Váci u. 20, tel. 1384-989, telex 22-7707; **TOT**, 1121 Normafa út 54, tel. 1754-011, telex 22-7057; **Volga**, 1134 Dózsa Gy. út 85, tel. 1290-200, telex 22-5120.
**
Bartók, 1113 Bartók B. út 152, tel. 1851-188, telex 22-6089; **Építők**, 1148 Nagy Lajos király út 15–17, tel. 1840-677; **Ifjúság**, 1024 Zivatar u. 1–3, tel. 1353-331, telex 22-5102; **Metropol**, 1074 Rákóczi út 58, tel. 1421-175, telex 22-6209; **Medosz**, 1061 Jókai tér 9, tel. 1531-700, telex 22-7000; **Minol**, 1039 Batthyány u. 45, tel. 1800-777, telex 22-5270; **Park**, 1087 Baross tér 10, tel. 1131-420, telex 22-6274; **Számalk**, 1115 Szakasits Á. út 68, tel. 1669-377, telex 22-5463; **Vénusz Motel** (seasonal), 1031 Dósa u. 2–4, tel. 1687-252,

telex 22-5112; **Wien**, 1118 Budaörsi út 88–90, tel. 1665-400, telex 22-4469
*
Citadella, 1118 Gellérthegy, Citadella sétány, tel. 1665-794. **Express**, 1126 Beethoven u. 7–9, tel. 1753-082, telex 22-4510; **Lidó**, 1031 Nánási u. 67, tel. 1886-865, telex 22-7350; **Polo**, 1033 Mozaik u. 1–3, tel. 1803-022, telex 22-3131; **Strand**, 1038 Pusztakúti út 3, tel. 1671-999, telex 22-4482; **Studium**, 1104 Harmat u. 129, tel. 1474-147
Inns:
Aquincum, 1033, Szentendrei út 105, tel. 1889-930 (1 April–31 Oct.); **Bara**, 1112, Hegyalja út 34–36; **Cinege**, 1121, Cinege u. 1–3, tel. 1759-975; **Haladás**, 1044, Üdülősor 7, tel. 1891-114, telex 22-7350 (15 Apr.–15. Oct.); **Jäger-Trió**, 1112, Ördögorom út 20/d, tel. 1865-742 (15 Apr.–15 Oct.); **Korona**, 1112, Sasadi út 127, tel. 1862-460; **Lidó Üdülőház**, 1031, Nánási út 25, tel. 1886-865, telex 22-7350; **Panorama**, 1026 Fullánk u. 7; **Pál Vendégház**, 1037, Pálvölgyi-köz 15; **Rosella**, 1125, Gyöngyvirág út 21, tel. 1150-576; **Paradiso**, 1125, Istenhegyi út 40/a; tel. 1561-988; **Sport**, 1021, Szépjuhászné út 9; **Unikum**, 1112, Bod P. u. 13; **Vadvirág**, 1025 Nagybányai út 18, tel. 1762-038; **Panorama** (bungalows, apartments), 1121, Rege út 21, tel. 1750-533; **Citadella Tourist Hotel** (cat. B) 1118, Citadella sétány, tel. 1665-794, telex 22-7648; **ÉSZV "Szegedi Hotel"**, 1135, Szegedi út 27, tel. 1296-689, telex 22-3116; **Strand Tourist Hostel** (Cat. B), 1038, Pusztakúti út 3, tel. 1671-999, telex 22-4482 (15 Apr.–15 Oct.).

Campsites

Caravan, 1121, Konkoly-Thege út 18/b (1 Apr.–30. Oct.); **Expo-autocamp**, 1101, Dobi I. u. 10, tel. 1470-990, telex 22-4525 (June–31 Aug.); **Hárshegyi**, 1021, Hárshegyi út 5–7, tel. 1151-482, telex 22-5113 (24 March–20 Oct.); **Metro-Tenisz**, 1162, Csömöri út 158 (1 Apr.–31 Oct.); **Mini**, 1039, Vörös Hadsereg útja 307 (1 May–30 Sept.); **Római**, 1031, Szentendrei út 189, tel. 1686-260, telex 22-5112 (1 Jan.–31 Dec.); **Római Mini**, 1031, Rozgonyi Piroska u. 19 (1 May–31 Oct.); **Rosengarten**, 1106, Pilisi út 7 (1 Apr.–15 Oct.); **Tündérhegyi "Feeberg"**, 1121, Szilassy út 8 (1 Jan.–31 Dec.); **Zugligeti "Niche"**, 1121, Zugligeti út 101 (15 March–15 Oct.).

Restaurants

Alabárdos, I. Országház u. 2 (an exclusive restaurant open only in the evening, medieval atmosphere, lute music, reservations recommended; **Aranyhordó**, I. Tárnok u. 16. (traditional atmosphere); **Aranyszarvas**, I. Szarvas tér 1 (game dishes); **Fehér Galamb**, I. Szentháromság u. 9–11 (poultry dishes); **Fortuna**, I. Fortuna u. 4 (exclusive restaurant, gypsy music); **Halászbástya**, I. Hess A. tér 1–3 (restaurant, tavern, disco); **Márványmenyaszszony**, I. Márvány u. 6 (Hungarian style interior, garden wine cellar); **Pest-Buda**, I. Fortuna u. 3 (Biedermeyer interior, traditional music); **Régi Országház**, I. Országház u. 17 (small rustic interior, garden wine cellar); **Aranyfácán**, II. Szilágyi Erzsébet fasor 33 (Slovakian restaurant); **Buda Gyöngye**, II. Vöröshadsereg útja 36 (exclusive restaurant, disco); **Hársfa**, II. Vöröshadsereg útja 132 (game dishes, gypsy music); **Kis-Buda étterem**, II. Frankel Leó u. 34; **Náncsi néni vendéglője**, II. Ördögárok 83; **Margitkert**, II. Margit u. 15 (a small restaurant with garden); **Paksi halászcsárda**, II. Mártírok útja 14 (fish specialities); **Vadrózsa**, II. Pentelei Molnár u. 15 (exclusive restaurant); **Kerék**, III. Bécsi út 103 (schrammel music); **Postakocsi**, III. Fő tér 2 (in the cellar of a Baroque building: **Sipos Halászkert**, III. Fő tér 6 (fish specialities; **Vasmacska**, III. Laktanya u. 3 (schrammel music, wine cellar); **Megyeri csárda**, IV. Váci út 102 (Hungarian csárda-inn, gypsy music); **Apostolok**, V. Kígyó u. 4–6 (decorated in early 20th-century style, booths); **Bajkál**, V. Semmelweis u. 1 (Russian cuisine); **Berlin**, V. Szent István krt. 13 (German cuisine); **Dunakorzó**, V. Vigadó tér 3 (Hungarian dishes); **Kárpátia**, V. Károlyi Mihály u. 4–8 (Hungarian decor, garden, gypsy music); **Lidó**, V. Szabadsajtó út 5 (amusement centre, restaurant, bar, programmes, gypsy music, ice-dance, jazz music, folklore programme, show); **Mátyás Pince**, V. Március 15. tér 7 (traditional restaurant with booths, a famous gypsy band in the evenings); **Nimród**, V. Münnich F. u. 24 (game specialities); **Pilvax**, V. Pilvax köz (gypsy music); **Százéves**, V. Pesti Barnabás u. 2 (antique interior, booths, gypsy music); **Szecsuán**, V. Roosevelt tér 5 (Chinese cuisine); **Szindbád**, V. Markó u. 74; **Szófia**, V. Kossuth Lajos tér 13–15 (Bulgarian cuisine); **Vigadó**, V. Vigadó tér (Hungarian and other continental dishes); **Havanna**, VI. Bajcsy-Zs. u. 21 (Cuban food specialities; **Opera**, VI. Népköztársaság útja 44; **Vörös sárkány**, VI. Népköztársaság útja 80 (Chinese cuisine); **Hungária**, VII. Lenin krt. 9–11 (successor to the "New York" coffee-house, restaurant); **Prágai Svejk Vendéglő**, VII. Kürt u. 16 (Czech cuisine); **Háry**, VIII. Bródy Sándor u. 30 (tavern with gypsy music); **Búsuló juhász**, XI. Kelenhegyi út 58 (the Gellérthegy terrace, gypsy music); **Citadella**, XI. Gellérthegy (situated on the top of the hill in the casemates of the former

fortress, gypsy music); **Bukarest**, XI. Bartók Béla út 48 (rustic interior, Rumanian speciality; fish soup); **Szeged**, XI. Bartók B. út 1 (Hungarian style restaurant with gypsy music); **Ezüst ponty**, XII. Németvölgyi út 96 (a small restaurant with cosy atmosphere:; **Ördögorom csárda**, XII. Edvi I. u.; **Étoile**, XIII. Pozsonyi út 4 (French cuisine); **Gundel**, XIV. Állatkerti út 4 (high-class restaurant traditionally famous for its cuisine, garden); **Borkatakomba**, XXII. Nagytétényi út 64 (situated where an old wine cellar once stood in a recess hewn out of the rock, gypsy music).

Large bistros and self-service restaurants

McDonald's, V. Régiposta u. 10; **Muskétás snack bar**, I. Dísz tér 8; **Mézes Mackó**, V. Kígyó u. 4–6; **Pilvax**, V. Városház u. 10; **City-grill** krt. V. Váci u. 20; **City-grill**, V. Tolbuhin körút 6; **City-grill**, V. Szent István körút 13; **Abbázia**, VI. Népköztársaság útja 49; **Carmen**, VI. Bajcsy-Zsilinszky út 15; **City-grill**, VI. Népköztársaság útja 33; **Savoy**, VI. Népköztársaság útja 48; **City-grill**, VI. Bajcsy-Zsilinszky út 70; **Centrál**, VII. Tanács krt. 7; **McDonald's** VI. Lenin krt. 111.; **Casino**, XIII. Margitsziget; **City-grill**, XIII. Jászai Mari tér 3

Popular confectioner's

Angelika, I. Batthyány tér 7; **Korona**, I. Dísz tér 6; **Pierrot Café**, I. Fortuna u. 14; **Gerbeaud**, V. Vörösmarty tér 7; **Jégbüfé**, V. Petőfi S. u. 2; **Anna**, V. Váci u. 7; **Lukács**, VI. Népköztársaság útja 70; **Művész**, VI. Népköztársaság útja 29; **Hauer**, VIII. Rákóczi út 49; **Stefánia**, VII. Rákóczi út 90

Bars and night clubs

Casanova, I. Batthyány tér 4; **Fortuna**, I. Hess A. tér 4; **Old Firenze**, I. Táncsics M. u. 26; **Halászbástya**, I. Hess A. tér 1–3; **Horoszkóp**, I. Krisztina krt. 41–43 (Hotel Penta); **Európa**, II. Hárshegyi út 5–7 (Hotel Európa); **Pipacs**, V. Aranykéz u. 5; **Nirvána**, V. Szent István krt. 13–15; **Bellevue Supper Club**, V. Apáczai Cs. J. u. 19 (Hotel Astoria); **Lidó**, V. Szabadsajtó út 5; **Moulin Rouge**, VI. Nagymező u. 17; **Maxim**, VII. Akácfa u. 3; **Étoile**, XIII. Pozsonyi út 4; **Havanna Club**, XIII. Margitsziget (Hotel Thermal); **Szép Ilonka**, I. Fő u. 20; **Phönix bár** (Grand Hotel Hungária), VII. Rákóczi út 90; **Orfeusz bár** (Hotel Béke), VI. Lenin krt. 97

Museums

Museum of Fine Arts, XIV. Dózsa Gy. út 41 (Hősök tere); **Hungarian National Gallery**, I. Dísz tér 17 (Buda Castle Palace B, C and D Buildings); **Hunga-**

rian National Museum, VIII. Múzeum krt. 14–16; Ethnographical Museum, V. Kossuth L. tér 12; Museum of Budapest History, I. Szent György tér 2 (Buda Castle Palace E Building); Aquincum Museum, III. Szentendre út 139; Buda Castle Labyrinth, I. Uri u. 9; Nagytétény Castle Museum, XXII. Nagytétény, Csókási P. u. 9; Museum of Applied Arts, IX. Üllői út 33–37; Art Gallery, XIV. Hősök tere; Semmelweis Museum of Medical History, I. Apród u. 1–3 (10.30–6); Legújabbkori Történeti Múzeum, I. (Buda Castle Palace A Building); Museum of Military History, I. Tóth Árpád sétány 40; Museum of Hungarian Commerce and Catering, I. Fortuna u. 4; Golden Eagle Pharmacy Museum, I. Tárnok u. 18; Transport Museum, XIV. Városligeti krt. 11; Museum of Agriculture, XIV. Városliget, Vajdahunyad vára; Hopp Ferenc Museum of Eastern Asiatic Art, VI. Népköztársaság útja 103; Ráth György Museum, VI. Gorkij fasor 12; Post Office Museum, VI. Népköztársaság útja 3; Ecclesiastical Collection of the Matthias Church, I. Szentháromság tér; Underground Railway Museum, V. in the underpass at the Deák tér Metro station; Tomb of Gül Baba, II. Mecset u. 14; Ady Memorial Museum, V. Veres Pálné u. 4–6; Bartók Béla Memorial House, II. Csalán út 29; Liszt Ferenc Memorial Museum, VI. Népköztársaság útja 67; Vasarely Museum, III. Corvin Ottó tér 1; Home Museum, III. Fő tér 4; Kiscelli Museum, III. Kiscelli u. 106–108; Lutheran National Museum, V. Deák tér 4; Kassák Memorial Museum, III. Fő tér 1 (Zichy Castle); National Jewish Religious and Historical Collection, Jewish Museum, V. Dohány u. 2 (Mon.-Thur. 2–6, Tue.-Fri. 10–1, from May 15 to Oct. 15); Hungarian Museum of Architecture, I. Táncsics M. u. 1; Museum of Stamps, VII. Hársfa u. 47; The Hercules Villa of Aquincum, III. Meggyfa u. 19–21; Petőfi Literary Museum, V. Károlyi M. u. 16; Museum of Musical History, I. Táncsics u. 7; Aquincum Military Settlement Museum, III. Korvin Ottó u. 63–65; Museum of the Aquincum Baths, III. Flórián tér 4–5 (display at the Metro stop).

Exhibition rooms (see p. 272)

Musical, theatres, opera, concerts, cultural centres: Booking for opera and theatre performances at the central ticket office: VI. Népköztársaság útja 18, tel. 1120-000 or at the theatre box offices. concert tickets: V. Vörösmarty tér 1, tel. 1176-222, or at the concert halls.
Hungarian State Opera House, VI. Népköztársaság útja 22; Erkel Theatre, VIII. Köztársaság tér 30;

Academy of Music, VI. Liszt Ferenc tér 8; Pesti Vigadó, V. Vigadó tér 1; Budapest Congress Centre, XII. Jagelló u. 1–3; Zenélő udvar (Musical Courtyard), I. Uri u. 62; Municipal Operetta Theatre, VI. Nagymező u. 17; State Puppet Theatre, VI. Népköztársaság útja 69 and VI. Jókai tér 10; Open Air Theatre, XIII. Margitsziget; Budai Park Theatre, XI. Kosztolányi D. tér; Városmajori Színpad, XII. Városmajor; Circus, XIV. Állatkerti krt. 7; Planetárium, Népliget (terminal of trolleybus No. 75), tickets at the box office; Youth Cultural Centre, Petőfi Csarnok, XIV. Városliget, Zichy M. u., Dripstone cave: Pálvölgyi barlang, II. Szépvölgyi út 162.

Swimming-pools, open-air swimming-pools and medicinal baths

Rudas medicinal baths, I. Döbrentei tér 9; Rác medicinal baths, I. Hadnagy u. 8–10; Komjádi Béla swimming-pool, II. Frankel L. út 35; Lukács medicinal baths, II. Frankel L. út 25–29; Király medicinal baths, II. Fő u. 84; Római open-air swimming-pool, III. Lőpormalom dűlő (summer only); Csillaghegy open-air swimming-pool, III. Pusztakúti út 3; Pünkösdfürdő open-air swimming-pool, III. Vöröshadsereg útja 272 (summer only); Újpest medicinal baths, IV. Árpád út 114–120; Gellért medicinal baths and open-air swimming-pool, XI. Kelenhegyi út 4; Nemzeti swimming-pool, XIII. Margitsziget; Széchenyi medicinal baths and open-air swimming-pool, XIV. Állatkerti krt. 13.

CEGLÉD, H-2700

Information: IBUSZ, Szabadság tér 1, tel. 20/10-479, telex 22-5088
Accommodation: Hotel Kossuth*, Rákóczi u. 4, tel. 20/11-812
Restaurants: Kossuth, Rákóczi út 1; Magyar, Rákóczi út 6; Zöld Hordó, Hajó u. 11; Alföld, Szabadság tér 7
Museum: Kossuth Museum, Marx u. 5
Sports: Municipal open-air swimming-pool, Rákóczi út 33.

CSONGRÁD, H-6640

Information: Szeged Tourist, Felszabadulás útja 14, tel. 63/31-232, telex 82-665
Accommodation: Hotel Erzsébet**, Felszabadulás útja 3, tel. 63/31-960, Köröstorok campsite***, Köröstorok, tel. 63/31-185
Restaurant: Csuka csárda, Szentesi út 1; Halásztanya, Kossuth tér 17; Kemence Csárda, Öregvár u.
Museum: Csongrádi Museum, Iskola u. 2; Regional House, Gyökér u. 1
Sports: Medicinal baths and open-air swimming-pool, Bacsó Béla u. 3–5;

Open-air swimming: Köröstoroki Ti-
sza-part, Holt Tisza-ág; Köröstorok
campsite – water sports, tennis.

DEBRECEN

Information: Hajdu Tourist, 4025 Barna u. 16, tel. 52/13-355, telex 72-361;
and 4024 Vörös Hadsereg útja 20, tel.
52/10-820, telex 72-636; IBUSZ, 4025
Vörös Hadsereg útja 11–13, tel. 52/15-
555, telex 72-244; Cooptourist, 4025
Holló J. u. 4, tel. 52/10-770; Volántourist, Batthyány u. 3, tel. 52/19-384, telex
72-711
Accommodation: Hotel Aranybika***, 4025 Vörös Hadsereg útja
11–15, tel. 52/16-777, telex 72-263;
Hotel Főnix*, 4025 Barna u. 17, tel.
52/13-355, telex 72-361; Hotel Debrecen*, 4025 Petőfi tér 9, tel. 52/16-550,
telex 72-271; Hotel Thermal*, 4032
Nagyerdei krt. 9–11, tel. 52/11-888,
telex 72-403; Hotel Sport*, 4025 Oláh
G. u. 3, tel. 52/17-456; Thermal Campsite** and bungalows, 4032 Nagyerdei krt. 102, tel. 52/12-456, telex 72-
361; 47. FIC Rally Campsite*** and
bungalows, Erdőspuszta, tel. 52/13-
500, telex 72-775; Aqua Thermal Pen-
sion, 4025 Sámsoni út 109, telex
52/19-842; Kerekestelepi Camp*, 4030
Lemnic u. 2–4, tel. 52/21-299
Restaurants: Hungária, Vörös Hadsereg útja 53; Óbester borozó
(taverns), Péterfia u. 61; Régi-posta,
Széchenyi u. 6; Szabadság, Vörös
Hadsereg útja 29; Új Vigadó, Lenin
park; Gambrinus, Vörös hadsereg útja
28/b; Bóbitás, on the Vekeri-tavi
campsite; Borsodi söröző (beer
house), Mester u. 1–3; Hortobágyi
csárda, Hortobágy; Kaparó csárda,
Patkó csárda, Hortobágy
Museums: Déri Museum, Déri tér 1;
Debrecen Literary Museum, Borsos
József tér 1; Medgyessy Ferenc
Memorial Museum, Péterfia u. 28; De-
lizsánsz Exhibition Room, Bethlen G.
u. 3; Collection of College and Ecclesiastical History of the Reformed
Church; Erdőspuszta Regional House,
Fancsika, 93/a
Sports: Hotel Főnix, riding; on the
campsites water sports and riding;
open-air swimming-pools; Szávai Gy.
u. 22 and Szabadság út 23; Nagyerdei
medicinal baths, Nagyerdei krt. 9–11.

DUNAÚJVÁROS, H-2400

Information: Dunaújváros Tourist Office, Korányi Sándor u. 1, tel. 25/16-
607, telex 29-363; IBUSZ, Vasmű u.
10/a, tel. 25/16-487, telex 29-234;
Cooptourist, Apáczai Csere J. u. 4–6,
tel. 25/16-691
Accommodation: Hotel Aranycsillag**, Vasmű út 39, tel. 25/18-045,
telex 29-321; Szélkakas Inn,
Lokomotív u. 1/a, tel. 25/16-989; If-

júsági-sziget campsite** and inn (seasonal), Ifjúság-sziget, tel. 25/17-627
Restaurants: Aranyhordó, Erdősor
31; Béke, November 7. tér 7; Duna-
gyöngye Halászcsárda (Fishermen's
Inn), Sziget u. 2; Réz-rák, Ifjúsági-
sziget; Kékcsillag, Vasmű u. 39
Museums: Intercisa Museum, Lenin
tér 4–3; Domanovszky Gallery,
Komócsin liget 11. Museum of Roman
Stonework Remains, Római krt. (at the
new watertower).

EGER, H-3300

Information: Eger Tourist, Bajcsy-
Zsilinszky u. 9, tel. 36/11-724, telex 63-
378; Cooptourist, Dobó tér 3, tel.
36/11-998, telex 63-258; IBUSZ, Bajcsy-Zsilinszky u., tel. 36/12-526, telex
63-336; Delta Tours, Lenin út 6, tel.
36/20-345
Accommodation: Hotel Unicornis*,
Hubay u. 2, tel. 36/12-455; Hotel
Eger***, Szálloda u. 1, tel. 36/13-233,
telex 63-355; Szenátor-Ház***, Dobó
u. 11, tel. 36/20-466; Hotel Park***,
Klapka u. 8, tel. 35/13-233, telex 63-
365; Buttler-ház (tourist "A", "B"),
Kossuth L. u. 26, tel. 36/12-455; Fortuna Inn (seasonal), Kapási u. 35/a, tel.
36/16-480; Kőkút guest-house, Kőkút
u. 11, tel. 36/10-292. Inn, campsite**
and bungalows (seasonal), Rákóczi u.
79. tel. 36/10.558
Restaurants: Széchenyi, Marx u. 3;
Fehér Szarvas, Klapka u. 6; Belvárosi,
Bajcsy-Zsilinszky u. 8; Vadászkürt,
Marx u. 4; Express, Felszabadulás tér
4; Három Farkas, Lenin u. 16; Mecset,
Knézich K. u. 3; Kazamata, Mártírok
tere; Szépasszony-völgye wine cel-
lars; Agria Taverna, Trinitárius u. 1;
Ételbár, Dobó I. tér 3; Lajosvári, Lenin
u. 168
Museums: Műemlék Pince (ancient
cellar), Szépasszony-völgye; Dobó Ist-
ván Castle Museum, Vár I; Spekula
Observatory, Szabadság tér 2; Gár-
donyi Géza Memorial Museum, Gár-
donyi G. u. 28; Spekula Observatory
Treasury of Cathedral (Basilica),
Szabadság tér
Sports: Municipal baths, Fürdő u. 1;
Open-air swimming-pool, Petőfi tér;
Indoor swimming-pool, Petőfi tér.

ESZTERGOM, H-2500

Information: Komtourist, Széchenyi
tér 13, tel. 33/12-082, telex 22-6606;
IBUSZ, Mártírok u. 1, tel. 33/12-552,
telex 22-5407
Accommodation: Hotel Eszter-
gom***, Prímás-sziget, tel. 33/12-555,
telex 27-765; Hotel Fürdő**, Bajcsy-
Zsilinszky u. 14, tel. 33/11-688, telex
27-721; Hotel Volán*, József A. tér 2,
tel. 33/11-257, telex 27-752; Vadvirág
Campsite*** and Motel (seasonal),
Bánomi-dűlő, tel. 33/12-234; Tourist

Hostel ("B"), Dobozi M. u. 8; Grand Tours Holiday Settlement, Prímás-sziget, Nagydunasétány, tel. 33/11-327, telex 22-477
Restaurants: Kispipa, Kossuth L. u. 19; Kettőspince restaurant and tavern, Bánomi-dűlő; Úszófalu Halászcsárda (fishermen's inn), Esztergom-sziget, Szabad Május sétány 14; Hévíz, Aradi Vértanúk tere; Fürdő, Bajcsy-Zsilinszky út 14
Museums: Balassa Bálint Museum, Bajcsy-Zsilinszky u. 28; Cathedral Treasury, Szent István tér 1; Christian Museum, Berényi u. 2; Castle Museum, Szent István tér 1; Babits Mihály Memorial House, Babits M. u. 15
Sports: Open-air swimming-pool, Bajcsy-Zsilinszky u. 14.

FONYÓD-BÉLATELEP, H-8640

Information: Siótour, Railway Station, tel. 84/61-214, telex 22-7400; IBUSZ, Szent István u. 4, tel. 84/60-449, telex 22-5422; Volántourist, Ady E. u. 31, tel. 84/60-830, telex 22-7401; Cooptourist, Bethlen G. u. 1, tel. 84/60-635; Delta Tours, Komjáth A. u. 21, tel. 84/61-835
Accommodation: Hotel Sirály* (seasonal), Alsóbélatelep, Bartók B. u. 2, tel. 84/60-125; Napsugár Camping site**, inn and bungalows (seasonal), Bélatelep, tel. 84/61-211, telex 22-4622; Liget guest-houses (seasonal), Fonyódliget, Szemere u. 2
Restaurants: Delta, Ady E. u. 7; Sirály, Bartók B. u. 3; Présház, Lenke u. 17; Gyöngyhalász, Fürdő u. 1.

GYŐR

Information: Ciklámen Tourist, 9021 Aradi Vértanúk u. 22, tel. 96/11-557, telex 24-616; IBUSZ, 9021 Tanácsköztársaság u. 29–31, tel. 96/14-224, telex 24-243; Volántourist, 9022 Árpád u. 51/b, tel. 96/17-133, telex 24-383; Cooptourist, 9022 Jedlik Á. u. 8, tel. 96/20-801, telex 24-431
Accommodation: Hotel Rába***, Árpád u. 34, tel. 96/15-533, telex 24-365; Hotel Klastrom***, 9021 Fürst S. u. 1, tel. 96/15-611, telex 24-731; Corvin guest-house, 9023 Csaba u. 22, tel. 96/12-171; Fehérhajó guest-house, 9025 Kiss E. u. 4, tel. 96/18-050; Kisrózsa guest-house, Tessedik u. 27; Inn, campsite*** and bungalows (seasonal), tel. 96/18-986, telex 24-458; Hotel Aranypart*, 9026 Áldozat u. 12, tel. 96/26-033
Restaurants: Hungária, Lenin u. 23; Vaskakas, Köztársaság tér 3; Park, Tanácsköztársaság útja 19; Aranyfácán beer house, Ady E. u. 21; Zöldfa, Hunyadi u. 2; Halászcsárda (fishermen's inn), Rózsa F. u. 4; Vár Taverna, Alkotmány u. 9; Camping, Kiskútliget, Rábaparti, Fürst S. u. 15; Tó, Ifjúság

krt. 113; Pozsonyi Beer House, Vági I. u. 14; Márka, Aradi Vértanúk u. 22; Kristály, Bartók B. u. 9
Museums: Xantus János, Széchenyi tér 5; Kovács Margit, Rózsa F. u. 1; Borsos-ház (Borsos-house), Martinovics tér 3; Picture Gallery, Alkotmány u. 4; Museum of Roman and Modern Stonework Finds, Köztársaság tér 5; Széchenyi Pharmacy Museum, Széchenyi tér 9
Sports: Medicinal baths, Ország u. 4–6. Thermal baths, swimming-pool, Országút u. 4.

GYULA, H-5700

Information: Gyulatourist, Eszperantó tér 2, tel. 66/61-192, telex 83-619; Békés Tourist, Kossuth u. 16, tel. 66/62-261, telex 83-560
Accommodation: Arany Kereszt Hotel***, Eszperantó tér 2, tel. 66/62-144, telex 83-619; Hotel Park*, Part u. 15, tel. 66/62-622; Komló Inn, Béke sugárút 6, tel. 66/61-041; Benedeki Inn, Szent Benedek u. 83, tel. 66/62-057; Szíves Inn, Kossuth L. u. 16, tel. 66/61-450; Campsite**, motel and bungalows (seasonal), Vadaskert u. 2, tel. 66/62-690; Thermal campsite***, and bungalows, Szélső út 16, tel. 66/62-240.
Restaurants: Budrio, Béke sugárút 69; Komló, Béke sugárút 6. Park, Part u. 15; Arany-Kereszt, Eszperantó tér 2
Museums: Erkel Ferenc Memorial House, Apor tér 7; Castle Museum, Kossuth u. 17
Entertainment: events organized by the Gyula Castle Theatre every summer.

HAJDÚSZOBOSZLÓ, H-4200

Information: Hajdutourist, József A. u. 2, tel. 52/62-214, telex 72-559; IBUSZ, Hősök tere 4, tel. 52/62-037, telex 72-553; Cooptourist, Vörös Hadsereg u. 44, tel. 52/62-041, telex 72-540; Volántourlst, Wesselónyi u. 36, tel. 52/61-761
Accommodation: Hotel Délibáb***, József A. u. 4, tel. 52/62-366, telex 72-439; Hotel Gambrinus*, József A. u. 3, tel. 52/62-054, telex 72-439; Hotel*, campsite** and bungalows (seasonal), Debreceni útfél, tel. 52/62-427
Restaurants: Alföldi, Hősök tere 19; Szigeti Halászcsárda (fishermen's inn), on the grounds of the medicinal baths; Halászcsárda (fishermen's inn), on the grounds of the medicinal baths; Halászcsárda (fishermen's inn), Jókai sor 12–14; Magyar, Lenin u. 3
Museums: Bocskai István Museum, Bocskai u. 12; Fazekas-ház (Pottery house), Ady E. u. 2; Gönczy Pál Memorial Room, Kálvin tér 7.

HARKÁNY, H-7815

Information: Mecsek Tourist, Kossuth L. u. 5, tel. 72/80-307, telex 12-276; IBUSZ, Bajcsy-Zsilinszky u. 2, tel. 72/80-163, telex 12-357; Cooptourist, Kossuth u. 37, tel. 72/80-102, telex 12-593 **Accommodation:** Hotel Baranya*, Bajcsy-Zsilinszky u. 3, tel. 72/80-160; Hotel Dráva**, Bajcsy-Zsilinszky u. 3-5-7, tel. 72/80-434; Hotel Napsugár*, Bajcsy-Zsilinszky u. 5, tel. 72/80-300; Campsite***, tourist hostel and holiday houses (seasonal), Bajcsy-Zsilinszky u. 4, tel. 72/80-117 **Restaurant:** Zöldkert, Arany J. u. 12.

HÉVÍZ, H-8380

Information: Zalatour, Rákóczi út 8, tel. 11-084, telex 35-248; Cooptourist, Rákóczi út 4, tel. 11-348, telex 35-263; Volántourist, Somogyi B. u. 2/a, tel. 13-381 **Accommodation:** Hotel Thermál****, Kossuth L. u. 9, tel. 11-180, telex 35-286; Thermál Hotel Aqua****, Kossuth L. u. 13–15, tel. 11-090, telex 35-247; Hotel Napsugár**, Tavirózsa u. 3–5, tel. 13-307, telex 35-313; Piroska guest-house, Kossuth L. u. 10, tel. 12-698; **Restaurants:** Debrecen, Rákóczi út 3; Rózsakert, Rákóczi út 19; Piroska, Kossuth L. u. 10; Gyöngyösi csárda, Rezi, Kültelek 5; Vadaskert csárda, Vadaskert; Badacsony, Kossuth L. u. 7.

HÓDMEZŐVÁSÁRHELY, H-6800

Information: Szeged Tourist, Szőnyi u. 1, tel. 64/41-325; IBUSZ, Lenin u. 5–7, tel. 64/41-220, telex 84-230 **Accommodation:** Hotel Fekete Sas*, Kossuth tér 2, tel. 64/42-019; Hotel Fáma*, Szeremlei u. 7, tel. 64/44-444, telex 84-285 **Restaurants:** Akvárium, Ady E. u. 1; Borozó (tavern), Városház u. 3; Alföldi, Vidra u. 2; Hódtava, Hóvirág u. 4/b; Halászcsárda (fishermen's inn), Táncsics M. u. 28; Bagolyvár, Malinovszkij u. 23; Kaszinó beer house, Városház u. 2 **Museums:** Tornyai János Museum, Szántó Kovács János u. 16–18; Csucsi Potter's House, Rákóczi u. 102; Tájház (regional folklore house), Árpád u. 21; Detached Farmstead Museum, Kopáncs (7 km from Hódmezővásárhely) **Sports:** Open-air swimming-pool and medicinal baths, Ady E. u. 1.

JÁSZBERÉNY, H-5100

Information: Tiszatour, Serház u. 3, tel. 57/12-051; IBUSZ, Lehel vezér tér 17, tel. 57/11-042, telex 23-579 **Accommodation:** Touring Hotel**, Serház u. 3, tel. 57/12-051, telex 23-535 **Restaurants:** Lehel, Lehel vezér tér 34; Márka ételbár, Déryné u. 4 **Museums:** Jász (Jazygian) Museum, Táncsics u. 5 **Sports:** Swimming-pool and thermal baths, Hatvani út 5.

KALOCSA, H-6300

Information: Pusztatourist, István király u. 35, tel. 779, telex 26-661; IBUSZ, István király u. 28, tel. 303, telex 26-241 **Accommodation:** Hotel Pirosarany*, István király u. 37, tel. 200, telex 26-483; Hotel Kalocsa**, Szabadság tér 4, tel. 78/11-931, telex 29-901 **Restaurants:** Kalocsai csárda, István király u. 87; Halásztanya (fish restaurant), Széchenyi housing estate; Juca néni csárdája, István király u. 37; Matthias, Petőfi u. 2 **Museums:** Museum of Hungarian Seasoning Paprika, Marx tér 6; Regional folklore house of the Cooperative for Folk Art and Homecrafts, Tompa M. u. 7; Nicolas Schöffer Memorial House, István király u. 76.

KAPOSVÁR, H-7400

Information: Siótour, Május 1. u. 1, tel. 82/11-509, telex 13-350; IBUSZ, Tanácsház u. 1–3, tel. 82/13-797, telex 13-355; Cooptourist, Kossuth u. 8, tel. 82/12-038, telex 13-224 **Accommodation:** Hotel Dorottya**, Engels u. 2, tel. 82/16-022, telex 13-244; Hotel Kapos**, Ady E. u. 2, tel. 82/16-022, telex 13-244; Csokonai guest-house, Május 1. u. 1, tel. 82/12-011, telex 13-350; Rákóczi guest-house, Vörös Hadsereg u. 4, tel. 82/17-213; Campsite**, Kaposvár-Topavár, Deseda-tó **Restaurants:** Park, Lenin u. 29; Cser, Cseri park; Sziget, Bartók B. u. 2; Béke beer house, Petőfi S. u.; Halászcsárda (fishermen's inn), Jókai liget **Museums:** Rippl-Rónai Memorial Museum, Róna-hegy; Somogy Gallery, Május 1. u. 12; Latinca Sándor Memorial Museum, Latinca S. u. 3; Gallery, Rákóczi tér 4 **Sports:** Thermal baths and swimming-pool, Jókai liget, Csik Ferenc sétány.

KAPUVÁR, H-9330

Information: Ciklámen Tourist, Fő tér 14, tel. 97/42-311, telex 24-415 **Accommodation:** Hotel Hanság**, Fő tér 27, tel. 97/42-311, telex 24-264 **Museums:** Rábaköz Museum, Fő tér 1; Pátzay Pál Exhibition of Statues, Kába sor 1.

KARCAG, H-5300

Information: Tiszatour, Vöröshadsereg u. 10, tel. 221

Accommodation: Otthon guest-house, Vöröshadsereg u. 33, tel. 60.

KAZINCBARCIKA, H-3700

Information: Borsod Tourist, Tavasz u. 7, tel. 48/14-390.; IBUSZ, Lenin út 46, tel. 48/10-657, telex 64-235 Accommodation: Hotel Polimer**, Ifjúság körtér 2, tel. 48/11-911, telex 62-265.

KECSKEMÉT, H-6000

Information: Pusztatourist, Szabadság tér 2, tel. 76/29-499, telex 26-555, IBUSZ, Széchenyi tér 1–3, tel. 76/20-557, telex 26-212, Cooptourist, Kéttemplom köz 9, tel. 76/20-357, telex 26-479 Accommodation: Hotel Aranyhomok**, Széchenyi tér 2, tel. 76/20-011, telex 26-327; Hotel Szauna*, Sport u. 3, tel. 76/28-700, telex 26-672; Sport Inn, Tó***, Sport u. 7, tel. 76/28-700; Szőlőfürt Inn, István király krt. 23, tel. 76/21-239; Andi guest-house, Bácskai u. 13–15, tel. 76/47-002; Hotel Három Gúnár***, Batthyány u. 7, tel. 76/27-077; Campsite for motorists** and bungalows (seasonal), Sport u. 5, tel. 76/28-700, telex 26-672 Restaurants: Hírös, Rákóczi u. 3; Strand, Sport u. 2/B; Snack-bars, Petőfi S. u. 1, Kéttemplom köz 3, and Széchenyi tér 1–3; Kisbugaci csárda, Munkácsy u. 10; Jalta tavern, Batthyány u.; Szőlőfürt, István király krt. 23; Aranyszarvas, Széchenyiváros, Hitel u.; Bugac csárda, Bugacpuszta; Sasfészek, by Road 52 to Dunaföldvár; Tanya csárda, 20 km from Kecskemét, by the village museum; Szélmalom csárda, Városföld, 127 km by Road No. 5 Museums: Katona József Museum, Bethlen körút 75; Museum of the Protestant Diocese on the Danube, Szabadság tér 7; Katona József Memorial House, Katona József u. 5; Gallery, Rákóczi u. 1; Museum of Hungarian Naive Artists, Gáspár A. u. 11; Museum of Hungarian Folk Crafts, Külső Szabadság u. 18; Szórakaténusz Toy Workshop and Museum, Gáspár A. u. 11 Sports: Indoor swimming-pool, Izsáki u. 1; Széktó Sauna Baths, Sport u. 1; Summer open-air swimming-pool, Sport u. 3.

KESZTHELY, H-8360

Information: Zalatour, Fő tér 1, tel. 12-560, telex 35-253; Solar Utazási Iroda, Fő tér 1, tel. 11-345, telex 35-301; IBUSZ, Széchenyi u. 1, tel. 12-951, telex 35-305; Lokomotív Tourist, Kossuth L. u. 22, tel. 11-535; Cooptourist, Tanácsköztársaság u. 26, tel. 12-441; Express, Kossuth L. u. 22, tel. 12-032, telex 35-233

Accommodation: Hotel Hullám***, Balatonpart, tel. 12-644, telex 35-338; Hotel Helikon***, Balatonpart 5, tel. 11-330, telex 35-276; Hotel Phoenix**, Balatonpart, tel. 12-630, telex 35-276; Hotel Amazon*, Szabadság út 11, tel. 12-448; Castrum campsite*** (seasonal), Móra F. u. 48, tel. 12-120; Campsite** and bungalows (seasonal), Balatonpart, tel. 12-782, telex 35-319. Restaurants: Béke, Kossuth L. u. 50; Gösser, Kossuth L. u. 35; Georgikon, Fő tér; Halászcsárda, Balatonpart; Hungária, Kossuth u. 35 Museums: Balaton Museum, Múzeum u. 26; Georgikon Manor Museum, Bercsényi u. 67; Helikon Castle Museum, Szabadság u. 1.

KISKUNFÉLEGYHÁZA, H-6100

Information: IBUSZ, Petőfi tér 2, tel. 76/62-150, telex 26-749 Accommodation: Kiskunság Inn, Petőfi tér 1, tel. 76/61-751; Borostyán Inn, Szőlő u. 1, tel. 76/62-573 Restaurants: Halászcsárda (fishermen's inn), Petőfi tér 2; Aranyhegyi csárda, Páka u.118 Museums: Kiskun Museum (Museum of Little Cumania), Vörös Hadsereg u. 9; Móra Ferenc Memorial Museum, Móra F. u. 19 Sports: Public swimming-pools, Blaha L. tér 1.

KISKUNHALAS, H-6400

Information: Pusztatourist, Semmelweis tér 16, tel. 21-455, telex 26-688; IBUSZ, Köztársaság u. 10–12, tel. 21-217, telex 26-633 Accommodation: Hotel Alföld*, Lenin tér 6, tel. 77/21-140, telex 26-460; Hotel Csipke**, Semmelweis tér 16, tel. 77/21-455, telex 26-688; Sóstó Motel, Sóstó, tel. 77/22-020; Campsite*** (seasonal), Brinkus L. u. 1, tel. 77/22-555, telex 26-402 Restaurants: Halasi csárda, Szász K. u. 5; Malom Inn, Malom sor 2; Tölgyfa, Brinkus u. Museums: Thorma János Museum, Köztársaság u. 2; Csipkeház (Lace house), Kossuth u. 37/a; Kiskunság National Park, Csárda Museum Sports: Open-air swimming-pool and medicinal baths, Brinkus L. u. 1.

KŐSZEG, H-9730

Information: Savaria Tourist, Várkör 57, tel. 94/60-238, telex 37-376; IBUSZ, Köztársaság tér 4, tel. 94/60-376, telex 37-419 Accommodation: Hotel Írottkő**, Köztársaság tér 4, tel. 94/60-373, telex 37-419; Hotel Park*, Felszabadulási park, tel. 94/60-363, telex 37-278; Hotel Strucc*, Várkör 124, tel. 94/60-

323; Kóbor Macska Inn, Várkör 100;
Napsugár Tourist Hotel, Szabó-hegy,
tel. 94/60-490; Jurisics Tourist Hotel,
Rájnis J. u. 9, tel. 94/60-227
Restaurants: Kulacs, Béke út 12;
Gesztenyés, Rákóczi u. 23; Turista,
Szabó-hegy
Museums: Jurisics Miklós Castle
Museum, Rajnis u. 9; Tábornokház,
Jurisics tér 4; Öregtorony (The Old
Tower), Chernel út 16; Pharmacy
Museum, Jurisics tér 11.

MAKÓ, H-6900

Information: Szeged Tourist, Lenin tér
10, tel. 65/12-384, telex 82-625; IBUSZ,
Lenin tér 8, tel. 65/11-410, telex 82-637
Accommodation: Hotel Korona*, Lenin tér 10, tel. 65/11-384; Campsite***
and inn (seasonal), Wekerle út 30, tel.
65/12-232, telex 82-625; Campsite for
motorists** and bungalows (seasonal), Marospart, tel. 65/11-914
Restaurants: Autós csárda, Bonyó-
liget
Museums: Espersit-ház, Kazinczy F. u.
6; József Attila Museum, Felszabadulás u. 4.

MEZŐKÖVESD, H-3400

Information: Borsod Tourist, Tanácsköztársaság u. 117, tel. 40/12-614,
telex 62-558; IBUSZ, Tanácsköztársaság u. 74, tel. 40/12-481, telex 62-632
Accommodation: Hotel Hőfürdő*, tel.
40/12-227; Thermál campsite for
motorists*** and bungalows, Zsórifürdő, tel. 40/11-436
Restaurants: Matyórózsa, Tanácsköztársaság u. 79
Museums: Matyó Museum, Béke tér
20.

MISKOLC

Information: Borsod Tourist, 3525,
Széchenyi u. 35, tel. 46/88-036, telex
62-273; in Miskolctapolca, 3519, Mar-
tos F. u. 7, tel. 46/68-917, telex 62-605
Accommodation: Hotel Pannónia***,
Kossuth u. 2, tel. 46/88-022; Hotel
Aranycsillag*, 3530, Széchenyi u.
22–24, tel. 46/35-114; In Miskolctapolca, Hotel Juno***, Csabai u. 2, tel.
46/64-133, telex 62-332; Hotel Park,
Bak D. u., tel. 46/60-811, telex 62-641;
Hotel Lidó*, Kiss József u. 4, tel. 46/69-
800; Tapolca Inn, Iglói út 15, tel. 46/67-
171, telex 62-605; Fenyő guest-house,
Görömbölyi u. 85, tel. 46/85-577;
Campsite for motorists and bungalows (seasonal), Iglói út 13, tel.
46/67-171; Éden Nyaralótelep: campsite*** and bungalows (seasonal),
Károlyi M. út 1, tel. 46/68-421, telex 62-
405
Restaurants: Alabárdos, Kisava, Első
sor 15; Tokaj, Győri kapu 47; Bükk,
Marx K. u. 24; Anna, Miskolctapolca;

Kisvadász, Győri út 15; Vadászkürt,
Miskolc-Lillafüred, Palota u. 80; Egye-
tem, Testvérvárosok útja 1; Palotás,
Kossuth u. 1; Diófa, Árpád u. 2; Ma-
gyaros, Augusztus 20. u. 12
Museums: Borsod-Miskolc Museum,
Kossuth u. 13; Diósgyőri Castle
Museum, Vár u. 24; Gallery of the Her-
man Ottó Museum, Felszabadítók u.
28. Herman Ottó Museum, Papszer u.
1; Déryné Memorial House, Vár u. 24;
Central Museum of Metallurgy, Mis-
kolc-Hámor, Palota u. 22; Hungarian
Orthodox Church Museum, Deák tér 7.

MOHÁCS, H-7700

Information: Mecsek Tourist, Tolbuhin u. 2, tel. 10-961, telex 12-343
Accommodation: Hotel Csele**, Kisfaludy tér 6–7, tel. 10-825; Hotel Korona*, Jókai tér 2, telex 10-049
Restaurants: Pannónia, Dózsa Gy. u.
31; Révkapu csárda, Kisfaludy tér;
Wernesgrüner beer house, Dózsa Gy.
u. 7; Csele csárda, Szőlőhegy; Halászcsárda, Kisfaludy tér
Museums: Kanizsai Dorottya
Museum, Szerb u. 2; Mohács Historical Memorial Place, Sátorhely.

MOSONMAGYARÓVÁR, H-9200

Information: Ciklámen Tourist, Lenin
u. 88, tel. 98/11-078, telex 24-341;
IBUSZ, Engels F. u. 4, tel. 98/15-135;
Volántourist, Móra Ferenc housing
project, Building D/1, tel. 98/15-992
Accommodation: Hotel Fekete Sas*,
Lenin u. 93, tel. 98/15-842; Hotel
Minerva*, Engels út 2, tel. 98/15-602,
telex 24-464; Szent Flórián***, Lenin
út 127, tel. 98/13-177, telex 24-786;
Solaris*, Lucsony u. 19, tel. 98/15-300,
telex 24-568; Lajta Tourist Hotel, Lenin
út 119, tel. 98/11-780; Autóklub campsite*** (seasonal), Gabona-rakpart 6,
tel. 98/15-883, telex 24-550
Restaurants: Széchenyi restaurant
and beer house, Városház u. 2; Várpince, Vár u. 2; Szigetkör, Engels út 5;
Béke, Lenin út 267; Borostyán, Bartók
B. u. 4
Museums: Hanság Museum, Lenin út
136; Exhibition of Fine and Applied
Arts, Lenin út 103; Museum of the Flo-
ra and Fauna of the Hanság, Vár 2,
Building D.

NAGYKANIZSA, H-8800

Information: Zalatour, Lenin u. 13, tel.
93/11-185, telex 33-255; IBUSZ,
Szabadság tér 21, telex 93/11-296;
Cooptourist, Dél-Zala department
store, tel. 93/11-383
Accommodation: Hotel Central**,
Szabadság tér 23, tel. 93/14-000, telex
33-264; Hotel Pannónia*, Vöröshad-
sereg u. 4, tel. 93/12-188, telex 33-264;
Campsite and Motel for motorists**

(seasonal), Vár u. 1, tel. 93/19-119, telex 33-255
Restaurants: Rózsakert, Szabadság tér 18; Béke, Lenin u. 7; Park, Városi Park; Várpince beer house, Lenin u. 7; Ady, Ady út 5; Kanizsa, Balatoni út 2; Fortuna, Zemplén Gy. u. 2; Tó, at the Csónakázó tó (boating lake); Halászcsárda (fishermen's inn), Lazsnakpuszta; Önkiszolgáló (self-service), Deák tér 18
Museums: Gallery of the Thury György Museum, Szabadság tér 11.

NAGYKŐRÖS, H-2750

Information: Dunatours, Széchényi tér 2, tel. 20/50-794
Accommodation: Hotel Központi*, Széchenyi tér 1, tel. 20/50-778, telex 22-6640
Restaurants: Kalamáris, Széchenyi tér 7
Museums: Arany János Museum, Ceglédi út 19.

NAGYVÁZSONY, H-8291

Information: Balatontourist, Kinizsivár, tel. 80/31-015, telex 32-350
Accommodation: Hotel Kastély*, Kossuth u. 12, tel. 80/64-109, Vázsony Inn, Sörház u. 2, tel. 80/64-344
Restaurants: Vázsonykő, Kinizsi u. 84; Várcsárda, Temető u. 7
Museums: Museum of the Kinizsi Castle; Post Office Museum, Temető u. 3; Open-Air Ethnographical Museum
Sports: riding.

NYÍREGYHÁZA, H-4400

Information: Nyírtourist, Dózsa Gy. u. 3, tel. 42/11-544, telex 73-385; IBUSZ, Lenin tér 10, tel. 42/12-122, telex 73-300
Accommodation: Hotel Szabolcs Korona**, Dózsa Gy, u. 1–3, tel. 42/12-333, telex 73-401; Hotel Krúdy**, Sóstó, tel. 42/12-424, telex 73-401; Svájcilak (Swiss cottage)*, Sóstó, tel. 42/12-424; Hotel KEMÉV*, Bethlen G. u. 58–60, tel. 42/10-606; Igrice Holiday village and campsite (seasonal), Sóstó, Blaha L. sétány, tel. 42/13-235; Palermo panzió, Széchenyi u. 16, tel. 42/15-777; Fenyves campsite and bungalows**, Sóstórfürdő, tel. 42/16-750, telex 73-385
Restaurants: Aranyszarvas, Szarvas u. 56; Borsod beer house, Rákóczi u. 4; Tisza Snack-bar, Luther House; Rácz, Búza tér 6; Tölgyes csárda, Sóstói u. 60; Zöld Elefánt, Körút 1
Museums: Jósa András Museum, Benczúr tér 21; Museum village, Nyíregyháza-Sóstó, Görögkatolikus Egyházi Gyűjtemény (Uniate Church Collection), Bethlen u. 5
Sports: Sóstó salt lake baths, Bernát u. 2.

OROSHÁZA, H-5900

Information: Békés Tourist, Kossuth L. u. 9, tel. 68/12-506; IBUSZ, Szabadság tér 12, tel. 68/11-023, telex 83-455
Accommodation: Hotel Alföld***, Szabadság tér 12, tel. 68/12-166, telex 83-504
Restaurants: Béke, Táncsics M. u. 15; Alföld, Szabadság tér 12
Sports: Gyopárosfürdő — medicinal baths and open-air swimming-pool.

ÓZD, H-3600

Information: IBUSZ, Vöröshadsereg u. 1, tel. 47/11-443, telex 64-216
Accommodation: Hotel Kohász**, Ív út 9, tel. 47/11-334, telex 64-206.

PÁPA, H-8500

Information: Balatontourist Nord, Fő tér 12, tel. 89/24-282, telex 24-584
Accommodation: Hotel Platán**, Fő tér 2, tel. 89/24-688
Restaurants: Sport, Kossuth L. u. 22; Béke, Fő tér 27; Aranykalász, Korvin u. 17; Hódoska, Gyimóti u; Bakony, Kerekes testvérek u. 10
Museums: Museum of Local History, Fő tér 1, the Castle; Museum of Ecclesiastical History and Art of the Transdanubian Diocese of the Reformed Church, Fő u. 6; Pharmacy Museum, Jókai u. 5–7; Kékfestő (bluedye) Museum, Március 15. tér 12.

PÉCS

Information: Mecsek Tourist, 7621 Széchenyi tér 1, tel. 72/14-866, telex 12-238; IBUSZ, 7621 Széchenyi tér 8, tel. 72/12-148, telex 12-234; Cooptourist, 7621 Bem J. u. 22, tel. 72/13-407, telex 12-411; Pannon Tourist, 7621 Déryné u. 1, tel. 72/11-326, telex 12-214
Accommodation: Hotel Hunyor**, Jurisics M. u. 16, tel. 72/15-677; Hotel Palatinus***, Kossuth u. 5, tel. 72/33-022, telex 12-652; Hotel Pannónia***, Rákóczi u. 3, tel. 72/13-322, telex 12-469; Hotel Fenyves*, Szőlő u. 64, tel. 72/15-996; Hotel Főnix, Hunyadi u. 2, tel. 72/11-680; Agóra Inn, Apáczai Csere körtér, tel. 72/41-604; Mecsek Mandulás campsite**, hotel, inn and bungalows (seasonal), Báránytető, tel. 72/15-981; Dozso Kemping**, Felsővámház u. 72, tel. 72/14-600; Batthyány Castle Inn, Pécs-Üszögpuszta, tel. 72/10-311, telex 12-325
Restaurants: Minaret, Sallai u. 35; Eszék, Bajcsy-Zsilinszky u. 14–16; Kazinczy, Kazinczy u. 6; Arma, Kossuth L. u. 13; Elefántos Ház, Jókai tér 6; Szliven (Bulgarian Cuisine), Mezőszél u. 1; Sopianae, Rákóczi út 73/C; Vadásztanya (game dishes), Jakabhegy út 69

Museums: Csontváry Museum, Janus Pannonius u. 11; Jakováli Hasszán Dzsámi (Turkish temple), Rákóczi út 2; Amerigo Tot Museum, Káptalan u. 2; Vasarely Museum, Káptalan u. 3; Zsolnay pottery exhibition, Káptalan u. 2; Museum of Renaissance Stonework Finds, Káptalan u. 2; Modern Magyar Képtár, Káptalan u. 4
Music: Liszt Ferenc concert hall, Kossuth L. u. 83
Sports: Balokány Baths, Zsolnay V. u. 46; Hullám (swimming-pool with artificial waves), József A. u. 12; Nagy Lajos swimming-pool, Széchenyi köz; Úszögpuszta Fogadó (inn): riding and tennis.

RÉVFÜLÖP, H-8253

Information: Balatontourist, Halász u. 5, tel. 87/44-309, telex 22-350; Volántourist, Csárda u. 1, tel 87/17-150, telex 22-6948
Accommodation: Ottó Inn (seasonal), Petőfi u. 38, tel. 87/44-207; Napfény campsite** (seasonal), Halász u. 5, tel. 87/44-309
Restaurants: Birka csárda, Füredi út 17; Hullám, Füredi út 6.

SALGÓTARJÁN, H-3100

Information: Nógrád Tourist, Palócz I. tér 3, tel 32/10-660, telex 22-9106; IBUSZ, Tanácsköztársaság tér 9, tel. 32/14-356, telex 22-9146
Accommodation: Hotel Karancs**, Tanácsköztársaság tér 21, tel. 32/10-088, telex 22-9103; Hotel Salgó*, Eresztvény, tel. 32/10-558; Dornyai Inn, Eresztvény, tel. 32/10-558, telex 22-9106; Campsite**, bungalows and motel (seasonal), Tóstrand, tel. 32/11-168
Restaurants: Tarján, Vöröshadsereg út 143; Salgó, Lenin tér 9; Beszterce, Vöröshadsereg út 60; Borsodi beer house, Arany J. út 1; Napsugár, Eresztvény; Turista, Eresztvény
Museums: Underground Mine Museum, Bajcsy-Zsilinszky u. 1; Nógrádi Sándor Museum, Nógrádi Sándor tér 8.

SÁROSPATAK, H-3950

Information: Borsod Tourist, Kossuth u. 46, tel. 41/11-073; IBUSZ, Kossuth u. 50, tel. 41/11-620, telex 62-517
Accommodation: Hotel Borostyán**, Kádár K. u. 28, tel. 41/11-611, telex 62-717; Hotel Bodrog**, Rákóczi u. 58, tel. 41/11-744, telex 62-786; Tengerszem campsite and bungalows (seasonal), Herczeg u. 2, tel. 41/11-753, telex 62-786
Restaurants: Borostyán, Kádár K. u. 26; Vadászkürt, Kossuth u. 87; Pince borozó, Szabadság tér 2
Museums: Sárospatak Picture Gallery, Szt. Erzsébet tér 4; Domján Ex-

hibition, Kazinczy u. 23; Rákóczi Museum, Kádár u. 21; Roman Catholic Ecclesiastical Collection, Szt. Erzsébet tér 7; Várgaléria (Castle Gallery), Szt. Erzsébet tér 21; Tiszamenti Református Egyházkerület Múzeuma (Museum of the Calvinist Church District on the Tisza), Rákóczi u. 1.

SÁTORALJAÚJHELY, H-3980

Information: IBUSZ, Kossuth tér 24–26, tel. 14–29
Accommodation: Hotel Zemplén*, Széchenyi tér 5/7, tel. 41/22-522; Kossuth tourist Hotel, Várhegy u. 10, tel. 41/21-164;
Restaurants: Kinizsi, Ady tér 9; Ezüstponty, Kossuth tér 10; Zemplén, Széchenyi tér 5/7; Várhegy, Esze T. u. 25.

SIÓFOK, H-8600

Information: Siótour, Szabadság tér 6, tel. 84/10-801, telex 22-4002; IBUSZ, Kele u. 1–3, tel. 84/11-107, telex 22-6075; Cooptourist, Fő u. 148, tel. 84/10-279, telex 22-6474
Accommodation: Hotel Lidó*** (seasonal), Petőfi S. u. 11, tel. 84/10-633, telex 22-4108; Hotel Balaton*** (seasonal), Petőfi S. u. 9, tel. 84/10-695, telex 22-4108; Motel* (seasonal), Kinizsi u. 6, tel. 84/10-644; Hotel Hungária*** (seasonal) Petőfi S. u. 13, tel. 84/10-677; Hotel Napfény** (seasonal), Mártírok u. 8, tel. 84/11-408, telex 22-4837; Hotel Vénusz*** (seasonal), Kinizsi u. 12, tel. 84/10-660, telex 22-4837; Hotel Európa*** (seasonal), Petőfi S. u. 15, tel. 84/13-411, telex 22-4108; Oázis Inn, Szigligeti u. 56, tel. 84/12-012; OKGT Holiday Hotel**, Beszédes J. sétány 92, tel. 84/11-633, telex 22-5680; Hotel Touring*, Fokihegy, tel. 84/10-684; Campsites: Camping**, Balatonszéplak, Zichy M. tér, tel. 84/11-364 (15 May–15 Sept.); Ezüstpart**, Balatonszéplak, tel. 84/11-374 (15 May–15 Sept.) Fűzfa**, Fő u. 7/a (1 June–31 Aug.); Ifjúság**, Sóstó, Pusztatorony tér, tel. 84/11-471 (15 May–15 Sept.); Kék Balaton**, Darnay tér, tel. 84/10-851 (15 June–31 Aug.); Strand**, Fürdő-telep, Szt. László u. 183, tel. 84/11-804 (15 May–15 Sept.); Aranypart**, Beszédes sétány 62, tel. 84/11-801, telex 22-7614 (1 May–30 Sept.); Mini*, Fürdő-telep, Szt. László u. 74 (1 May–30 Sept.); TOT*, Fürdő-telep, Viola u. 19–21 (1 June–31 Aug.)
Restaurants: Motel, Kinizsi u. 6; Fogas, Fő u. 114; Csárdás, Fő u. 105; Delta, Fő u. 88/A; Matróz, at the port; Csülök, Bajcsy-Zsilinszky u. 38; Hableány, Széplak, Erkel u. 75/A; Piroska csárda, Széplak-felső by Road 70, Kálmán Imre, Kálmán Imre sétány
Museums: Beszédes József Museum of Water Management, Sió u. 2; Szán-

tódpuszta Tourist and Cultural Centre; Kálmán Imre Memorial House, Kálmán Imre sétány 5 **Music, entertainment:** Maxim Variety, Batthyány u. 15; Éden bár, Petőfi sétány 15; Pipacs bár, Mártírok útja 11; Open-air Theatre, Dimitrov park; Siófok Holiday Resort Club (Siófoki Üdülőhelyi Klub); Cultural Centre, Fő tér 2; Csikó bár, Petőfi sétány.

SOPRON, H-9400

Information: Ciklámen Tourist, Ógabona tér 8, tel. 99/12-040, telex 24-9174; IBUSZ, Várkerület 41, tel. 99/13-281, telex 24-9175; Lokomotív Tourist, Városház u. 4, tel. 99/11-111, telex 24-9157; VOLÁN head office, Lackner K. u. 1, tel. 99/11-041, telex 24-9108; Soptour, Ötvös u. 9, tel. 99/12-448 **Accommodation:** Hotel Lővér***, Várisi út 4, tel. 99/11-061, telex 24-9123; Hotel Sopron***, Fövényverem u. 7, tel. 99/14-254, telex 24-9200; Hotel Palatinus***, Új u. 23, tel. 99/11-395, telex 24-9146; Hotel Pannónia*, Várkerület 73–75, tel. 99/12-180, telex 24-9116; Átrium guest-house, Kőszeg u. 3, tel. 99/13-799; Kállai guest-house (seasonal), Ferenczi I. u. 60, tel. 99/14-435; Lővér campsite and bungalows, tel. 99/11-715, telex 24-9193; Tourist hostel, Ferenczy J. u. 4, tel. 99/12-228; Tourist hostel, Új u. 8, tel. 99/12-185; Inns: Jégverem u. 1, tel. 99/12-004; Patkó, Kossuth Major, Somfalvai út, tel. 99/14-648, telex 24-9127 **Restaurants:** Deák, Erzsébet u. 20; Gambrinus, Új u. 2; Alm, Hársfa sor 48; Szélmalom restaurant and coffee house, Fraknói u. 4; Kaszinó, Liszt F. u. 1; Bécsikapu, Bécsi u. 6; Generális snack-bar, Fő tér 7; Vöröskakas, Várkerület 25; Hubertus, Bécsi u. 6; BISTROS: Várkerület 25; Várkerület 7; Várkerület 104; Cézár wine cellar, Hátsókapu u. 2; Gyógygödör, Templom u. 2; Hungária snack-bar, Lackner K. u. 60; Kékfrankos, Széchenyi tér 12 **Museums:** Fabricius Ház (Fabricius house), Fő tér 6; Lábasház, Orsolya tér 5; Liszt Ferenc Museum, Deák tér 1; Old Synagogue, Új u. 22; Pharmacy House, Fő tér 2; Baker House, Bécsi u. 5; Fire watch-tower, Fő tér; Museum of Mining, Templom u. 2; Zettl-Largo Collection, Balfi u. 11 **Sports:** Lővér fürdő (indoor swimming-pool), Szabadság krt. 83; Tómalom fürdő (from May 15 to Aug. 31); Balf (18 km) medicinal baths for rheumatic diseases; riding, tennis, bowling and skiing opportunities **Entertainment:** Sopron Days, Sopron Festive Weeks (in March).

SÜMEG, H-8330

Information: Balatontourist, Kossuth u. 29, tel. 114

Accommodation: Hotel Vár*, Vak Bottyán u. 2, tel. 164; Hotel Kisfaludy*, Kossuth u. 13, tel. 129, telex 32-221

SZARVAS, H-5540

Information: IBUSZ, Szabadság u. 6–10, tel. 67/12-520, telex 82-388 **Accommodation:** Hotel Árpád**, Szabadság u. 32, tel. 67/12-120, telex 82-595; Aranyszarvas campsite*** and bungalows, Erzsébet-liget, tel. 423, telex 83-697 **Museums:** Dry Mill, Ady E. u. 1; Slovakian Regional Folklore House, Hoffmann u. 1; Ruzicska Collection, Erzsébet-liget; Tessedik Sámuel Museum, Vajda P. u. 1

SZEGED

Information: Szeged Tourist, 6720 Klauzál tér 7, tel. 62/21-800, telex 82-648; IBUSZ, 6720 Klauzál tér 2, tel. 62/26-533, telex 82-231; Alföld Tours, 6720 Bajcsy-Zs. u. 28, tel. 62/12-070, telex 82-415; Volántourist, Dani I. u. 7, tel. 62/21-341, telex 82-591 **Accommodation:** Hotel Hungária***, 6721 Komócsin Z. tér 2, tel. 62/21-211, telex 82-403; Hotel Tisza**, 6720 Wesselényi u. 1, tel. 62/12-466, telex 82-358; Hotel Royal**, 6720 Kölcsey u. 1, tel. 62/12-911, telex 82-403; Hotel Napfény**, 6728 Dorozsmai út 4, tel. 62/25-800, telex 82-536; Sárkány Inn, 6725 Indóház tér 1, tel. 62/10-514; Napfény Campsite*** and bungalows, 6728 Dorozsmai út 2, tel. 62/25-800, telex 82-536; Partfürdő Campsite**, Középkikötő sor, tel. 62/53-795; Sziksós Campsite***, Kiskundorozsma. tel. 62/61-050 **Restaurants:** Alabárdos, Oskola u. 13; Hági, Kelemen u. 3; Szeged, Széchenyi tér 9; Debrecen, Széchenyi tér 13; Tiszagyöngye, Partfürdő (Új-Szeged); Halász-csárda (fishermen's inn), Felső-Tisza; Halász-csárda (fishermen's inn), Felső-Tisza; Halász-csárda (fishermen's inn), Roosevelt tér 14; Camping csárda, Dorozsmai út 2; Gambrinus beer house, Deák F. u. 24; Fehértói Halászcsárda, Külterület 41; HBH Pub, Deák F. u. 4 **Museums:** Móra Ferenc Museum, Roosevelt tér 1–3; Castle Museum with stonework finds, the Castle **Sports:** Liget thermal baths, Torontál tér–Fürdő u; Municipal Medicinal Baths, Lenin krt. 24; Partfürdő (on the bank of the river Tisza; Alsókikötő sor; Úszóházak (swimming houses), Szeged-Tisza-part; Swimming-pool, Székelysor; Kiskundorozsma-Sziksósfürdő (salt baths).

SZÉKESFEHÉRVÁR, H-8000

Information: Albatours, Szabadság tér 6, tel. 22/12-494, telex 21-235;

IBUSZ, Ady E. u. 2, tel. 22/11-510, telex 21-339; Cooptourist, Rákóczi u. 3, tel. 22/14-391, telex 21-291
Accommodation: Hotel Alba Regia***, Rákóczi u. 1, tel. 22/13-484, telex 21-295; Hotel Magyar Király**, Március 15. u. 10, tel. 22/11-262, telex 21-293; Két Góbé Inn, Gugásvölgyi u. 4
Restaurants: Szabadság, Vörösmarty tér 1; Ősfehérvár, Szabadság tér 3; Árpád, József A. u. 57; Kiskulacs, Népköztársaság u. 56; Aranyszarvas, Horváth I. u. 6; Gorsium (10 km), by highway M7
Museums: István Király (King Stephen) Museum, Gagarin tér 3; Budenz House, Arany J. u. 12; Csók István Picture Gallery, Bartók B. tér 1; Fekete Sas Pharmacy Museum, Március 15. u. 5; Bory Castle, Máriavölgyi út; Franciscan Church, Szabadság tér 8; Schaár Erzsébet Collection, Jókai u. 11
Entertainment: Open-air theatre
Sports: Open-air swimming-pool (seasonal), Szabadságharcos út 18; Árpád Turkish bath and swimming-pool, Kossuth u. 12; Tennis and water sports at Lake Velence (15 km).

SZEKSZÁRD, H-7100

Information: Tolnatourist, Széchenyi u. 38, tel. 74/12-144, telex 14-222; IBUSZ, Széchenyi u. 19, tel. 74/11-947, telex 14-218; Cooptourist, Kölcsey housing estate, 160, tel. 74/11-722, telex 14-372
Accommodation: Hotel Gemenc***, Mészáros L. u. 2, tel. 74/11-722, telex 14-240; Hotel Alisca*, Kálvária u. 1, tel. 74/12-228; Sió motel and campsite** (seasonal), by highway 6, tel. 74/12-458
Restaurants: Sió csárda, by highway 6; Szász beer house, Garay tér; Kispipa, Széchenyi u. 51; Kiskulacs, Zalka M. u. 6; Baktai tavern, Fáy u; Krokodil, Cseri J. u. 114
Museums: Béri Balogh Ádám Museum, Mártírok tere 26; Babits M. Memorial House, Babits u. 13
Sports: Municipal swimming-pools, Toldi u. 6; tennis and riding.

SZENTENDRE, H-2000

Information: Dunatours, Somogyi-Bacsó part 6, tel. 26/11-311, telex 22-5423
Accommodation: Hotel Danubius**, Ady E. u. 28, tel. 26/12-511, telex 22-4300; Hotel Party*, Ady E. u. 5, tel. 26/12-491; Hubertus guest-house (seasonal), Tyúkos dűlő 10, tel. 26/10-616; Coca-Cola guest-house, Dunakanyar krt. 50, tel. 26/10-410; Ságvári Endre tourist hostel, Lajosforrás, tel. 26/10-683; Papsziget inn, hotel, bungalows and campsite (sea-

sonal), Papsziget, tel. 26/10-697; Dominó, Ady E. u. 80; Márka, Szabadkai u. 9, tel. 26/12-788; Kőhegyi, Kőhegy u. 16, tel. 26/12-292
Restaurants: Béke, Fő tér 19; Teátrum, Rév u. 10; Görög Kancsó, Görög u. 1; Határcsárda, Ady E. u. 43; Szigetgyöngye, Papsziget; Duna, Dózsa György út; Aranysárkány, Bogdányi u. 21; Nosztalgia coffee-house, Bogdányi u. 21; Olasz étterem, Somogyi-Bacsó part 6; Muskátli, Rakodczay P. u. 1; Régimódi, Futó u. 3; Vidám szerzetesek, Bogdányi u. 9
Museums: Barcsay Collection, Dumtsa J. u. 10; Czóbel Museum, Templom tér 1; Ferenczy Museum, Fő tér 6; Kerényi Jenő Memorial Museum, Ady E. u. 5; Kmetty Museum, Fő tér 14; Anna Margit and Ámos Imre Memorial Exhibition, Bogdányi u. 10; Bornemissza Memorial Room, Somogyi-Bacsó part 4; Kovács Margit Museum, Vastagh Gy. u. 1 (9–7 every day except after official holidays); Open-air Ethnographical Museum, Szabadságforrás út
Sports: Papsziget open-air swimming-pool, Leányfalu open-air swimming-pool, Móricz Zs. u.; water sports and riding.

SZENTES, H-6600

Information: IBUSZ, Kossuth tér 5, tel. 331, telex 82-261
Accommodation: Hotel Petőfi*, Petőfi S. u. 2, tel. 254; Strandfürdő bungalow, Széchenyi liget, tel. 334, telex 82-208.

SZERENCS, H-3900

Information: Borsod Tourist, Kassai út 10/B
Accommodation: Hotel Huszárvár*, Huszárvár u. 11, tel. 41/31-58.

SZOLNOK, H-5000

Information: Tiszatour, Ságvári E. krt. 32, tel. 56/44-803, telex 23-373; IBUSZ, Kossuth u. 18, tel. 56/30-510, telex 23-306; Cooptourist, Ságvári krt. 31, tel. 56/32-403, telex 23-404
Accommodation: Hotel Pelikán***, Vízpart körút 1, tel. 56/43-855; Hotel Tisza***, Marx park 2, tel. 56/31-155, telex 23-370; Hotel Touring**, Tiszaliget, tel. 56/35-805, telex 23-401; Hotel Student**, Mártírok u. 2, tel. 56/39-688; Motel Pelikán, Vízpart körút 2, tel. 56/33-284, telex 23-403; Tiszaliget campsite**, inn and bungalows (seasonal), tel. 56/18-596, telex 23-401
Restaurants: Nemzeti, Ságvári krt. 22; Museum, Kossuth tér 5; Aranylakat, Tiszaliget; Szolnok, Jubileum tér 2; Evezős csárda, Holt-Tisza-part, Vízpart krt 1

Museums: Szolnoki Gallery, Koltói Anna u. 2; Damjanich János Museum, Kossuth tér 4.

SZOMBATHELY, H-9700

Information: Savaria Tourist, Mártírok tere 1, tel. 94/12-348, telex 37-342; Cooptourist, Savaria u. 1, tel. 94/14-766, telex 37-404; IBUSZ, Savaria u. 3, tel. 94/14-141, telex 37-307
Accommodation: Hotel Claudius****, Bartók B. krt. 39, tel. 94/13-760, telex 37-262; Hotel Isis**, Rákóczi F. u. 1, tel. 94/14-990, telex 37-385; Hotel Savaria**, Mártírok tere 4, tel. 94/11-440, telex 37-200; Hotel Tourist*, Jókai park, tel. 94/14-168; Campsite*** and bungalows (seasonal) Kondics u. 4, tel. 94/14-766, telex 37-343
Restaurants: Pannonia, Köztársaság tér 29; Gyöngyös, Savaria u. 8; Pelikán, Vörös Hadsereg útja 6; Tó, Kondics u.; Halászcsárda (fishermen's inn), Rumi út 18; Önkiszolgáló (self-service), Mártírok tere 5/B; Fészek beer bar, Petőfi S. u. 49; Vadász, Vörös Zászló út 59
Museums: Vasi Museum Village, Árpád u. 30; Observatory, Vörös Zászló út 112; Savaria Museum, Kisfaludy S. u. 8; Szombathely Gallery, Rákóczi u. 12; Smidt Museum, Hollán Ernő u. 2; Iseum Romkert, Rákóczi u. 1
Sports: Lake baths, Kondics u; Thermal baths, Tanácsköztársaság liget; Indoor swimming-pool, Bartók B. krt.; Bükfürdő (16 km), bus service, for rheumatic, gynaecological, orthopaedical and traumatological diseases.

TAPOLCA, H-8300

Information: Balatontourist, Deák F. u. 7, tel. 87/11-179, telex 32-657
Accommodation: Hotel Gabriella*, Batsányi tér 7, tel. 87/12-642
Restaurants: Tavaszbarlang, Arany J. u. 16; Balaton, Deák F. u. 2.

TATA, H-2890

Information: Komtourist, Ady E. u. 9, tel. 34/81-805, telex 27-223; and Tatabánya, Győri út 12, tel. 34/11-936; Cooptourist, Tópart sétány 18, tel. 34/81-602, telex 27-356; IBUSZ, Tatabánya, Felszabadulás tér 18/B, tel. 34/12-869, telex 27-249
Accommodation: Hotel Diana***, Remeteségpuszta, tel. 34/80-388, telex 27-237; Hotel Kristály*, Ady E. u. 22, tel. 34/80-577, telex 27-259; Hotel Malom*, Szabadság tér 8, tel. 34/81-530; Hotel Pálma*, Néppark, tel. 34/80-577, telex 27-259; Öregtó campsite*** and bungalows (seasonal), Fáklya u. 1, tel. 34/80-496; Fényes fürdő campsite** and bungalows (sea-

sonal), Fényes fasor, tel. 34/81-591, telex 27-291; Hotel Árpád***, Tatabánya, Újváros, Felszabadulás u. 1, tel. 34/10-299, telex 27-361; Rozmaring Inn, Tatabánya, Árpád u. 17, tel. 34/10-825; Nomád campsite**, Tatabánya, Tolnai út 14, tel. 34/11-907
Restaurants: Fényes, Görög Hősök útja 2; Fenyves, Nagytó-park; Vár, Rákóczi u. 22; Jázmin, Bacsó B. út 70; Aranyponty, Vértesszőlősi út; Forrás, Fényesfürdő; Barátok asztala taverna, Bartók B. út 1; Zsigmond wine cellar, Öregvár fishermen's inn, Nagytó
Museums: Museum of replicas of ancient Greek and Roman statues, Rákóczi út; Kuny Domokos Museum, Néppark; Museum of Ethnic Germans, Alkotmány u. 1
Sports: Fényesfürdő, Fényes fasor; Kristály fürdő, II. Erzsébet tér; riding, tennis and water sport opportunities.

TIHANY, H-8237

Information: Balatontourist, Kossuth u. 20, tel. 86/48-519
Accommodation: Club Tihany Hotel**** and bungalows, Rév u. 3, tel. 86/48-088, telex 32-272; Tihany Center, Kenderföld u. 19, tel. 86/48-707, telex 32-675
Restaurants: Önkiszolgáló (self-service) at the port; Sport, Fürdőtelep 34 (at the inner port); Fogas, Kossuth L. u. 1; Kecskeköröm csárda, Kossuth L. u. 13; Halásztanya (fishermen's inn), Visszhang u. 11; Rege confectionery, Batthyány u. 38
Museums: Tihanyi Museum; Open-air Ethnographical Museum, Batthyány u. 36; Potters' house, Visszhang u. 10
Music: organ concerts in the church of the Tihany Abbey
Sports: water sports and riding opportunities.

TOKAJ, H-3910

Information: TOKAJ Wein Tours, Rákóczi u. 39, tel. 240, telex 62-467
Accommodation: Hotel Tokaj**, Rákóczi u. 5, tel. 58-201, telex 62-741; Tisza campsite**, bungalows and tourist hostel (seasonal), Tiszapart, tel. 17
Restaurants: Rákóczi, Bethlen G. u. 35,; Tiszavirág, Halászcsárda (fishermen's inn), Münnich F. u. 4; ÁFÉSZ Halászcsárda (fishermen's inn), Rákóczi u. 5; Taverna, Hősök tere
Museums: Cellar Museum, Petőfi u.; Tokaj Museum, Bethlen G. u. 7
Sports: water sports.

VÁC, H-2600

Information: Dunatours, Széchenyi u. 14, tel. 27/10-940, telex 28-2260; OMNIBUSZ, Szabadság tér, tel. 27/13-411
Accommodation: Tabán guest-

house, Corvin lépcső 3, tel. 27/11-607; Lovaspanzió (guest-house for horsemen), Váchartyán, Veres Pálné u. 3; Hotel Express** (seasonal), Verőcemaros, tel. 27/50-166, telex 28-2202
Restaurants: Halászkert (fish restaurant), Liszt F. sétány 9; Pokol csárda, Szentendrei sziget; Fehér Galamb, Lenin u. 37; Kőkapu, Dózsa Gy. u. 5; Snack bar, Széchenyi u. 33
Museums: Vak Bottyán Museum, Múzeum u. 4; Greek Church exhibition room, Március 15. tér 19; Hincz Gyula Collection, Lőwy S. u. 16.

VESZPRÉM, H-8200

Information: Balatontourist, Münnich F. u. 3, tel. 80/26-277, telex 32-350; IBUSZ, Kossuth u. 6, tel. 80/25-402, telex 32-284; Cooptourist, Vörös Hadsereg tér 2, tel. 80/22-313, telex 32-456
Accommodation: Hotel Veszprém**, Budapesti út 6, tel. 80/24-876, telex 32-501; Erdei bungalows (seasonal), Kittenberger Kálmán u. 14, tel. 80/26-751
Restaurants: Halle beer house, Lenin tér 2; Stadion, Csermák A. u. 13; Magyaros, Kossuth L. u. 6; Vadásztanya, József A. u. 22; Cserhát önkiszolgáló (self-service), Kossuth Lajos u. 6; Snack-bar in the shopping centre; Viadukt, Pápai u. 37; Betyár csárda, at Nemesvámos (5 km); Kiskukta, Március 15. u. 4; Egri, Vadaspark; Marica Café, Kossuth L. u. 5
Museums: Bakony House, Lenin liget 5; Castle Museum; Gizella Chapel, Vár; Herend China Museum, Kossuth út 140; Szent György Chapel; Bakony Museum of Natural Science, Zirc (22 km), Rákóczi tér 1.

VISEGRÁD, H-2025

Information: Dunatours, Fő u. 3/A, tel. 26/28-330, telex 22-4180
Accommodation: Hotel Silvanus***, Fekete-hegy, tel. 26/28-311, telex 22-5720; Tourist hostel (seasonal), Széchenyi u. 7; Campsite** and bungalows (seasonal), Széchenyi u. 7; Jurta campsite*** and bungalows (seasonal), Mogyoróhegy, tel. 26/28-217, telex 22-6205
Restaurants: Vár, Fő u. 13; Sirály, Rév u. 15; Diófa, Fő u. 48; Erdei Vendéglő, Nagyvillám; Fekete Holló, Rév u. 12
Museums: King Matthias Museum of the Hungarian National Museum, Fő u. 23; Solomon Tower, Fő u. 23; Zsigmondy Vilmos Collection, Visegrád-Lepence
Sports: Erdei open-air swimming-pool. Lepence-völgy; riding, tennis and water sports.

ZALAEGERSZEG, H-8900

Information: Zalatour, Kovács K. tér 1, tel. 92/11-443, telex 33-236; IBUSZ, Dísz tér 4, tel. 92/11-458, telex 33-291; Cooptourist, Kossuth u. 36, tel. 92/11-331
Accommodation: Hotel Balaton**, Balatoni út 2/A, tel. 92/14-100, telex 33-408; Hotel Aranybárány**, Széchenyi tér 1, tel. 92/14-100, telex 33-325; Göcsej Inn, Kaszaházi u. 2, tel. 92/11-580; Göcsej tourist hostel, Kaszaházi u. 2, tel. 92/11-580
Restaurants: Sport, Kosztolányi u. 8; Halász-Vadász csárda (fish and game restaurant), Kaszaházi u. 2; Göcsej, Dózsa-liget; Napfény, Landorhegyi út 10; Erdőgyöngye, Alsó-erdei út; Nefelejcs, Dísz tér; Önkiszolgáló (self-service), Dísz tér 3; Piccoló beer house, Petőfi u. 16
Museums: Potters' House, Kazinczy F. u. 20; Göcsej Village Museum, Falumúzeum u. 5; Göcsej Museum, Batthyány u. 2; Kisfaludy Strobl Collection, Batthány u. 2
Sports: Indoor and open-air swimming-pools, Mártírok u. 76; riding, tennis, water sports, bathing Mártírok u. 76; riding, tennis, water sports; bathing and water sport opportunities at Lake Gébárt.

ZAMÁRDI-SZÁNTÓD, H-8621

Information: Siótour, Kossuth u. 12, tel. 84/31-072; Cooptourist, Zamárdi, Petőfi u. 1, tel. 84/31-179
Accommodation: Hotel Touring** (seasonal), Zamárdi, Petőfi u. 146, tel. 84/31-088; Hotel Touring**, Szántód, Rév, tel. 34/31-096, telex 32-6471; Campsite for motorists I**, Zamárdi, Balatonpart, tel. 84/31-163; Campsite for motorists II**, Zamárdi, Balatonpart, tel. 84/31-158; Campsite Rév**, Szántód, Rév, tel. 84/31-159
Restaurants: Pannónia, Zamárdi, Batthyány u. 13; Rév csárda, at the Szántód ferry; Neszebár, Nagyváradi u. 11; Kék-Tó (self-service), Zamárdi, István u. 76; Ménes csárda, Szántódpuszta, at highway 7; Kakukk, Szántód, Tavasz u. 12.; Paprika, Zamárdi, Honvéd u. 1; Part bistro, Zamárdi, Zöldfa u.; Muskátli, Zamárdi, Zalka M. u.; Önkiszolgáló (self-service), Zamárdi, Jegenye tér; Halász és Birka csárda (fish and lamb dishes), Zamárdi, Batthyány u. 3
Museum: Village Museum in the territory of the Foreign Tourist and Cultural Centre
Sports: riding and water sport opportunities.

DIRECTORY OF PLACE NAMES

Abaliget 151
Abaújvár 254
Ábrahámhegy 173
Adony 144
Agárd 133
Agárdpuszta 133
Aggtelek see Jósvafő
Ajka 143
Almásfüzitő 112
Alsónyék 146
Alsóörs 161
Ásványráró 116
Aszód 233
Aszófő 171

Bábolna 112
Badacsony 173
Badacsonyörs 176
Badacsonytördemic 173
Baja 197
Bakonybél 142
Balácapuszta 138
Balassagyarmat 229
Baláta (lake) 154
Balaton (lake) 155
Balatonakali 171
Balatonakarattya 158
Balatonaliga 183
Balatonalmádi 160
Balatonarács 165
Balatonberény 192
Balatonboglár (Boglárlelle) 189
Balatonederics 176
Balatonfenyves 191
Balatonföldvár 187
Balatonfüred 162
Balatonfűzfő 159
Balatongyörök 178
Balatonkenese 159
Balatonkeresztúr 191
Balatonlelle (Boglárlelle) 188
Balatonmáriafürdő 191
Balatonrendes 173
Balatonszárszó 187
Balatonszemes 187
Balatonszentgyörgy 192
Balatonszepezd 172
Balatonszéplak 185
Balatonudvari 171
Balatonújhely 185
Balatonvilágos 189
Balf 122
Bálvány 242
Bánk 104
Barcs 151
Báta 146
Bátaszék 198
Békés 216
Békéscsaba 214
Bélapátfalva 242
Berekfürdő 218
Bicske 108
Bodajk 137
Boldogkőváralja 253
Bonyhád 146
Börzsöny (mountains) 104
Budakalász 84

Budapest 31
Aquincum 53
Buda Hills 59
Castle District 36
Gellért Hill 57
Inner City 60
Kiskörút 69
Margaret Island 52
Nagykörút 73
Népköztársaság útja 75
Óbuda 51
Rákóczi út 80
Víziváros 47
Bugac-puszta 201
Buják 233
Buzsák 190
Bükfürdő 128
Bükkszék 237
Bükkszentkereszt 249

Cegléd 209
Csaroda 228
Csenger 228
Csesznek 142
Csisztapuszta 191
Csobánc (mountain) 178
Csókakő 137
Csongrád 202
Csopak 162
Csorna 116

Dabas 199
Debrecen 220
Decs 146
Devecser 143
Diósgyőr 247
Diósjenő 104
Dobogókő 98
Dombóvár 153
Dorog 112
Dömös 91
Dörgicse 172
Drávaiványi 152
Dunaföldvár 144
Dunakeszi 98
Dunakömlőd 145
Dunaújváros 144

Edelény 252
Eger 237
Egervár 132
Egregy 189
Érd 133, 144
Érdliget 133
Erdőbénye 259
Eresztvény 234
Esztergom 92

Fadd-Dombori 146
Farkasgyepű 142
Fehér-tó (lake) 209
Feldebrő 237
Felsőbagod 131
Felsőörs 161
Fenékpuszta 157, 181
Fertőboz 122
Fertőd 122

Fertőrákos 122
Fonyód 190
Fót 98
Füzér 260

Galgagyörk 233
Galgahévíz 233
Galgamácsa 233
Galyatető 236
Gárdony 133
Gemenc (forest) 146
Gorsium see Tác
Gyenesdiás 178
Göcsej 131
Göd 99
Gödöllő 232
Gönc 254
Gyoma 217
Gyopárosfürdő 214
Gyöngyös 235
Győr 112
Gyula 215
Gyulaj (forest) 154

Hajdúböszörmény 225
Hajdúdorog 225
Hajdúság 218
Hajdúszoboszló 219
Harkány 151
Hasznos 233
Hatvan 233
Hédervár 116
Hegyeshalom 117
Herend 142
Hévíz 182
Hidegség 122
Hódmezővásárhely 213
Hollóháza 260
Hollókő 232
Hollós-tető 249
Hortobágy 223

Igal 154
Inota 138
Ipolytarnóc 231

Ják 128
Jánkmajtis 228
Jászberény 209
Jávorkút 249
Jósvafő (Baradla Caves) 250

Kalocsa 196
Kám 129
Kaposvár 154
Káptalanfüred 160
Kapuvár 116
Karancs-hegy (mountain) 234
Karcag 218
Karcsa 260
Kazincbarcika 249
Kecskemét 199
Kékestető 236
Keszthely 178
Kiliántelep 171
Kiskőrös 198
Kiskunfélegyháza 202
Kiskunhalas 198
Kismaros 193
Kisoroszi 99
Kisterenye 233

Kisújszállás 218
Kisvárda 228
Kiszombor 213
Komárom 112
Komló 153
Kórós 152
Körmend 130
Kőszeg 124
Kövesd 171

Lábatlan 112
Leányfalu 88
Lébénymiklós 116
Lenti 132
Lillafüred 247
Litér 160
Little Balaton (lake) 192
Lovas 157, 162

Mád 257
Majk-puszta 109
Makó 212
Mánfa 153
Máriabesnyő see Gödöllő
Mártély 214
Martonvásár 133
Mátészalka 228
Mátrafüred 236
Mátraháza 236
Mátraszentimre 236
Mátraszentistván 236
Mátraszentlászló 236
Mátraszőlős 233
Mátraverebély 233
Mecseknádasd 146
Mezőkövesd 243
Mezőtúr 218
Mikófalva 242
Miskolc 244
Miskolctapolca 248
Mohács 159
Monok 253
Mór 137
Mosonmagyaróvár 117
Murakeresztúr 132

Nádudvar 218
Nagybörzsöny 104
Nagycenk 123
Nagykálló 227
Nagykanizsa 132
Nagykőrös 202
Nagymaros 103
Nagyvázsony 166
Nemeskér 124
Nemesvámos 141
Neszmély 112
Nógrád 104
Noszvaj 243
Nova 131
Nyírbátor 227
Nyíregyháza 226
Nyírség 226

Olaszliszka 259
Ópusztaszer 203
Orfű 151
Ormánság 152
Orosháza 214
Oroszlány 109
Ózd 250

Ozora 145
Öcsény 146
Őriszentpéter 131
Őrség 131
Örvényes 171
Öskü 138

Pácin 260
Pákozd 134
Paks 145
Paloznak 162
Pannonhalma 115
Pápa 142
Parád 236
Parádfürdő 236
Parádhuta 236
Parádsasvár 236
Pásztó 233
Pécs 147
Pécsvárad 146
Pétfürdő 138
Pilis (mountains) 98
Pilisszentkereszt 98
Pócsmegyer 99
Pomáz 84
Putnok 250
Püspökladány 218

Rábafüzes 130
Ráckeve 196
Rádiháza 132
Rajka 117
Rédics 132
Révfülöp 173
Rezi 181
Rudabánya 252

Ságvár 185
Salgótarján 234
Salgó (castle) 234
Sárköz 144
Sárospatak 257
Sárpilis 146
Sárvár 128
Sátoraljaújhely 260
Sellye 152
Siklós 152
Simontornya 145
Siófok 183
Sirok 237
Solt 196
Sóly 160
Som 185
Somlóvásárhely 143
Somogyvár 190
Somoskő (castle) 234
Sopron 118
Sopronbánfalva 122
Sopronhorpács 124
Sóstó-fürdő 226
Sümeg 157, 177
Süttő 112

Szabadbattyán 137
Szabolcs 256
Szalonna 252
Szántód 186
Szántódpuszta 186
Szarvas 216
Szarvaskő 242
Szécsény 231

Szeged 204
Székesfehérvár 134
Szekszárd 145
Szenna 154
Szentendre 84
Szentendre Island 99
Szentes 203
Szentgotthárd 130
Szentkirályszabadja 161
Szentkútpuszta 233
Széphalom 260
Szerencs 253
Szigetköz 116
Szigetmonostor 99
Szigetvár 151
Szigliget 176
Szikszó 252
Szilvásvárad 242
Szob 103
Szolnok 210
Szombathely 126
Sződliget 99
Szőlősgyörök 190
Szőny 112

Tab 185
Tác 137
Tahitótfalu 99
Tákos 228
Tállya 256
Tápé 208
Tapolca 176
Tarcal 257
Tarnaszentmária 237
Tata 109
Tatabánya 109
Telkibánya 254
Tihany 167
Tiszafüred 225
Tokaj 254, 256
Tokod 112
Tolcsva 257
Törökszentmiklós 218
Tura 233
Türje 178
Túrkeve 218

Újmassa 248
Újmecsekalja 150

Vác 100
Vácrátót 99
Vaja 228
Vajszló 152
Vámosatya 228
Várgesztes 109
Várpalota 138
Vasvár 130
Velemér 131
Velence 133
Velence (lake) 133
Velencefürdő 133
Verőce 103
Verőcemaros 103
Verpelét 237
Vértesszőlős 109
Veszprém 138
Villány 152
Vilonya 160
Visegrád 88
Vizsoly 253

Vonyarcvashegy 178
Vörösberény 160
Vörs 192

Zala 185
Zalaegerszeg 131
Zalakaros 132
Zalalövő 131
Zalaszántó 183

Zalavár 158
Zamárdi-Szántód 186
Zánka 172
Zebegény 103
Zirc 142

Zsámbék 108
Zsámbok 233
Zsórifürdő 243

Printed in Hungary, 1990
Printing House "Kner", Gyoma